Managing the Social Studies Curriculum

Managing the Social Studies Curriculum

Kent Freeland, Ph.D.

TECHNOMIC
PUBLISHING CO., INC.

LANCASTER · BASEL

Managing the Social Studies Curriculum

a **TECHNOMIC** publication

Published in the Western Hemisphere by
Technomic Publishing Company, Inc.
851 New Holland Avenue
Box 3535
Lancaster, Pennsylvania 17604 U.S.A.

Distributed in the Rest of the World by
Technomic Publishing AG

Printed in the United States of America
10 9 8 7 6 5 4 3 2 1

Main entry under title:
  Managing the Social Studies Curriculum

A Technomic Publishing Company book
Bibliography: p.
Includes index p. 373

Library of Congress Card No. 90-71263
ISBN No. 87762-709-6

CONTENTS

PREFACE

This book is designed for professional educators—principals, curriculum supervisors, school district personnel in charge of curriculum, state department of education administrators and specialists, department heads, teachers and classroom practitioners, and university teacher educators.

Its purpose is to serve as a guide for educators in the elementary and middle grades who desire assistance in managing the social studies curriculum. One of the main themes of the book is that the social sciences need to be emphasized more in the elementary and middle grades; social studies needs to be more than just a blank mixture of topics.

Some of the helpfulness of this book is illustrated by such features as:

(1) *Checklists*, which allow the reader to decide if certain conditions have been met

(2) *Lesson Plans*, which are placed in most chapters to illustrate early elementary and middle grade curriculum recommendations

(3) *Assistance Points*, which provide information on such topics as (a) sources of social studies information, (b) review questions on the chapters, and (c) practical implications of research dealing with social studies

(4) *Bibliographies*, which appear at the end of each chapter

(5) *Appendices*, which supply information regarding social studies units, social studies skills, and program of studies

The book is organized in the following manner.

Chapter 1 looks at how social studies evolved over the years and highlights some of the problems it faces today.

Chapter 2 focuses on unit and lesson planning.

Chapter 3 provides advice on what makes a good history component in social studies.

Chapter 4 presents help on structuring geography in the curriculum.

Chapter 5 sets out a political science ingredient for the students.

Chapter 6 proffers a plan for handling sociology.

Chapter 7 delivers suggestions for those who want to know why anthropology is essential to social studies.

Chapter 8 extends ideas on infusing economics in the social studies for elementary and middle grades.

Chapter 9 presents help on teaching social studies to children with special needs (to include mainstreaming, gifted and talented, and critical thinking).

Chapter 10 shows a way for a curriculum decision maker to select social studies materials, such as textbooks, computer software, audiovisual materials, etc.

Chapter 11 supplies guidance for identifying what topics (among those that don't neatly fit into the six social sciences) should be included in the social studies curriculum, such as international education, environmental education, current events, psychology, philosophy, writing in the social studies, women's studies, peace studies, etc.

Chapter 12 gives recommendations for educators regarding evaluation in social studies. It deals not only with evaluation of students, but also evaluation of programs.

A book is seldom the product of one person who works entirely by himself. Therefore, I wish to acknowledge the support of and timely suggestions by my wife, Kay, during the writing of this book.

1 | A BIRD'S-EYE VIEW FOR THE ADMINISTRATOR

Chapter Preview of Key Ideas

★ *Social studies is a relatively new subject in the school's curriculum.*

★ *The 18th and 19th centuries provided for just a few of the areas in social studies.*

★ *The National Council for the Social Studies was created in 1921.*

★ *There is no unified view of what social studies should be.*

★ *Professionals, university students, and public school students all have different impressions of social studies.*

★ *This book defines social studies as "the use of the social sciences to promote citizenship, along with an understanding of our world and the people who live in it."*

★ *Decision makers in education need to work with "scope and sequence" in the social studies curriculum.*

WHAT'S WRONG?

A sentiment has appeared across the country in the 1980s, namely, that our schools need to "beef up" the content of the curriculum and that this needs to be done by educators who are competent in their subjects. Educational reform has become the battle cry of parents and legislators as they have sought to revamp the curriculum.

In 1982 Mortimer Adler's book *The Paideia Proposal: An Educational Manifesto* was published, which espoused a core curriculum in the schools. Adler felt that there were too many electives in the curriculum.

Three significant reports came out in 1983. *A Nation at Risk* (National Commission on Excellence in Education, 1983) asked for a longer school

1

day and school year, as well as a core curriculum consisting of English, mathematics, science, social studies, and computer science. *The Failure of Our Public Schools* (University of Dallas, 1983) struck the same theme with a more detailed inspection. *Action for Excellence* (Education Commission of the States, 1983) urged states to take an active role in strengthening the curriculum.

A Study of Schooling (Goodlad, 1984) recommended lowering the age (to four) when children start school. His recommendations also included "increasing local site control; more planning time for teachers; a core curriculum in the areas of language, math/science, social studies, art, and vocations; ungraded classes that maximize interaction between older and younger children; the use of peer teaching and cooperative learning; and the creation of schools-within-schools where teachers work in teams with small groups of students over several years" (Newman, 1985, 3).

A Nation Prepared: Teachers for the 21st Century (Carnegie Task Force on Teaching as a Profession, 1986) itemized steps to strengthen the teaching force. More recently, the United States Office of Education has outlined its recommendations for improving education. Former Secretary of Education, William J. Bennett (1986), in his *First Lessons*, criticized social studies for being full of "ersatz" social science while slighting history, geography, and other traditional topics.

In December 1987 Bennett unveiled a core curriculum that he felt would stiffen secondary schools. He called it the James Madison High School plan. In the fall of 1988 he presented his corresponding vision for James Madison Elementary School.

The Closing of the American Mind (Bloom, 1987) lamented what was seen as a decline in the education and morality of youth in the United States. In a recent Gallup Poll (*Education Week*, August 3, 1988) the respondents ranked education as the most important issue in the 1988 Presidential race.

School districts throughout the nation are concerned with demonstrating high performance, often by way of showing how well their students perform on competency or achievement tests. Despite this desire, many schools are experiencing severe problems in controlling their own situation. The takeover of the Jersey City public schools' fiscal and personnel operations by the state of New Jersey (*Education Week*, August 3, 1988) is an indication of the seriousness of the situation.

Many businesses and private corporations have felt the need to collaborate and lend support to improve education. National Geographic Society sponsors summer workshops on geography for teachers across the country. Ashland Oil has undertaken a television campaign in the state of Kentucky to encourage students to stay in school.

The general population is looking for a way to change the schools so that students will be well educated. The public fumes when they hear that one in three 17 year olds do not know when Columbus discovered America. Schools seem to be sympathetic to the call for reform but are often unsure about how to proceed. How has the development of social studies over the years led to the problems it now faces? How should social studies be taught? What social studies content knowledge should an educator possess? These are some of the questions that this chapter and the following ones will address.

SOCIAL STUDIES PRIOR TO THE 20TH CENTURY

Schools are nothing new, but in many ways social studies is. The Greeks provided education for some of their youth: reading, writing, and counting formed the basis of a young boy's schooling. Social studies, however, was not included in the subjects of study. Moving along in time—to the Romans, the Middle Ages, and the Renaissance—we are still not able to see a subject with the name of "social studies." Even if we look at formal schooling during our own country's Colonial period, we will not see social studies listed in the curriculum. Young boys (and a few girls) would have studied geography and history as they sat in uncomfortable, 17th century wooden buildings.

The practice of having distinct subjects of history and geography taught from separate books continued through the 18th, 19th, and into the 20th centuries. Moral education was included in a young person's training because of the emphasis on society's religious sentiments during the early years of the United States. As our country pushed its frontiers westward, civics became an important component of the curriculum because it was felt that our youth needed to be indoctrinated into nationalistic principles. The important point to keep in mind, however, is that social studies was not a term used by educators because it had not yet been coined. Students were studying separate subjects of geography, history, and civics as late as World War I.

SOCIAL STUDIES IN THE 20TH CENTURY

In 1916 the National Education Association's (NEA) Commission on the Reorganization of Secondary Education recommended the following high school sequence of topics, which, by and large, has stayed with us until today (Gross and Dynneson, 1983, 20 and 21):

Grade 7   European history and geography

Grade 8	American history
Grade 9	Civics
Grade 10	European history
Grade 11	American history
Grade 12	Government or problems of democracy

In 1921 the National Council for the Social Studies was created. Although social studies now was represented by a national group, history (and the American Historical Association) assumed the dominant, "big brother" role. The other social studies areas really did not get much attention until the 1960s. The Soviet Union had launched *Sputnik* in 1957, resulting in millions of dollars being pumped into education in the United States in the hope that our country could catch up to the Soviets in science. While the physical sciences and mathematics were the prime benefactors of this infusion of money in the late 1950s and early 1960s, the social sciences benefited by a similar windfall later in the 1960s.

The result was a revised look for the social studies. History and geography remained "the big two"; civics, moral education, and citizenship were subsumed under the name of political science or government. Economics, sociology, and anthropology were added. These six, history, geography, political science, economics, sociology, and anthropology, formed the new social studies and have remained the center of social studies into the 1980s.

Utilizing these six areas has resulted in either a multidisciplinary or an interdisciplinary approach to social studies. The multidisciplinary position suggests a "separate subject" orientation (Skeel, 1979, 73), whereas the interdisciplinary position indicates that the various disciplines are intertwined.

HOW SOME PEOPLE VIEW SOCIAL STUDIES

Professionals' Viewpoints

A survey was conducted (Smith and Smith, 1984) of educational professionals (public school teachers, school district curriculum supervisors, and university professors) who are primarily responsible for teaching social studies. They were asked to state their major concerns in the teaching of social studies.

All three of the above groups agreed on certain concerns:

(1) The vastness of the subject area, i.e., social studies includes so many things, it's hard to define

(2) The perceived value of social studies in the curriculum, i.e., not

enough interest is given to social studies in relation to other curriculum areas

(3) Lack of emphasis in teaching methods on problem solving and inquiry

The social studies teachers had an additional concern: motivating students.

University Students' Perceptions

How do college students in a teacher education program view social studies? Weible and Evans (1982) attempted to find out by asking preservice teachers to respond to certain statements about social studies. Table 1.1 shows percentages for the sixty-six students who had enrolled in an ele-

Table 1.1 University students' perceptions of NCSS guidelines.

Guideline 1: Relationship of Program to the Maturity and Concerns of Students					
	Strongly Agree	Agree	Don't Know	Disagree	Strongly Disagree
Students should be involved in selecting goals for their school's social studies program.	30%	58%	12%	—	—
Students should have some choice in selecting learning activities in the social studies class.	45%	55%	—	—	—
The social studies program should be designed to meet the needs and concerns of all students.	73%	24%	2%	2%	—
Social studies should be an important part of the K–6 school curriculum.	70%	30%	—	—	—

Guideline 2: Relationship of Program to the Real Social World					
	Strongly Agree	Agree	Don't Know	Disagree	Strongly Disagree
Students should have an opportunity to study and discuss values which may be different from their own in social studies.	65%	33%	—	—	2%
An analysis of controversial global problems (racism, sexism, world resources, and ecological imbalance) should be included in the social studies program.	38%	41%	13%	—	8%
Local issues should be included as a topic of study in the social studies program.	59%	38%	3%	—	—
The social studies program should promote actual student involvement in local issues.	46%	45%	3%	—	6%

(continued)

Table 1.1 (continued).

Guideline 3:
Relationship of Program to Currently Valid Knowledge
Representative of Human Beings' Experience, Culture, and Beliefs

	Strongly Agree	Agree	Don't Know	Disagree	Strongly Disagree
An understanding of the past is an important aspect of the social studies program.	32%	66%	2%	—	—
A balance of local, state, national, and international topics should be included.	48%	50%	2%	—	—
The social studies program should provide the opportunity for students to examine potential future conditions and problems at the local, state, national, and international levels.	38%	59%	2%	—	1%
Human achievement and failure should be included in the social studies program.	41%	55%	3%	—	1%

Guideline 4:
Selection of Objectives; How Objectives Guide Program

	Strongly Agree	Agree	Don't Know	Disagree	Strongly Disagree
The school's social studies program should be continuously evaluated to keep pace with the ever changing world.	77%	23%	—	—	—

Guideline 5:
Nature of Activities

	Strongly Agree	Agree	Don't Know	Disagree	Strongly Disagree
Learning activities should be sufficiently varied and flexible to appeal to many kinds of students.	77%	21%	2%	—	—
Students' ideas, feelings, and opinions should be respected in all social studies activities.	76%	23%	1%	—	—
Activities should encourage students to investigate and seek additional information on their own about the topics they are studying in social studies.	70%	30%	—	—	—

Table 1.1 *(continued).*

Guideline 6: Relationship between Instruction and Range of Learning Resources				
	Strongly Agree	Agree	Don't Know	Disagree	Strongly Disagree

	Strongly Agree	Agree	Don't Know	Disagree	Strongly Disagree
Many reading resources (literature, newspapers, magazines, and maps) are required for social studies; no one textbook is sufficient.	73%	23%	1%	3%	—
Reading resources should accommodate a wide range of reading abilities and interests.	68%	30%	—	2%	—
Films, filmstrips, field trips, and guest speakers are necessary resources for a good social studies program.	68%	26%	3%	3%	—
Social studies activities should require students to work in small and large group situations.	41%	55%	4%	—	—

Guideline 7: Relationship of Social Studies Program to Students' Experiences				

	Strongly Agree	Agree	Don't Know	Disagree	Strongly Disagree
Social studies should provide students with skills necessary to learn about their world independent of classroom instruction.	53%	47%	—	—	—

Taken from Tom Weible and Charles Evans, "The Elementary Social Studies Curriculum," *Southern Social Studies Quarterly*, pp. 33–38 (Fall 1982).

mentary methods course. In general, their perceptions were consistent with selected standards of the NCSS Curriculum Guidelines.

Elementary and Middle Grade Students' Views

Shaughnessy and Haladyna (1985) surveyed 3,000 students in grades 1–8 to see how they liked social studies. Student rankings revealed "social studies was very low and actually declined from grade 4 to grade 8" (p. 692).

Freeland and Dickinson (1984) asked 441 students in grades 4, 5, and 6 to indicate their favorite subject among the following: reading, arithmetic/mathematics, language/English, social studies, spelling, and science. Social studies did not rank in the top three favorites for any of the grades, with the exception of grade 5, where it was ranked second. (Incidentally, math was ranked first in all three grades.)

Shaver et al. (1979) drew the following conclusions from the attitudes of public school students toward social studies:

(1) The teacher is the key to what social studies will be for the student.

(2) New materials created for social studies are not being used.

(3) The dominant instructional tool is the textbook.

(4) The curriculum is mostly history and government.

(5) Instruction tends to be group-controlled recitation and lecture.

(6) Knowledge of information is considered to be important.

(7) Teachers tend to rely on external motivation; students learn in order to get good grades and approval, not because they want to learn.

(8) Social studies does not inspire student interest.

(9) Affective goals are not explicit parts of the social studies curriculum.

Social studies educators feel that a "scope and sequence for the teaching of social studies would help to identify some of the essential information that students should learn" (Smith and Smith, 1984, 45). It would also be helpful if there were a definition of social studies. Let's discuss "definition" before we discuss "scope and sequence."

HOW IS SOCIAL STUDIES DEFINED?

One of the oldest and most oft-quoted definitions of social studies is the one Edgar Wesley delivered in 1937: "The social studies are the social sci-

[*Social Education*, p. 428 (October 1981).] Reprinted with permission.

"Welcome to Tag Team Wrestling!"

ences simplified for pedagogical purposes" (Wesley, 1937, 4). This suggests to some people that social studies is just a watered-down version of social sciences. Most social studies educators, such as Stanley Wronski (1982), deny that this is the case.

In fact, many educators will distinguish between social studies and social sciences. History is sometimes thought of as being part of the first term but not the second. Wilma Longstreet (1985) complains that "our crucial terminology keeps shifting on us, and the role of social science in the social studies remains obscure" (p. 356).

Throughout this book, we will consider social studies and social sciences to be the same, and we will also consider history to be part of both. It can be argued that history should be included in the social sciences because historians make use of the scientific method in their investigations and are capable of creating new knowledge about the past.

Barr, Barth, and Shermis (1977) suggest that a definition of social studies should be based upon instructional goals, not upon content. They feel the goal of social studies is the development of citizenship and have therefore proposed the following definition:

> The social studies is an integration of experience and knowledge concerning human relations for the purpose of citizenship education [p. 69].

John Michaelis (1980) refers to other definitions, which are characterized by attention to (1) developing a student's thinking and decision-making ability, (2) developing knowledge and skills needed to improve society, and (3) developing the whole child, thereby making social studies focus on the personal development of the individual. There is no shortage of definitions; in fact, the variety of descriptions prompts some people to refer to social studies as "social stew."

A DEFINITION FOR YOU

This book will use the following definition of social studies: *Social studies is the use of the social sciences to promote citizenship, along with the understanding of our world and the people who live in it.*

This definition makes use of a finding by the following six national reports that were delivered during the 1980s (Newman, 1985, 5):

(1) The Paideia Proposal: An Educational Manifesto

(2) High School: A Report on Secondary Education in America

(3) Academic Preparation for College: What Students Need to Know and Be Able to Do

(4) A Place Called School: Prospects for the Future

(5) A Nation at Risk: The Imperative for Educational Reform

(6) Horace's Compromise: The Dilemma of the American High School

These reports all identify citizenship, or civic understanding, as central to education.

What about the National Council for the Social Studies itself? Does it give us any guidelines as to what should be the definition or goal of social studies? It really doesn't give us a definition, but it does list some essential ingredients.

First, it says that students must be provided knowledge in social studies. This knowledge should come from the history and culture of our nation and the world, from geography, from government, from economics, from social institutions, from intergroup and interpersonal relationships, and from worldwide relationships of all sorts.

Second, students need to have democratic beliefs presented to them and discussed with them, but not indoctrinated blindly into them.

Third, students need to develop thinking skills, which include data-gathering skills, intellectual skills, decision-making skills, and interpersonal skills.

Fourth, students need participation skills, i.e., a chance to connect the classroom with the community.

Fifth, students need to develop civic action, which can be described as the willingness to take part in public affairs (NCSS, 1981).

SCOPE AND SEQUENCE

As we talk about the social studies curriculum, we use two terms: scope and sequence. Simply stated, **scope** refers to what is taught throughout a single year (or throughout the total K–12 years), while **sequence** refers to the order in which the topics are taught. The sequence of topics within a school year is normally determined by each individual school district, by the building, or sometimes by the teacher. The scope, however, is often decided on a larger scale. The state departments of education in our nation normally decide on the scope of topics for a K–12 arrangement. (See Appendix A for a sample program of studies.) A two-year study by the Social Science Education Consortium in Boulder, Colorado, emphasized how close the curricula are in the various states (Superka et al., 1980).

Project SPAN

Project SPAN (Social Studies/Social Science Education: Priorities and Needs) began in 1978 and ended in 1980. The purpose of this study was to examine social studies education and to make recommendations for its future.

Project SPAN commented on the uniformity of topics taught throughout the country. Look at Table 1.2 and notice the similarity to the 1916 high school curriculum described earlier in this chapter.

The staff members of the SPAN project recommended that the K–12

Table 1.2 Examples of unit topics for each grade level.

Kindergarten

Kindergarten programs deal with topics that help to familiarize children with their immediate surroundings. The home and school provide the setting for these studies. With some kindergarten children it is possible to include, in a simple way, references to the world beyond the immediate environment.

Learning about Myself
Rules for Safe Living
Learning How My Family Buys Goods and Services
Working Together at School
Continents and the Globe
People Change the Earth

Grade One

Grade one studies are based in the local area, such as the neighborhood, but provision is often made to associate the local area with the larger world. A major criticism of first grade units in particular and primary units in general has been that they have tended to be too confining and that their content has been thin. Units should provide for easy transition from the near-at-hand to the faraway and back again at frequent intervals—when it is established that the backgrounds of children warrant such movement. Neighborhood and community services can be stressed in this grade.

The Shopping Center
Families at Work
Great Americans
A Japanese Family (comparative study)
Scarcity and Demand
Families: Size and Structure
Families and Their Needs
Dividing the Work

Grade Two

The grade two program provides for frequent and systematic contact with the world beyond the neighborhood. Through the study of transportation, communication, food distribution, and travel, the children begin to learn how their part of the world is connected to other places on earth.

Suburban Neighborhoods
Transportation and Communication: Our Links to the World
Rural and Urban Communities
Where and How We Get Our Food
People Working Together
How Neighborhoods Change

(continued)

Table 1.2 (continued).

Grade Three

The grade three program often emphasizes the larger community concept: what a community is, types of communities, why some communities grow though others do not, and how communities provide for basic needs. Many programs include an outside community for purposes of comparison. Schools are giving a great deal of attention to the large, urban community at this grade level.

Our City's Government
Food for the Community
Keeping Cities Up-to-Date—Change
Communities at Home and Abroad (comparative cultures study)
Life in Early American Settlements
Why a City Is Where It Is
The Parts of a City
Natural Surroundings and People's Actions

Grade Four

In grade four the world as the home of people, showing various geographical features of the earth along with variety in ways of living, is often stressed. These studies help children understand some of the adaptive and innovative qualities of human beings. Home-state studies are popular in grade four; often they are included to meet legislative requirements. Comparative studies are commonly recommended.

Historical Growth and Change of the Home State
The Pacific Northwest (regional study)
Deserts of the World (regions)
Others Who Share Our World (comparative cultures study)
Kenya and Its African Neighbors (comparative study)
India, a Society in Transition (comparative study)
Regions Make a World

Grade Five

Almost everywhere the fifth grade program includes the geography, history, early development, and growth of the United States. The program may focus on the United States alone or on the United States and Canada or on the United States, Canada, and Latin America. The latter option makes the fifth grade program a heavy one. The fifth grade emphasis should be coordinated with the eighth and eleventh grades in order to avoid repetitive treatments.

Founding of the New World
The Native Americans
The Making of Our Nation
The War between the States
An Early American Mining Community
History of the Great Plains
Completion of National Expansion
One Nation; Many Heritages

Grade Six

The sixth grade program may include the study of Latin America and Canada or of cultures of the Eastern Hemisphere. Both of these patterns are in common use. A major limitation of sixth grade programs is that they attempt to deal with too many topics. Often this results in a smattering of exposures without developing significant depth of understanding. The same criticism applies to the seventh grade. Stronger programs emerge where teachers carefully select a few units that are representative of basic concepts that have wide and broad applicability. For example, a class need not study all the Third World nations in order to gain some understanding of the problems of newly developing countries.

Table 1.2 (continued).

Grade Six

Western Hemisphere Emphasis
    Cooperation in the Americas
    The Prairie Provinces
    Three Inca Countries
    The Saint Lawrence Seaway and Its Effect on Canadian Growth
    The Organization of American States

Eastern Hemisphere Emphasis
    Ancient, Classical, and Medieval Civilizations
    The Birthplace of Three Religions
    The U.S.S.R. and Eastern Europe in Recent Times
    Great Discoveries
    The Renaissance and Reformation
    Empires and Revolutions
    The People's Republic of China

Grade Seven

The nature of the seventh grade program depends on the content of grade six. Either Latin America or culture regions of the Eastern Hemisphere are popular choices for this grade. Some schools are developing exciting programs in anthropology in grade seven. World geography is also included in some districts as are studies of the home state.

    Rise of Modern Civilization
    Africa: Yesterday, Today, and Tomorrow
    The Home State
    Challenges of our Times
    World Resources: Who Has Them? Who Uses Them?
    The Age of Technology—Its Effects on People
    Environmental Problems
    Principles of Geography
    A Look at Tomorrow: The Future

Grade Eight

The study of the United States and of the American heritage is widespread in grade eight. The program usually stresses the development of American political institutions and the development of nationality. The approach typically consists of a series of units arranged chronologically. The fifth and eleventh grades also include elements of American history. Defining the emphasis for each of these grades and differentiating appropriately among them in terms of content and approach is necessary in order to avoid unwarranted duplication in the three grades.

    Old Nations in the New World
    A Free and Independent Nation
    A Strong and Expanding Nation
    A Divided Nation
    Birth of an Industrial Giant
    A World Power in the Space Age

John Jarolimek. *Social Studies in Elementary Education*, 7th ed. NY:Macmillan (1986).

social studies curriculum should be organized around the major social roles of our society. All seven roles should be taught in the K–6 grades:

(1) Citizen
(2) Worker
(3) Consumer
(4) Family member
(5) Friend
(6) Member of social groups
(7) Self

The seventh grade course should focus on the more personal roles: self, family member, friend, and member of social groups. The eighth grade course should be changed from a chronological United States history survey to a topical treatment of the social roles, and the ninth grade course should deal essentially with the societal roles of citizen, consumer, and worker (Morrisett et al., 1980).

Current Curriculum

A few pages ago you read about the similarity that exists across the nation when it comes to scope (or topics taught in social studies). In Table 1.2 John Jarolimek supplies us with some frequently taught topics for grades K–8 (Jarolimek, 1986, 12–14).

The elementary grade topics in Table 1.2 reflect the "expanding horizons" approach of Paul Hanna from the 1930s. Hanna's sequence builds upon the belief that a child's expanding experiences enable him to learn about topics that get progressively farther away from his own self. That sequence is arranged as follows (Hanna, 1963, 191):

Grade 1	The child's family community; the child's school
Grade 2	The child's neighborhood community
Grade 3	The child's local communities: city, county, metropolis
Grade 4	The child's state community; the child's region-of-states community
Grade 5	The United States national community

Areas of Content

While Jarolimek's table reflects the traditional topics, there are individuals and groups who advocate alternatives. A study begun by the NCSS in

1977, and carried into the early 1980s, identified twenty-three areas that should be taught in grades K–12 (Herman, 1983):

Anthropology	Legal education
Career education	Moral education
Citizenship education	Multicultural education
Consumer education	Philosophy
Contemporary issues	Political science
Death and dying	Psychology
Economics	Religion studies
Energy education	Science in society
Future studies	Sexism education
Geography	Social psychology
Global education	Urban studies
History	

This study did not assign the above topics to a specific grade, but rather stated that they should be taught in a range of levels between grades K–12. (Any topic included in the grade 10–12 range was also mentioned in the K–9 range.)

Recent Alternatives

The November/December 1986 issue of *Social Education* presents five scope and sequence ideas: the first one uses history and geography as the basis (Downey, 1986); the second one utilizes seven broad themes (Hartoonian and Laughlin, 1986); the third one adopts a problem-solving rationale (Engle and Ochoa, 1986); the fourth one encourages a transformation of our society through social education (Stanley and Nelson, 1986); and the fifth one reflects a focus on global education (Kniep, 1986).

William Bennett, the former United States Secretary of Education, released reports concerning what he considers to be a model curriculum for elementary and high school social studies. Following are his ideas for K–8 (*Lexington Herald-Leader*, August 1988):

K–3	Introduction to history, geography, and civics (significant Americans, explorers, native Americans; American holidays; customs and symbols; citizenship and landscape; climate and map work)
Grade 4	United States history to Civil War
Grade 5	United States history since 1865
Grade 6	World history to the Middle Ages

Grade 7   World history from the Middle Ages to 1900

Grade 8   World geography and U.S. constitutional government

The state of California has recently adopted a new K–12 scope and sequence (see Figure 1.1) in social studies (Alexander and Crabtree, 1988). There are three broad goals: (1) knowledge and cultural understanding, (2) democratic understanding and civic values, and (3) skills attainment and social participation. Each of these goals contains a number of strands (see Figure 1.2). The framework for this scope and sequence seems to rely upon an interdisciplinary approach, giving history and geography more attention than in recent years.

RECOMMENDATIONS FOR A CURRICULUM

Although there is no agreed upon social studies curriculum that experts feel is right for all elementary and middle grade schools throughout the country, there are a number of ideas which this book considers to be essential:

(1) The main focus of social studies in the schools should be to foster good citizenship.

(2) Social studies needs to emphasize the six social science disciplines (history, geography, political science, economics, anthropology, and sociology). Students must have content knowledge in these areas.

(3) Social studies should be either interdisciplinary or multidisciplinary. It needs to combine the various social science disciplines.

(4) Social studies should begin in the primary grades with concrete learning experiences. That is, students should have a chance to handle real objects and see actual situations.

(5) Social studies should build upon experiences that students already have. New learning should be related to what the students have previously learned.

ASSISTANCE POINTS

Questions for Action for the Administrator

1. Assume a parent came to your office and wanted to know if there were a uniform K–8 social studies curriculum that all fifty states follow. How would you respond?

Kindergarten	Learning and Working Now and Long Ago
Grade 1	A Child's Place in Time and Space
Grade 2	People Who Make a Difference
Grade 3	Continuity and Change
Grade 4	California: A Changing State
Grade 5	United States History and Geography: Making a New Nation
Grade 6	World History and Geography: Ancient Civilizations
Grade 7	World History and Geography: Medieval and Early Modern Times
Grade 8	United States History and Geography: Growth and Conflict
Grade 9	Elective Courses in History–Social Science
Grade 10	World History, Culture, and Geography: The Modern World
Grade 11	United States History and Geography: Continuity and Change in the 20th Century
Grade 12	Principles of American Democracy (one semester) and Economics (one semester)

Figure 1.1 History-social science course titles, K–12 [Alexander, Francie and Charlotte Crabtree. "California's New History-Social Science Curriculum Promises Richness and Depth," *Educational Leadership*, p. 12 (Sept. 1988)]. Reprinted with permission.

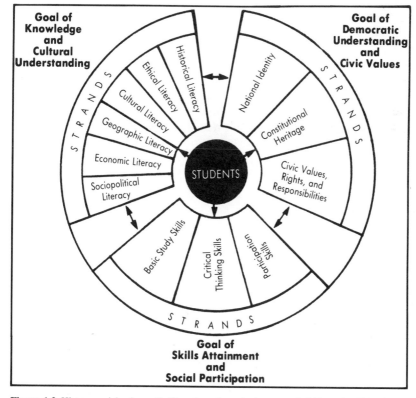

Figure 1.2 History-social science K–12 goals and curriculum strands [Alexander, Francie and Charlotte Crabtree. "California's New History-Social Science Curriculum Promises Richness and Depth," *Educational Leadership*, p. 11 (Sept. 1988)]. Reprinted with permission.

2. Respond to the statements in Table 1.1. As a school administrator, how do your answers compare with those of the students in the survey?

3. If you observed a social studies class where a teacher was utilizing history material in her lesson, what "scope and sequence" criteria would you refer to in order to justify teaching this history content?

4. In what ways is there dissatisfaction with social studies in the school systems of our country?

5. Assume that your school district is rewriting its curriculum guides and needs to include a rationale statement for teaching social studies. What is the central purpose of teaching social studies in the elementary and middle grades?

Names and Addresses of Professional Organizations

1. National Council for the Social Studies
   3501 Newark St., N.W.
   Washington, DC 20010
   (The NCSS publishes *Social Education, Theory and Research in Social Education,* and *Social Studies and the Young Learner.*)

2. Association for Supervision and Curriculum Development
   225 North Washington
   Alexandria, VA 22314
   (The ASCD publishes *Educational Leadership.*)

3. Phi Delta Kappa
   Eighth & Union Streets
   P.O. Box 789
   Bloomington, IN 47402
   (PDK publishes *Phi Delta Kappan.*)

4. National Association of Elementary School Principals
   1615 Duke Street
   Alexandria, VA 22314
   (NAESP publishes *The Principal.*)

5. National Association of Secondary School Principals
   1904 Association Dr.
   Reston, VA 22091
   (NASSP publishes *Bulletin.*)

6. American Association of School Administrators
   1801 N. Moore St.
   Arlington, VA 22209
   (AASA publishes *The School Administrator.*)

7. ERIC/ChESS
   Indiana University
   2805 East 10th St., Suite 120
   Bloomington, IN 47405

8. Social Science Education Consortium
   855 Broadway
   Boulder, CO 80302
   (SSEC publishes *Social Studies Curriculum Materials Data Book.*)

9. National Middle School Association
   4807 Evanswood Dr.
   Columbus, OH 43229
   (NMSA publishes *Middle School Journal.*)

10. National School Boards Association
    1680 Duke St.
    Alexandria, VA 22314
    (NSBA publishes *American School Board Journal.*)

11. Association for Childhood Education International
    11141 Georgia Ave.
    Wheaton, MD 20902
    (ACEI publishes *Childhood Education.*)

12. Association for Early Childhood Education
    212 King St. W.
    Toronto, Ontario M5V 1K5
    Canada
    (AECE publishes *Journal of Early Childhood Education.*)

13. American Association of Colleges for Teacher Education
    One Dupont Circle
    Washington, DC 20036
    (AACTE publishes *Journal of Teacher Education.*)

14. Association of Teacher Educators
    Suite ATE, 1900 Association Dr.
    Reston, VA 22091
    (ATE publishes *Action in Teacher Education.*)

15. National Education Association
    1201 16th St., N.W.
    Washington, DC 20036
    (NEA publishes *Today's Education.*)

16. American Federation of Teachers
    11 Dupont Circle, N.W.
    Washington, DC 20036
    (AFT publishes *American Teacher.*)

17. American Educational Research Association
1230 17th St., N.W.
Washington, DC 20030
(AERA publishes *American Educational Research Journal.*)

18. National Association for Middle School Administration
Box 16149
Columbus, OH 43216
(NAMSA publishes *American Middle School Education.*)

A Social Studies Professional Library

What books should an administrator consider if he wants to compile a professional library for social studies? The following list represents just one possibility and is adapted from a longer list that appeared in *Social Education* (Hass, 1987):

1. Foundations of social studies education
The Project SPAN Reports. Boulder, CO:SSEC (1982).

2. History
Downey, Matthew T. *Teaching American History: New Directions*. Bulletin 67, Washington, DC:NCSS, 115 pp. (1982).

3. Anthropology
Johanson, Donald and Edey Matiland. *Lucy: The Beginnings of Humankind*. New York:Warner Books, 389 pp. (1982).

4. Economics
Helburn, Suzanne and James E. Davis. *Preparing to Teach Economics: Approaches and Resources* (revised and expanded edition). Boulder, CO:SSEC, 116 pp. (1982).

5. Geography
Manson, Gary A. and Merrill K. Ridd, eds. *New Perspectives on Geographic Education: Putting Theory into Practice*. Washington, DC:National Council for Geographic Education, 218 pp. (1977).

6. Political science
Heater, Derek and Judith A. Gillespie, eds. *Political Education in Flux*. London, UK:Sage Pubs., 302 pp. (1981).

7. Psychology and social psychology
Benjamin, Ludy T., Jr. and Kathleen D. Lowman. *Activities Handbook for the Teaching of Psychology*. Washington, DC:American Psychological Association, 244 pp. (1981).

8. Sociology
Geertsen, Reed, ed. *Eighty-One Techniques for Teaching Sociological Concepts*. Washington, DC, 148 pp. (1980).

9. Basic reading/writing/thinking skills
   Beyer, Barry K. *Back-to-Basics in Social Studies*. Boulder, CO: SSEC, 49 pp. (1977).

10. Future studies
    Fitch, Robert M. and Cordell M. Svengalis. *Futures Unlimited*. Washington, DC:NCSS, 88 pp. (1979).

11. Global studies
    Hoopes, David S. *Global Guide to International Education*. Yarmouth, ME:Intercultural Press, 704 pp. (1985).

12. Law-related studies
    Turner, Mary Jane and Lynn Parisi. *Law in the Classroom, Revised Edition*. Boulder, CO:SSEC, 484 pp. (1984).

13. Multicultural studies
    Banks, James A. *Multiethnic Education: Theory and Practice*. Boston:Allyn and Bacon, Inc., 326 pp. (1981).

14. Peace and nuclear studies
    Sloan, Douglas, ed. *Education for Peace and Disarmament: Toward a Living World*. New York:Teachers College Press, 288 pp. (1983).

15. Science/technology/society studies
    Patrick, John J. and Richard C. Remy. *Connecting Science, Technology, and Society in the Education of Citizens*. Boulder, CO:SSEC, 90 pp. (1985).

16. Values education
    Shaver, James P. and William Strong. *Facing Value Decisions, 2nd ed*. New York:Teachers College Press, 179 pp. (1982).

17. Women's studies
    Grambs, Jean D., ed. *Teaching about Women in the Social Studies: Concepts, Methods, and Materials*. Bulletin 48, Washington, DC: NCSS, 117 pp. (1976).

18. Social studies instruction: curriculum organization patterns
    Davis, James E. *Planning a Social Studies Program: Activities, Guidelines, and Resources*. Boulder, CO:SSEC, 284 pp. (1983).

19. Social studies instruction: goals and objectives
    Remy, Richard C. *Handbook of Basic Citizenship Competencies*. Alexandria, VA:Association for Supervision and Curriculum Development, 108 pp. (1980).

20. Social studies instruction: teaching methods
    Dobkin, William S., Joel Fischer, Bernard Ludwig, and Richard Koblinger. *A Handbook for the Teaching of Social Studies, 2nd ed*. Sponsored by the Association of Teachers of Social Studies in the

City of New York/United Federation of Teachers, Boston:Allyn and Bacon, 323 pp. (1985).

21. Social studies instruction: instructional materials
    Social Studies Curriculum Materials Data Book, Vol. 1–X. Boulder, CO:SSEC (1971–1985).

22. Social studies instruction: computer instruction
    Abelson, Robert B., ed. *Using Microcomputers in the Social Studies Classroom*. Boulder, CO:SSEC, 140 pp. (1983).

23. Social studies instruction: evaluation
    Williams, Paul L. and Jerry R. Moore. *Criterion-Referenced Testing for the Social Studies*. Bulletin 64, Washington, DC:NCSS, 92 pp. (1980).

24. Change processes in social studies
    Hahn, Carole L., Gerald W. Marker, and Thomas J. Switzer. *Three Studies on Perception and Utilization of "New Social Studies" Materials*. Boulder, CO:SSEC, 116 pp. (1977).

25. Sources on sources
    Armento, Beverly. "Research on Teaching Social Studies," in *Handbook of Research on Teaching, 3rd ed*. Merlin C. Wittrock, ed. New York:Macmillan, pp. 942–951 (1986).

REFERENCES

Adler, Mortimer, J. *The Paideia Proposal: An Educational Manifesto*. New York:Macmillan (1982).

Alexander, Francie and Charlotte Crabtree. "California's New History-Social Science Curriculum Promises Richness and Depth," *Educational Leadership*, pp. 10–13 (September 1988).

Barr, Robert D., James L. Barth, and S. Samuel Shermis. *Defining the Social Studies*. Bulletin 51, Washington, DC:National Council for the Social Studies (1977).

Bennett, William J. *First Lessons: A Report on the Elementary Education in America*. Washington, DC:U.S. Government Printing Office (1986).

Bloom, Allan. *The Closing of the American Mind*. New York:Simon and Schuster (1987).

Carnegie Task Force on Teaching as a Profession. *A Nation Prepared: Teachers for the 21st Century*. Washington, DC:Carnegie Task Force (1986).

Downey, Matthew T. "Time, Space and Culture," *Social Education*, pp. 490–501 (November/December 1986).

Education Commission of the States. *Action for Excellence*. Denver, CO:Education Commission of the States (1983).

Education Week (August 3, 1988).

Engle, Shirley and Anna Ochoa. "A Curriculum for Democratic Citizenship," *Social Education*, pp. 514–526 (November/December 1986).

Freeland, Kent and George Dickinson. "Elementary Students' Rankings for Favorite Subjects and Subjects of Highest Grades," *Educational Review*, pp. 1–5 (Spring 1984).

Goodlad, John I. *A Place Called School: Prospects for the Future.* New York:McGraw-Hill (1983).

Goodlad, John I. *A Study of Schooling.* New York:McGraw-Hill (1984).

Greene, Elizabeth. "Proponent of 'Cultural Literacy' Finds Disciples in the Nation's Schools," *The Chronicle of Higher Education*, pp. A13, A16, A17 (November 16, 1988).

Gross, Richard E. and Thomas L. Dynneson. *What Should We Be Teaching in the Social Studies?* Bloomington, IN:Phi Delta Kappa Fastback Series, No. 199 (1983).

Hanna, Paul R. "Revising the Social Studies: What Is Needed?" *Social Education* (April 1963), p. 191, as discussed in Thomas L. Dynneson and Richard E. Gross, "A Century of Encounter," *Social Education*, pp. 486–488 (November/December 1986).

Hartoonian, H. Michael and Margaret A. Laughlin. "Designing a Scope and Sequence," *Social Education*, pp. 502–512 (November/December 1986).

Herman, Wayne L., Jr. "What Should Be Taught Where?" *Social Education*, pp. 94–100 (February 1983).

Hirsch, E. D., Jr. "Restoring Cultural Literacy in the Early Grades," *Educational Leadership*, pp. 63–70 (December 1987/January 1988).

Hirsch, E. D., Jr. *Cultural Literacy: What Every American Needs to Know.* Boston: Houghton Mifflin (1987).

Jarolimek, John. *Social Studies in Elementary Education*, 7th ed. New York:Macmillan Publishing Co., Inc. (1986).

Kniep, Willard M. "Social Studies within Global Education," *Social Education*, pp. 536–542 (November/December 1986).

Lexington Herald-Leader. Newspaper article entitled "Bennett: Beef up Grade School Classes," Lexington, Kentucky (August 31, 1988).

Longstreet, Wilma S. "Social Science and the Social Studies: Origins of the Debate," *Social Education*, pp. 356–359 (May 1985).

Michaelis, John U. *Social Studies for Children: A Guide to Basic Instruction*, 7th ed. Englewood Cliffs, NJ:Prentice Hall (1980).

Morrissett, Irving, Douglas P. Superka, and Sharryl Hawke. "Recommendations for Improving Social Studies in the 1980s," *Social Education*, pp. 570–576 (November/December 1980).

National Commission on Excellence in Education. *A Nation at Risk: The Imperative for Education Reform.* Washington, DC:U.S. Government Printing Office (1983).

National Council for the Social Studies Position Statement. "Essentials of the Social Studies," *Social Education*, pp. 162–164 (March 1981).

Newman, Fred M. *Educational Reform and Social Studies: Implications of Six Reports.* Boulder, CO:Social Science Education Consortium, Inc. (1985).

Shaughnessy, Joan M. and Thomas M. Haladyna. "Research on Student Attitude Toward Social Studies," *Social Education*, pp. 692–695 (November/December 1985).

Shaver, J. P., O. L. Davis, Jr., and S. W. Helbrun. "The Status of Social Studies Education: Impressions from Three NSF Studies," *Social Education*, Vol. 43, pp. 150–153 (1979) [cited in Joan M. Shaughnessy and Thomas M. Haladyna. "Research on Student Attitude Toward Social Studies," *Social Education*, pp. 692–695 (November/December 1985)].

Skeel, Dorothy J. *The Challenge of Teaching Social Studies in the Elementary School, 3rd ed.* Santa Monica, CA:Goodyear Publishing Co., Inc. (1979).

Smith, Dennie L. and Lana J. Smith. "Concerns of Teachers, Supervisors, and Teacher Educators for Teaching Social Studies." *Southern Social Studies Quarterly*, pp. 36–47 (Spring 1984).

Stanley, William B. and Jack L. Nelson. "Social Education for Social Transformation," *Social Education*, pp. 528–534 (November/December 1986).

Superka, Douglas P., Sharryl Hawke, and Irving Morrissett. "The Current and Future Status of the Social Studies," *Social Education*, pp. 362–369 (May 1980).

University of Dallas. *The Failure of Our Public Schools*. Irving, TX:University of Dallas (1983).

Weible, Tom and Charles S. Evans. "The Elementary Social Studies Curriculum: Preservice Teacher Perceptions," *Southern Social Studies Quarterly*, pp. 32–39 (Fall 1982).

Wesley, Edgar B. *Teaching the Social Studies: Theory and Practice*. Boston:D. C. Heath (1937).

Wronski, Stanley P. "Edgar Bruce Wesley (1891–1980): His Contributions to the Past, Present and Future of the Social Studies," in *Journal of Thought*, Virginia Atwood, ed. Norman, OK:University of Oklahoma, pp. 55–67 (Fall 1982).

2 | ESSENTIALS OF INSTRUCTIONAL PLANNING

Chapter Preview of Key Ideas

★ A resource unit is an example of a long-range plan.

★ There are eight parts to a resource unit: (1) An "Overview" is an introduction to the unit. (2) "Concepts, Generalizations, and Facts" show the relationships among ideas, broad statements, and specific information. (3) "Understandings, Attitudes, and Skills" present goals (or objectives) for the teacher to follow. (4) "Motivational Activities" usually introduce the unit. (5) "Developmental Activities" enable the students to carry out the day-to-day work of the unit. (6) "Evaluation Techniques" allow the teacher to assess the learning that is taking place. (7) A "Bibliography" is a list of the printed materials used for the unit. (8) The "Other Sources" section contains nonprint materials.

★ Lesson plans are developed from a longer unit plan and cover one day's instruction.

★ One way to write a lesson plan is the five-step approach: (1) purpose, (2) motivation, (3) development, (4) conclusion, and (5) materials.

★ Teaching methods are instructional strategies.

★ Joyce and Weil present a classification of methods into four main families: (1) information processing, (2) personal, (3) social, and (4) behavioral.

THE NEED FOR PLANNING

There is a passage from *Alice's Adventures in Wonderland* where Alice asks the Cheshire Cat for help in finding her way (Carroll, 1941):

25

"Would you tell me, please," said Alice, "which way I ought to walk from here?"

"That depends a good deal on where you want to get to," said the Cat.

"I don't much care where . . . ," said Alice.

"Then it doesn't matter which way you walk," said the Cat.

". . . so long as I get *somewhere*," Alice added as an explanation.

"Oh, you're sure to do that," said the Cat, "if you only walk long enough."

Knowing the destination might not have been important for the Cheshire Cat, but it is for educators. Operating with a purpose or a plan is essential if we intend to take the correct paths.

Although there are pedagogically correct models to follow when writing curriculum plans, these models are often not followed by practitioners (Neale et al., 1983).

Wanda May suggests some of the reasons why educators do not often use models that are espoused in textbooks (May, 1986):

(1) A model often requires a sophisticated knowledge base in the subject matter.

(2) The complexity of actual classroom life often is not congruous with the systematic approach of a model.

(3) A model often does not take into account personality factors or learning style preferences.

This chapter will try to explain how planning is actually carried out in social studies. Utilizing an eight-part scheme, this model avoids the above-mentioned three problems.

Social studies planning takes three forms: **long-range plans**, **intermediate plans**, and **short-term plans**. Resource and teaching units cover a long period of time; weekly plans cover an intermediate period of time; and daily lesson plans cover a short period. All three kinds of plans are used in social studies.

A **resource unit** is a collection of materials, activities, techniques, and so on, which are organized around topics. When implemented, the above items enable a person to teach a social studies unit. Resource units are not prepared with a particular group of students in mind, primarily because each year a teacher receives a new group of students and needs to prepare a slightly different unit for each class. Since the resource unit is a collection of materials, activities, and techniques, each year the teacher can pick and choose from it to arrive at a unit tailored for that year's students.

Besides being a collection, a resource unit is an organizational tool that allows a teacher to relate learnings to one another and to avoid a program that is highly fragmented by isolated daily lessons. Phillip Heath and Thomas Weible (1979) list advantages to teaching with a unit:

(1) Unit planning puts the teacher in control of the teaching–learning situation.

(2) Unit planning makes instruction relevant to the experiences and needs of individual students.

(3) Unit instruction provides decision-making opportunities directed toward socially responsible behavior.

(4) Unit instruction translates learning into social action.

(5) Unit planning provides for development and utilization of diverse competencies among teachers and is a vehicle for bringing these together in meeting common goals.

(6) Unit instruction promotes basic skills development.

(7) Unit instruction fosters independent student inquiry and learning.

(8) Unit instruction permits exploration, application, and integration of the personal interests and abilities of students regardless of content area.

THE PARTS OF A RESOURCE UNIT

Think of a resource unit as being divided into eight parts:

I.	Overview
II.	Concepts, Generalizations, and Facts
III.	Understandings, Attitudes, and Skills
IV.	Motivational Activities
V.	Developmental Activities
VI.	Evaluation Techniques
VII.	Bibliography
VIII.	Other Sources

I. Overview

An overview is an introduction to the unit. Written in narrative, paragraph form, the overview includes such items as

What is the topic of the unit?
What is the grade level of the unit?
Why was this topic selected?
How long will the unit be taught?

> Why is it important that students
> study this topic?
> What are some important things
> the students will study in this unit?

II. Concepts, Generalizations, and Facts

The function of this section is to provide an outline of what the students
will be studying. Social studies is such a vast subject that a teacher can
easily be confused about how to arrange all the material. This part of the
unit will allow a teacher to operate with an organized plan.

CONCEPTS

A concept can be defined simply as an idea. It should be brief—no more
than a few words. The social science disciplines provide us with innumer-
able examples of concepts:

History	chronology, early settlements, the present, heirlooms, change, old
Geography	mountains, population explosion, zoning practice, land use, metropolis, river
Political Science	government, political power, freedom of speech, democracy, dictatorship
Economics	consumers, scarce resources, money, division of labor, production, wants
Sociology	role, primary group, belonging, social class, leadership, fads, cooperation
Anthropology	customs, artifacts, primitive people, ways of life, culture, tool

As you can see, concepts can be everyday terms (river) or they can be
terms that children perhaps have not studied before (division of labor).
They can refer to tangible things (tool) or they can refer to abstractions
(cooperation). Concepts form the basis for a teacher's lesson. If you ask a
teacher what she is going to teach in social studies tomorrow afternoon,
she might say, "I'm teaching about fads," or "My students will be studying
about freedom of speech."

Because concepts are tossed around so freely and are used so commonly, there is a danger that teachers will expect their students to comprehend them very quickly. Concepts are ideas and, as such, they summon
different images in students' mind. A lesson on rivers might mean that

Jimmy will visualize the wide Mississippi River (because his family crossed it on their vacation last summer); it might mean that Susie will envision a busy waterway, filled with barges and boats (because that is what she saw on television last week); and to Frank it might mean a peaceful place to cast a fishing line (because he and his grandfather often go to a nearby river to fish). The teacher's job then is to teach about "river" as a very general idea, one that addresses all the characteristics that are in the minds of her students.

USES OF CONCEPTS. Using concepts in teaching has several benefits (besides helping to organize information): first, they show a relationship or association. In the above example of rivers, a primary teacher can point out that all rivers have common qualities, i.e., contain water, have a source and a head, have banks, move in a meandering way, have currents, etc.

Second, the use of concepts can reduce relearning. If a middle grade student is introduced to the concept of monarchy when 17th century England is studied, then he will have an easier time learning about the Romanoffs of 19th century Russia.

SPIRAL APPROACH. Concepts can be handled at varying levels of complexity. A five-year-old child would learn about adaptation as she participates in a social studies lesson involving the need to wear warm clothing during the winter. On the other hand, an eleven-year-old student would deal with this same concept in a more complex way. She might discuss it in terms of 19th century Americans adapting to the effects of the Industrial evolution.

The late Hilda Taba illustrates how a concept can spiral up in complexity. In Figure 2.1 the concept of modification is taken from grade one through grade eight.

Although there are countless concepts, some are easier to teach than others, and some are easier to use in a spiral approach from grade to grade. Hilda Taba has identified eleven of them as essential for a grade 1–8 social studies progam. They are (Taba, 1971, 24)

causality	conflict	cooperation
cultural change	differences	interdependence
modification	power	societal control
tradition	values	

GENERALIZATIONS

A generalization is a statement that is usually true and applicable. Each of the six social science disciplines yields countless generalizations. Some examples are listed on page 31.

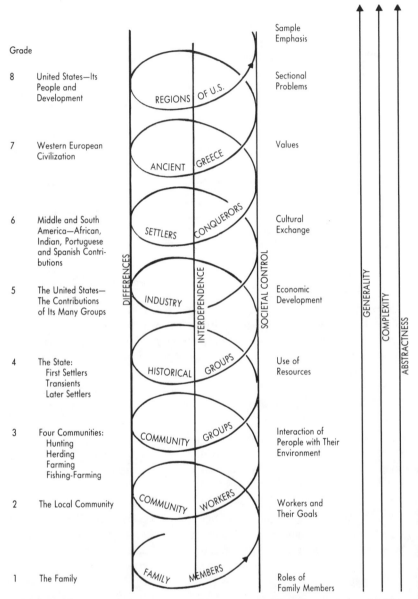

Figure 2.1 The spiral development of three key concepts. Reprinted by permission of Addison-Wesley Pub. Co. Taken from *A Teacher's Handbook to Elementary Social Studies, 2nd ed.* by Hilda Taba, et al., © 1971.

(1) *History*
Change has always been with us throughout the centuries.

(2) *Geography*
Areas of the earth develop relationships with other areas.

(3) *Political Science*
Every known society has some kind of authority structure called a government.

(4) *Economics*
Economic resources can be used in various ways.

(5) *Sociology*
The family is the basic social unit in most societies.

(6) *Anthropology*
The art and architecture of a group of people help create a national identity.

Generalizations always contain one or more concepts. For example, generalization number (1) above contains the concept of change; number (2) has the concept of relationships; number (3) has society, authority structure, and government; number (4) has economic resources; number (5) has family, social unit, and societies; and number (6) has art, architecture, and national identity. Often a generalization will show a relationship between the concepts, such as in number (6) above. In this case, students need to be aware that a country's national identity is shaped by factors such as art and architecture.

CHOOSING GENERALIZATIONS FOR THE UNIT. After a number of concepts are seleced for the unit, the generalizations are chosen. For example, if a third grade teacher selects a unit entitled "Getting Food to Our Community," he might select the concepts of transportation, production, and cooperation. The last concept of cooperation could lead to a study of the following generalizations:

(1) Many groups work to produce food.

(2) Producers must find a way to get their goods to the consumers.

FACTS

A fact is a specific piece of verified information. Examples of facts are listed below:

George Washington was the first president of the United States.
Amelia Earhart was the first woman to fly alone across the Atlantic Ocean.

> During the Great Depression in our country, the
> unemployment rate for Blacks was twice as high as
> that for Whites.
> The Nile River flows toward the north.
> The basic unit of money in Mexico is the peso.

THE RELATIONSHIP AMONG CONCEPTS, GENERALIZATIONS, AND FACTS

It was mentioned earlier in this chapter that a teacher organizes lessons around concepts—ideas representing abstract or concrete entities. These concepts are then linked with broad statements (called generalizations) to either provide a description of the concept or to depict a relationship among several concepts. Facts are used to provide supporting detail to the generalization and to make the concept meaningful.

A unit on "rivers" would deal with several concepts; one of them might be "movement." Several generalizations could be used to teach the concept of movement; one of them might be, "Rivers take a variety of paths as they proceed from the source to the mouth." The students would then need to study a large number of facts that would present different situations in which the generalization would be true; some facts might be: (1) The beginning of a river is called a source. (2) The end of a river is called a mouth. (3) The Mississippi River flows from north to south. (4) The Nile River flows from south to north. (5) The Amazon River flows from west to east. (6) The Congo River flows from east to west.

Other facts could be added to illustrate how rivers in the world do indeed travel in many kinds of paths: long rivers, short rivers, straight rivers, meandering rivers, gently flowing rivers, rapidly rushing rivers, etc. When the unit is completed, each student should be able to realize the diversity in the routes of rivers around the world. It isn't expected that a student memorize the generalization. The expectation is for the student to be able to verbalize—in his own words—the essence of the generalization. For example, if a student were to tell the teacher, "I didn't know there were so many rivers in the world, and it seems like they all look a little different from each other," then the student has apparently understood that the rivers he has studied move in a variety of ways.

Another important point regarding concepts, generalizations, and facts is that the first two are transferable; that is, a concept and a generalization have meanings relative to many settings. What students know about "representative government" in one situation can be applied to another situation. A student who realizes that "people who live in a country with a representative government are involved in decision making" can apply this to many situations in the world. Facts, on the other hand, are not transferable. They are applicable only to a specific situation. *"The United States has a representative government"* is a fact that is true in just one instance. Concepts and generalizations, then, supply a framework for learning, while facts supply the details to fill out the framework.

III. Understandings, Attitudes, and Skills

PURPOSES VS. OBJECTIVES

The importance of this part of the resource unit is that it relates specifically to purposes and objectives. A purpose is a general statement that establishes a goal for the lesson. For example, a teacher who selects the topic of "river transportation" might feel that her purpose for that lesson will be for the students to learn about the ways that rivers facilitate transportation.

Such a broadly stated purpose has its place. It is appropriate when a teacher wants to think about the general direction for the unit; it is acceptable when a teacher needs to communicate to other people the overall nature of the lesson. It is not sufficient, though, when a teacher wants to measure student achievement in a certain lesson exactly.

Specific goals call for more precise objectives. Robert Mager (1962, 3) defines an objective as

> . . . an intent communicated by a statement describing a proposed change in a learner—a statement of what the learner is to be like when he has successfully completed a learning experience. It is a description of a pattern of behavior (performance) we want the learner to be able to demonstrate.

A behavioral objective is often created with an A-B-C-D approach. The "A" stands for actor; the "B" stands for behavior; the "C" stands for conditions; and the "D" stands for degree of mastery. In the situation above, where the teacher stated her purpose as wanting her students to learn about the ways that rivers facilitate transportation, the A-B-C-D approach can be used to create a more precise behavioral objective:

> The student will write, and correctly spell, the names
> of three kinds of watercraft used on the ocean, which
> carry cargo from one part of the world to another.

The "A" (actor) is represented by the student. The "B" (behavior) is indicated through the verb *write*. The "C" (conditions) are simply given by stating that the student must use watercraft which travel the ocean—rather than lakes or rivers. The "D" (degree of mastery) is designated by requiring the student to spell the names of the watercraft correctly. By elaborating upon and lengthening a purpose, it is apparent that a teacher can create an objective stated in behavioral terms.

Here is another example. A lesson might have as its purpose: The students will understand how the United States depends upon other countries for certain raw materials. This could be transformed into an objective—using behavioral terms—in the following manner:

> Using pictures from *Newsweek* and *Time*, the student will create a collage showing products used in our country that are made from raw materials supplied from foreign countries. The raw materials will be correctly listed at the bottom of the collage.

Actor:	the student
Behavior:	make a collage
Conditions:	use pictures from magazines
Degree of mastery:	correctly list the raw materials

In summary, there are times when a purpose is appropriate and there are times when an objective is appropriate. It all depends upon the specificity desired by the teacher. Ronald T. Hyman (1974, 37–52) provides a good summary of the pro and cons for using objectives rather than purposes.

Because the use of "objective" or "purpose" is often a philosophical preference by the teacher, this book will use a neutral term to refer to either—or both. The term *goal* will be used when referring to what the student is expected to learn in a lesson.

Administrators should be aware that there are three main areas where teachers can write goals; they are understandings, attitudes, and skills.

UNDERSTANDINGS

An understanding is defined as a piece of knowledge that has been comprehended. This is something that a student will know or remember—something which would derive from the cognitive domain of learning (Bloom, 1956).

A teacher who is preparing a unit on "Games around the World" would make a list of the understandings he wants his students to attain. Some of these might be

(1) The student will learn the names of five games played in countries in the Eastern hemisphere.
(2) The student will list a game played in the U.S. and then list the name of a similar game from another country.
(3) The student will identify the equipment needed to play the Spanish game "Pelele."

ATTITUDES

An attitude is defined as "a feeling the student has toward something or someone." Attitudes emanate from the affective domain. In the unit on "Games around the World," the teacher might include the following on his list:

(1) The student will enjoy participating in a game he has not tried before.

(2) The student will demonstrate respect for the rules of the games.

(3) The student will develop a curiosity about the origin of the games she is playing.

SKILLS

A skill is defined as "the ability to do something." Skills originate in the psychomotor domain and suggest movement requiring a mind/motor connection. In this same unit on games, a teacher would prepare a list of skills, some of which might appear as follows:

(1) The student will develop leadership ability by serving as a captain for one of the team games.

(2) The student will develop listening skills when the directions for a new game are delivered.

(3) Using a world map, the student will be able to locate the countries for the games that the class plays.

This part of the resource unit is designed to be a collection of the teacher's objectives from all three domains. It is often convenient to have such a list. For example, during a parent/teacher conference a parent might ask, "Could you tell me what my son will be learning this year in social studies?" It's simply a matter of the teacher turning to one of his units and reading some of the goals from Part III. At times a teacher wishes to use a newsletter sent to the homes to communicate to parents some of the plans for social studies that semester. Again, the teacher can list some of the understandings, attitudes, and skills from Part III.

Furthermore, since social studies is such a vast topic, it is comforting for a teacher to be able to look at Part III and realize that there are certain definite goals which she is trying to accomplish during a period of instruction. The teacher is also able to keep a balance among the three domains by making sure that all three areas of Part III are represented with an adequate number of goals.

It is impossible to list all the understandings and attitudes that students should learn in grades K–8. On the other hand, it is possible to find lists of skills that have been created for elementary and middle grade students.

The National Council for the Social Studies (NCSS, 1963) published in its 33rd yearbook a social studies skills chart, which has endured for over twenty-five years. The 221 skills are listed in Appendix D.

John Jarolimek has established a grouping for the social studies skills, which appears in Table 2.1.

IV. Motivational Activities

This section of the resource unit is concerned with the opening day of the unit. What will the teacher do with the class to initiate the study of this

Table 2.1 Social studies skills. *

Social Skills

1. Living and working together; taking turns; respecting the rights of others; being socially sensitive.
2. Learning self-control and self-direction.
3. Sharing ideas and experiences with others.

Study Skills and Work Habits

1. Locating and gathering information from books, the library, and from a variety of other sources and special references.
2. Making reports; speaking before a group; listening when others are reporting; listening to and following directions.
3. Reading social studies materials for a variety of purposes, e.g., to get the main idea; to locate a particular point or fact; to predict outcomes; to detect author bias; to compare and contrast.
4. Using maps, globes, charts, graphs, and other graphic and pictorial materials.
5. Organizing information into usable structures such as outlining; making charts; making time lines; classifying pictures or data; arranging ideas, events, or facts in a sequence; taking notes; keeping records; and preparing summaries.
6. Conducting an inquiry on a problem of interest.

Group Work Skills

1. Working together on committees and assuming various roles in small groups such as being chairperson, secretary, or group member.
2. Participating in a group discussion; leading a discussion.
3. Participating in group decision making.

Intellectual Skills

1. Defining and identifying problems; relating prior experiences to a present inquiry.
2. Forming and testing hypotheses; drawing conclusions based on information.
3. Analyzing and synthesizing data.
4. Distinguishing between fact and opinion; learning to separate relevant from irrelevant information and to recognize bias in persuasive materials such as advertising, political statements, and propaganda.
5. Sensing cause and effect relationships.
6. Comparing and contrasting differing points of view.
7. Recognizing the value components in decision making.

* From John Jarolimek, *Social Studies in Elementary Education, Seventh* ed. NY:Macmillan, pp. 6, 7 (1985).

new topic? Motivational theory tells us that educators must utilize interest to get the students to participate eagerly. Therefore, this part of the unit will contain a number of activities that will create excitement with the students because they are interested and curious about what is occurring.

There are some characteristics a motivational activity must possess:

(1) It must be an attention grabber. As mentioned above, students need to have their interest aroused.

(2) It must be relatively short. A motivational activity will occur within a single class period and might last just a few minutes.

(3) Normally, the activity will be executed by the teacher. The reason for this is that the class will have no or little knowledge about the topic at the inception of the unit; therefore, it is unwise to require the students to perform with a scanty background. Although the teacher is the major actor in a motivational activity, it is acceptable for the students to participate if it means that they contribute only within their limits.

(4) A motivational activity should set the stage for the unit, making it clear what the rest of the unit is going to be about.

(5) A motivational activity can also be used at a later point in the unit if the teacher finds that the students need a shot in the arm. We don't like to think about the students' interest waning, but it does happen. At that point, the teacher can carry out another motivational activity to boost the students' enthusiasm.

EXAMPLES OF MOTIVATIONAL ACTIVITIES

A kindergarten teacher might initiate a unit on safety in the following manner, which would only take a few minutes. The teacher asks the students who ride a school bus to raise their hands. Then she asks them to tell her the things they have done on the bus this week to create a safe ride. Among the first mentioned things might be, "I sit in my seat and do not stand in the aisle." If the students are unable to come up with ideas quickly, the teacher can prompt them by asking, "Do you think it's a good idea to stick your arms outside the window on the bus?"

This activity qualifies as a motivational activity because (1) it gets the attention of the students since a school bus is a familiar part of their lives; (2) it is short, taking only a portion of the class period; (3) it is essentially carried out by the teacher (the students' contributions do not call for knowledge beyond their capabilities); and (4) it introduces the rest of the class period, which will focus on safety.

A second motivational activity for a seventh grade class might be as follows, lasting an entire class period. The teacher announces to the class that they will spend the next three weeks studying the classical world of ancient Greece and Rome. The students are instructed to take out a sheet of paper and fold it in half lengthwise. At the top of the left column should be written the heading "Things about Greece and Rome," and at the top of the right column should be written "The Number of Students in Class Who Agree."

Each student should make a list in the left column of any pieces of information he thinks are true about Greece or Rome. The information could be something he has read, seen on television, or obtained from other sources. A tally mark should be entered in the right column for each item the student has written. This indicates that the item has been mentioned one time.

Once all the students have had a chance to prepare a number of items, the teacher would ask each student to read his or hers. If another student reads the same item, then a second tally mark is made in the right column. At the end of the class period, a student will have a long list of items in the left column, along with a record of the total number of students in class who had agreed with the items.

This also qualifies as a motivational activity because (1) it is an attention getter by way of involving the students; (2) it is short, taking no longer than a single class period; (3) the activity only requires students to do what they are capable of doing; and (4) it is a good beginning for the unit. The teacher can quickly look at the tally totals to see what are the most prevalent ideas about Greece and Rome. In addition, these totals can be compared to the students' opinions at the completion of the unit to see which of their conceptions have changed.

V. Developmental Activities

This section of the resource unit contains the heart and soul of the unit, for it contains the activities in which the students will actually be engaged. A developmental activity is used after the motivational activity is finished. Many of them should be used during the course of the unit because they will allow the students to develop a thorough familiarity with the topic being studied. A developmental activity could be completed in less than a single class period, although it will usually take one or more class periods.

A third grade teacher who is teaching a unit on "Our Community" might decide to spend one class period on a developmental activity: having the students view a filmstrip on communities. The introduction to the filmstrip, the actual viewing, and the follow-up discussion could fill up a half-hour lesson.

Later in the unit, that teacher might decide to have her third graders go on a field trip as a developmental activity. This time the activity might take three days: one day for a preview of what the students will see, a second day for the trip itself, and a third day for a review of the trip they took.

The developmental activities should be chosen so that they coincide with the previous three parts of the unit—the introduction of Part I, the items of Part II, and the purposes of Part III. Kenworthy has compiled a good collection of activities (see Figure 2.2), some of which can be motivational while others can be developmental.

Activity or method	**Am using this now**	**Should try or use more**
1. Bulletin boards		
2. Buzz groups		
3. Cartoons		
4. Chalkboard		
5. Charts and graphs		
6. Choral speaking		
7. Collecting		
8. Committee or group work		
9. Cooking food of places studied		
10. Crossword puzzles		
11. Current events		
12. Dances of places or periods studied		
13. Debates (for older pupils only)		
14. Diaries		
15. Dioramas		
16. Discussions		
17. Dramatics		
18. Exhibits		
19. Films		
20. Filmstrips		
21. Flags		
22. Flannelboards		
23. Flash cards		

Figure 2.2 Ideas for motivational and developmental activities [taken from Leonard Kenworthy, *Social Studies for the Eighties, 3rd ed.* NY:John Wiley, pp. 81–84 (1981)].

Activity or method	Am using this now	Should try or use more
24. Flowcharts (especially of economic processes)		
25. Games		
26. Halls of Fame		
27. Interviews (sometimes tape-recorded)		
28. Jigsaw puzzle maps		
29. Listening activities of many kinds		
30. Making models		
31. Maps of many kinds, and globes		
32. Mobiles		
33. Mock panels, broadcasts, and telecasts		
34. Mock-ups (enlargements to more than life-size)		
35. Modeling in various media		
36. Montages and/or collages		
37. Murals		
38. Music		
39. Newspapers and magazines		
40. Notebooks		
41. Open textbook study		
42. Panels and round tables		
43. Pen pals		
44. People as resources		
45. Photographs taken by pupils		
46. Pictures		
47. Plays		
48. Poetry		
49. Posters		
50. Problem-solving or inquiry		
51. Puppets		
52. Questioning of many kinds		
53. Radio programs		
54. Reading of many kinds		
55. Recordings		

Figure 2.2 (continued). Ideas for motivational and developmental activities [taken from Leonard Kenworthy, *Social Studies for the Eighties, 3rd ed*. NY:John Wiley, pp. 81–84 (1981)].

Activity or method	Am using this now	Should try or use more
56. Reporting		
57. Reproductions or facsimiles		
58. Role-playing or sociodrama		
59. Sand tables		
60. School affiliations		
61. Scrapbooks (individual and/or class)		
62. Service projects (like Trick or Treat)		
63. Sewing		
64. Slides		
65. Sociometric devices for grouping		
66. Source materials		
67. Stamps, coins, and other hobbies		
68. Story-telling		
69. Surveys		
70. Talks by teachers, pupils, visitors		
71. Tape recordings		
72. Television		
73. Tests of various kinds		
74. Textbooks		
75. Time-lines		
76. Transparencies		
77. Trips		
78. Word-association device		
79. Workbooks or response books		
80. Writing for materials		
81. Written work of various kinds		

Figure 2.2 (continued). Ideas for motivational and developmental activities [taken from Leonard Kenworthy, *Social Studies for the Eighties, 3rd ed.* NY:John Wiley, pp. 81–84 (1981)].

VI. Evaluation Techniques

The sixth part of the resource unit is a collection of techniques that an administrator could recommend to a teacher to evaluate the students. These evaluation ideas could be used at the end of the unit or at any time throughout. More will be written later in this book about evaluation of students in social studies.

To provide one example of an entry in this evaluation section, suppose that a teacher had taken his third grade class on a field trip (developmental activity) to visit one of the town's local merchants. One of the purposes for that trip was to have the students realize the variety of merchandise that a store owner must keep on hand to satisfy his customers' needs. An evaluation technique for that part of the unit might be for the teacher to have the class create an experience summary. Asking the students, upon returning to the school, to supply the names of the objects they saw at the store, the teacher would write their responses on some large sheets of butcher paper. This technique would allow the teacher to evaluate how well the class recalled what they had seen on the field trip. The summary might appear as shown in Figure 2.3.

VII. Bibliography

This section of the resource unit contains a list of written materials that could be used by the teacher or the students. Examples include fiction books, newspaper articles, poems, encyclopedias, textbooks, diaries, letters, bills of sales, census records, brochures, etc. Some of these would be

---

An Experience Chart Summarizing a Field Trip

1. Pens   I can buy ball point pens at Murphy's Hardware Store.

2. Light bulbs   There are light bulbs that give lots of light and there are light bulbs that give off little light.

3. Hammer   If I need to buy a hammer, I can buy it at Murphy's Store.

4. Lawn mower   Mr. Murphy sells heavy items. One of these is a lawn mower.

5. Paint   My mother wants to paint our house. She can find the paint she needs at Murphy's.

6. Extra things   Mr. Murphy has many things in his store. Some of them he keeps in the back room because he doesn't have space for them anywhere else.

Figure 2.3

used by the students as they work through the unit while others would be utilized by the teacher as she constructs the unit.

As much descriptive information as a teacher desires can be placed under a bibliographic entry, for example:

(1) Author
(2) Title
(3) Publication date
(4) Publisher
(5) Publisher's address
(6) Call number
(7) Short description of the material
(8) Is this intended for teacher, student, or both?

A teacher who is doing a fifth grade unit on the U.S. Revolutionary War period might have the following entry in Part VII:

> Lawson, Robert. *Mr. Revere and I.* New York:Dell
> Publishing Co., Inc. (1953). A student will appreciate
> this humorous account of a great moment in our
> country's history. Paul Revere's horse tells about some
> of the happenings during the American Revolution.

VIII. Other Sources

This last part of a resource unit reflects the nonprint materials that are not included in Part VII: Bibliography. Examples of entries include filmstrips, photographs, films, special maps, phonograph records, videocassettes, guest speakers, kits, games, etc. Some of the same information can be included for each entry as mentioned in Part VII.

An example of a resource unit on Mexico, for the fifth grade, is shown in Appendix C.

LESSON PLANS

The first part of this chapter discussed how to construct a long-range teaching plan: a resource unit. The resource unit covers a period from several days to several weeks; therefore, it needs to be broken down into daily instructional experiences, which are called lesson plans. Johann Herbart, a 19th century German, was one of the first educators to develop a systematic approach to lesson planning. He structured a lesson into five parts:

(1) *Preparation*
Students are prepared for the lesson by referring to previous experiences.

(2) *Presentation*
The new material is presented to the students.

(3) *Association*
Analogies are made between the new material and prior learning.

(4) *Generalization*
New and old learning is combined to produce a new principle.

(5) *Application*
The student's grasp of the new principles is applied to a variety of situations.

There are many ways to write lesson plans. Among the many approaches to lesson planning that have been advanced, Madeline Hunter's lesson design stands out as one of the most popular this past decade. It is based on putting theory (what social scientists have found out about the psychology of learning) into practice. Hunter's model consists of seven parts:

(1) *Establish Anticipatory Set*
This allows the students to focus on what will be learned.

(2) *Objective and Purpose*
The teacher needs to state what will be learned.

(3) *Input*
Students acquire new information about the knowledge, procedures, and skills they will be taught.

(4) *Modeling*
The teacher provides demonstrations of the procedure or product they are expected to learn.

(5) *Checking for Understanding*
The teacher ascertains that the students know how to do what is expected of them.

(6) *Guided Practice*
Students practice their knowledge or skill under direct supervision.

(7) *Independent Practice*
The students perform the new knowledge or skill on their own.

Through personal experiences of teaching elementary and middle grade students, teaching undergraduate methods students, and working with classroom teachers, I use a five-part lesson plan, which contains the essential characteristics of the lesson plans previously described. This five-part format contains (1) purpose, (2) motivation, (3) development, (4) conclusion, and (5) materials. All of the lesson plans presented in this book have been prepared according to this style.

(1) *Purpose*

This tells what the intent of the lesson is. The information can be written either in broadly stated goals or in precise objectives. In the accompanying lesson plan the purpose is fairly broad, i.e., "locate places" and "discern ties."

(2) *Motivation*

This describes how the teacher will begin the lesson. The motivation component can occupy a period of time as short as a few minutes, or it can take more of the class period. In the accompanying lesson plan, the class is asked to do something that is easy, namely, to define a term which they have heard and used before. The intent of the motivation section is to stimulate the students for the upcoming lesson.

(3) *Development*

This part of the lesson plan occupies the bulk of the class period, for it is a description of what the students (and the teacher) will be doing. The accompanying lesson devotes about half of the period to the development component. The teacher guides the class for a part of it, while the students independently work on some of it.

(4) *Conclusion*

The conclusion is the wrap-up, which can include review, testing, summary, or extension activities. It is also a time for previewing the next lesson. The accompanying lesson is concluded by having the class do an activity that requires them to use the skills they learned in the lesson.

(5) *Materials*

This is a list of all the materials the teacher will need to conduct that day's lesson.

MIDDLE GRADE LESSON PLAN

Topic: **Making Connections**

Grade: **6th**

Date: **February 5, 1:30–2:15**

I. *Purpose*: tells what a student will learn

The student will be able to locate places on a map. The student will be able to discern the ties that connect various places in the world.

II. *Motivation*: tells how to begin the day's lesson

The teacher should write the word "classify" on the board. Ask the students what this word means. An example can be provided of sorting playing cards into four piles (hearts, diamonds, clubs, and spades) according to suit. When the class has satisfactorily understood that it signifies putting things into certain groups that are alike, the lesson can proceed.

III.   *Development*: tells how to conduct the day's lesson

Hand out the accompanying document entitled "Making Connections" (see p. 47). As the class reads it silently, they should look for the five different kinds of connections among people in the world.

While they are reading, the teacher should put the following table on the chalkboard.

Connections	
Category of Connection	**Characteristics of That Category**
1.	
2.	
3.	
4.	
5.	

As the members of the class finish reading, have five people come to the board and put their connection in the left-hand column. At this point the teacher will lead a discussion so that the right-hand column can be completed. It should be the *most important* characteristic of that kind of connection. For example, a "technological" connection category should have as its characteristic something about people in one part of the world quickly being in communication with people in another part of the world. Students might have several characteristics which they feel are the most important, but they should be able to justify their opinions.

Ask the class how they have proceeded to classify. Their responses should be elaborated on until it has been suggested that a person must look for all the characteristics of the items; different categories should be established to accommodate groups of these characteristics; and then the items are placed in the appropriate category.

IV.   *Conclusion*: tells how to close or evaluate the day's lesson

(a) Kuwait and U.S.S.R. Sign Arms Deal

(b) China Increases Purchases of U.S. Wheat

(c) Bulgaria Denies It Stole Japanese Trade Secrets

(d) Head of Roman Catholic Church Plans to Tour Canada

ACTIVITY
60 MAKING CONNECTIONS

Technology Has Changed Our World in Many Ways. One important way has been to connect the parts of the world more closely than ever before. For example, rapid communication makes it possible for news to spread from one region to another in minutes. Cures for diseases discovered in one region are quickly shared with others.

Regions Are Also Linked Politically and Economically. Technological connections are not the only links between regions. Two others are political links and economic links. Political links are connections between governments. Some political links are alliances, or friendships. Other political links are not friendly at all. Some political links are organizations that nations belong to, like the United Nations.

Economic links involve trading of goods and services. Economic links have been important since people first sailed the oceans. They are even more important today. The complex machines in industrialized countries need resources from other regions to run. Large populations in areas with poor farmland need to buy food from other regions to survive.

Another Kind of Link Is a Cultural Link. A cultural link involves shared customs, language, music, art, religion, or other element of culture. Because the United States is a nation of immigrants, it has cultural links with many other regions. Technology has also increased cultural links. New inventions let television programs, recordings, movies, and books be shared more readily than ever.

Finally, Regions Share Geographic Links. A geographic link could be a shared climate, body of water, landform, or resource. For example, Northern America and Western Europe have always been linked by the North Atlantic Ocean. The North Atlantic has been an important transportation route between the two regions. It has also been a resource. The shared resource of oil links the nations of the Middle East with oil-producing countries in Southern Africa, Asia, and Latin America, as well.

There are so many connections between regions that some people describe today's world as a global village. This means that people around the world depend on each other, just like the people of a small town or village do.

In this activity, you will identify some of the connections that link regions into one world.

★ BUILDING SKILLS: CLASSIFYING CONNECTIONS

As you know, classifying means grouping items according to their characteristics. Classifying can be simple. For example, you can sort playing cards according to their color, their number, or whether they are hearts, spades, clubs, or diamonds.

Classifying world connections is harder. The characteristics of connections are not as easy to see. First, you must decide what groups or categories you are going to use. Then you must define the characteristics that match each category. Third, you look at the connections to see what characteristics they have. Finally, you sort the connections into the categories you picked.

(e) U.S. State Department Calls for More Aid to Central America

(f) U.S. Space Shuttle Launches Indonesian Satellite

(g) Central American Volcano Affects Climate in Faraway Lands

(h) Little Leaguers Meet for World Series in Taiwan

(i) France Sells Nuclear Technology to Middle Eastern Countries

(j) Scientists Cooperate in Antarctica

The above represent headlines that could possibly appear in the newspaper. Read headline "a" to the class and ask someone to come to the world wall map and point out where Kuwait and the Soviet Union are. Then ask them to decide which of the five connections is suggested by this headline: (a) technological, (b) political, (c) economic, (d) cultural, or (e) geographic. The student should not only be able to give a reason why a headline falls in a certain category but should also be asked to explain why it is not an example of another category.

V. Materials: tells what is needed for the day's lesson

World wall map, handout entitled "Making Connections" (see page 47).

Note: This lesson plan has been adapted from an activity entitled "Making Connections," published by Graphic Learning Corporation, Tallahassee, FL.

The lesson plan "Making Connections" is interdisciplinary because it utilizes information from a number of the social sciences. Geography is prevalent with references to places in the world, but economics (trading of goods), political science (governments), and anthropology (culture) are also present. Some of the lesson plans presented in later chapters focus almost entirely on just a single social science discipline, but that is done just for clarity of presentation. In reality, social studies at the early elementary and middle grade levels should be taught by combining a number of the social sciences in each lesson.

Tips on Planning Lessons

When executing the lesson plans they have made, teachers are encouraged (McKenzie, 1986) to utilize the following suggestions, for they lead to increased student achievement.

INTRODUCE LESSONS WITH CLEAR GOALS

Sometimes a lesson has too much poorly organized information for a student to learn. In these cases the teacher needs to inform the pupils of the lesson's objective, display a list of questions that should be answered as a result of the lesson, give an outline of points to be made in the lesson, show relations between ideas to be introduced and material previously learned, etc.

MAKE IDEAS CLEAR AND USEFUL

Students often find material difficult to understand or impossible to apply. In these cases the teacher needs to substitute precise terms for vague terms. Say "only ten cities" instead of "a few cities" or say "in six out of eight cases" instead of "usually."

Defining concepts as a dictionary does can provide little help to students as they try to grasp the meaning. A vertical listing of attributes is more successful. For example, it is easier to understand the meaning of the concept "capitalism" if it appears in the following manner.

Capitalism is an economic system where

(1) Land, factories, and other means of production are owned by private individuals or groups of individuals.

(2) Competition among businesses takes place.

(3) Hired labor produces goods and services.

(4) Profits are made from a business.

Principles or generalizations that do not state precisely when they are applicable are stumbling blocks to students' comprehension. A teacher should restate these rules in "if-then" style. The unclear generalization "in a market economy, consumer economic wants exert a major influence on production" could be restated as "if consumers make their economic wants known in a market economy, then production can be influenced."

ENSURE ELABORATION

A teacher should broaden the meaning of a concept or generalization by giving both examples and nonexamples. If the concept is "peninsula," then the formations of Florida and Spain/Portugal can be shown on the map as examples of land with water on three sides. Conversely, Madagascar would be a nonexample because it is completely surrounded by water. Another way to elaborate is to read a story as an illustration of the material being taught.

GUIDE PROCESSING WITH QUESTIONS

A teacher should try to involve the entire class when a question is asked. One technique to do this is to have the pupils give a nonverbal signal (put your thumb down if the answer is no or put your thumb up if the answer is yes.)

METHODS OF INSTRUCTION

Teaching methods are instructional strategies. Educators are concerned with methods because appropriate methods lead to effective learning. Just as with lesson plans, methods are described in a variety of ways. One of the leading books which describes methods is by Joyce and Weil (1986). These authors classify methods into four families:

(1) The information processing family
(2) The personal family
(3) The social family
(4) The behavioral system family

Methodology is obviously of paramount importance to teachers, and it often assumes a similar role for principals (as instructional leaders in the building), central office supervisors (whose primary role is to monitor curriculum), and assistant superintendents (in charge of the district's instructional needs). The upcoming pages of this chapter briefly describe the various social studies methodologies that are subsumed under the four families.

The Information Processing Family

This family of models deals with how students acquire and organize data. Information processing is concerned with how a person's experiences are organized into meaningful patterns into long-term memory.

CONCEPT LEARNING

Concept learning is the general term used to help students learn how to use concepts to organize information. It can be further subdivided into (1) concept formation, whereby students observe differences and similarities of gathered data, group the data, and label the groups; (2) concept reception, whereby the students receive the definition of the concept to be learned, receive examples and nonexamples of the concept, and supply additional examples and nonexamples of the concept, giving reasons for their selections; and (3) concept attainment, whereby students are presented examples and nonexamples of the concept to be learned. They then try to attain the definition or rule pertaining to the concept. Ultimately, the students supply their own examples and nonexamples of the concept. Bruner, Goodnow, and Austin (1967) have written on concept learning.

INDUCTIVE THINKING

This thinking process is achieved by drawing conclusions from specific observations. Inferences are drawn by the students as they are presented with examples and nonexamples of the concept to be learned. Hilda Taba (1967) established a reputation for teaching inductively.

INQUIRY TRAINING

This method is designed to teach students how to find out the answers to puzzling situations. Sometimes it is called problem solving, discovery learning, reflective inquiry, or reflective thought. Regardless of the term, it contains a series of steps: (1) perceiving a problem, (2) developing a hypothesis, (3) gathering and evaluating data to test the hypothesis, (4) confirming or rejecting the hypothesis, and (5) formulating a conclusion. Barry Beyer (1971) has written extensively on inquiry teaching.

ADVANCE ORGANIZERS

This method is suitable when the teacher is presenting large amounts of information and the student can benefit by having some kind of structural organization. Examples of advance organizers are an outline, a film, a demonstration, a statement of relationship, an illustration, etc. The most noted proponent (Ausubel, 1963) says that an advance organizer relates new information to what the student already knows.

MEMORIZATION

This is a mnemonic technique to improve memory. Human beings develop this ability in a number of ways, e.g., acronyms (HOMES signifies the Great Lakes of Huron, Ontario, Michigan, Erie, and Superior); jingles or rhymes (in 1492 Columbus sailed the ocean blue); rote (simply memorizing word for word what is to be remembered); link system (to label the European countries on a map, a person can think "Italian boots" and know that Italy is the country shaped like a boot). Lorayne and Lucas (1974) have written a book that provides examples of memory techniques.

The Personal Family

This family of methods focuses on the individual so that he can more readily take responsibility for his actions and have more self-awareness.

NONDIRECTIVE TEACHING

This method emphasizes a partnership between student and teacher. The teacher can help the students take a more active role in directing their education. One instance would be when a student plans an independent study project. Carl Rogers (1969) has been a pioneer in this area.

SYNECTICS

This method is designed to foster creativity in search of solutions to problems. This can be done by helping students view old problems, ideas, or products in a new light; or by helping them to see unfamiliar ideas in a more meaningful way. William Gordon (1961) has done a great deal with synectics at the elementary and secondary levels.

Joyce and Weil (1986, 163) describe a situation involving synectics in a seventh grade class, which is preparing a campaign in opposition to a change in Forest Service regulations that would permit a large part of a grove of redwood trees to be cut down as part of a lumbering operation. The class has made posters but considers them to be too dull. The class decides to try synectics by discussing analogies to the redwood trees. One student asks, "How is a redwood tree like a toothpick?" to which another responds by saying, "You use them to pick the teeth of the gods." After a period of time during which the class uses analogies to look at the redwood tree situation in a different perspective, they are ready to use some of their new ideas to redo the posters.

THE CLASSROOM MEETING

This procedure allows students to meet as a group to discuss and work out problems. The point of the meetings is not to criticize each other, but to find ways to help each other. Used as a way for students to take responsibility for their social and behavioral situations, it addresses the students' needs for self-worth, self-awareness, and respect for other students. William Glasser (1965) is an authority in this area.

The Social Family

Social family methods are synergistic, i.e., they operate on the theory that collective benefits occur by having individuals work together cooperatively.

GROUP INVESTIGATION

"The model is designed to lead students to define problems, explore various perspectives on the problems, collect relevant data, develop hypotheses, and test them. The teacher organizes the group process and disciplines it, helps the students find and organize information, and ensures that there is a vigorous level of activity and discourse" (Joyce and Weil, 1986, 10). Herbert Thelen (1960) has written on this topic, stressing the benefits of democratic life in the classroom.

ROLE-PLAYING

This may be used to have students act out the roles of other people to facilitate their understanding of human relations in problem situations. Fannie and George Shaftel (1982) have written about this manner of teaching empathy.

JURISPRUDENTIAL INQUIRY

Cases are studied involving social problems in a way that promotes systematic thinking. Its primary aim is to investigate controversial issues and determine how citizens should negotiate differences. Oliver and Shaver (1971) have developed this method.

SOCIAL SCIENCE INQUIRY

This method teaches students to use the methods of social scientists. Byron and Massialas (1966) have illustrated six phases to this process: (1) present a problem or puzzling situation to the students, (2) develop a hypothesis from which to explore or solve the problem, (3) define and clarify the terms in the hypothesis, (4) examine the hypothesis in terms of its assumptions, implications, and logical validity, (5) gather facts and evidence to support the hypothesis, and (6) formulate a solution of or statement about the problem.

The Behavioral Systems Family

Models in this family have one thing in common, namely, that people adjust their behavior in response to information about how successfully they are completing tasks.

MASTERY LEARNING AND DIRECT INSTRUCTION

Mastery learning, as described by Benjamin Bloom (1971, 47–63), has the following characteristics:

(1) Mastery of a subject is described with reference to major objectives established for the unit.

(2) The material is then divided into small segments, each one having its own objectives.
(3) Learning materials are selected, along with the teaching strategy.
(4) Each segment of learning has diagnostic tests to determine how well the student is progressing.
(5) The information obtained from the diagnostic tests is used to refine the lessons for the student.

Direct instruction is a teacher-directed approach. It is characterized by large-group instruction, with classroom time highly structured by the teacher. Learning tasks are broken down into small steps. Corrective feedback by the teacher is essential as the student engages in guided practice.

LEARNING SELF-CONTROL

This method uses feedback to modify the student's behavior. Contingency management and programmed learning are two examples. Students are taught to take responsibility for their own behavior.

SIMULATION

In a simulation, students are put into a nearly real-life situation. Usually, the students are asked to role-play within a set of guidelines. Individuals are typically required to utilize decision-making skills.

APPLICATION OF METHODOLOGY

We can refer back to the middle grade lesson plan from the first part of this chapter to see how teaching methods can be used. First of all, the motivation part of "Making Connections" is an example of the information processing family. Narrowing it down, it is also an example of the advance organizer method because it relates information that the student knows (sorting playing cards) to the term that the class will study that day (classification of connections).

The development part of the lesson plan utilizes the concept learning method as the students are presented with information from which they must find examples of five kinds of connections.

The conclusion part of the lesson plan is a continuation of the concept learning method because the students are asked to classify various examples of the connections.

ASSISTANCE POINTS

Questions for Action for the Administrator

1. Assume you are conferencing with one of your teachers and he wants to know where he can obtain a resource unit on a topic he wants to strengthen. Which resource units has your district prepared that can be shared among the teachers in various buildings?

2. Look through the curriculum guidelines that are distributed by your state department of education. Are there any unit topics listed in these guidelines that your district does not currently teach in grades K–8?

3. Assume you are evaluating a first-year teacher and she has the feeling she is being overwhelmed by all the material she must teach. You attempt to make things more manageable for her. How can you explain the following statement which classifies the multitude of material into just three, easy to remember areas?

   Anything a student learns must be either an understanding, an attitude, or a skill.

4. Compare the five-step lesson plan in this chapter with the lesson plans your teachers are required to submit. Are your teachers' plans complete enough to reflect what they are teaching?

5. How can you have your teachers develop proficiency in "concept learning"?

6. The basic methods of instruction are (1) information processing, (2) personal, (3) social, and (4) behavioral. Are students in your district given a chance to experience all four?

Research about Planning: Implications for Educators

1. Experienced teachers do not plan in a linear fashion; that is, they do not proceed from a consideration of goals first, activities second, resources third, and so on. Instead, they operate in a simultaneous fashion (May, 1986). This means that they consider several elements interactively (content, activities, student abilities, student needs, curriculum resources, etc.).

2. McKenzie (1986, 123) says that direct instruction, which is teacher centered and product oriented (imposing high structure on the class, having pupils practice on common assignments, carefully monitoring and correcting pupil errors during lessons, asking frequent recall and comprehension questions, and explaining new material to groups of students), works well when teachers wish to teach facts, concepts,

principles, and routine skills up to the application level in elementary social studies and when the teachers are working with a low ability, low SES (socioeconomic status), or heterogeneous class.

3. The elements of effective teaching have been outlined by various researchers. Labonty and Danielson (1988) have summarized some of the findings by these researchers:

   (a) A teacher needs to monitor or be aware of several things at once, which are happening in the classroom (Kounin, 1970).

   (b) Praise of desired behavior is effective if it is spontaneous, genuine, and specific (Brophy and Putnam, 1979).

   (c) Feedback on behavior should be immediate (Bloom, 1976).

   (d) Students should be paced in accordance with their ability (Bruning, 1984).

   (e) Effective teachers give appropriate seatwork (Kounin, 1970).

   (f) Effective teachers solicit active participation by the students (Bloom, 1976).

   (g) Effective teachers model the behavior they desire in their students (McDaniel, 1986).

   (h) Effective teachers make smooth transitions between activities (Kounin, 1970).

   (i) Effective teachers can get everyone's attention prior to instruction (McDaniel, 1986).

   (j) Flexibility in adapting is characteristic of effective teachers (Laminack and Long, 1985).

   (k) Effective teachers make efficient use of time (Blair, 1984).

   (l) Effective teachers utilize the assertive discipline techniques of praise, limits, expectations, and rules (McDaniel, 1986).

   (m) Effective teachers use cuing practice to alert students to what is ahead (McDaniel, 1986).

   (n) Effective teachers have "with-it-ness," or the ability to deal with potential disruptions (Kounin, 1970).

   (o) Effective teachers have a sense of humor (Ziegler, 1985).

4. Teachers' plans serve as "scripts" for carrying out instruction in the classroom. These scripts exert such a strong influence on teachers that they tend not to deviate from them once they have begun teaching (Kentucky State Department of Education, 1985, 3).

5. Planning leads to confidence, direction, and security in a teacher's performance in the classroom (McCutcheon, 1980).

Selecting Teaching Methods

The following criteria have been adapted from Hyman's (1974, 63–64) criteria for selecting teaching methods. The criteria represent a way of looking at three factors: the teacher, the situation, and the students.

1. The method should suit the teacher's abilities, knowledge of subject matter, and interests.

2. The method should suit the students' abilities—verbal and psycho-motor.

3. The method should suit the type of teaching aimed at: teaching how to . . . (skill-oriented); teaching that . . . (knowledge-oriented), or teaching to be . . . (value-oriented). If the teacher wants to teach note-taking, for example, then he should provide the students with opportunities to take notes.

4. The method should suit the time and place context of the teaching situation. For example, if it is 2 P.M. on a Friday afternoon and the class is comprised of fifth graders who are performing during halftime at a school basketball game that evening, it would be unwise to choose a method that requires the students to sit quietly and attentively for fifty minutes. Rather, have them engage in an activity that allows them to move around.

5. The method should suit the subject matter at hand. For example, to teach the students the effects that running water has on eroding loose soil, it would seem inappropriate to set up a debate on the issue. Demonstrations or laboratory exercises would be more to the point.

6. The method should suit the number of students being taught. For example, the laboratory method works best if there is sufficient equipment for the entire class.

7. The method should suit the interests and experiences of the students. For example, if most of the previous lessons have been conducted according to the discussion method, it might prove worthwhile to employ the lecture method. Students are often eager to listen to a carefully reasoned lecture in a class in which a discussion or inquiry method has generally been used. Variety in methods is advantageous.

8. The method should suit the students' relationship with the subject matter. For example, for the first few days in a new unit, the teacher could choose a method that will familiarize the students with fundamental terms and skills.

Information Processing Family	Essential Characteristics	Classroom Structure			Number of Students			Age of Students		Ability of Students		Difficulty of Use	
		Teacher Initiates Most of the Action	Student Initiates Most of the Action	Both Teacher and Student Initiate Action	Used well with Individual Students	Used Well with Small Groups of Students	Used Well with Large Groups of Students	Works Well with Younger Students	Works Well with Older Students	Desirable for Low Ability Students	Desirable for Average and Above Average Ability Students	Requires Much Training and Practice by the Teacher	Requires Little or Moderate Training and Practice by the Teacher
Concept Learning	Student learns how to assign objects to classes having similar functions			✓		✓	✓	✓	✓	✓	✓		✓
Inductive Thinking	Student makes a series of responses that are linked together			✓		✓	✓	✓	✓	✓	✓		✓
Inquiry Training	Student learns a variety of specific responses and chains, learns how to sort them out appropriately	✓				✓	✓	✓	✓	✓	✓		✓
Advance Organizers	Student relates data to concepts and theories	✓				✓	✓	✓	✓	✓	✓		✓
Memorization	Student learns to give a specific response to a particular stimulus		✓		✓	✓	✓	✓	✓	✓	✓		✓

The Personal Family	Essential Characteristics	Classroom Structure			Number of Students			Age of Students		Ability of Students		Difficulty of Use	
		Teacher Initiates Most of the Action	Student Initiates Most of the Action	Both Teacher and Student Initiate Action	Used well with Individual Students	Used Well with Small Groups of Students	Used Well with Large Groups of Students	Works Well with Younger Students	Works Well with Older Students	Desirable for Low Ability Students	Desirable for Average and Above Average Ability Students	Requires Much Training and Practice by the Teacher	Requires Little or Moderate Training and Practice by the Teacher
Nondirective Teaching	Student gains self-understanding		✓		✓	✓			✓	✓	✓	✓	
Synectics	Student learns how to increase his creativity			✓		✓	✓		✓		✓	✓	
The Classroom Meeting	Student analyzes his behavior			✓			✓	✓	✓	✓	✓		✓

(continued)

	Characteristic	Classroom Structure			Number of Students			Age of Students		Ability of Students		Difficulty of Use	
	Essential Characteristics	Teacher Initiates Most of the Action	Student Initiates Most of the Action	Both Teacher and Student Initiate Action	Used well with Individual Students	Used Well with Small Groups of Students	Used Well with Large Groups of Students	Works Well with Younger Students	Works Well with Older Students	Desirable for Low Ability Students	Desirable for Average and Above Average Ability Students	Requires Much Training and Practice by the Teacher	Requires Little or Moderate Training and Practice by the Teacher
Group Investigation	Student learns how to apply rules to a new problem		✓			✓	✓	✓	✓	✓	✓		✓
Role-Playing	Student learns to take the view of others		✓			✓	✓	✓	✓	✓	✓		✓
Jurisprudential Inquiry	Student develops citizenship skills by analyzing social values	✓				✓	✓		✓		✓		✓
Social Science Inquiry	Student learns how to reflect on significant social problems			✓		✓	✓		✓		✓		✓

The Social Family

	Characteristic	Classroom Structure			Number of Students			Age of Students		Ability of Students		Difficulty of Use	
The Behavioral Systems Family	Essential Characteristics	Teacher Initiates Most of the Action	Student Initiates Most of the Action	Both Teacher and Student Initiate Action	Used well with Individual Students	Used Well with Small Groups of Students	Used Well with Large Groups of Students	Works Well with Younger Students	Works Well with Older Students	Desirable for Low Ability Students	Desirable for Average and Above Average Ability Students	Requires Much Training and Practice by the Teacher	Requires Little or Moderate Training and Practice by the Teacher
Mastery Learning and Direct Instruction	Student achieves learning in small, incremental steps	✓			✓	✓		✓		✓		✓	
Learning Self-Control	Student reacts to stimulus control and positive reinforcement			✓	✓	✓		✓		✓		✓	
Simulation	Student experiences a nearly real-life situation			✓		✓	✓		✓		✓	✓	

61

9. The method should suit the teacher's relationship with the students. For example, if the teacher has not yet established mutual trust, the role-playing method might not be the best choice.

Comparison of Teaching Models

The preceding matrix (see pages 58–61) is designed to help the educational decision maker compare the teaching models of Joyce and Weil (1986) described in this chapter.

REFERENCES

Ausubel, David. *The Psychology of Meaningful Verbal Learning*. New York:Grune and Stratton (1963).

Beyer, Barry. *Inquiry in the Social Studies Classroom*. Columbus, OH:Merrill (1971).

Beginning Teacher Internship Program—Domains: Knowledge Base of the Florida Performance Measurement System. Frankfort, KY:Kentucky State Department of Education (1985).

Blair, T. R. "Teaching Effectiveness: The Know-How to Improve Student Learning," *Reading Teacher*, 38:138–142 (November 1984).

Bloom, Benjamin. *Human Characteristics and School Learning*. New York:McGraw-Hill (1976).

Bloom, Benjamin. "Mastery Learning," in *Mastery Learning: Theory and Practice*. J. H. Block, ed. New York:Holt, Rinehart, and Winston (1986).

Bloom, Benjamin, ed. *Taxonomy of Educational Objectives*. New York:Longmans, Green and Co., Inc. (1956).

Brophy, Jere and J. Putnam. "Classroom Management in the Elementary Grades," in *Classroom Management*, 78th Yearbook of the National Society for the Study of Education, part II. D. Dukes, ed. Chicago:University of Chicago Press (1979).

Bruner, Jerome, J. J. Goodnow, and G. A. Austin. *A Study of Thinking*. New York: Science Editions, Inc. (1967).

Bruning, R. H. "Key Elements of Effective Teaching in the Direct Teaching Model," in *Using Research to Improve Teacher Education*. Washington, DC:ERIC Clearinghouse on Teacher Education, pp. 78–88 (1984).

Carroll, Lewis. *Alice's Adventures in Wonderland*. New York:Heritage Press (1941).

Gagne, Robert M. "The Learning of Concepts," *School Review*, pp. 187–196 (Autumn 1965).

Glasser, William. *Reality Therapy*. New York:Harper and Row (1965).

Gordon, William. *Synectics*. New York:Harper and Row (1961).

Heath, Phillip A. and Thomas D. Weible. *Developing Social Responsibility in the Middle School: A Unit Teaching Approach*. Washington, DC:National Education Association (1979).

Hunter, Madeline. "Knowing, Teaching, and Supervising," in *Using What We Know about Teaching*. P. Hosford, ed. Alexandria, VA:Association for Supervision and Curriculum Development (1984).

Hyman, Ronald T. *Ways of Teaching, 2nd ed.* Philadelphia, PA:J. B. Lippincott Co. (1974).

Jarolimek, John. *Social Studies in Elementary Education, 7th ed.* New York:Macmillan (1986).

Joyce, Bruce and Marsha Weil. *Models of Teaching, 3rd ed.* Englewood Cliffs, NJ: Prentice Hall (1986).

Kenworthy, Leonard S. *Social Studies for the Eighties: In Elementary and Middle Schools, 3rd ed.* New York:John Wiley & Sons (1981).

Kounin, J. *Discipline and Group Management in Classrooms.* New York:Holt, Rinehart, and Winston (1970).

Labonty, Jan and Kathy E. Danielson. "Effective Teaching: What Do Kids Say?" *The Clearing House*, pp. 394–398 (May 1988).

Laminack, L. L. and B. M. Long. "What Makes a Teacher Effective—Insight from Preservice Teachers," *Clearing House*, 58:268–269 (1985).

Lorayne, Harry and Jerry Lucas. *The Memory Book.* New York:Briercliff Manor (1974).

Mager, Robert F. *Preparing Instructional Objectives.* Palo Alto, CA:Fearon (1962).

Martorella, Peter H. *Elementary Social Studies.* Boston:Little, Brown and Co. (1985).

Massialas, Byron and Benjamin Cox. *Inquiry in the Social Studies.* New York: McGraw Hill (1966).

May, Wanda T. "Teaching Students How to Plan: The Dominant Model and Alternatives," *Journal of Teacher Education*, pp. 6–12 (November/December 1986).

Maxim, George W. *Social Studies and the Elementary School Child, 3rd ed.* Columbus, OH:Merrill (1987).

McCutcheon, Gail. "How Do Elementary School Teachers Plan Their Courses?" *Elementary School Journal*, 81:4–23 (1980).

McDaniel, T. R. "A Primer on Classroom Discipline: Principals Old and New," *Phi Delta Kappan*, 68:63–67 (1986).

McKenzie, Gary R. "Learning and Instruction," in *Elementary School Social Studies: Research as a Guide to Practice.* Bulletin No. 79, Virginia Atwood, ed. Washington, DC:NCSS, pp. 119–136 (1986).

McKinney, C. Warren. "The Effectiveness of Three Methods of Teaching Social Studies Concepts to Sixth-Grade Students," *Journal of Educational Research*, pp. 35–39 (September/October 1984).

Merrill, M. D. and R. D. Tennyson. *Concept Teaching: An Instructional Design Guide.* Englewood Cliffs, NJ:Educational Technology Productions (1977).

National Council for the Social Studies. *Skill Development in Social Studies.* The Thirty-Third Yearbook of the NCSS. Washington, DC, pp. 15–34 (1963).

Naylor, David T. and Richard Diem. *Elementary and Middle School Social Studies.* NY:Random House (1987).

Neale, D. C., A. J. Pace, and A. B. Case. "The Influence of Training, Experience, and Organizational Environment on Teachers' Use of the Systematic Planning Model," Paper presented at the annual meeting of the American Educational Research Association, Montreal (April 1983).

Neely, A. "Teacher Planning: Where Is It Going?" *Action in Teacher Education*, 7:25–29 (1985).

Oliver, D. and James Shaver. *Cases and Controversy: A Guide to Teaching the Public Issues Series.* Middletown, CT:American Education Publisher (1971).

Rogers, Carl. *Freedom to Learn*. Columbus, OH:Merrill (1969).

Servey, Richard E. *Elementary Social Studies: A Skills Emphasis*. Boston:Allyn & Bacon (1981).

Shaftel, Fannie and George Shaftel. *Role Playing in the Curriculum*. Englewood Cliffs, NJ:Prentice Hall (1982).

Taba, Hilda. *Teacher's Handbook for Elementary Social Studies*. Reading, MA:Addison Wesley (1971).

Thelen, Herbert. *Education and the Human Quest*. New York:Harper and Row (1960).

Ziegler, V. G., G. Boardman, and D. Thomas. "Humor, Leadership, and School Climate," *Clearing House*, 58:346–348 (1985).

3 | HISTORY: FOR THE YOUNG AND THE OLD

Chapter Preview of Key Ideas

★ "History readiness" is important for young children.

★ They need to develop a background in sequencing events, telling time, and developing a vocabulary.

★ History cannot be taught logically, i.e., young children cannot start with the earliest events in history.

★ History needs to focus on people, so that it becomes social history.

★ Various teaching strategies need to be used for history.

★ Primary sources are actual objects of historical significance, such as artifacts, documents, personal investigation, and audio-visual materials.

★ Secondary sources are accounts written by people according to their interpretations of historical events.

"Those who don't use history are doomed to repeat its mistakes" is a paraphrase of a familiar saying. There are some benefits to studying history; chief among them is developing an understanding of human heritage. In addition to this cognitive knowledge, students also can develop an appreciation for other people if more of their background is known. It was stated earlier that a major reason for including social studies in the school curriculum is to foster citizenship. It is easier to exhibit good attitudes toward our fellow citizens in the world if we know something about them and their past. It follows, then, that a definition of history can be *the study of the record of people's past*.

HISTORY IN THE CURRICULUM

History as a subject has been a feature of our school curriculum since Colonial days. In 1884 the American Historical Association was formed, increasing the stature of history among the other social sciences. Educators must beware of assuming that all people learn history in the same manner, regardless of the age or developmental level of the individual.

The work of Roy Hallam (1972) illustrates the extreme view that a young person is not capable of understanding history in any meaningful way until about the age of sixteen. He points out that the abstractness of history requires the high-level thinking of Piaget's formal operations stage.

Richard Lidberg conducted a study with young children whereby he asked them to explain the meaning of various terms such as *long ago* and *in the distant past*. The results indicated that the children had a distorted impression of time. *Long ago* for a first grader might be as recent as last year.

HISTORY READINESS FOR EARLY ELEMENTARY STUDENTS

While the preceding few paragraphs pose a cautious approach for including history in the elementary curriculum, the position of this book is that history should be taught to students as early as the primary grades. Seefeldt (1984) and Elkind (1981) agree with this. The Bradley Commission (1988) has recommended that the K–6 social studies curriculum be history-centered.

A knowledge of young children's capabilities and limitations is essential to planning the proper lessons. Young children do not begin school with a well-defined sense of time. Therefore, a teacher must engage the students in activities that are suitable for a preoperations stage or a concrete operations stage. *History readiness* seems to be an appropriate term for this.

Readiness suggests preparation. In reading, this is achieved by having the preschool–primary child follow a left-to-right progression (to prepare for reading a line on a page), trace with his finger the outline of an object (to prepare him to realize that letters have shapes, too), etc. Following are some examples of activities that an administrator can suggest to a teacher in order for primary students to achieve history readiness.

Daily Schedule

The teacher should put the date on the chalkboard every day. Beneath it should be the events for the day:

8:15	School begins
9:00	Reading
10:15	Recess
10:30	Arithmetic
11:30	Lunch
12:30	Story time
1:00	Spelling
1:30	Science
2:00	Recess
2:15	Health
2:30	Social studies
3:00	School ends

A child looks at the above schedule and sequences events. The schedule can also be used to instruct students in telling time: "Sally, what time of the day do we have spelling?" "Evan, do we have social studies in the morning or in the afternoon?"

Telling Time

Some children begin kindergarten with the ability to tell time. Most of them, however, do not. The teacher should use arithmetic and social studies time to instruct her students in this area. A large play clock makes an excellent instructional device, as the students can move the hands to the desired positions. Ask a child to move the hands of the clock to show the time when they come back from lunch or the time when they have science.

Chronology

After children understand that events happen in a sequence during a day, they can be presented with a series of events that occur over several days or weeks. One second grade teacher had her class—at the end of the day— cut out a smiling sun, a raindrop, a dark cloud, etc., to depict the weather on that particular day. These would be taped to the top of each child's desk. At the conclusion of the week, the students would discuss the weather by looking at the cutouts, recalling the series of events. This is the beginning of a sense of chronology, or time.

Vocabulary

Simple vocabulary should be emphasized by the teacher. *Month, hour, calendar, clock, minute hand, after, today, yesterday, tomorrow, fall, winter, noon, first, afternoon, midnight, Monday,* and *October* are all terms that have a relationship to time. The teacher should use them in her conversations with the students and determine if they know the meanings.

Since abbreviations are introduced in the primary grades, this would be an opportune time to choose some abbreviations that deal with time, for example:

Wed.,   Feb.,   min.,   hr.,   yr.,   wk.,   A.M.,   P.M.

Passage of Time

History is fundamentally concerned with chronology and the eventful passage of time. Since young children cannot comprehend the broad sweep of long time periods, it is helpful if a teacher can provide examples of shorter, self-contained time periods. For example, the duration of even a human life is too long for a youngster to truly understand; therefore, an example should be introduced that presents life on a smaller scale.

One way to do this is to bring insects, plants, or animals into the classroom and watch them develop from newborns into adults. Caterpillars are commonly caught by children and brought to school. As they develop into the cocoon and chrysalis stages, the teacher can point out how they are getting older, until one day they become an adult.

The class can plant bean seeds, which quickly start to sprout. Within weeks the students can see the young plants grow into large plants. Another example could be drawn from tadpoles maturing into frogs. Young children can see an entire life span of a living creature played out before their eyes in a matter of months. This is history compacted and made understandable.

Time Line

Young children can work with time lines to help them visualize the order in which events occur. The usual horizontal time line marked off into centuries or decades is totally inappropriate for young children. Rather, a child's first time line should depict familiar happenings in his or her own life. The teacher could construct a time line for a second grade class on a large sheet of butcher paper taped to the chalkboard. The beginning point might be 6:00 in the morning, and the ending point might be 9:00 at night.

The line would be marked off into fifteen divisions, each one representing an hour's time. The teacher would ask the class what they might be doing at each of these times. For example, at 6:00 A.M., a child might be getting out of bed. Therefore, the class could look through magazines in the room to find a picture of a bed, which could be taped beneath the

"6:00" point. If a child is eating breakfast at 7:00, then a picture of a box of cereal could be placed beneath that point (see Figure 3.1). This process would continue until all of the hours on the time line have some illustration depicted underneath.

AFTER HISTORY READINESS

After the history readiness experiences, as students get older, the teacher can begin more advanced lessons. These could include vocabulary such as the following—all of which require more sophisticated understanding: *generation, centennial, ancestor, prehistoric, decade, fiscal year, descendant, millenium, era, eon, annual, ancient, medieval, dynasty,* and indefinite terms (e.g., *presently, shortly, recently*).

As was done in the early primary grades for readiness experiences, lessons in later primary grades should be crafted to allow students to think in concrete terms about the concepts. As an example, if a teacher is working with the concept of "generation," it would be valuable for a student to bring photographs from home: a photograph of the child, a photograph of the parents, and a photograph of the grandparents. Place these in tiers so that the bottom row is the child's, the row above that is the parents', and the top row is the grandparents'. In this way the student can associate each row with a different generation. Birth dates could be connected to each of these people so that a rough idea could be attained of how many years separate one generation from another. This activity will point out to the students how the length of a generation varies from one example to another.

The Bradley Commission (1988) feels that no fewer than four years of history should be allotted to grades seven through twelve. This exposure to history should represent three areas: "American history to tell us who we are and who we are becoming; the history of Western civilization to reveal our democratic political heritage and its vicissitudes; world history to acquaint us with the nations and people with whom we shall share a common global destiny" (p. 7).

TEACHING HISTORY ILLOGICALLY

One of the points of the preceding examples in this section of Chapter 3 is that history really cannot be taught in a logical manner. If it could be taught logically, then you would start at the beginning of recorded history when teaching young children who are beginning school. In other words, the student would start at the inception of history and march along—grade by grade—toward the 1990s. In reality, the opposite occurs. Students in the

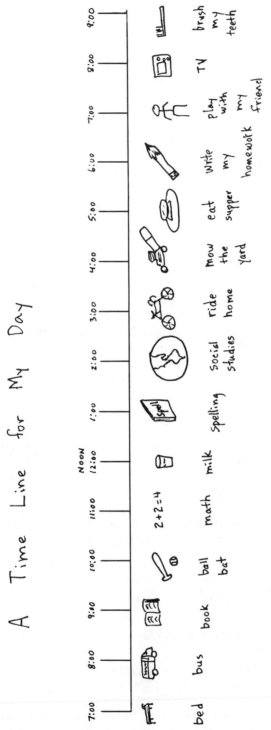

Figure 3.1 A time line for my day.

primary grades are taught chiefly about recent events, whereas older students are taught history that goes farther back in time.

There are exceptions to this rule of illogicalness. One of the exceptions says that students at a very young age can study historical topics that go far back in time if these topics are celebrated observances. Holidays are prime examples. They are such a familiar part of young children's lives that the students already have a foundational knowledge of the event. A study by Johnston (1979) found that the most popular holidays were

> Christmas (December 25)
> Halloween (October 31)
> Valentine's Day (February 14)
> Thanksgiving (fourth Thursday in November)
> Easter (varying dates from March through April)
> Lincoln's Birthday (February 12)
> Washington's Birthday (February 22)
> Mother's Day (second Sunday in May)
> St. Patrick's Day (March 17)
> Columbus Day (second Monday in October)

Additional holidays during the school year include

> Martin Luther King, Jr.'s Birthday (January 15)
> Hannukah (varying dates in December)
> Veterans Day (November 11)
> Arbor Day (usually observed on the last Friday of April)
> Chinese New Year (varying dates in January or February)
> American Indian Day (fourth Friday in September)

Seefeldt (1984, 161–162) suggests that the following be done to make holiday celebrations meaningful and enjoyable for young children:

(1) Work the celebration into the regular routine of the child's school day.

(2) Involve the children in planning the celebration.

(3) Keep the activities simple and low-keyed.

(4) Involve the parents and resource persons in the celebration.

(5) Focus on only a few concepts for a holiday.

Separation of church and state dictates that certain religious holidays must be treated carefully. For example, Christmas must not be turned into a religious ceremony; rather, it should be an objective study "about" the socially significant occasion.

A second exception (besides holidays) to the rule of illogicalness is young children's natural fascination with *random details* and *limits of reality*. These are terms that Egan (1982) uses as he explains why history is essential for social studies in the early grades. Egan's ideas are presented in the following section.

HISTORY CURRICULUM FOR YOUNG CHILDREN

Chapter 1 explained how the "expanding horizons" approach is commonly used in social studies programs throughout the nation. The justification behind this approach is that children can use their background experiences as building blocks to expand their knowledge of social studies. For example, once a child has been taught about *families* (including her own), then she is better able to study how families of people form neighborhoods. The second is difficult to do if the first has not been accomplished.

However, expanding horizons should not be carried to its extreme. A child should not be prevented from discussing neighborhoods if the study of the family has not been done. Kieran Egan applies this to the teaching of history as he points out that young children are impulsively drawn to the exotic and fantastic—even though these are beyond the relevant experiences of the children.

Egan feels that history is abundant with examples of concepts that fill children's lives at a very young age: *love, hate, fear, security, good, bad, courage, cowardice*, etc.

> If children are not encouraged to apply these basic concepts to new content, the concepts will surely fail to undergo refinement or elaboration. The act of embodying a concept in different content begins the process of conceptual elaboration. The story of Robin Hood helping the poor against rapacious barons led by the Sheriff of Nottingham is comprehensible to young children because they know what those relationships mean most basically; they know courage and daring, they know oppression and resentment, they know greed and anger. At the same time, they elaborate their concept of oppression, for example, by using it to make sense of this content, which is quite different from their own experience. We might see it too as the encouragement of imagination: using concepts derived from immediate experience to make new worlds and relationships meaningful [Egan, 1982, 440].

TEACHING STRATEGIES FOR HISTORY

History is about people, which Jarolimek (1986, 148) calls "social history." This approach to history goes beyond the "famous people–famous events" scheme by enabling students to investigate both ordinary people and the well-known ones. The concepts and generalizations listed below are examples that teachers in a school district can incorporate into social studies lessons dealing with history.

Concepts

change	chronology	cause and effect
continuity	heirlooms	generation
prehistoric	leadership	conflict
nationalism	exploration	

Generalizations

- Events of the past influence those of the present.
- Many civilizations have risen and fallen in the history of human existence.
- Interdependence has increased rapidly in recent times.
- Multiple causes and consequences must be considered in studying events.
- Human existence is characterized by change.

TEACHING IDEAS

Following are some teaching ideas—using primary sources and secondary sources—which can be used with early elementary and middle grade students.

Primary Sources

These are actual objects, which can be viewed, handled, or inspected by the students to give them a better sense of their historical significance. Examples of primary sources might be (1) an exhibit of costumes or clothing in a museum, (2) a collection of Indian arrowheads, (3) an old photograph showing how a town looked fifty years ago, or (4) a letter from a mother to her son who was fighting in World War I. Whatever form the primary sources take, they are a fountainhead of information that tells us about events, the places where they occurred, and the people who were affected by them. Strategies for teaching some of these primary sources are described below.

ARTIFACTS

These are objects used in the past, such as tools, dishes, and clothing. The following lesson plan demonstrates how artifacts can be used to teach the concept of *antiques*.

EARLY ELEMENTARY GRADE LESSON PLAN

Topic: **Objects from the Past**

Grade: **3rd**

Date: **April 14, 2:00–2:30**

I. *Purpose*: tells what a student will learn

The students will learn about life in the past by looking at some objects that were used in communities years ago. Students will learn the names of these objects, how they were used, and how they have been replaced in today's society.

II. *Motivation*: tells how to begin the day's lesson

An old cherry pitter will be shown to the class. Since the pitter has an unusual appearance, the class will be asked to guess what this object might have been used for. After a number of students have tried to identify it, the teacher will tell the students that this was once used to remove the pits from cherries after they had been picked from the tree.

III. *Development*: tells how to conduct the day's lesson

Several more objects will be shown to the class. All of these will be articles that had a common use around the house or farm during the first part of this century, before the students' grandparents were born. These objects are as follows:

(a) *Apple Butter Scoop*

This utensil was used in the making of apple cider and apple butter, which were considered to be America's national drink and national spread at the turn of the century. The scoop was made of wood because it was thought that if apples made contact with metal, it would spoil the flavor.

(b) *Butter Mold*

After butter was churned, it was placed into this mold. The design on the top of the mold was imprinted into the butter.

(c) *Salt Holder*

These small glass containers were placed on the table at each person's setting. The idea was for each person to pinch out the salt as he needed it for his food. Salt used to be a very expensive commodity, hence the phrase "worth your weight in salt."

(d) *Carpenter Plane*

These wooden tools resembled a box, and carpenters had many of them to shave wood. (Figure 3.2 shows what some of them look like.)

(e) *Calf Yoke*

This device is hung around the neck of a high-spirited calf to keep it from climbing through fences. It is made from three pieces of wood, one of them bent in a U-shape to fit over the calf's head.

As each object is displayed, the class should attempt to determine how it was used. They should conjecture whether the object would be found more frequently in a wealthy person's home or in the home of a person of ordinary income. They could decide whether it would be used in a city or on a farm.

IV. *Conclusion*: tells how to close or evaluate the day's lesson

The students will be given a handout prepared by the teacher. On the left side of the paper will be sketches of the five objects that were discussed previously in Part III of the lesson. Each student will be asked to write the correct names of the objects on the right-hand side of the sheet. On the back of the handout, each student will pick one of the objects to compare to modern life, describing how people in this decade have found modern practices to replace these antique objects.

V. *Materials*: tells what is needed for the day's lesson

Cherry pitter, butter mold, salt holder, carpenter plane (apple butter scoop and calf yoke—if they are obtainable), handout, illustration of planes.

DOCUMENTS

Birth certificates, deeds, census reports, contracts, membership rolls, treaties, marriage certificates, stock certificates, telegrams, and passenger manifests provide raw data, which students can compile, analyze, and explain. Since students will often arrive at different conclusions, documents are excellent for showing how written history is a subjective product. People write history based upon their interpretation of the facts. Carey and Greenberg (1983) encourage that the following questions be answered when students use these formal documents:

(a) What kind of a document is it? Is it a legal paper, newspaper, policy report, letter, or telegram?
(b) When was the document written, and what was happening in the world?
(c) Who is mentioned in the document?
(d) What effect did the document have?
(e) Can I use this document as a primary source?
(f) How can I present the information? Should it be in a written report?

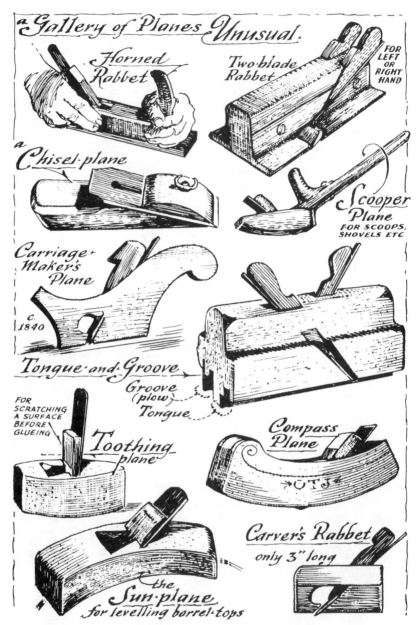

Figure 3.2 Antique tools [taken from Eric Sloane, *A Museum of Early American Tools*, NY:Ballantine Books, pp. 64, 65 (1964)].

Oral report? Or can I present the information on a chart, on slides, in a graph, or as a survey?

A great many document reproductions are printed in *Social Education*, and teachers are encouraged to use them in their classes. An example letter (Figure 3.3) and the middle grade lesson plan could be used to teach a lesson about the constitutional issue of federalism.

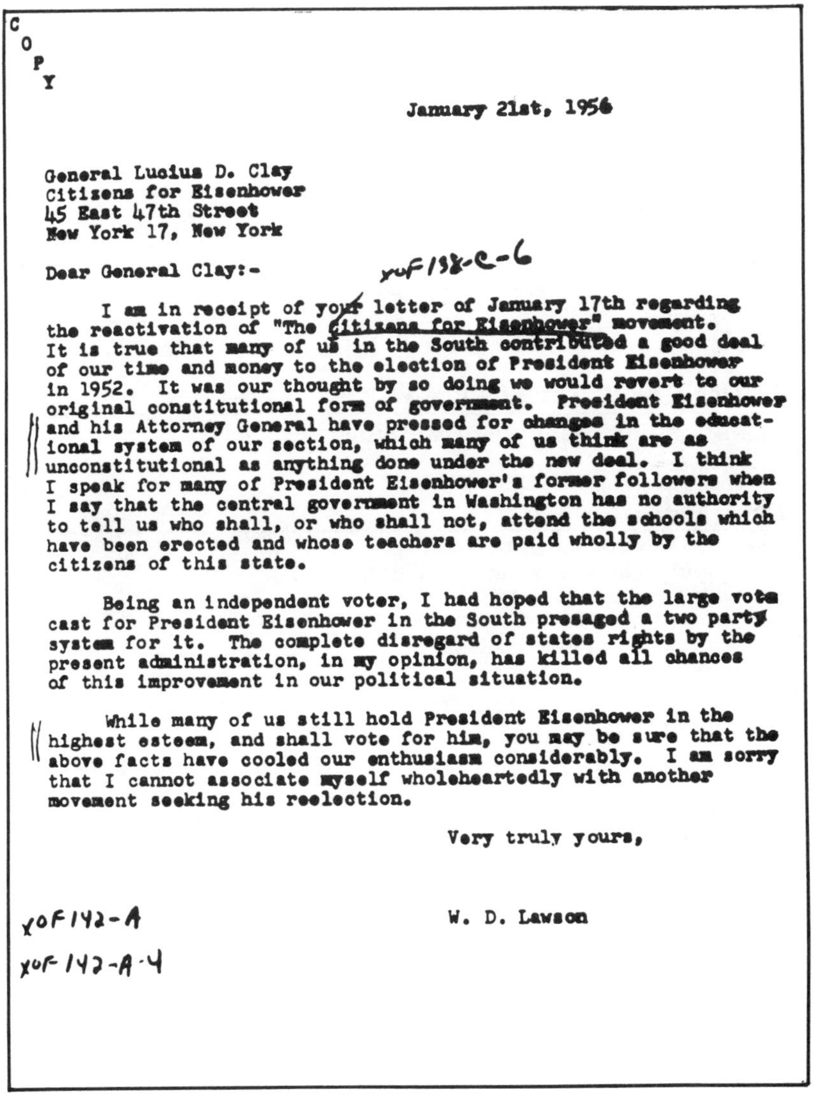

C
O
P
Y

January 21st, 1956

General Lucius D. Clay
Citizens for Eisenhower
45 East 47th Street
New York 17, New York

Dear General Clay:-

yuf 138-C-6

I am in receipt of your letter of January 17th regarding the reactivation of "The Citizens for Eisenhower" movement. It is true that many of us in the South contributed a good deal of our time and money to the election of President Eisenhower in 1952. It was our thought by so doing we would revert to our original constitutional form of government. President Eisenhower and his Attorney General have pressed for changes in the educational system of our section, which many of us think are as unconstitutional as anything done under the new deal. I think I speak for many of President Eisenhower's former followers when I say that the central government in Washington has no authority to tell us who shall, or who shall not, attend the schools which have been erected and whose teachers are paid wholly by the citizens of this state.

Being an independent voter, I had hoped that the large vote cast for President Eisenhower in the South presaged a two party system for it. The complete disregard of states rights by the present administration, in my opinion, has killed all chances of this improvement in our political situation.

While many of us still hold President Eisenhower in the highest esteem, and shall vote for him, you may be sure that the above facts have cooled our enthusiasm considerably. I am sorry that I cannot associate myself wholeheartedly with another movement seeking his reelection.

Very truly yours,

yoF 142-A
xof 142-A·4

W. D. Lawson

Figure 3.3

The generation of the 1950s...had to define...[the] relationship between states and national government. Because of the centralization of federal power following two world wars and the social welfare legislation of the New Deal, the national government was left with greatly expanded powers. Against this background were set the tensions created by state segregation laws that violated the rights of black Americans under the Constitution. Unlike the crisis of the 19th century, this crisis was settled by the Supreme Court. Beginning with the Brown decision, the Supreme Court struck down all state segregation laws that came before it, effectively dismantling long-established customs of the South. On March 12, 1956, 101 members of Congress signed a "Declaration of Constitutional Principles" in which they decried "the Supreme Court's encroachment on rights reserved to the States and to the people, contrary to established law and to the Constitution."

Many white Southerners had broken with Southern political tradition when they voted for the Republican candidate Dwight Eisenhower in 1952 because they believed he would favor states' rights. ...W.D. Lawson was "a very highly regarded cotton merchant," who had served as chair of the Citizens for Eisenhower Movement in Gaston County, N.C., in 1952. In his letter Lawson refers to this crisis in federalism. This document is taken from the Eisenhower Presidential Library, Dwight D. Eisenhower; Records as President (White House Central Files 1953-1961), Official File.

Figure 3.4 Political events in the 1950s.

MIDDLE GRADE LESSON PLAN

Topic: **Constitutional Issues: Federalism**

Grade: **8th**

Date: **April 21, 1:45–2:35**

I. *Purpose*: tells what a student will learn

The students will develop a more thorough understanding of how states rights can be an issue for some citizens.

II. *Motivation*: tells how to begin the day's lesson

Show the class a photograph of Dwight D. Eisenhower and ask them to identify him. Then have the students name some of the things this man is famous for. Tell the class they will be examing a letter by a man who was disappointed in some of President Eisenhower's actions as the chief executive of our country.

III. *Development*: tells how to conduct the day's lesson

Read to the class the information that appears in the accompanying Figure 3.4.

Distribute copies of Mr. Lawson's letter, which is shown in Figure 3.3. Students should answer the following questions:

(1) What did Lawson hope would happen when he supported President Eisenhower in 1952?

(2) What events had happened to cool his enthusiasm?

(3) What might he mean by the following phrases?
- "revert to our original constitutional form of goverment"
- "pressed for changes in the educational system of our section"
- "disregard of states rights by the present administration . . . has killed all chances of this improvement in our political situation"

IV. *Conclusion*: **tells how to close or evaluate the day's lesson**

Tell the class that they will prepare to write a letter of response to William Lawson, specifically regarding Lawson's concern about school desegregation. Before the class starts to write the letter, however, they need to investigate President Eisenhower's position on school desegregation. At the end of class this day, each student will look in the textbook for references to Dwight Eisenhower. Tomorrow they will go to the library and locate further sources about the life of this president. The class will then read from the sources they have located to prepare the letter of response.

V. *Materials*:

Illustration providing background information of the 1950s, illustration showing William Lawson's letter.

Note: Some of the ideas of this lesson plan are found in the article by Leslie Gray and Wynell Burroughs, "Teaching with Documents," *Social Education*, pp. 162, 163 (March 1987).

LETTERS, DIARIES, AND JOURNALS

These items are less formal than the documents mentioned above. What do letters, diaries, and journals have in common? All of them are written, firsthand records of the past. A letter is a piece of corresondence to one or more people; a diary is a personal record of one's thoughts, written on a daily basis; and a journal (or log) is usually a less personal account of daily events.

Reading a letter, diary, or journal is a thrilling way to experience history, because the reader is living the times as another person understood them. *The Diary of Anne Frank* is one of the most popular examples of a diary kept by a young person.

Interact, a company in California, has published a simulation entitled "Puzzle." It enables middle grade students to perform the tasks of a biographer-historian. One of the simulated letters, which are created from American colonial and antebellum times, appears in Figure 3.5.

Ⓐ

April 17, 1769

My Dearest Wife;

At last we are under full sail again. Since we left Africa it has been storm one minute, clear the next, and becalmed after that.. I have never seen such a plague of Nature's moods. Thrice I have ordered jolly-boats over the side to row us in search of Wind. We daren't lie along this coast to tempt any Corsairs, or worse, the French.

The men are daily growing surly at the fickle aspect of the Weather. It distresses me that some, including good Kelly, the cook, are assigning the blame to our new adopted navvy, a brown sprig of a girl whom I have named Molly.

She is a fine-featured African who came to us in a queer way. While we frolicked at our last port by Tunis, a child of nine or ten years burst into the tavern followed by a scoundrel with as cutthroat a visage as ever I saw. We shielded her from the slave-dealer and brought her aboard. Though she is brown, her features, particularly the darting black eyes, remind me of our lost Louise.

I am determined to try Molly as our cabin-girl. There has been no proper cabin-boy since young Ned Boswell died of the Mortification after a runner nearly cut his leg in twain.

Molly is quick to learn our English words. She trusts us and works hard to gain everyone's favour.

As always long days and nights at sea remind me of the great depth of my love for you and the babes. Do kiss them for me.

With tenderest love,
Richard [ANDREWS]

Ⓐ
[NEWSPAPER CLIPPING -- DATE AND NEWSPAPER UNKNOWN.]

It was heartening to see the crowd who turned out to hear Mrs. Molly Andrews speak of her experiences as a slave. A most singular individual is Mrs. Andrews. Though she is not above the average height, her fund of knowledge, and her stories of the good and bad sides of slavery are superlative and unusual to the highest degree for a person her age. She commanded the attention of all, even the babes in arms, it seemed, for none cried out during her two hour recital.

Mrs. Andrews was not the first speaker to our community concerning that dread institution, slavery, nor is she (unfortunately) likely to be the last. Mr. William Brown will be remembered for his account of the Southern lash that fell upon brown backs. But while Mr. Brown brought tears to our eyes, he also caused grown men to beat themselves on the chest and swear to bring slavery down!

Figure 3.5 Reprinted with permission of Interaction Publishers, Inc. © 1972. Lakeside, CA 92040.

Copies of authentic correspondence that could be used by students to investigate historical conditions are shown in Figures 3.6, 3.7, and 3.8.

PERSONAL ROOTS IN THE PAST

To facilitate a student's understanding that history is part of his or her own life or that it is part of the local surroundings, Hennings, Hennings, and Banich (1980, 396–402) describe the following techniques:

(a) *Family Tree*

Primary-age students can informally talk about parents and grand-

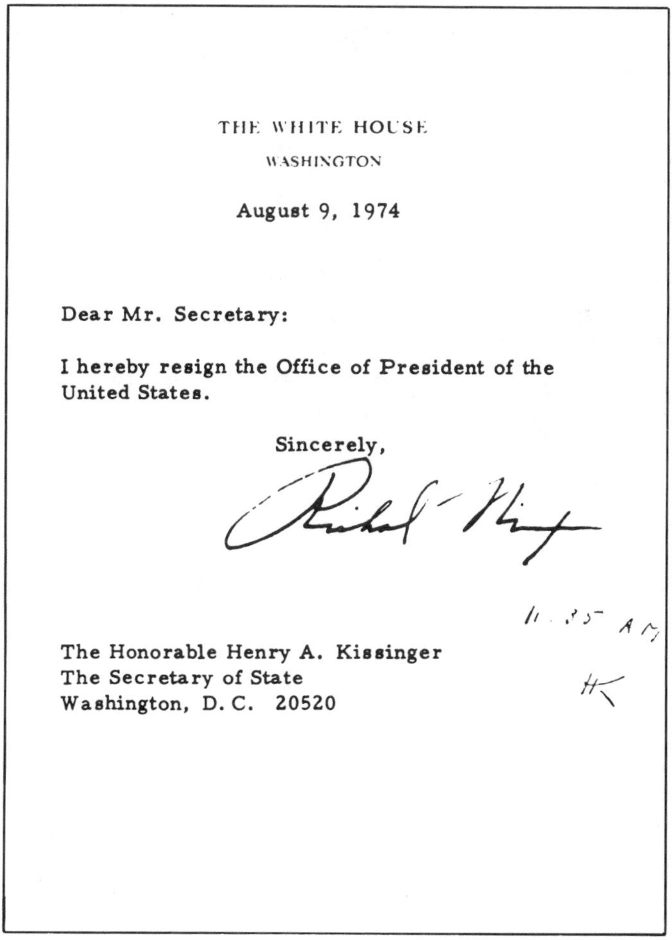

THE WHITE HOUSE

WASHINGTON

August 9, 1974

Dear Mr. Secretary:

I hereby resign the Office of President of the United States.

Sincerely,

Richard Nixon

The Honorable Henry A. Kissinger
The Secretary of State
Washington, D. C. 20520

Figure 3.6 [Taken from *Social Education*, p. 344 (May 1982).] Reprinted with permission.

Chieko E
Period II, English I

My Last Day At Home

The month of May when I was attending school, all the residents of Hood River county, as well as the people of the whole western coast was surprised to receive such an unexpected order of evacuation.

Promptly after hearing about the order I with my folks went to register and then for a brief physical examination. Then I helped my folks pack and prepared to leave my dear home on May 13, 1942.

On May 8, 1942 I withdrew from P   Grade School, where all my friends and teachers bid me farewell with sorrowful face and tears. Our packing never seem to cease, we kept on packing then finally we were finished. Then came May 13th, my most dreaded day which I shall never forget the rest of my life. On the afternoon of the 13th, I board the train headed for P   , California.

On the night of the 15th we arrived. The weather was pretty hot. In P   I lived in the D-section which had forty barracks, which had vie apartments to a .barrack.

I stayed at the P   Assembly Center about two months. Then around July 15, 1942 we received our order to evacuate for Tule Lake. Then on July 18th we evacuated for Tule Lake and spent a night on the train. I arrived in Tule Lake. At present I am living in Block 58. The residents of this block is most Tacoma folks which I am not very much acquainted with as yet. Being that my cousin lives in Block 57 I am always visiting them.

I am always hoping that this war will end, so that I will be able to go back to P   , my home town and see all my old friends, and live to my dying days in my old home in P   , Oregon.

Figure 3.7 A composition by a high school student of Japanese ancestry who is being relocated in 1942 [Taken from *Social Education*, p. 355 (May 1981)]. Reprinted with permission.

parents, resulting in the construction of diagrams that show the three generations.

(b) *Family Roots*

Primary-age students can inquire from parents about what part of the world his or her ancestors came from. These countries can be located on a globe or on a map.

(c) *Family Biographies*

In the intermediate grades, students could compose short family biographies that set forth their family's past.

(d) *Memory Walk*

Primary students work from their own memory of their local com-

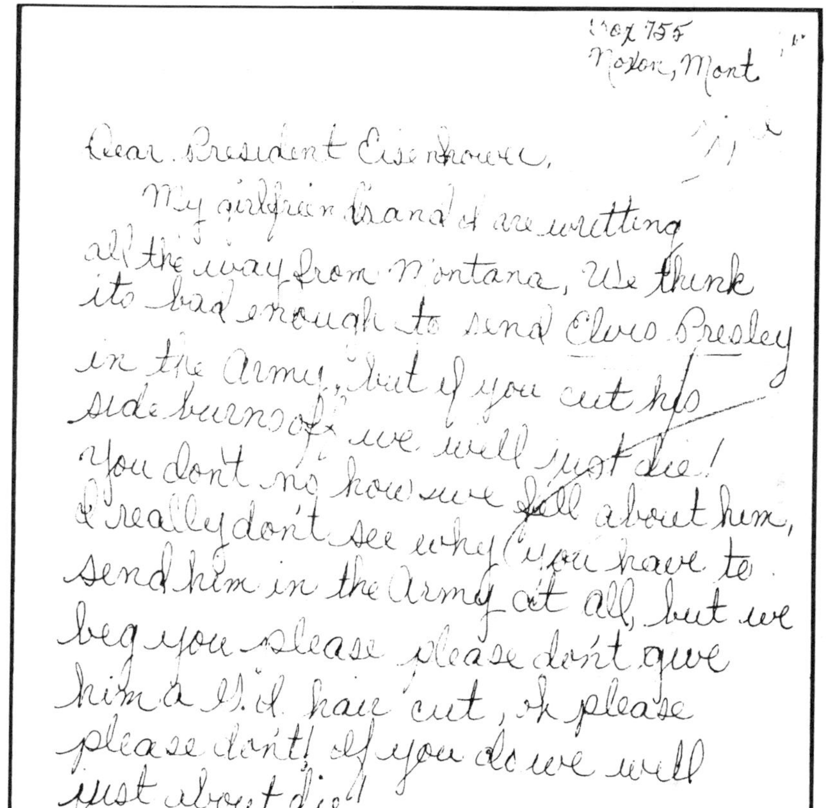

Box 755
Noxon, Mont.

Dear President Eisenhower,

My girlfriend and I are writting all the way from Montana. We think its bad enough to send Elvis Presley in the army, but if you cut his side burns off we will just die! You don't no how we fell about him, I really don't see why you have to send him in the army at all, but we beg you please please don't give him a G.I. hair cut, oh please please don't! If you do we will just about die!

PRESLEY
PRESLEY
IS CORCRY
P-R-E-S-L-E-Y

Elvis Presley
LOVERS

Linna Lilly
Sharon Bare
Vickie Mattson

Figure 3.8 Letter from young girls to President Eisenhower [Taken from *Social Education*, p. 407 (May 1985)]. Reprinted with permission.

munity to identify buildings and sites that are plotted on a map of the area. Students can discuss such questions as "Is the stone library older than the courthouse?" "Were these stores built about the same time, since they look so similar?"

(e) *A Map Comparison*
In the upper grades, students can compare an old town map with an up-to-date one. They can find specific examples of how the town has changed. For example, empty land thirty years ago has now been changed into a shopping center.

Several of the examples from the preceding section "Personal Roots in the Past" required students to ask individuals about past events. This leads to another technique called oral history.

ORAL HISTORY

As Mehaffy, Sitton, and Davis (1979) point out, oral history helps students become active, rather than passive; it also discloses to students that the stuff of history is all around them.

Engelhardt and Muir (1986) list the steps for a classroom teacher who prepares his class for collecting oral history data:

(1) Gather basic equipment (e.g., tape recorders, cords, release forms, etc.).

(2) Explain oral history concept to students.

(3) Teach students to use equipment.

(4) Provide practice in note-taking.

(5) Invite someone to visit the class for an interview.

(6) Select a topic for investigation by the entire class.

(7) Discuss tips for interviewing.

(8) Set up interview schedule.

(9) Choose several tapes to listen to in class as practice for transcribing.

(10) Develop a display of students' work and a newspaper to illustrate findings.

AUDIOVISUAL MATERIALS

Since it is impossible for a person to be magically transported back in time to witness occurrences and people involved in these happenings, the next best thing is to have audio or visual materials to capture the sight and/or sound. It is relatively easy to locate phonograph recordings of President John F. Kennedy giving his inaugural speech, wherein he challenges the U.S. citizenry to "ask not what your country can do for you, but what you can do for your country." Television allows the class to view firsthand debates among candidates for political office. Videotapes can be used to replay programs that deliver valuable lessons to young people.

When it is not possible to obtain materials that portray the actual people or events, then films, records, or recordings that recreate these events can be purchased or rented. The amusing film *Ben and Me* provides a glimpse into the contributions of Benjamin Franklin. Sometimes private companies will sponsor commercial works, which are available to schools. *Columbus* by IBM is an example of such a program that appeared on television and was also promoted in the schools. IBM supplied posters, a filmstrip, an audio cassette, and a teacher's guide to educators who requested them.

Secondary Sources

These are accounts written by people according to their interpretations of historical events. History textbooks are the obvious examples of secondary sources. An author reports on the facts that seem relevant and important to him or her. Textbooks are very helpful for presenting an easily obtained description of the past.

It is important that students are exposed to other written accounts besides those they find in their textbooks. Books of a historical nature can help children identify with the past. Stoddard (1984) concluded that books (historical fiction, folklore, biographies, and wordless picture books) can benefit a preoperational child by broadening his limited experiences.

Mildred Dawson (Jarolimek and Walsh, 1974, 117–118) very aptly sums up how good literature can enliven the social studies:

> An understanding of early peoples will result as children read authentically historical fiction such as Haugaard's *Hakon of Rogen's Saga* (early Vikings) or books about early Americans like McNeer's *The American Indian Story* and Haig-Brown's *The Whale People*. Colonial and pioneer times come to life as children admire the bravery of early colonists in Smith's *Pilgrim Courage*, see superstitions of witchcraft in Speare's *The Witch of Blackbird Pond*, fight Indians with Edmonds' *The Matchlock Gun*, go traveling in Coatsworth's *Away Goes Sally*, roam the fields with Mason's *Susannah, the Pioneer Cow*, live the pioneer life in Steele's *Westward Adventure* and Laura Ingalls Wilder's *Little House* books, colonize California in Politi's *The Mission Bell*, or see the sweep of history in Caudill's *Tree of Freedom*.

> The stress and strain, the horrors of battle will become real as child-readers identify with the Civil-War teen-ager in Keith's *Rifles for Watie*. Or, civics of today become intriguing through books such as Johnson's *The Congress*.

> Or let's turn to biography. Primary children will thoroughly enjoy the colorful and carefully authentic d'Aulaire biographies of great Americans of the

past or Daigliesh's *The Thanksgiving Story*. With older children, the past fairly glows as they read Daugherty's *Daniel Boone*, Sandburg's *Abe Lincoln Grows Up*, or the scholarly volumes by May McNeer, Genevieve Foster, and Clara Judson. There are remarkably fine series available, too, as for instance the *Landmark Books* or the *Childhood of Famous Americans*.

The early days of Poland and medieval England are vividly relived in Kelly's *Trumpeter of Krakow*, De Angeli's *The Door in the Wall*, and Gray's *Adam of the Road* (all beautifully literary in style). Or let the children turn to the old favorite, Pyle's *Otto of the Silver Hand* and to the recent book on Biblical times, Speare's *The Bronze Bow*.

Books such as the ones listed by Dawson can be found in *Social Education*. Once a year this journal publishes "Notable Children's Trade Books in the Field of Social Studies." The selections are based upon the following criteria:

(1) Are written primarily for children in grades K–8

(2) Emphasize human relations

(3) Present an original theme or a fresh slant on a traditional topic

(4) Are highly readable

(5) Have a pleasing format and, when appropriate, illustrations

In addition to title, publisher, and author, additional information is furnished: number of pages, ISBN book number, cost, grade level, and a synopsis of the book.

ASSISTANCE POINTS

Questions for Action for the Administrator

1. Assume you have observed a social studies lesson taught by one of your primary grade teachers. His lesson dealing with historical material seems to have gone "over the heads" of the children. How would you discuss with him the need to use "history readiness" in his lessons?

2. Textbooks often vary in their treatment of historical topics. The author's point of view can be an explanation for this. Obtain several different textbooks at the same grade level (e.g., fifth grade books) to see how they treat a historical topic. For example, look at two fifth grade books to see the differences in their coverage of the Civil War.

3. What possibilities are there in your school district for students to study oral history?

4. Assume that the curriculum committee in your school district has

been discussing the new social studies curriculum plan in California and wants to investigate how history can be given a more prominent place in the elementary grade curriculum. What comments can you make to support their attempt to emphasize history?

5. After visiting a sixth grade class, you (a supervisor) hold a conference with the teacher. You observed that the students had low time on task. Using information from this chapter, what suggestions might you make to increase their time on task?

Names and Addresses of Professional Organizations and Journals Dealing with History

1. American Historical Association
   400 A Street, S.E.
   Washington, DC 20003

2. Organization of American History Teachers
   c/o Marjorie Bingham, Pres.
   St. Louis Park HS
   6425 Thirty-Third Street
   St. Louis Park, MN 55426
   (The OAHT publishes the journal *OAH Magazine of History*.)

3. National Commission on Social Studies in Schools
   11 DuPont Circle, Suite LL4
   Washington, DC 20036

4. National History Day
   11201 Euclid Avenue
   Cleveland, OH 44106

5. Organization of American Historians
   112 N. Bryan St.
   Bloomington, IN 47401

6. Society for History Education
   California State Un., Long Beach
   1250 Bellflower Blvd.
   Long Beach, CA 90840

7. *History and Social Science Teacher*
   16 Overlea Blvd.
   Toronto, Ontario M4H 1A6
   Canada

Research about History: Implications for Educators

Linda Levstik (1986) feels that social studies educators need to utilize narrative-based history more frequently. If children's historical thinking is more akin to thinking in literature than to thinking in science and mathematics, then children can learn by making written responses to historical material.

REFERENCES

Bradley Commission on History in Schools. *Building a History Curriculum: Guidelines for Teaching History in Schools*. Washington, DC:Educational Excellence Network (1988).

Dawson, Mildred A. "Literature Enlivens the Social Studies," *Education*, pp. 294–297 (January 1965). Cited by John Jarolimek and Huber M. Walsh. *Readings for Social Studies in Elementary Education, 3rd ed.* New York:Macmillan, pp. 115–119 (1974).

Egan, Kieran. "Teaching History to Young Children," *Phi Delta Kappan*, pp. 439–441 (March 1982).

Engelhardt, Leah and Sharon Pray Muir. "Oral History in the Elementary School." Paper presented at the 1986 Annual Meeting of the National Council for the Social Studies, New York.

Elkind, David. "Child Development and the Social Science Curriculum of the Elementary School," *Social Education*, 45(6):435–437 (1981).

Gray, Leslie and Wynell Burroughs. "Teaching with Documents," *Social Education*, pp. 162, 163 (March 1987).

Hallam, R. N. "Thinking and Learning in History," *Teaching History*, 2:337–346 (1972).

Hennings, Dorothy Grant, George Hennings, and Serafina Fiore Banich. *Today's Elementary Social Studies*. Chicago:Rand McNally (1980).

Johnston, A. *School Celebrations: Teaching Practices Related to Celebration of Special Events, Grades 1–6, in the United States*. Knoxville:Bureau of Educational Research and the Department of Curriculum and Instruction, College of Education, University of Tennessee (1979).

Lidberg, Richard. "Reading Comprehension Difficulties in Fourth, Fifth, and Sixth Grade Social Studies Textbooks," unpublished doctoral dissertation, The University of Iowa (1966).

Mehaffy, George L., Thad Sitton, and O. L. Davis, Jr. "Oral History in the Classroom," *How to Do It*, Notebook Series 2, No. 8. Washington, DC:National Council for the Social Studies (1979).

Seefeldt, Carol. *Social Studies for the Preschool–Primary Child, 2nd ed.* Columbus: Merrill (1984).

Sloane, Eric. *A Museum of Early American Tools*. NY:Ballantine Books (1964).

Stoddard, Ann H. "Teaching Social Studies in the Primary Grades with Children's Literature," paper presented at the Annual Meeting of the Florida Reading Association (October 1984).

4 | GEOGRAPHY: HERE, THERE, AND EVERYWHERE

Chapter Preview of Key Ideas

★ *Citizens of the United States are being criticized for their lack of geographical knowledge.*

★ *Maps and globes are the backbone of geography.*

★ *Maps need to be selected with an eye to the developmental level of the student.*

★ *Globes are manufactured with a variety of information, so they need to be carefully selected, too.*

★ *There is no precise order in which all map and globe skills must be taught.*

★ *An NCSS skills sequence chart has been in widespread use across the country for about twenty-five years.*

★ *A new focus on geographical themes has been developed by the Association of American Geographers and the National Council for Geographic Education.*

A short while ago the front page headlines of a newspaper read, "Lost in America: U.S. adults' geography skills rated low" (*Lexington Herald-Leader*, 1988). The article summarized the results of a Gallup Poll that was sponsored by the National Geographic Society. Gilbert Grosvenor, president and chairman of the Society bemoaned the fact that 75 percent of adult Americans did not know where the Persian Gulf is; 25 percent could not identify the Pacific Ocean; and 14 percent could not locate their own country on a map of the world. Grosvenor, speaking to the National Press Club, stated that, "If we are to be influential in resolving atmospheric and ocean pollution, deforestation, global hunger, nuclear arms control, and a whole host of other issues, we must be geographically literate" (*Lexington Herald-Leader*, July 1988).

GEOGRAPHY IN THE CURRICULUM

Geography is one of the oldest social science disciplines, dating back to Egyptian and Greek thinkers. Eratosthenes was a Greek geographer of the third century B.C. who very accurately calculated the circumference of the earth and suggested the possibility of reaching India by sailing west.

Today, geography is taught in nearly all elementary schools; many states require a geography course in high school; and 90 percent of colleges/universities that have teacher certification programs require their students to have a geography course (Dumas and Weible, 1983, 18). Despite this long-standing attention to geography, it seems that United States students and adults are not as literate as they should be about world geography (see Grosvenor's comments above).

Part of the problem might be the way in which geography is viewed by the average citizen. Too often, it is considered to be only the study of earth's natural features by using maps and globes. However, this view of geography is much too narrow, and perhaps this partially explains why Americans do poorly with questions such as those asked by the Gallup Poll.

In recent years educators have realized the need to expose people to a much broader approach to geography. It must be both physical geography and human geography. To that end, the National Council for Geographic Education and the Association of American Geographers (Joint Committee on Geographic Education, 1984) have created K–12 guidelines that focus on five themes:

(1) *Location: Position on the Earth's Surface*
Absolute location (coordinates of latitude and longitude) and relative location (the interdependence of these places) are two ways of describing the positions of people and places on the earth. For example, the city of Beaumont is located in southeast Texas, 30 degrees south latitude and 94 degrees west longitude. How does its location in this oil-field area of the Gulf of Mexico affect its appearance (oil wells, refineries, etc.)?

(2) *Place: Physical and Human Characteristics*
Geographers describe a place by using its special characteristics. For example, a place has distinctive physical characteristics (landforms, climate, vegetation, etc.) and human characteristics (transportation network, population composition, architecture, etc.).

(3) *Relationships within Places: Humans and Environments*
Human beings represent a vital component in the appearance of their environment; they can modify it or adapt to it. For example, people level mountains to build interstate highways. They have also taken advantage of flat, fertile land to establish farms.

(4) *Movement: Humans Interacting on the Earth*

Humans display a great amount of mobility. For example, tens of thousands of people traveled to Seoul, South Korea, to view the 1988 Summer Olympic Games. However, movement does not have to be demonstrated by actual travel of people from one country to another. It could simply be shown through the interaction of a person in Arizona eating an apple that was grown by a person in the state of Washington.

(5) *Regions: How They Form and Change*

The basic unit of geographic study is the region, which can be limited to an area as small as a neighborhood or can be expanded to include an area as large as the Pacific Rim. A region is a spatial unit that can be characterized by political criteria, cultural criteria, economic criteria, etc.

Barbara Winston (1986, 43) has a host of suggestions to gain a broad perspective of geography, which is essential to today's citizens:

(1) Formulate enlightened opinions on complex global issues related to peace, hunger, trade, environment, refugees, development, or overpopulation, to name a few.

(2) Cast informed votes for government leaders with stands on the above issues, and evaluate whether records of leaders' actions reflect that they know and take account of geographic realities surrounding the issues.

(3) Make informed decisions about personal foreign policies and evaluate related individual and group behaviors.

(4) Gain perspectives about similarities and differences in ways people in other societies live and interact with each other and their environments—a preliminary step to reduce ethnocentric and stereotypic thinking.

(5) Understand and find creative solutions to problems such as those in community or urban planning.

(6) Deal with regional issues such as open space or transportation problems.

(7) See ways in which apparently local, regional, or national issues are linked inextricably to global issues.

(8) Gain skills to select and use maps with understanding because comprehension of so many issues depends on one's ability to use media that answer questions about "where?" "how far?" or "in what direction?"

It is clear, then, that we can no longer think of geography simply as being able to point to a place on a map or globe. A more comprehensive definition would be "Geography is the *study of the earth and how humans interact with it.*"

GEOGRAPHY AND THE DEVELOPMENT OF THE STUDENT

Jean Piaget and Bärbel Inhelder (1967) conducted a study with young children to show that spatial understanding is something that students must develop. Piaget and Inhelder had children look at a cluster of three miniature papier-mâché mountains. The youngsters were asked to imagine the views of other people who had different vantage points of these mountains, which were placed on a table where the children were seated. The subjects—up to the age of seven—were not able to visualize this. Instead, they seemed to liken every perspective to their own viewpoint. In Piagetian terms, this means the children at this age are *egocentric.*

Rice and Cobb (1978) looked at a number of studies concerning whether or not young children should receive geographic instruction. They concluded that primary-age children can learn geographic concepts, but the knowledge and presentation by the classroom teacher is the key. One of the studies they reviewed revealed that first graders can read some maps and that even kindergarteners can learn cardinal directions.

Sharon Pray Muir (1985) has included many points to facilitate the development of map reading skills in children. She bases her information on Bruner's (1966) three developmental stages: enactive, iconic, and symbolic. Enactive experience requires concrete interaction with the concept; iconic representation uses graphic or mental images; and symbolism forces children to use abstract verbal or written symbols.

Muir suggests that a teacher can assist the student; for example, she can make an iconic map enactive by having the students walk in the area the map shows, or she can make a symbolic map iconic by showing an aerial photograph of the map area.

The point to be emphasized is that there is no prescribed age at which students should be introduced to geographic concepts and skills. School administrators should be sure that exposure is started as soon as children are in kindergarten, although cognitive development will limit what they are able to comprehend.

GLOBES AND MAPS

Globes and maps are essential to the study of geography because they are representations of the world on which we live. Both of these materials should be used with early elementary and middle grade students, but it might be asked which of these should be used before the other when introducing a new lesson to early elementary students. Several arguments can be made for using a globe prior to a map.

Globes

(1) A globe shows the earth as a round object. The concept of *roundness* is important for early elementary students because it is essential for their later understanding of night and day, time zones, seasons, travel, etc. For thousands of years people thought the earth was flat—as a map is; young children do not need to repeat this misconception.

(2) The globe is a model of the real earth. Young students are familiar with various kinds of models. They have enjoyed model trains, assembled model airplanes, and played with doll houses. All of these are similar to the real objects but designed as a smaller version. Building on the background knowledge that children have of model toys, they can perceive that the globe is a small replica of the earth.

(3) The globe shows the earth as a whole. With a glance, the child can see an actual object that appears as the earth really would. Mountains, lakes, cities, continents, etc., are all there to give a three-dimensional impression much more complete than a two-dimensional map.

(4) The globe shows true direction. As you will find out later in this chapter, it is much easier to teach directions using a globe than using a map. Essentially, this is because the north pole can be easily used as a reference point on a globe.

(5) The globe shows the earth accurately. Maps often distort the shape of an area or the distance between places. To illustrate this, look at Figures 4.1 and 4.2, which show a comparison of Greenland with the United States. The globe indicates that the United States is *much larger* than Greenland, whereas the map erroneously depicts the U.S. as being *much smaller* than the island. The following lesson plan can be used to teach why a map is sometimes deceptive.

MIDDLE GRADE LESSON PLAN

Topic: **Comparing Maps and Globes**
Grade: **6th**
Date: **November 12, 2:00–2:40**

I. *Purpose*: **tells what a student will learn**

The students will be able to use a scale and determine the distance between

Figure 4.1 The western hemisphere.

points on a map and a globe. They will be able to analyze why distance and size are sometimes different on a globe versus a map.

II. *Motivation*: tells how to begin the day's lesson

Pull down the classroom wall map showing the world. Write the cities New York and Moscow on one part of the chalkboard and Quito and Nairobi on the other part of the chalkboard. Tell students that they are going to find out how far it would be if they had to fly between these two pairs of cities. First, though, the teacher should point out where each of these cities is on the map. Next, he should ask the students to guess the distances. The teacher should solicit about three guesses for each pair of cities. After the first guess, the teacher should inform the class that it is about 25,000 miles around the earth at the equator, and perhaps that will help them estimate the distance between the cities.

III. *Development*: tells how to conduct the day's lesson

Now that the class has given their guesses about the distances, they should compute the actual distances. Prior to this class, the teacher should have bor-

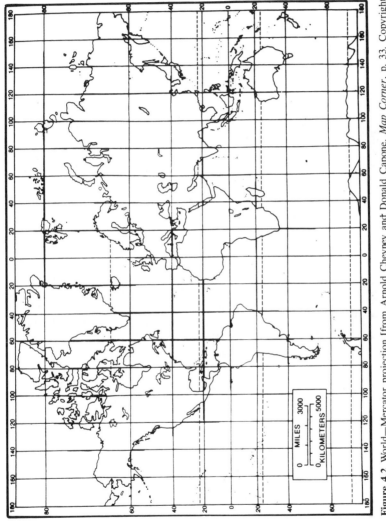

Figure 4.2 World—Mercator projection [from Arnold Cheyney and Donald Capone, *Map Corner*, p. 33. Copyright © 1983 Scott, Foresman and Company]. Reprinted with permission.

rowed enough globes from other classrooms in the building so that about four students can work at one globe. Then give each group a Mercator world map projection. Be sure that both the globes and map have a scale.

Using the scale, each group should find out how far it really is between the two pairs of cities. While the class is doing this, the teacher should copy on the chalkboard the chart in Figure 4.3. This will be used to record some of the distances. Select about three of the groups to come to the board and record their four distances in the correct cell on the chart.

The true calculations should have resulted in about 11,000 miles for both the globe and map distances between Quito and Nairobi. The globe distance between New York and Moscow should have been about 4,500 miles, with the map distance being about 7,000 miles. Using the Mercator projection map, all of the groups should have encountered the dissimilarity. Pose this problem to the class: "Why should Quito and Nairobi have the same figures while there is a large discrepancy between the globe and map distances for New York and Moscow?" Many students will have no idea why this is so. Others might realize that the answer lies in the fact that a globe and a map must be different somehow. A few might be able to perceive that some of the areas on the globe do not look the same as those areas on the map.

The answer lies in the fact that some maps misrepresent distances because they do not show the true shapes and sizes of land and water bodies. The Mercator map of Figure 4.2 has lines of longitude which are parallel—they never meet—whereas a globe will have the lines of longitude converge at both poles. This means that the greatest distortion occurs in the extreme northern and southern latitudes; it occurs to a lesser extent in the middle latitudes; and it is nonexistent at the equator.

		Distance in Miles		
		Group A	Group B	Group C
Quito, Ecuador	Globe			
to				
Nairobi, Kenya	Map			
New York	Globe			
to				
Moscow	Map			

Figure 4.3

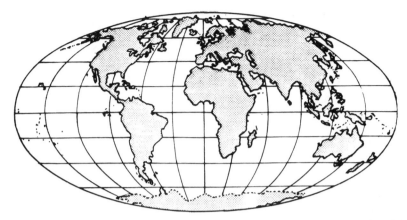

Figure 4.4 [Taken from *Map Reading*, St. Louis, MO:Milliken Publishing Co., p. 12. Copyright © 1970.] Reprinted with permission.

IV. *Conclusion*: tells how to close or evaluate the day's lesson

Present the class with an analogy. Have them imagine cutting an orange in half and hollowing out the pulp so that they have a hemisphere in each hand. Place one of these hemispheres on a table so that the rounded side is towards the ceiling. Then try to flatten it with the palm of the hand. What happens? The orange rind will tear along the edges. The class should understand that cartographers are faced with a similar problem as they try to make a flat map using a round globe. The map will tear in places. Rather than leave jagged gaps, cartographers fill these in with water or land (where no water or land should have existed!). This increase of land and water on the map consequently results in increased distance.

If we would use maps that have their lines of longitude converge at the poles, the distortion would not be a problem. Some maps, such as the one in Figure 4.4 try to do this. Others (as shown in Figure 4.5) try to preserve the image that the earth "tears" at the northern and southern latitudes. It is difficult, however, to measure distances on the map in Figure 4.5 because you can only use the areas that contain water or land.

Conclude the lesson by having each group of students make two lists of pairs of cities. One of the lists should contain pairs that would result in the same distance, regardless of whether a globe or map is used. The other list should contain pairs of cities whose distances are different depending on whether a globe or a map is used to determine them.

V. *Materials*: tells what is needed for the day's lesson

Globes, Mercator maps, classroom wall map.

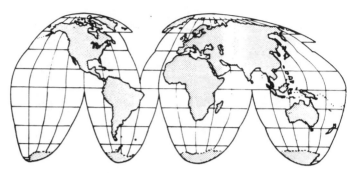

Figure 4.5 [Taken from *Map Reading*, St. Louis, MO:Milliken Publishing Co., p. 12. Copyright © 1970.] Reprinted with permission.

CONCEPTS AND GENERALIZATIONS

The previous lesson plan taught the concepts of *location, scale, distance*, and *distortion*. Students would be able to understand the generalization "A round earth cannot always be shown accurately on a flat map."

Examples of other concepts and generalizations from geography are listed below.

Concepts

latitude	longitude	land use
climate	tropical region	areal differentiation
movement	contour	mountain
time zones	landscape	rotation of the earth

Generalizations

- Ways of living are influenced by geographic factors.
- The global location of a region contributes to its importance in international affairs.
- Areas of the earth develop bonds with other areas.
- Places on the earth have a distinctiveness about them that differentiates them from all other places.

YOUNGER STUDENTS AND GLOBES

Size

Early elementary students should be presented first with globes that are twelve inches in diameter or smaller. "Little hands need small objects" is a saying that has relevance in this case. It is much easier for a young child to handle a small globe than to wrestle with a larger one.

A small globe allows a young child to see the entire earth at a single glance. If a larger globe is placed before the child, he will be drawn to parts of it and not see the whole.

Markings

Globes with diameters up to twelve inches don't require numerous colors. It is desirable for such a globe to have water represented with just one color: blue. The land, similarly, should be depicted with few colors. One, two, or three colors are common to show desert areas, high mountainous areas, etc. If one of the first skills a young child learns on a globe is to distinguish water from land, it makes sense to have just one color for land areas.

A twelve-inch globe should have only important cities, rivers, lakes, etc., labeled. Confusion results if a globe has too many places on it.

OLDER STUDENTS AND GLOBES

Size

Students in the upper primary, intermediate, and middle grades can progress to globes that are twelve inches in diameter or larger. Sixteen-inch globes are commonly found in school supply catalogs. Occasionally, globes that are several feet in diameter can be purchased. These project globes can have a slate surface so that groups of students can gather around and write on it with chalk.

Markings

Larger globes can accommodate more information. Instead of having just one shade of blue for water, it can be helpful to have several shades of blue. Deep blue shows deep water, ranging to a light blue for shallower water.

Land can be divided into different colors. Elevation (mountains, hills, low-lying areas, etc.) and political boundaries (continents, countries, states, etc.) are the most frequent uses for colors.

Color can also be used for particular reasons, resulting in *special purpose* maps. Population density, crops, vegetation, rainfall, etc., are examples of features that can be shown on one of these maps.

A bigger globe is suitable for placing rivers, cities, lakes, mountains, etc., that are not considered of major importance. Cluttering is not a problem when you have a larger globe.

MAPS

Maps are used to communicate ideas, data, and relationships in spatial form. They are a two-dimensional representation of the earth's surface. Since they are flat, they can be likened to a photograph. This comparison allows a teacher to have students discuss the purpose of a photograph (small; shows what something looks like; is a picture of a real object; can't carry the real, big object around with you; etc.) and connect that to the purpose of a map. A critical factor for children to understand a map is that it is made from an aerial perspective.

There are many kinds of maps, but they all start with the same first step, namely, making a flat projection from a globe. There are basically three kinds of projections:

(1) *Cylindrical* (see Figure 4.6)

Imagine a roll of paper is slid over a globe made out of glass with a light bulb inside the globe. The only points where the paper touches the globe are on the equator. If the light is turned on, the grid lines of the globe cast shadows on the paper tube, resulting in latitude and longitude lines that are straight up and down or straight across. A cartographer could then trace these shadows with a pen, unroll the cylinder and have a map such as the Mercator projection. The benefit of this projection is that it shows travel routes clearly. For example, a ship traveling due north would appear to keep exactly on the same longitude line.

(2) *Tangential Plane* (see Figure 4.7)

Imagine the same glass globe with light bulb as mentioned in the description of the cylindrical projection. A flat sheet of paper is placed on the globe this time, touching at only one point. The shadows from the grid line are traced with a pen. The most common type of tangential plane projection is the polar map, depicted as though a person saw either the North or South Pole from directly overhead.

(3) *Conical* (see Figure 4.8)

This time imagine a paper cone is placed over a globe so that it touches the globe at a certain line of latitude. The benefit of using the conical projection is that it is very useful and accurate when depicting a small area in the middle latitudes, such as the United States.

In actuality, maps are not made in the simple way described above. Instead of using a light bulb shining from within a glass globe, cartographers utilize mathematics.

Just as there are advantages to globes over maps, there are advantages that work the other way: maps are less expensive, they do not occupy much storage space, they can show more detailed features, and they can depict a wider variety of geographical areas (street map, town map, state map, etc.).

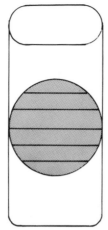

Figure 4.6 Cylindrical projection.

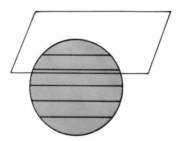

Figure 4.7 Tangential plane projection.

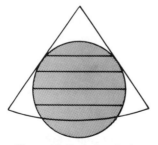

Figure 4.8 Conical projection.

RAISED RELIEF FOR GLOBES AND MAPS

It makes it easier for students at both the early elementary and middle grades to visualize topographic features if they can apply a tactile learning style. Therefore, globes and maps that have raised surfaces to indicate hills and mountains, or surface depressions to show low-lying areas, greatly assist geographic learning. These globes and maps are more expensive for administrators to purchase, but they are worth the price. There is a danger of misinterpretation, though, because the raised elevation heights are often not in the correct proportion to the horizontal distances of the earth's surface. For example, a child who runs his fingers over the small bumps of the Himalayas might think that they are not very high at all. Teachers should point out to the students that the raised relief is sometimes exaggerated or underestimated only to indicate where some land is lower or higher than other land.

YOUNGER STUDENTS AND MAPS

The central problem with young children working with maps is that maps are abstract representations of real places in the world. Since children starting school are still in the developmental stage that Piaget calls preoperations—ready to move into the next stage of concrete operations—these children demonstrate the inability to conserve. This means that they cannot easily understand that two shapes which look different might have the same area (see Figure 4.9). In this figure, both North Carolina and Arkansas cover approximately the same area—53,000 square miles. Teachers need to be aware of the problems young children have with conservation of number, matter, length, and area because these impinge on their ability to comprehend maps.

Seefeldt (1984) feels that a place to start would be for teachers to focus on the child and the immediate environment:

(1) Take the students for a walk around the neighborhood and point out things that might be found on a map (trees, houses, stores, etc.). Later, collect pictures of the things that are on the list.

(2) Have the children identify different land surfaces on their neighborhood walk (a grassy playfield, a concrete street, a hill down the block, etc.). Point out that these would have to look different if they were drawn on a map.

(3) Encourage children to use boxes, doll houses, sticks, and paper, for these provide valuable concrete experiences for the later tasks of making and interpreting maps.

Figure 4.9 United States southeast states [from Arnold Cheyney and Donald Capone, *Map Corner*, p. 88. Copyright © 1983 Scott, Foresman and Company]. Reprinted with permission.

Maxim (1987) recommends informal play with blocks to help them conceptualize space. As they work on their creations, the teacher should assume the role of observer and encourager. Appropriate comments or questions might be (Maxim, 1987, 326)

"Which automobile will fit through the garage door?"
"How can you make this road longer?"
"Does your road have curves or is it straight?"

"Where would that car go if this road was closed?"

"What made your building fall down?"

"Let's see if that building is as tall as this tower."

"Jimmy's foot is two blocks long. How many blocks long is my foot?"

"How can you build a bridge so that the truck can get to the other side of the river?"

"Are these blocks the same size?"

"I wonder what would happen if you put a round block here."

It is also a wise practice to encourage them to talk about what they are building. Verbalization allows children to describe the relationships they see in space.

OLDER STUDENTS AND MAPS

Older students are able to refine beginning map skills and advance to more sophisticated work. Children in the early grades have primarily used maps that

(1) Are fanciful in nature (usually depicting familiar places such as a zoo, park, or neighborhood and imaginary places such as Playland, Fantasyland, or Spaceland)

(2) Contain mostly pictorial or semipictorial symbols

(3) Often represent a real environment shared by all the children

(4) Begin to introduce children to the locations of people or places under study in other contexts, such as in literature or reading books (Maxim, 1987, 341)

Outline maps, travel maps, satellite maps, and special purpose maps can be used to take the student from a three-dimensional world of reality to a two-dimensional one on paper. They will be increasingly able to gather and interpret information and solve problems.

Spatial Development

Spatial development in students progresses along three stages: topological, projective, and Euclidean (Cohen, 1986, 162). A student who perceives topologically would view two large, unequal, grassy areas as being equal in size if they both were merely bounded by some kind of enclosure. A more developed student who perceives projectively would consider two yards of unequal area as being equal (1) if they both had a fence surrounding them, (2) if they both had a gate opening in the same corner of each yard, and (3) if they both had equipment in about the same position in each yard. A student who perceives in a Euclidean manner would claim that two areas were equal in size only if an additional condition were present: the pieces of equipment in the two yards would have to be the same distance from each other and from the fences. Most intermediate and middle grade students are in the projective stage—ready to move into the Euclidean stage. Teachers should help students comprehend map representations by encouraging them (Cohen, 1986, 163)

> . . . to observe and draw many and varied things—objects, people, animals, and landscapes. Encourage them to manipulate all shapes of things. They should feel them, hold them, turn them, build with them, match objects with pictures, observe them from many perspectives. Encourage the children to imagine what the objects would look like from many viewpoints.
> . . . Whenever possible, expose children to activities accompanied by written and pictorial representations.

SOME DIFFICULT CONCEPTS

All maps depict *scale*, i.e., they show a distance on paper which bears some relationship to the actual distance on the ground. Somewhere in the late primary grades students will be able to use the concept of scale to determine distances between points on a map—and later on a globe. There are three basic ways to use a scale to determine distance:

(1) *Graphic Scale*
   In its simplest form, this scale just requires the students to read the number that appears at the bottom of a strip of paper such as the one below:

   Sometimes a student may have to add numbers if he needs to move the strip of paper along the path between two points.

(2) *Inches-to-Miles (or Kilometers-to-Meters) Scale*
   This is a bit more advanced than the graphic scale because it requires that a student use fractions to compute distance. For example, if "one inch equals 500 miles" is written at the bottom of a map, and the student measures four inches between two cities, then she must use the algorithm "1 to 500 = 4 to *x*." Occasionally, a student can get the measurement just by adding successive 500-mile segments.

(3) *Representative Fraction Scale*
   This is the most difficult of the scales and appears as follows:

$$1 : 200,000$$

This is interpreted as meaning that for every unit on the map there are 200,000 of these same units on the ground. Of course, the complexity of this scale lies with the huge numbers that are involved.

The second concept to pose special challenges to students in the middle grades is *time zone*. The earth's rotation on its axis, from west to east, creates day and night. There is one hour's difference between each fifteen degrees longitude; hence, there are twenty-four time zones in the world. An understanding of longitude lines is tied closely to that of time zones. Globes are much more effective than maps to display the time differences around the world.

The third concept that presents difficulties for middle grades is *contour line*. Contour maps have closed, curved lines so that all the points on each line are at the same elevation. Raymond Muessig (1985) explains how a three-dimensional mountain can be constructed from balsa wood so that it is built in layers. The individual layers provide a good illustration for the meaning of contour lines.

MAP AND GLOBE SKILL CATEGORIES

For three and one-half decades, the established listing of skills for map and globe instruction has been the one that appeared in the Twenty-Fourth Yearbook of the National Council for the Social Studies (Kohn, 1953, 146–147). The major skill areas in this skills chart are:

(1) Orient the map and note directions.
(2) Recognize the scale of a map and compute distances.
(3) Locate places on maps and globes by means of grid systems.
(4) Recognize and express relative locations.
(5) Read symbols and look through maps to see the realities for which the symbols stand.
(6) Correlate patterns that appear on maps, and make inferences concerning the association of people and things in particular areas.

Ten years later, the NCSS slightly reworked these skills and created the following subskills (Kennamer, 1963, 157–168 and 322–325):

(1) Orient the map and note directions (11 subskills listed).
(2) Locate places on maps and globes (18 subskills listed).
(3) Use scale and compute distances (10 subskills listed).
(4) Interpret map symbols and visualize what they represent (7 subskills listed).
(5) Compare maps and draw inferences (7 subskills listed).

This 1963 document showed that just five skills should be taught at the kindergarten, first, or second grade level:

(1) Use relative terms of location and direction, e.g., near, far, above, below, up, down.

(2) Learn to make simple sketch maps to show location.

(3) Use small objects to represent large ones, such as a photograph compared to actual size.

(4) Make simple large-scale maps of familiar areas, such as classroom, neighborhood.

(5) Understand that real objects can be represented by pictures or symbols on a map.

This is a very small number, and many educators today feel that early elementary students are able to handle more map and globe instruction than this would imply.

A joint committee of the National Council for Geographic Education (NCGE) and the Association of American Geographers (AAG) came up with its own sequence of skills in 1984. It was organized around the five major geographic themes that were discussed earlier in this chapter. It is interesting to note that these *Guidelines* contain thirty skills which should be taught in kindergarten, first, and second grades.

SEQUENCE OF SKILLS

This section of the chapter will present a sequence of map and globe skills adapted from the NCGE/AAG *Guidelines for Geographic Education*. Each of the K-6 skills are followed in brackets by concepts from the five geographic themes mentioned earlier in this chapter—(1) location, (2) place, (3) relationships within places, (4) movement, and (5) regions.

Kindergarten: Focus on Self in Space

(1) Knows and uses terms related to location, direction, and distance (up/down, left/right, here/there, near/far) {*location*}

(2) Recognizes a globe as a model of the earth {*location*}

(3) Recognizes and uses terms that express relative size and shape (big/little, large/small, round/square) {*characteristics of place*}

(4) Identifies school and local community by name {*location* and *characteristics of place*}

(5) Recognizes and uses models and symbols to represent real things {*location* and *characteristics of place*}

(6) Makes simple observations and describes weather, seasons, the school, the neighborhood, and the route to school and to home {*characteristics of place*}

First: Focus on Homes and School in Different Places

(1) Knows geographic location of home in relation to school and neighborhood {*relative location* and *characteristics of micro environments*}

(2) Knows the layout of the school campus {*location* and *characteristics of micro environments*}

(3) Uses simple classroom maps to locate objects {*relative location*}

(4) Identifies state and nation by name {*characteristics of micro environments*}

(5) Identifies seasons of the year {*relative location*}

(6) Describes characteristics of seasons and discusses their impact on people {*characteristics of micro environments*}

(7) Follows and gives verbal directions (here/there, left/right) {*relative location*}

(8) Distinguishes between land and water symbols on globes and maps {*relative location* and *characteristics of micro environments*}

(9) Relates location on map/globe to location on earth {*relative location*}

(10) Describes similarities and differences among people in their own community {*relative location* and *characteristics of micro environments*}

(11) Describes similarities and differences between people in their own community and in other places {*relative location* and *characteristics of micro environments*}

(12) Observes, describes, and builds simple models and maps of the local environment {*relative location* and *characteristics of micro environments*}

Second: Focus on Neighborhoods— Small Places in Larger Communities

(1) Makes and uses simple maps of school and home neighborhoods {*location* and *place*}

(2) Interprets map symbols using a legend {*location* and *place*}

(3) Knows and uses cardinal directions {*location*}

(4) Locates one's community, state, and nation on maps and globes {*location* and *place*}

(5) Identifies local landforms {*place*}

(6) Identifies a variety of types of transportation and communication within the community {*location* and *place*}

(7) Describes effects of seasonal change on the local environment {*environmental changes*}

(8) Differentiates between maps and globes {*location*}

(9) Locates other neighborhoods studied on maps {*location, place,* and *neighborhoods as regions with similarities and differences*}

(10) Explains that neighborhoods depend on other neighborhoods to satisfy their wants and needs {*interdependence across space, interaction within and between neighborhoods,* and *neighborhoods as regions with similarities and differences*}

(11) Traces routes within and between neighborhoods using a variety of maps and models {*interdependence across space, interaction within and between neighborhoods,* and *neighborhoods as regions with similarities and differences*}

(12) Compares pictures and maps of same area {*place*}

Third: Focus on Community—Sharing Space with Others

(1) Uses distance, direction, scale, symbols {*relative location*}

(2) Prepares physical and human profile of community, including ethnic diversity and some of the historical dimensions of this diversity {*characteristics of landscapes* and *environmental relationships*}

(3) Compares community with other communities {*characteristics of landscapes* and *community as a region*}

(4) Compares rural and urban environments {*characteristics of landscapes* and *environmental relationships*}

(5) Analyzes various environmental situations in terms of positive/negative consequences {*environmental relationships*}

(6) Describes how people depend on each other in communities including focus on children, adults, and elderly men and women {*interdependence and interaction within community*}

(7) Describes interaction in community in terms of transportation/communication {*interdependence and interaction within community*}

(8) Describes how community interacts with other communities and areas {*community as a region*}

(9) Determines the characteristics of a region and explains why the local community can be considered a region {*community as a region*}

Fourth: Focus on the State, Nation, and World

(1) Interprets pictures, graphs, charts, and tables {*location*}

(2) Works with distance, direction, scale, and map symbolization {*location*}

(3) Relates similarities and differences between maps and globes {*location*}

(4) Uses maps of different scales and themes {*location* and *nature and characteristics of places*}

(5) Recognizes the common characteristics of map grid systems (map projections) {*location*}

(6) Discusses how regions are defined and how the regional concept might be used {*the nature of regions*}

(7) Compares and contrasts regions on a state, national, or world basis {*the nature of regions*}

(8) Locates and describes major geographical features and regions {*nature and characteristics of places* and *interaction of the human and physical environments*}

(9) Compares and contrasts major geographical features and regions using case studies of countries having different peoples, cultures, and environments {*human interactions within and between the state, nation, and world; global interdependence;* and *the nature of regions*}

(10) Notes how regions change through time {*interaction of the human and physical environments*}

(11) Demonstrates how humans interact within and between the state, nation, and world {*interaction of the human and physical environments and global interdependence*}

(12) Describes how people have adapted to and have modified their environments in keeping with their values, and understands how personal choices or behaviors are related to conditions of people in other places {*interaction of the human and physical environments*}

(13) Examines the impact of technological advances on the human and physical environments {*global interdependence*}

(14) Discusses how personal behavior could be changed to solve a particular environmental problem {*nature and characteristics of places; human interactions within and between the state, nation, and world;* and *global interdependence*}

(15) Discusses how people of the world are linked by transportation and communication and how they help fulfill each other's needs and are dependent on each other {*place* and *relationships within places*}

(16) Recognizes the relationships between human activities and various locations, i.e., work, recreation, shopping, education, religion {*relationships within places*}

Fifth: Focus on United States, Canada, and Mexico

(1) Recognizes distance, direction, scale, map symbols, and the relationship of maps and globes {*location*}

(2) Works with latitude and longitude {*location* and *comparative analysis of places*}

(3) Uses maps, charts, graphs, and tables to display data {*location* and *comparative analysis of places*}

(4) Discusses location in terms of where and why {*location* and *comparative analysis of places*}

(5) Maps the corresondence between resources and industry {*location*}

(6) Compares physical and cultural areas and regions within the United States with each other {*comparative analysis of places* and *human interaction in the United States with Canada and Mexico*}

(7) Maps physical and cultural regions in North America. Explains how these regions were outlined {*comparative analysis of places; quality of life; human interaction in the United States with Canada and Mexico; and physical and cultural regions of the United States, Canada, and Mexico*}

(8) Identifies, locates, and describes well-known economic areas such as Pittsburgh, Atlanta, the Central Valley of California, etc. {*location, quality of life, and human interaction in the United States with Canada and Mexico*}

(9) Compares the quality of life in various regions (e.g., economic prosperity, including comparisons across age, sex, and ethnic groups {*quality of life*}

(10) Outlines regions within the United States and Canada on the basis of movement and concentrations of different cultural groups {*human interaction in the United States with Canada and Mexico; and physical and cultural regions of the United States, Canada, and Mexico*}

(11) Compares and contrasts life in Anglo-America with life in Mexico, and understands the interrelationships between these areas {*physical and cultural regions of the United States, Canada, and Mexico*}

(12) Positive and negative consequences of having other nations to the north and south of the United States {*relationships within places*}

(13) Describes how there has been environmental deterioration in the United States, Mexico, and Canada related to industrial growth and economic prosperity {*quality of life*}

(14) Discerns ways in which personal choices and public decisions influence environmental quality {*quality of life* and *human interaction in the United States with Canada and Mexico*}

(15) Identifies local, regional, national, and international problems that have geographic dimensions {*comparative analysis of places; quality of life; human interaction in the United States with Canada and Mexico*; and *physical and cultural regions of the United States, Canada, and Mexico*}

(16) Comprehends how United States, Mexico, and Canada grew into their present territorial areas {*human interaction in the United States with Canada and Mexico*; and *physical and cultural regions of the United States, Canada, and Mexico*}

Sixth: Focus on Latin America, Europe, USSR, Middle East, Asia, and Africa

(1) Improves understanding of location, relative location, and the importance of location {*location*}

(2) Uses maps, globes, charts, and graphs {*location*}

(3) Readily uses latitude, longitude, map symbols, time zones, and basic earth–sun relations {*location*}

(4) Gains insights into the interaction of climate, landforms, natural vegetation, and other interactions in physical regions {*physical and cultural geographic characteristics*}

(5) Uses cultural regions to study change in regions through time {*physical and cultural geographic characteristics*}

(6) Examines human–land adaptations in difficult environments {*human–environmental interactions*}

(7) Perceives and analyzes migration patterns, including rural to urban and between regions of different levels of development {*spatial interrelationships*}

(8) Maps trade routes, particularly those connecting developed and developing nations {*spatial interrelationships*}

(9) Divides several large regions, such as the USSR or Africa, into smaller regions based on race, language, nationality, religion, or

some other cultural characteristic {*regions and subregions of the world*}

(10) Identifies important global problems with geographic dimensions, i.e., deforestation, desertification, pollution, overfishing, and offers suggestions for improvement. Does this for developed and developing nations. {*physical and cultural geographic characteristics; human–environmental interactions; spatial interrelationships*; and *regions and subregions of the world*}

(11) Plots distributions of population and key resources on regional maps {*physical and cultural geographic characteristics; human–environmental interactions; spatial interrelationships*; and *regions and subregions of the world*}

(12) Examines relationships between personal and national choices and their consequences for people in other world regions {*physical and cultural geographic characteristics; human–environmental interactions; spatial interrelationships*; and *regions and subregions of the world*}

(13) Explains problems with geographic dimensions. Suggests possible solutions. {*physical and cultural geographic characteristics; human–environmental interactions; spatial interrelationships*; and *regions and subregions of the world*}

INSTRUCTIONAL ACTIVITIES FOR THE GEOGRAPHY THEMES

Location

Early elementary students can start out by being taught the proper meanings of *up* and *down*, which do not mean at the top of a map and at the bottom of a map. *Up* means away from the earth and *down* means toward the earth. Therefore, a teacher should use and explain such common phrases as "up the hill," "down the stairs," etc.

Young children should learn to distinguish among the following items on a map or globe: continent, ocean, equator. They should see that the shapes are different, that some are near to or far away from where they live.

These students need to see the location of items on a map representing something they have experienced. Have them construct a map of their classroom (see Figure 4.10). Ask them, "Where should the classroom door be located?" "Is this the correct place for Sally's desk?" or "Do you think that the bookcase should be located closer to the teacher's desk on the map?"

Jigsaw puzzle maps can either be purchased or made. Commercially

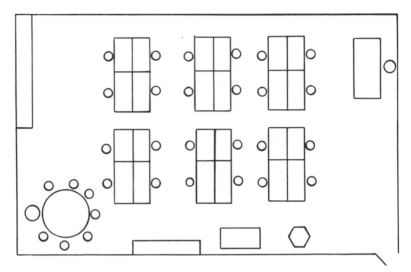

Figure 4.10 Classroom map.

The map below shows some of our state's important highways and parkways. Use the map to answer the questions that follow it.

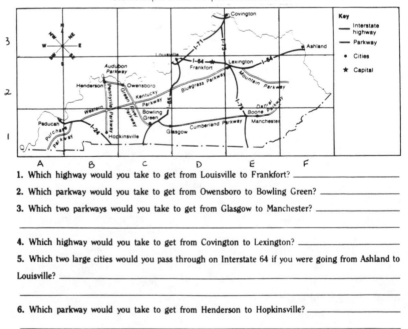

1. Which highway would you take to get from Louisville to Frankfort? _____

2. Which parkway would you take to get from Owensboro to Bowling Green? _____

3. Which two parkways would you take to get from Glasgow to Manchester? _____

_____

4. Which highway would you take to get from Covington to Lexington? _____

5. Which two large cities would you pass through on Interstate 64 if you were going from Ashland to Louisville? _____

_____

6. Which parkway would you take to get from Henderson to Hopkinsville? _____

_____

Figure 4.11 Some important highways and parkways in Kentucky (Laidlaw Brothers).

prepared ones are good for letting students learn where various places are in the world. Those that are constructed by the teacher or the students out of cardboard enable children to reconstruct a map by matching shapes and outlines.

Somewhere during the transition between early elementary and middle grades, the students can be instructed in the use of latitude and longitude lines. This skill can be associated with the ability to work with graphs in mathematics class, for both require that the student be able to use a combination of horizontal and vertical eye/hand coordination. They must be able to follow a line going along a left–right plane, while at the same time keeping in mind a line going along a top–bottom direction.

In the middle grades students can be taught to use coordinates to locate places. A highway road map can be a very appealing way for students to locate sites they have heard about or perhaps have traveled to. Figure 4.11 shows a state map with the common 1–8 vertical numbering and the A–H horizontal lettering on the grid lines.

Have the students consult an almanac to make a list of the twenty most populous cities in the world. They should then try to describe where they are in relation to something else. For example, a student might write that fifteen of the cities are north of the equator, six of the cities are in Asia, only three of the cities are south of the 40 degrees south latitude line, fifteen of the cities are on a body of water, etc.

Place

Activities associated with this theme concern both physical and human characteristics. Students just beginning school can be taken outside to look at the objects that are around their school, e.g., sidewalk, parking lot, sand box, merry-go-round, softball field, bushes, etc. They could discuss which ones they use most often during the day.

Make a list of the various bodies of water that can be found on the earth, e.g., pond, creek, river, lake, ocean, canal, etc. Discuss how each of these is similar to and different from another; e.g., a creek is so little that a person can quickly walk across it, but a lake is big and deep. Then have students discuss the different uses for each of them; e.g., we go water skiing on the lakes, but we can look for smooth rocks on the bottom of a creek.

Older students in the middle grades can work with the generalization that "all places on earth have special features that distinguish them from other places." An issue of *Update* (Peterson, 1987) includes a lesson plan that has students work in groups to draw an imaginary island that contains at least ten of the following land and water formations:

basin	bay	canyon
cape	cove	delta

gulf	hill	inlet
lake	mountain	mountain range
peninsula	plateau	river
sea	valley	

The students could then add latitude and longitude lines and describe the climate for their island.

Relationships within Places

This theme stresses how much humankind has changed the earth's environment. It deals with the interrelationships between people and geographical features such as climate, soils, topography, etc. The earliest grades should have some exposure to this. The teacher could do the following:

- Refer to maps and globes whenever students discuss people and places around the world.
- Use as many photographs as possible to show how people have modified their environment (ancient pyramids in Egypt, dikes in the Netherlands, interstate highways blasted through mountains in Appalachia, etc.).
- Draw comparisons between humans and other animals. Purchase an ant farm for the classroom and observe how the ants work together to build tunnels and carry the dirt.

The accompanying lesson plan utilizes the theme of "location" and "relationships within places." To make it easier for these third graders to identify with the concepts of *relative location* and *environmental relationships*, animals are the focus, rather than people.

EARLY ELEMENTARY GRADE LESSON PLAN

Topic: **Living in the World**

Grade: **3rd**

Date: **April 2, 1:15–1:45**

I. *Purpose*: tells what a student will learn

Students will locate where certain circus animals are from and will learn the location of these animals in relation to the equator, the tropics, and the poles. The students will investigate what type of climate prevails in these three areas of the earth. The students will understand why certain locations are suitable for certain animals.

II. *Motivation*: tells how to begin the day's lesson

Students will be asked about their experiences with the circus; for example, have they ever been to one, what is their favorite part, and what animals did they see?

III. *Development*: tells how to conduct the day's lesson

Students will first examine the names of seven circus animals printed on the chalkboard: bear, elephant, lion, monkey, zebra, poodle, and seal. The students will be asked to read these names and tell one thing that they know about them. Questions will be used to stimulate thought before each animal is discussed:

(1) Do you know where this animal is from?

(2) What about the animal might give you a clue as to the type of climate it might be suited for? (For example, polar bears have thick fur, which allows them to live comfortably in the Arctic region.)

(3) Using these clues, can you guess where this animal might be from?

Each animal will be discussed individually. For example, when discussing the bear, students will be told that most kinds of bears live north of the equator. Students will be asked to define and point out the equator on a globe. They will also be asked to show where north of the equator would be. Students will then be told, more specifically, where the animal is from, for example, brown bears in Alaska, American black bears in the wooded areas of North America, and polar bears in regions bordering the Arctic Ocean. These places will be pointed out on the globe to the class.

Each animal will be discussed in a similar fashion, using the globe for as many references as possible. Some pertinent facts will be included, such as:

(1) Of the two kinds of elephants, African and Asiatic, most trained elephants come from Asia.

(2) African elephants are fiercer and more difficult to train.

The tropics will be introduced with the monkey since most monkeys live in the tropics. The poles will be introduced with the polar bears.

IV. *Conclusion*: tells how to close or evaluate the day's lesson

Students will be divided into groups, with each group having a globe. As the name of an animal is stated, each group can discuss among themselves where it is from. At the end of a designated period of time, a spokesperson from each group must point to that location on the globe.

V. *Materials*: tells what is needed for the day's lesson

School circus kit containing photographs and coloring pages, globes, reference materials on animals.

Note: Some ideas for this lesson were developed by Nina Goecke and Vickie Sandlin.

Students in the upper grades can investigate how persons use their space:

- Study one of our country's dams, e.g., the Hoover Dam. Investigate how it was built, how it holds back the Colorado River, and what the positive and negative effects of it are.
- Announce to the class that a shopping center is being planned for the local area. It is their responsibility to decide how many stores should be built and what kind they should be. They could even create a 3-D replica of the shopping center.
- List the following terms on the board: coastal land erosion, earthquake, hurricane, flood, Arctic snowstorm, and desert heat. Students should search for photographs that depict how people have adapted to these forces of nature. For example, a photograph could show an igloo, which keeps the cold winds out; or a picture could be shown of a southern California beach house built on stilts to keep it above the eroding land.

Movement

People around the world interact with one another by traveling, communicating, or relying upon each other. This theme focuses on the movement of goods, people, and ideas.

Students in the primary grades should be encouraged to talk about vacations they have taken. This movement could be plotted on a map.

The names of the cardinal directions (north, south, east, and west) should be displayed on the walls so that the class can visualize where people are traveling when the students hear about these directions.

The teacher could cut out small boats, trains, cars, planes, or other vehicles. As news stories are brought to class recounting how people, goods, or ideas travel from one place to another, the miniature vehicles could be affixed to the map or globe at the appropriate points. If an English rock star is making a United States tour, a plane could be taped over London, England, and another plane over New York City, where he lands.

A lesson plan (O'Donnell, 1987) details how a student who progresses from an early elementary grade to a middle grade (fourth) can learn about movement. Students in the class are given candy bars. They list the main ingredients from the wrapper and use maps, charts, and magazine articles to locate where the ingredients came from. Discuss what modes of transportation might have been used to move the ingredients from one place to another. Students in the upper grades can use a map or globe scale to determine how far products have been shipped to arrive at their hometown.

Students can read about the proposed "Chunnel" (from the words channel and tunnel) that is being built between England and France. They could evaluate whether this will be a superior way to move people. The class could examine the ways in which ideas move from one country to another. Fast-food restaurants began in America, but now you can find McDonald's in many countries. Students could write to McDonald's headquarters to obtain a list of those cities in the world and determine what they have in common.

Regions

Regions can be large or small areas. A region must, however, be defined with a criterion that unifies it. Africa is a region because it is a body of land called a continent; a neighborhood is a region because it has a school that all the children attend. A region can share more than one criterion, e.g., the Arab world shares ethnic, religious, linguistic, and environmental features that distinguish it from Southeast Asia.

Early elementary students can study their region by making a map of their neighborhood. After taking a walking tour of the area, they can make the appropriate symbols to place on their maps: churches, fire hydrants, police station, school, city hall, trees, etc.

The teacher should present the class with a variety of regions, e.g., coal mining, dairy farming, crop farming, inner city, fishing, etc., and students should discuss what kind of stores these regions might have. What are some they all share? What are some that are unique to each?

Smith et al. (1988) present a lesson plan on Middle America with the following objectives:

(1) Students learn the meaning of the concept of migration.
(2) Students learn about the volume of immigrants, their destination, and the reason they chose to emigrate to a particular country.
(3) Students will construct a map utilizing a table of data.

Creating and using thematic maps is the topic for one lesson (Longmire, 1987) whereby students look up the per capita income of South American countries. They then do quartile ranking, which is achieved by ranking the per capita incomes from highest to lowest, dividing the ranked data into four equal parts (or quartiles), and defining the range of each quartile. Assign a color to each quartile—darkest colors for the highest figures and lightest colors for the lowest figures. Create a key that shows the per capita income range represented by each color. Students color an outline map of the continent using the colors from the key. They speculate on the factors that could be related to the per capita income of a country, e.g., population, literacy, GNP, etc.

ASSISTANCE POINTS

Questions for Action for the Administrator

1. Assume you are in charge of a vertical K–8 organization. The teachers know that children are different in maturation and cognitive development through this range. However, they are not sure what this means in terms of the kinds of materials that would be needed. Use the information from this chapter to describe how maps and globes for younger children should be different from maps and globes for older students.

2. Assume that the annual standardized test score results for your district are low in the area of social studies. After further investigation, you feel that the problem lies in the primary grades. They are not getting enough map and globe instruction. Develop a plan to strengthen the geography area; part of your plan might be to gather a list of commercial maps and globes that you would present to your teachers, encouraging them to use this list to prepare an order for their room.

3. After conferencing with a teacher, she complains that teaching geography is so difficult because there are so many different skills that can be taught. Prepare a response whereby you give her an alternative way of looking at geographic education. Specifically, discuss organizing lessons around the five geographic themes established by the National Council for Geographic Education and the Association of American Geographers.

4. As an administrator, you might want to get your district involved in the Geographic Alliance. Write the National Geographic Society in Washington, DC and find out how this can be done.

Addresses for Maps and Globes

Following are some addresses you can use to obtain information on maps and globes:

1. To obtain 2″ × 2″ slides of major U.S. metropolitan areas, write to the U.S. Geological Survey, EROS Data Center, Sioux Falls, SD 57198.

2. Topographic maps are published for each state and can be obtained from Branch of Distribution, U.S. Geological Survey, 1200 South Eads Street, Arlington, VA 22202.

3. Information on landsat maps (color images of the earth's surface) can be obtained from Educational Programs Office, NASA Goddard Flight Center, Greenbelt, MD 20771.

4. Standard maps and globes can be purchased from major companies, such as (a) C. S. Hammond, Inc., 515 Valley Street, Maplewood, NJ 07040, (b) A. J. Nystrom and Co., 333 Elston Avenue, Chicago, IL 60618, (c) Rand McNally and Co., 8255 N. Central Park Avenue, Skokie, IL 60076, (d) George F. Cram Co., 730 East Washington St., Indianapolis, IN 46206.

Names and Addresses of Professional Organizations and Journals Dealing with Geography

1. National Geographic Society
Educational Services
Washington, DC 20036
(The Society sponsors summer workshops for teachers across the country. It also sponsors a "Geography Bee.")

2. Association of American Geographers
1710 16th Street, N.W.
Washington, DC 20009

3. National Council for Geographic Education
Western Illinois University
Macomb, IL 61455
(The NCGE publishes *Journal of Geography*.)

Research about Geography: Implications for Educators

Most elementary grade students are in Piaget's concrete operations stage. This means they need to use manipulative materials that stimulate exploration. They should also be provided with a variety of hands-on experiences (Muir and Frazee, 1986, 202).

REFERENCES

Barth, James L. "Elementary Curriculum," *Social Education*, pp. 204–206 (March 1986).

Bruner, Jerome S. "On Cognitive Growth," in *Studies in Cognitive Growth*. J. S. Bruner, R. R. Oliver, and D. M. Greenfield, eds., New York:Wiley, pp. 1–67 (1966).

Buggey, JoAnne and James Kracht. "Geographic Learning," in *Elementary School Social Studies: Research as a Guide to Practice*. Bulletin No. 79, Virginia Atwood, ed., Washington:NCSS, pp. 55–67 (1986).

Cheek, Helen N. "Activities for Intermediate Grades," *Social Education*, pp. 207–211 (March 1986).

Cohen, Herbert G. "First Lessons in Map Use: The Primary Grades," *The Social Studies*, pp. 162–164 (July/August 1986).

Council of Chief State School Officers. "Geography Education and the States," A report on a 1988 geography education survey of state education agencies. Washington, DC:CCSSO.

Dumas, Wayne and Tom Weible. "Certification of Social Studies in Twelve Southern States," *Southern Social Studies Quarterly*, pp. 12–19 (Spring 1983).

Frazee, Bruce M. "Foundations for an Elementary Map Skills Program," *The Social Studies*, pp. 79–82 (March/April 1984).

Joint Committee on Geographic Education. *Guidelines for Geographic Education: Elementary and Secondary Schools*. Washington, DC:Association of American Geographers and the National Council for Geographic Education (1984).

Kennamer, Lorrin. "Developing a Sense of Place and Space," in *Skill Development in Social Studies*. Thirty-third Yearbook of the National Council for the Social Studies, Helen M. Carpenter, ed., Washington, DC:NCSS, pp. 157–168 and 322–325 (1963).

Kohn, Clyde. "Interpreting Maps and Globes," in *Skills in Social Studies*. Twenty-fourth Yearbook of the National Council for the Social Studies, Helen M. Carpenter, ed., Washington, DC:NCSS, pp. 146–157 (1953).

Lexington Herald Leader. Front-page newspaper article entitled "Lost in America: U.S. Adults' Geography Skills Rated Low," Lexington, Kentucky (July 28, 1988).

Longmire, Joan Marie. "Patterns of Prosperity," lesson plan in *Update*. Newsletter No. 9 by the National Geographic Society. Washington, DC, pp. 7, 8 (Fall 1987).

Muessig, Raymond. "Building Higher-Level Geographic Skills with Topographic Maps," *Social Education*, pp. 34–37 (January 1985).

Muir, Sharon Pray and Bruce Frazee. "A Developmental Perspective," *Social Education*, pp. 199–103 (March 1986).

O'Donnell, Corine. "The World in a Candy Bar," lesson plan in *Update*. Newsletter No. 9 by the National Geographic Society, Washington, DC, pp. 5, 6 (Fall 1987).

Peterson, Julius E. "Creating an Island," lesson plan in *Update*. Newsletter No. 9 by the National Geographic Society, Washington, DC, pp. 9, 10 (Fall 1987)

Piaget, Jean and Bärbel Inhelder. *The Child's Conception of Space*. New York:W. W. Norton & Co. (1967).

Rice, M. J. and R. L. Cobb. *What Can Children Learn in Geography? A Review of the Research*. Boulder, CO:SSEC (1978).

Savage, Tom V. and David G. Armstrong. *Effective Teaching in Elementary Social Studies*. New York:Macmillan (1986).

Smith, Ben A. et al. "Middle America: Intra- and Interregional Connections," *Social Education*, pp. 93–102 (February 1988).

Whitmore, Paul M. "Mapping: A Course," *Science and Children*, pp. 14–16 (January 1988).

Winston, Barbara. "Teaching and Learning in Geography," in *Social Studies and Social Sciences: A Fifty-Year Perspective*. Bulletin No. 78, Stanley Wronski and Donald Bragaw, eds., Washington, DC:NCSS, pp. 43–58 (1986).

5 | POLITICAL SCIENCE: A PICTURE OF CONTROL

Chapter Preview of Key Ideas

★ *Political science is the study of how people govern themselves.*

★ *Political socialization begins at a very young age.*

★ *Young children personally identify with political leaders and look up to them.*

★ *Their view becomes more realistic as they get older.*

★ *Piaget's stages of development indicate an expanding capability by a student to understand political issues from a third-person perspective. This is not present in young primary students and is very difficult for intermediate students.*

★ *Citizenship has been a part of our school's curriculum since the beginning of our country. It started out by focusing on values of liberty, equality, and patriotism.*

★ *Community involvement has been added during the decades of the 1960s, 1970s, and 1980s.*

★ *Law-related education develops students' understandings, attitudes, and skills necessary to respond effectively to legal issues in our society.*

POLITICAL SCIENCE IN THE CURRICULUM

Political science goes beyond a narrow definition. It is more than the science of politics or the study of public policy. It can broadly be defined as *the study of how people govern themselves.* Banks and Clegg (1985, 328) describe five kinds of political scientists. One kind attempts to describe desirable political systems. Another kind focuses on the legal aspect— investigating laws, documents, etc., or looking at the jobs of governmental

123

bodies and officials, e.g., Congress, judges, mayors. A third kind is the behaviorist, who develops theories that can be used to predict and control behavior. A fourth kind studies how groups of people affect public policy decisions. Finally, a fifth kind attempts to solve social problems and improve the human condition. It is the task of education decision makers to select material from all of these approaches to political science.

A number of topics are closely connected to political science. Civics, or citizenship, is foremost and will be treated in this chapter. So will law-related education (application of the law to daily life—and politics). Current events in part discusses political events and figures; it will be handled in a later chapter.

Jarolimek (1986, 159) says that three ideas are essential to political science in the elementary and middle grades:

(1) All societies have developed ways of establishing and maintaining social order.

(2) The central order-maintaining instrument has great power over the lives of individuals subjected to it.

(3) All such systems demand and expect a loyalty to them when they are threatened by hostile opposing forces.

POLITICAL SCIENCE AND THE YOUNG CHILD

Children are politically socialized beginning at a very early age, which follows from the findings that 50 percent of an individual's intellectual ability is formed by the age of four and 80 percent by the age of eight (Bloom, 1964). Young children are politically socialized mainly by imitation and by what they are told.

In a recent study (Hepburn, 1979), third graders were tested on their political knowledge. The results showed that they had a grasp of just over one-half of what might be taught to students of that age. They were asked about the following topics:

(1) National material

(2) State and local material

(3) Law and individual rights

(4) Politics/political ethics

(5) Global affairs

(6) Participation skills

(7) Analytic skills

It is interesting to note that the highest score was in the category of "participation skills," while the lowest scores were obtained in "law and individual rights."

Preston and Herman (1981, 23–26) summarize some points about the political awareness of children in the primary grades as follow.

Ideas of Government

Children associate government with personal figures of authority, thus giving them an imperfect idea of government. Their knowledge becomes less sketchy as they progress through the primary grades so that fourth graders can rate the president's job as "the most important," but they cannot yet supply many duties that he performs. Fourth graders have, however, begun to associate government with legislative bodies, rather than with individuals.

We know from Hess's (1967) study that children in grades K–3 identify with and admire political figures in the following order: the president of the United States, the local officials, and the state officials.

Sophistication of Thinking

These primary students have relatively little political information, exhibit relatively inaccurate information, and possess relatively general

"Electoral College? Doesn't your sister go there?"

TAKEN FROM *NEWSCURRENTS*, MADISON, WI.

(rather than specific) ideas. Primary-age children mimic their parents' party partisanship, as illustrated when they say, "I'm a Democrat" or "I'm a Republican." As they leave the primary grades, they begin to drop their idealization of political figures and assume a more realistic view. The older children also develop an independent political outlook, rather than the partisan affinity they copied earlier from their parents.

Development of Political Socialization

Young children have limited sophistication about political matters for two reasons: (1) adults just don't discuss political realities with children; rather, they shield them from events and issues; and (2) children of this age are not yet capable of a sufficiently high level of ideological thinking.

POLITICAL SCIENCE AND THE OLDER STUDENT

As students move into the intermediate grades, they develop more political understanding. Conner and Singleton (1981) administered a 10-question survey to sixth graders:

(1) Has a woman ever been president of the United States?
(2) How old does one have to be to vote in an election in the United States?
(3) Which political party has the elephant as its symbol?
(4) Which political party has the donkey as its symbol?
(5) Do you remember if President Kennedy was a Democrat or a Republican?
(6) For how many years is the governor elected to serve?
(7) How many United States senators are there from Kentucky?
(8) How old does one have to be to become president of the United States?
(9) United States senators are elected to serve a term of how many years?
(10) How many members does the Supreme Court have?

Ninety-three percent of the students answered the first question correctly while only four percent answered the last question correctly.

When asked to choose the most powerful person among the list of people in Figure 5.1, 100 percent of the students said that the president of the United States had the most power. When asked to choose the most important person, 37 percent selected the president, 30 percent selected the father, and 21 percent selected the mother. Eighteen percent of the students

The following choices were available to sixth grade students as they were asked to select (1) the person with the most power and (2) the person who is the most important.

1. United States Senator
2. Father
3. Police officer
4. President
5. Mother
6. Grandparent
7. Other
8. Uncertain: no response

Figure 5.1 Sixth grade choices.

chose the categories of police officer, other, or uncertain. We can see that students are conforming to Hess's (1967) contention that, as children leave the primary grades, they no longer view the president as the most esteemed figure.

Students who are entering the intermediate grades can begin to discern the difference among city, state, and nation. No longer do they confuse the geographical identity of the three. As they develop formal thinking, the students can think abstractly about how other people view issues.

The following lesson plan illustrates how a middle grade class can think about our country. The methods used by the teacher are concept learning and advance organizers (see Chapter 2).

MIDDLE GRADE LESSON PLAN

Topic: **Examining the Constitution**

Grade: **5th**

Date: **May 19, 1:00–2:00**

I. *Purpose*: tells what a student will learn

The student will be able to explain the purpose and functions of the three branches of government and will be able to describe the concept of checks and balances and explain its necessity.

II. *Motivation*: tells how to begin the day's lesson

Divide the class into five groups and distribute a complete copy of the Constitution to each group, providing time for them to examine the document. In a large group, encourage the students to react and comment on the document and to share their own knowledge. Pose such questions as: Why was this document written? What do you know about the people who signed the

Constitution? How is the language of the Constitution different from the language in your textbook? Do you recognize any important ideas in this document?

III. *Development*: tells how to conduct the day's lesson

Ask the students to remember that one of the major fears at the Constitutional convention was that the central government would get too powerful. Explain that, in order to avoid this, the writers of the Constitution set up three branches of government.

Refer to the diagram of a stool in Figure 5.2 (which has previously been drawn on the chalkboard) and explain that when power is balanced among the three branches, the government is stable and works well, just like the stool. If one branch becomes too powerful, it is as though one leg of the stool suddenly became longer. The government becomes unbalanced and does not work as well. Also, no branch of government can work all by itself, just as the stool cannot stand on one leg.

Show the transparency (which has been made earlier) entitled "Our National Government—Checks and Balances" (see Figure 5.3). Develop the concept of checks and balances. By matching the shapes from one branch with those of another, the students will be able to discover examples of ways in which the branches check each other.

Distribute copies of "The Constitution: An Outline" (Figure 5.4) to each student. Using the outline, the students should identify what articles allow the branches to do their duties. For example, a student would say that the executive branch carries out the laws because of Article II.A. or that the legislative branch makes treaties because of Article I.C.2.

IV. *Conclusion*: tells how to close or evaluate the day's lesson

Distribute copies of the "Which Branch of Government?" sheet (Figure 5.5). Have each student complete the worksheet using the "The Constitution: An Outline" as a reference.

V. *Materials*: tells what is needed for the day's lesson

Five copies of a complete version of the Constitution, copies for the entire class of "The Constitution: An Outline" and "Which Branch of Government?" and transparency entitled "Our National Government—Checks and Balances."

Note: This lesson plan is adapted from "Examining the Constitution," which appeared in *The Constitution and the Early Republic*, published by the Fairfax County Public Schools, Office of Curriculum Services, Department of Instructional Services, Fairfax, VA 22003 (January 1985).

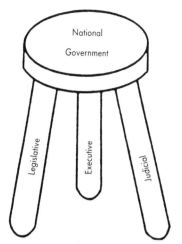

Figure 5.2 Three legs support a stool.

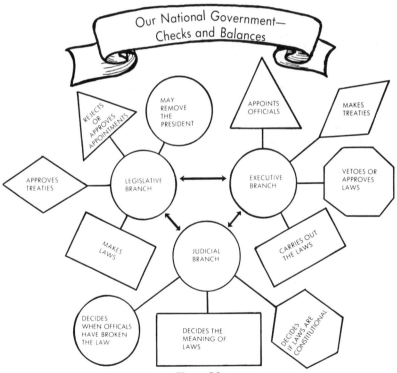

Our National Government—
Checks and Balances

REJECTS OR APPROVES APPOINTMENTS

MAY REMOVE THE PRESIDENT

APPOINTS OFFICIALS

MAKES TREATIES

APPROVES TREATIES

LEGISLATIVE BRANCH

EXECUTIVE BRANCH

VETOES OR APPROVES LAWS

MAKES LAWS

JUDICIAL BRANCH

CARRIES OUT THE LAWS

DECIDES WHEN OFFICALS HAVE BROKEN THE LAW

DECIDES THE MEANING OF LAWS

DECIDES IF LAWS ARE CONSTITUTIONAL

Figure 5.3

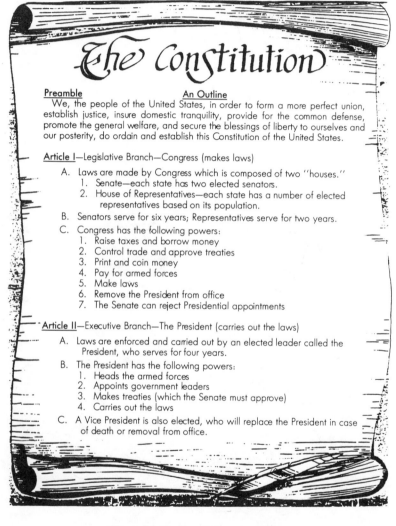

The Constitution

Preamble   **An Outline**

We, the people of the United States, in order to form a more perfect union, establish justice, insure domestic tranquility, provide for the common defense, promote the general welfare, and secure the blessings of liberty to ourselves and our posterity, do ordain and establish this Constitution of the United States.

<u>Article I</u>—Legislative Branch—Congress (makes laws)

A. Laws are made by Congress which is composed of two "houses."
1. Senate—each state has two elected senators.
2. House of Representatives—each state has a number of elected representatives based on its population.

B. Senators serve for six years; Representatives serve for two years.

C. Congress has the following powers:
1. Raise taxes and borrow money
2. Control trade and approve treaties
3. Print and coin money
4. Pay for armed forces
5. Make laws
6. Remove the President from office
7. The Senate can reject Presidential appointments

<u>Article II</u>—Executive Branch—The President (carries out the laws)

A. Laws are enforced and carried out by an elected leader called the President, who serves for four years.

B. The President has the following powers:
1. Heads the armed forces
2. Appoints government leaders
3. Makes treaties (which the Senate must approve)
4. Carries out the laws

C. A Vice President is also elected, who will replace the President in case of death or removal from office.

Figure 5.4 The Constitution: An outline.

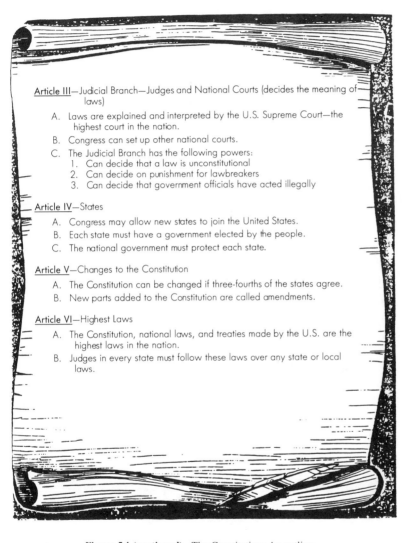

Article III—Judicial Branch—Judges and National Courts (decides the meaning of laws)

   A. Laws are explained and interpreted by the U.S. Supreme Court—the highest court in the nation.

   B. Congress can set up other national courts.

   C. The Judicial Branch has the following powers:
     1. Can decide that a law is unconstitutional
     2. Can decide on punishment for lawbreakers
     3. Can decide that government officials have acted illegally

Article IV—States

   A. Congress may allow new states to join the United States.

   B. Each state must have a government elected by the people.

   C. The national government must protect each state.

Article V—Changes to the Constitution

   A. The Constitution can be changed if three-fourths of the states agree.

   B. New parts added to the Constitution are called amendments.

Article VI—Highest Laws

   A. The Constitution, national laws, and treaties made by the U.S. are the highest laws in the nation.

   B. Judges in every state must follow these laws over any state or local laws.

Figure 5.4 (continued). The Constitution: An outline.

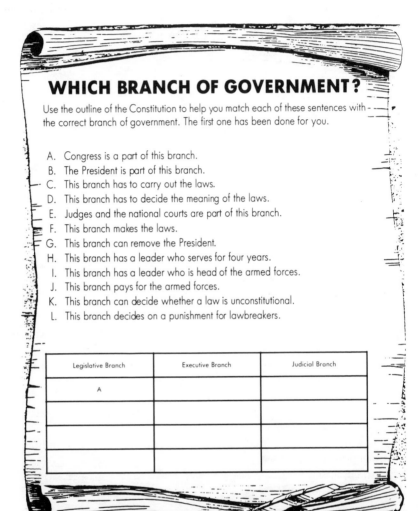

WHICH BRANCH OF GOVERNMENT?

Use the outline of the Constitution to help you match each of these sentences with the correct branch of government. The first one has been done for you.

A. Congress is a part of this branch.
B. The President is part of this branch.
C. This branch has to carry out the laws.
D. This branch has to decide the meaning of the laws.
E. Judges and the national courts are part of this branch.
F. This branch makes the laws.
G. This branch can remove the President.
H. This branch has a leader who serves for four years.
I. This branch has a leader who is head of the armed forces.
J. This branch pays for the armed forces.
K. This branch can decide whether a law is unconstitutional.
L. This branch decides on a punishment for lawbreakers.

Legislative Branch	Executive Branch	Judicial Branch
A		

Figure 5.5

TEACHING CONCEPTS AND GENERALIZATIONS

The following are some concepts and generalizations that can be taught to elementary and middle grade students in the area of political science. Administrators should make their teachers aware of them.

Concepts

power	freedom of speech	authority
Bill of Rights	democracy	elections
rules	laws	voting
justice	responsibility	citizen
government	political system	Constitution
freedom	separation of powers	due process
trial by jury	civil liberties	majority rule
taxes	autocracy	monarchy
dictatorship	branches of government	political parties
oligarchy	nationalism	equality
state	special interest group	city

Generalizations

- Every nation has some kind of authority structure that can be called its government.
- Political rights are meaningful only if they are counterbalanced by political responsibilities.
- Rules help keep us safe.
- Taxes are collected to help local, state, and national governments provide services to their citizens.
- Due process of law is needed to provide equal opportunity and protection for people.
- Throughout the world, many types of political systems exist to determine public policy.

Some young children feel that adults are omnipotent, to the point that they might think that a single political leader makes all the laws, controls all the money, and owns all the property. To teach the concept of *rules*, a teacher could allow students in a primary class to make some of their own rules to go with those of the teacher. This way the children see that rule-making can be a participatory process. Furthermore, they can see what is meant by the generalization "Rules are designed to help people."

As a fifth grade class studies the beginning of our country, they can learn about the different ways in which the European countries of France, England, and Spain ruled their North American colonies. Monarchy, parliament, governors, taxes, and other concepts would be applied to such generalizations as "Conflicts arise when individuals and groups interpet laws differently."

CITIZENSHIP EDUCATION

Citizenship in our schools had its beginnings in the founding of our country; liberty, equality, and patriotism were three important political values during that period. To these were added Christian morality and the middle class virtues of hard work, honesty, integrity, individualism, and obedience to legitimate authority. This was the form of citizenship at the end of the 19th century.

Freeland (1981) traced the path of citizenship in the 20th century be reviewing National Education Association Yearbooks from 1920–1978. The events of World War I, immigration, World War II, and worldwide growth of communism greatly channeled the direction of citizenship in the schools so that by the 1970s, student participation and community involvement appeared to be the key ideas.

Involving Young Children

A program in citizenship for young children should exhibit certain features, according to McGowan and Godwin (1986):

(1) It should foster active participation and involvement.

(2) It should utilize content that is relatively familiar to the students.

(3) It should have a strong skills component.

The following lesson plan entitled "What's Mine and What's Yours?" demonstrates these three features.

EARLY ELEMENTARY GRADE LESSON PLAN

Topic: **What's Mine and What's Yours?**

Grade: **Kindergarten or 1st**

Date: **May 15, 1:15–1:45**

I. *Purpose*: **tells what a student will learn**

By the end of the lesson, the students will be able to (1) name an item(s) that they own, (2) list several rights of ownership that they can exercise, (3) differentiate between items that they do and do not own, and (4) state reasons why property rights of others should not be violated.

II. *Motivation*: **tells how to begin the day's lesson**

The entire class sits on the floor with an object they have been asked to bring from home. This object is something which each child considers to be special. Several of the children share some of the reasons why the object is so important to them.

III. *Development*: **tells how to conduct the day's lesson**

The teacher now explains to the students that they own these special things and discusses the rights of ownership with the group. Some of these rights are

(a) The right to transport the item

(b) The right to use it whenever appropriate

(c) The right to let others use it

The teacher also discusses the responsibilities of ownership with the group. Some of these are

(a) The need to protect the item

(b) The responsibility to maintain it properly

Students offer personal illustrations of how each right and responsibility applies to them.

The students offer examples of items that they own and items that they use but do not truly own. The teacher helps students differentiate between things they own and things they may use. (Can you take it home? Must you take care of it?)

The class returns to their desks and draws four items that are their own special property, after which they present some of their drawings to the rest of the group. A student who presents her drawing should state reasons why these things are her property.

IV. *Conclusion*: **tells how to close or evaluate the day's lesson**

The success of the activity can best be measured by determining the relevance and accuracy of the discussions during the lesson and by examining the appropriateness of the items that have been included in the children's drawings.

V. *Materials*: **tells what is needed for the day's lesson**

Objects which the students have brought from home, drawing supplies.

Note: This lesson is adapted from a lesson by the same name, which originally appeared in *Teaching About Elections in Indiana* by C. W. Engelland, T. M. McGowan and V. Smith (1984), published in Indianapolis by the Indiana Department of Education.

Involving Older Students

Older students can get involved in a variety of ways (Conrad and Hedin, 1979). Social/political action allows a young person to influence public decision making. This is often reserved for older students who join local committees or groups working for political change.

Community projects is a second type of involvement mentioned by Conrad and Hedin. This type represents projects that have been initiated by students with little adult help, e.g., operating a recycling center, producing a community newspaper, and advising city government on where a biking trail should be placed.

Volunteer service is for students who donate their time in a social service agency. Helping to decorate rooms in a day-care center and bringing food to a relief center are two examples.

The accompanying checklist (Chart 5.1) presents a model citizenship program. Applicable for younger and older students, it contains the three elements of (1) understandings—content, (2) attitudes—involvement, and (3) skills which are found in the NCSS "Essentials Statements" of Figure 5.6.

LAW-RELATED EDUCATION (LRE)

Law-related education began in the 1960s, and the initial emphasis was on teaching the Bill of Rights. Today it is a part of the K–12 curriculum whereby pupils develop an understanding of our judicial system and develop a functional knowledge of the operation of our legal institutions. The most desirable plan for teaching it is to infuse it into the existing curriculum, since the following key concepts are so often taught, not only in social studies, but in other curriculum areas as well:

rules	laws	due process
authority	power	rights
justice	privacy	legal system
property	responsibility	equal protection

LRE is distinctive because of the pupil-involving techniques used to teach it: community research, police ride-alongs, mock trials, moot courts, roleplay, case study discussion, and debate. Maxey (1987) discusses the function of technology as a resource to teach LRE.

Computers in the Classroom

The *Medalists* series (Hartley Courseware in Dimondale, MI) for middle grades is a drill and practice program. *Lincoln's Decisions* (Educa-

MODEL CITIZENSHIP PROGRAM   **ASSESSMENT OF CURRENT PROGRAM**

	Current program does this (X)	Grade level(s) where this occurs	Evidence this occurs
• Is based upon objectives which are thoughtfully selected and are philosophically consistent with the "Essentials of the Social Studies" and are clearly stated in such a way as to furnish direction for the entire program.			
• Is built on a logical developmental K–12 sequence which attempts to develop the cognitive structure, skills, attitudes, and knowledge necessary for full participation in local, state, national and global communities.			
• Recognizes that while the primary responsibility for citizenship education resides with social studies educators, it is also an integral part of the total school program including school climate, procedures, and organization.			
• Is based upon learning experiences which are meaningful and practical to students and which enable them to discuss issues in an open, supportive environment, i.e., such instruction should be directly related to the age, maturity, and concerns of students.			
• Provides students with understanding and appreciation of the fundamental beliefs inherent in the Declaration of Independence, the U.S. Constitution, and the Universal Declaration of Human Rights through learning experiences which are rooted in the historical derivation as well as the contemporary application of these documents.			
• Provides formal instruction for all students in concepts related to the structures and function of local, state, and national government, international organizations, and processes and judicial systems at all levels.			
• Focuses instruction upon study of the United States in global and historical contexts.			
• Provides opportunities for investigation into public policy issues.			

Chart 5.1 Essential characteristics of a citizenship program: criteria checklist (developed by the NCSS Citizenship Committee, 1981–1983).

MODEL CITIZENSHIP PROGRAM ASSESSMENT OF CURRENT PROGRAM

	Current program does this (X)	Grade level(s) where this occurs	Evidence this occurs
• Enables students to practice civic participation in the total school program, including school governance, for development of skills for democratic political participation. Encourages students to participate in civic activities in the community.			
• Provides students with a broad range of educational experiences to insure that classroom settings are culturally rich, intellectually stimulating, and experientially based.			
• Provides opportunities for students to learn about and appreciate multicultural contributions to our civic heritage.			
• Helps students see themselves as members of various structures including family, other groups, the local community, the state, and the nation, and as inhabitants of a global society.			
• Provides students with opportunities to identify their rights and responsibilities as members of various groups, e.g., family, school, community, state, nation, and the human species in a global community.			
• Develops student competency in making socio/political decisions with consideration of consequences and which take into account the viewpoints of different individuals and groups.			
• Develops student competency in generating and using such standards of justice, ethics, morality, and practicality to make judgements about people, institutions, policies, and decisions.*			
• Is sensitive to parents, interested individuals and civic groups.			
• Includes comprehensive evaluation using a variety of measures to assess achievement of objectives.			
• Systematically, formally evaluates to maintain and upgrade program quality.			

*Richard C. Remy. *Handbook of Basic Citizenship Competencies*. Alexandria, VA:Association for Supervision and Curriculum Development, p. 86 (1980).

Chart 5.1 (continued) Essential characteristics of a citizenship program: criteria checklist (developed by the NCSS Citizenship Committee, 1981–1983).

Essentials of Social Studies

Citizen participation in public life is essential to the health of our democratic system. Effective social studies programs help prepare young people who can identify, understand, and work to solve the problems that face our increasingly diverse nation and interdependent world. Organized according to a professionally designed scope and sequence, such programs:

1. Begin in pre-school and continue throughout formal education and include a range of related electives at the secondary level.
2. Foster individual and cultural identity.
3. Include observation of and participation in the school and community as part of the curriculum.
4. Deal with critical issues and the world as it really is.
5. Prepare students to make decisions based on American principles.
6. Demand high standards of performance and measure student success by means that require more than the memorization of information.
7. Depend on innovative teachers, broadly prepared in history, the humanities, the social sciences, educational theory and practice.
8. Involve community members as resources for program development and student involvement.
9. Lead to citizenship participation in public affairs.

In 1979, National Council for the Social Studies joined with eleven other professional associations to reaffirm the value of a balanced education.[*] We now enumerate the essentials of exemplary social studies programs. Such programs contribute not only to the development of students' capacity to read and compute, but also link knowledge and skills with an understanding of and commitment to democratic principles and their application.

Knowledge

Students need knowledge of the world at large and the world at hand, the world of individuals and the world of institutions, the world past, the world present and future. An exemplary social studies curriculum links information presented in the classroom with experiences gained by students through social and civic observation, analysis, and participation.

Classroom instruction which relates content to information drawn from the media and from experience focuses on the following areas of knowledge:

- History and culture of our nation and the world.
- Geography—physical, political, cultural, and economic.
- Economics—theories, systems, structures, and processes.
- Social institutions—the individual, the group, the community, and the society.
- Intergroup and interpersonal relationships.
- World-wide relationships of all sorts between and among nations, races, cultures, and institutions.

From this knowledge base, exemplary programs teach skills, concepts, and generalizations that can help students understand the sweep of human affairs and ways of managing conflict consistent with democratic procedures.

[*]Essentials of Education Statement, Washington, D.C. 1980

Figure 5.6 The essentials statements (reprinted from the National Council for the Social Studies NCSS Tool Kit).

Democratic Beliefs

Fundamental beliefs drawn from the Declaration of Independence and the United States Constitution with its Bill of Rights form the basic principles of our democratic constitutional order. Exemplary school programs do not indoctrinate students to accept these ideas blindly, but present knowledge about their historical derivation and contemporary application essential to understanding our society and its institutions. Not only should such ideas be discussed as they relate to the curriculum and to current affairs, they should also be mirrored by teachers in their classrooms and embodied in the school's daily operations.

These democratic beliefs depend upon such practices as due process, equal protection, and civic participation, and are rooted in the concepts of:

- Justice
- Responsibility
- Diversity
- Equality
- Freedom
- Privacy

Thinking Skills

It is important that students connect knowledge with beliefs and action. To do that, thinking skills can be developed through constant systematic practice throughout the years of formal schooling. Fundamental to the goals of social studies education are those skills which help assure rational behavior in social settings.

In addition to strengthening reading and computation, there is a wide variety of thinking skills essential to the social studies which can be grouped into four major categories:

- **Data Gathering Skills.** Learning to:
  Acquire information by observation
  Locate information from a variety of sources
  Compile, organize, and evaluate information
  Extract and interpret information
  Communicate orally and in writing
- **Intellectual Skills.** Learning to:
  Compare things, ideas, events, and situations on the basis of similarities and differences
  Classify or group items in categories
  Ask appropriate and searching questions
  Draw conclusions or inferences from evidence
  Arrive at general ideas
  Make sensible predictions from generalizations
- **Decision Making Skills.** Learning to:
  Consider alternative solutions
  Consider the consequences of each solution
  Make decisions and justify them in relationship to democratic principles
  Act, based on those decisions
- **Interpersonal Skills.** Learning to:
  See things from the point of view of others
  Understand one's own beliefs, feelings, abilities, and shortcomings and how they affect relations with others
  Use group generalizations without stereotyping and arbitrarily classifying individuals
  Work effectively with others as a group member
  Give and receive constructive criticism
  Accept responsibility and respect the rights and property of others

Participation Skills

As a civic participant, the individual uses the knowledge, beliefs, and skills learned in the school, the social studies classroom, the community, and the family as the basis for action.

Connecting the classroom with the community provides many opportunities for students to learn the basic skills of participation, from observation to advocacy. To teach participation, social studies programs need

Figure 5.6 (continued). The essentials statements (reprinted from the National Council for the Social Studies NCSS Tool Kit).

to emphasize the following kinds of skills:

* Work effectively in groups—organizing, planning, making decisions, taking action
* Form coalitions of interest with other groups
* Persuade, compromise, bargain
* Practice patience and perserverance in working for one's goal
* Develop experience in cross-cultural situations

Civic Action

Social studies programs which combine the acquisition of knowledge and skills with an understanding of the application of democratic beliefs to life through practice at social participation represent an ideal professional standard. Working to achieve that ideal is vital to the future of our society. However, even if excellent programs of social studies education were in place, there would often remain a missing element—the will to take part in public affairs. Formal education led by creative and humane teachers can provide the knowledge, the tools, the commitment for a thoughtful consideration of issues and can even stimulate the desire to be active. But to achieve full participation, our diverse society must value and model involvement to emphasize for young people the merit of taking part in public life.

During the period of the bicentennial of our Constitution and Bill of Rights, is it not time for us to recommit ourselves as a nation to strong education for civic responsibility?

Figure 5.6 (continued). The essentials statements (reprinted from the National Council for the Social Studies NCSS Tool Kit).

ional Activities in Freeport, NY) is a tutorial program for middle grades. The *Decisions, Decisions* series (Tom Snyder Productions in Cambridge, MA) affords simulations for middle graders. *PFS: File* (Scholastic, Inc. in New York City) is a data base program for middle school pupils. *Survey Taker* (Scholastic, Inc. in New York City) enables a teacher to tabulate and present survey results, using tables or graphs.

Video Technology

Thinkabout (Agency for Instructional Technology in Bloomington, IN) is a television program for grades five and six. *Neighborhoods* (Great Plains National Instructional Television in Lincoln, NE) is designed for the primary grades.

Charlotte Anderson (1980) listed the learning outcomes from law-related education programs. Chart 5.2 portrays how an outcome is matched up with an activity that can bring about the desired outcomes.

MOCK TRIALS

Mock trials are used to teach middle grade students about the process of our political institutions. In a mock trial, students assume the roles of

Outcome from a Law-Related Education Program	Activities to Achieve the Corresponding Outcomes
1. Perceiving law as promotive, facilitative, comprehensible, and alterable	1. Have the students in a room construct a classroom constitution.
2. Perceiving people as having potential to control and contribute to the social order	2. Students analyze how laws are made and changed in various cultures and groups.
3. Perceiving right and wrong as issues all citizens can and should address	3. Students can dramatize with puppets what happens when a safety rule is broken and why people must abide by rules.
4. Perceiving the dilemmas inherent in social issues	4. Discuss the historic situation of the Puritans, who were faced with the dilemma of submitting to a law that went against their beliefs, or fleeing to another land. What political power was demonstrated? What political repercussions were there?
5. Being reflective decision makers and problem solvers who make grounded commitments	5. Have students identify a problem in their school, such as dangerous behavior on the playground, and ask them to devise a plan to help eliminate it.
6. being able to give reasoned explanations about commitments made and positions taken	6. Students will keep a log for a day, listing several instances where they have had to make a choice to follow or not to follow a rule.
7. Being socially responsible conflict managers	7. Students identify a situation which presents difficulty for students to cross. The class would identify the problem, arrive at a possible solution, and write a letter to the appropriate person or agency requesting their solution be considered.
8. Being critically responsive to legitimate authority	8. Ask the class to think of a law and list all the reasons in one column why it is good for him or her. Then they should list all the reasons why it is good for other people.
9. Being knowledgeable about law, the legal system, and related issues	9. Invite a judge to the classroom to tell about his/her job.
10. Being empathetic, socially responsible, and considerate of others	10. Read the story of *The Little Red Hen*. Discuss if the characters in the story were considerate of the hen. Then ask if the hen was considerate of them when she ate the bread.
11. Being able to make mature judgements in dealing with ethical and moral problems	11. Summarize for the class an important court case in our country's history, e.g., *Brown vs. Board of Education of Topeka, Kansas*. Ask the students to write a page describing how this decision has affected the lives of the people in this country.

Chart 5.2

various characters, namely, judge, prosecuting attorney, defense attorney, juror, and witness. Students learn essential aspects of courtroom procedure and rules of evidence. Michaelis (1988, 279) explains how a mock trial could be handled:

> An experienced group should begin with a simple mock trial in which a judge hears the case and makes the decision with no attorneys present, as in small claims court. After students have built up a background of knowledge and experience, a civil court mock trial may be simulated. The main steps in a mock trial are briefing (preparation), conducting the trial (simulation), and debriefing (evaluation). Briefing should be thorough so that participants understand their roles, the issue, and the facts. . . . Debriefing contributes much to learning as students evaluate the following: How were the roles played? How might they be changed? What was the issue? Which facts were relevant? How effectively were they presented? How sound were the arguments on each side? How might they be improved? Why do you agree or disagree with the decision? Can you think of sound reasons for an appeal?

ASSISTANCE POINTS

Questions for Action for the Administrator

1. You are head of a social studies department and your teachers make a request. They would like to investigate out-of-school experiences in your community. What concepts in political science could be enhanced by such experiences?

2. An administrator should be an instructional leader. What guidance would you supply to teachers with respect to the need for students to learn about local, state, and national government in our country?

3. Assume you are in charge of writing the rationale statement for your district's accreditation self-study. How could you explain that citizenship is the core of the social studies curriculum?

4. If a parent feels that the purpose of law-related education is to "make little lawyers out of all the children," how would you explain that this is not the intent?

Instructional Tips for Children Still in Concrete Operations

The ideas on the following pages are designed for students who are in Piaget's concrete operational development stage and have not yet moved into Piaget's formal operational stage. The material in the following chart and in the teacher–student dialogue is derived from Kitty Abraham's article in *Elementary School Journal* (November 1983, pp. 229, 230) entitled "Political Thinking in the Elementary Years: An Empirical Study."

Stage	Age	Characteristics	Instructional Tips
concrete operations	late primary and early intermediate grades 7–12 years of age	• Student needs chance to take another's point of view. • Student needs chance to solve problems he has not experienced directly. • Student has difficulty in reasoning about verbal propositions, e.g., "Can Mrs. Smith be a city council member *and* a Republican?"	• Involve students in direct-participation experiences in which they have the opportunity to role-play. • Provide instructions about political parties by allowing children to participate in formulating hypothetical party platforms and deciding on party affiliations.
		• As a student interacts with peers, he is liberated from egocentrism. • As a student interacts with peers, he is able to acquire rationality and objectivity by comparing his thoughts with those of others.	• Teacher should conduct political instruction as often as possible in open group discussion formats.
		• Student needs to critically examine his current political concepts and readjust them to a state of equilibrium on a higher level.	• Political instruction should involve the teacher's use of a direct and probing repartee with children that anticipates and spontaneously reacts to children's comments, while simultaneously compelling them toward cognitive reorganization. [see dialogue on next page]
		• Student has an inflexible cognitive system; things are viewed in black/white terms, not gray.	• Involve student in group games that facilitate children's ability to systematize, differentiate, and reason deductively. • Involve students in group games that facilitate their ability to classify, so that an object or person can be placed in more than one category.

Dialogue

Teacher:	We've been talking about political parties this week; we've mentioned the Republican party, the Democratic party, and the Independent party. But we haven't really talked about how you become a member of a political party. How do you become a Republican? Dan?
Dan:	Well, it's sorta the way you feel.
Teacher:	You mean like feeling happy or feeling sad?
Dan:	No, it's more like the things you do.
Teacher:	What kind of things?
Dan:	I'm not sure . . . sorta like make speeches and stuff.
Teacher:	Can you tell if a person is a Republican?
Dan:	Yeh, because they make speeches.
Teacher:	Well, I heard Mr. Jones [principal] make a speech at the teacher's meeting last week. Is he a Republican?
Sue:	He might be . . . if he votes.
Teacher:	Do you have to vote to be a Republican, or do you have to make speeches?
Dan:	Maybe you have to do both.
Teacher:	Oh, so if you vote and make speeches, you are a Republican. Is that right?
Children:	Yes.
Teacher:	Then how do you get to be a Democrat?
Jane:	Democrats vote too. And they make speeches at the Democratic party.
Teacher:	What kind of party is it?
Jane:	Probably like people all dressed up and balloons all over the place and music playing.
Children:	[laughter]
Jane:	Well, I saw the Democratic party on TV last summer!
Teacher:	The Democrats *did* meet last summer, didn't they? That was the Democratic convention—some of it looked like a party when they placed candidates in nomination. But Democratic *party* means something else—who thinks they know?
Bob:	It's sort of like their group or club—the people who want to be Democrats.
Teacher:	Okay. If you're a Democrat, can you be a teacher or a principal or something at the same time?
Children:	Yes.
Teacher:	If you're a Democrat, can you be an American at the same time?
Children:	Yes [perhaps less certainly so].
Teacher:	Well, if you're a Democrat, can you be a Republican at the same time?
Children:	[various uncertain responses]

Names and Addresses of Professional Organizations

Following are some names and addresses of organizations to which you can write for information about teaching political science:

1. American Bar Association
   1155 E. 60th St.
   Chicago, IL 60637
   (The ABA assists with the Mock Trial program and puts out a news-letter entited *Update*.)

2. American Civil Liberties Union
   22 East 40th St.
   New York, NY 10016

3. Mershon Center
   Citizenship Development and Global Education Program
   Ohio State University
   199 West 19th Ave.
   Columbus, OH 43201
   (The Mershon Center has available citizenship decision-making ma-terials.)

4. Center for Civic Education/Law in a Free Society
   Suite 1, 5115 Douglas Fir Rd.
   Calabasas, CA 91302
   (The Center publishes K–12 multimedia instructional units.)

5. Phi Alpha Delta Public Service Center
   Suite 325E
   7315 Wisconsin Ave.
   Bethesda, MD 20814
   (This organization offers technical assistance for program develop-ment and resource mobilization.)

6. Constitutional Rights Foundation
   602 S. Kingsley Dr.
   Los Angeles, CA 90005
   (The foundation puts out a newsletter.)

7. National Institute for Citizen Education in the Law
   25 East St., N.W.
   Suite 400
   Washington, DC 20001
   (This organization assists with the Mock Trial program.)

8. American Political Science Association
   1527 New Hampshire Ave.
   Washington, DC 20036

(The APSA publishes the journal *American Political Science Review*.)

9. Close Up Foundation
   1235 Jefferson Davis Highway
   Arlington, VA 22202
   (Close Up offers programs and materials on citizenship.)
10. Congressional Quarterly
    1414 22nd St., N.W.
    Washington, DC 20037
    (CQ offers books and materials on American politics.)

Research about Political Science: Implications for Educators

Administrators in education need to be aware of the fact that a person's base of political knowledge is fairly well established by the time a child leaves junior high or the middle grades (Easton and Hess, 1962). In other words, if a person at this age believes that democracy is a good political system, chances are that he will keep this opinion into adulthood.

Parker and Kaltsounis (1986, 18) summarize the research on children's political learning:

1. Political learning begins early and continues through early childhood, late childhood, and adolescence.
2. Different types of political learning take place at different points over the preadult years.
3. Basic attachments and identifications are among the first political outlooks to be acquired.
4. Early orientations toward political authorities seem to be indiscriminately positive and benevolent. They become less so as the child moves through late childhood and into adolescence.
5. Early conceptions of politics and government are highly personalized. The government, the president, the mayor, and other elements are understood initially in personal terms. This personalization fades and is replaced by more abstract perceptions by late childhood and early adolescence.
6. Affective orientations, or feelings, about political objects seem to be acquired before information or knowledge. One has feelings about the nation and the president (usually positive feelings) before one has much understanding of their functions.
7. During late childhood, children acquire information and knowledge about the political world. They begin to distinguish between different

political roles and acquire the basic factual information needed to map out the political world.

8. During adolescence, individuals increase their capacity to deal with abstractions and to engage in ideological thinking and ends–means analysis. They become more interested in following political events and more involved in partisan and electoral politics.

REFERENCES

Abraham, Kitty G. "Political Thinking in the Elementary Years: An Empirical Study," *Elementary School Journal*, pp. 221–231 (November 1983).

Anderson, Charlotte. "Promoting Responsible Citizenship through Elementary Law-Related Education," *Social Education*, pp. 383–386 (May 1980).

Anderson, Charlotte. "How Fares Law-Related Education?" Reston, VA:National Association of Secondary School Principals, ERIC document ED289789 (1987).

Arnoff, Melvin. "Added Depth to Elementary-School Social Studies," *Social Education*, pp. 335–336 (October 1964).

Arnold, George F. "Teaching Local Government Painlessly," *The Social Studies*, pp. 111–114 (May/June 1985).

Banks, James A. and Ambrose A. Clegg, Jr. *Teaching Strategies for the Social Studies, 3rd ed.* White Plains, NY:Longman, Inc. (1985).

Bloom, Benjamin. *Stability and Change in Human Characteristics.* New York:John Wiley and Sons (1964).

Coles, Robert. *The Political Life of Children.* Boston:The Atlantic Monthly Press (1986).

Curtis, Charles K. "Citizenship Education and the Slow Learner," in *Building Rationales for Citizenship Education*. Bulletin No. 52, edited by James Shaver. Arlington, VA:NCSS, pp. 74–95 (1979).

Dawson, R. E. and K. Prewitt. *Political Socialization.* Boston:Little, Brown (1977).

Easton, David and Robert Hess. "The Child's Political World," *Midwest Journal of Political Science*, 6:227–246 (1962).

Easton, David and Jack Dennis. *Children in the Political System.* New York:McGraw Hill (1969).

Engelland, C. W., T. M. McGowan and V. Smith. *Teaching about Elections in Indiana.* Indianapolis, IN:Indiana Department of Education (1984).

Freeland, Kent. "Citizenship: Changing over the Years," *Indiana Social Studies Quarterly*, pp. 34–38 (Spring 1981).

Greenstein, Fred I. *Children and Politics.* New Haven:Yale University Press (1965).

Hepburn, Mary. "What Do Students Know about Politics?" Paper presented at the 1979 Annual Meeting of the American Political Science Association, Washington, DC, ERIC document ED178443.

Hess, Robert D. and J. V. Torney. *Development of Political Attitudes in Children.* Garden City, NJ:Doubleday (1967).

Hunkins, Francis P., Jan Jeter, and Phyllis Maxey. *Social Studies in the Elementary School.* Columbus, OH:Merrill (1982).

Jarolimek, John. *Social Studies in Elementary Education, 7th edition*. New York: Macmillan (1986).

Johnson, Lynell and Robert D. Hess. "Kids and Citizenship: A National Survey," *Social Education*, pp. 502–505 (December 1984).

Krause, Merton S. "Schoolchildren's Attitudes toward Public Authority Figures," *Adolescence*, pp. 111–112 (Spring 1975).

Levitsky, Ronald and George Steffen. "Supreme Court Simulation Game," *The Social Studies*, pp. 89–92 (March/April 1983).

Maxey, Phyllis. "Tapping the New Technology," *The International Journal of Social Education*, pp. 79–85 (Autumn 1987).

McGowan, Thomas M. and Charles M. Godwin. "Citizenship Education in the Early Grades: A Plan for Action," *The Social Studies*, pp. 196–200 (September/October 1986).

Michaelis, John U. *Social Studies for Children, 9th edition*. Englewood Cliffs, NJ:Prentice Hall (1988).

Metz, Kathleen E. "Children's Thinking and Primary Social Studies Curricula," *Elementary School Journal*, pp. 115–121 (November 1978).

Parker, Walter C. and Theodore Kaltsounis. "Citizenship and Law-Related Education," in *Elementary School Social Studies: Research as a Guide to Practice*. Bulletin No. 79, Virginia Atwood, ed., Washington, DC:National Council for the Social Studies (1986).

Palonsky, Stuart. "Political Socialization in Elementary Schools," *Elementary School Journal*, pp. 493–506 (May 1987).

Preston, Ralph C. and Herman L. Wayne, Jr. *Teaching Social Studies in the Elementary School, 5th edition*. New York:Holt, Rinehart, and Winston (1981).

Remy, Richard C. *Handbook of Basic Citizenship Competencies*. Alexandria, VA: ASCD (1980).

Singleton, J. Allen and Mary Lou Conner. "Political Awareness of Sixth Graders in a Rural Kentucky County," *Indiana Social Studies Quarterly*, pp. 43–51 (Spring 1981).

6 | SOCIOLOGY: PEOPLE GETTING ALONG

Chapter Preview of Key Ideas

★ Sociology is the study of groups of people.

★ Sociology occupies a large part of the social studies curriculum in the primary grades.

★ Self, family, neighborhood, and community are important concepts.

★ Rules and truth are easily understood concepts for the young primary children.

★ Some techniques are better used with older students when teaching sociological material.

★ A case study is a detailed examination of an incident or an event.

★ Many sociological topics are essential to the students' lives, e.g., relating to older people in society, dealing with religion, coming to grips with crime and delinquency, reducing prejudice, and knowing one's values.

★ Educators need to exercise care when teaching some topics because they generate controversy.

★ Literature can be used to teach sociological concepts and generalizations.

Sociology is *the study of groups of people*. More exactly, it is concerned with how the individuals in these groups behave. Groups can be large or small. Technically, a group is constituted by two or more people who are assembled for a common purpose. Examples of groups might be a family, a baseball team, a class of students, or a mob.

TEACHING CONCEPTS AND GENERALIZATIONS

Following are some concepts and generalizations that can be taught to elementary and middle grade students. Administrators should make their teachers aware of them.

Concepts

norms	groups	socialization
society	status	role
class	social structure	social stratification
assimilation	values	sanctions
conflict	family	friendship
sharing	institution	social change
self concept	interdependency	population
urbanization	rural community	marriage
neighborhood	prestige	reward
organization	criminal behavior	discrimination
cooperation	peer pressure	poverty
moral conduct	conscience	ethical behavior
home		

Generalizations

- The family is the basic social institution in most societies.
- The goals of one group may be in conflict with the goals of another group.
- The group enforces its norms by the use of sanctions.
- All societies are in continual change.
- All members of a society are placed into layers of prestige and power called social classes.
- Population growth is one of the most challenging problems in our world.

THE YOUNG LEARNER

Social studies in the early elementary grades is primarily sociological (Banks and Clegg, 1985, 287). Kindergarten typically focuses on the self, first grade on the family, second grade on the neighborhood, and third grade on the community. Banks and Clegg recommend that an educator should teach with sociological concepts and generalizations in mind, rather than simply with topics. It facilitates comprehension, transfer, and mastery of content. The following early elementary lesson plan teaches "norms" and "sanctions" from the list of concepts, while also teaching the generalization "The group enforces its norms by the use of sanctions."

EARLY ELEMENTARY LESSON PLAN

Topic: **The Playground Incident**

Grade: **3rd**

Date: **September 4, 1:35–2:00**

I. *Purpose*: **tells what a student will learn**

Students will understand that a group enforces its norms by the use of sanctions.

II. *Motivation*: **tells how to begin the day's lesson**

The teacher should read the following situation to the class:

> During recess, the boys in Miss Jones's class hurried outside to play with the big, red ball that Miss Jones had just bought for her pupils. Miss Jones had wanted the boys to play a game with the girls that morning, but the boys, led by Joe, had begged her to let them play with the big, shining ball. When she pulled the ball out of the closet, Joe and Johnny grabbed it. They ran toward the large play area, which was a distance from where Miss Jones usually stood to watch the children play. Joe and Johnny threw the ball to each other and to their friends. Carl, who was not too well liked by some of the leaders in the crowd, didn't get a chance to catch the ball very often. When Carl and Joe were struggling for the ball, it ran out of the playground into the street. It was crushed by a speeding car. Stu ran and told Miss Jones exactly what had happened.

III. *Development*: **tells how to conduct the day's lesson**

The teacher should ask the following question:

(1) Did Joe and Johnny treat Carl in a way that would have been approved of by Miss Jones? Why or why not?

(2) When children are playing, what are some ways that adults expect them to act? (List norms on the board.)

(3) Did Stu act in a way the other boys would approve of? Why or why not?

(4) When children are playing, what are some things they expect each other to do and not to do? (List norms on the board.)

(5) What are some things that Miss Jones might do to make Joe and Johnny treat Carl differently? (List sanctions on the board.)

(6) What might the other boys do to make Joe and Johnny treat Carl differently? (List sanctions on the board.)

(7) What might the boys do to stop Stu from tattling? (List sanctions on the board.)

The words *norms* and *sanctions* do not have to be used in discussion with the students. The essential point is that students understand that (a) people are expected to act in certain ways and (b) rewards or punishments are used to assure that people act that way. Synonyms for these concepts can be used, e.g., "ways of acting," "rewards," and "punishments." Students should realize that sometimes the expectations that adults have for behavior are different from what peers expect.

IV.   *Conclusion*: tells how to close or evaluate the day's lesson

Ask the class to think of other incidents that might occur at school where groups of people are working or playing. What incidents might arise that would cause hurt feelings or might result in someone being treated unfairly? As an incident is mentioned, have the class identify what the desired behavior should be (norm) and what the other students could do (sanctions) to get the parties to act in the desired way.

V.   *Materials*: tells what is needed for the day's lesson

Copy of the story incident to be read to the class.

Note: The above lesson plan is adapted from *Teaching Strategies for the Social Studies*, 3rd ed., by James Banks and Ambrose Clegg, copyrighted by Longman, p. 289 (1985).

Are all concepts in sociology of equal importance? George Schuncke says "No." He indicates seven concepts that are considered to be most important and were derived from research studies with K–4 students themselves. Furthermore, children actually understand the meaning of these concepts. Table 6.1 lists and ranks them.

Nielsen and Finkelstein (1988) believe that there is a connection between the group climate (a sociological feature) and encouraging good citizenship. See Figure 6.1 for their model of democratic classroom interaction.

Their model lists the roles of both teacher and students and shows the types of instructional settings that best facilitate the desired results. The following middle grade lesson plan illustrates how Nielsen and Finkelstein's model can be applied. The communication and participation segments of the model can be found in the class discussion in Part II: Motiva-

Table 6.1 Most important concepts and their order of importance.

Order	K	1	2	3	4
			Grade		
1	rules	truth	truth	truth	truth
2	truth	rules	rules	rules	rules
3	property	promises	authority	authority	authority
4	authority	authority	promises	promises	friends
5	sharing	property	property	property	promises
6	friends	sharing	friends	sharing	property
7	promises	friends	sharing	friends	sharing

Note : This table is adapted from one that appears in "Values Concepts of Younger Children," by George M. Schuncke and Suzanne L. Krogh, in *The Social Studies*, p. 270 (Nov./Dec. 1982). Reprinted with permission by Heldref Publications.

tion in the lesson plan. Both the interaction and the application segments occur in Part III: Development of the lesson plan. The interaction segment of the model appears when the students list their reasons for getting into a fight and then compare and contrast lists. The application segment of the model takes place when the students prepare the survey and administer it. Finally, the reflection segment can be found in Part IV: Conclusion of the lesson plan, during which the students discuss the results of the survey.

MIDDLE GRADE LESSON PLAN

Topic: **Getting Angry**

Grade: **7th**

Date: **March 12, 1:05–1:45**

I. *Purpose:* **tells what a student will learn**

Students will be able to:

(a) Identify five causes of aggressive behavior within their school setting
(b) State their parents' views on the causes of disruptive behavior
(c) Compare and contrast their values and views about violent behavior with those of their peers and their parents

II. *Motivation:* **tells how to begin the day's lesson**

Discuss with the class if they have ever been "angry" with anyone and how it occurred. This will prepare the students to think about the concepts of anger and aggression that will follow.

Citizenship Processes	Teacher	Students	Instructional Setting
Communication	Establishes with group, rules for interaction Initiates problem Encourages shared interaction and decision making	State and refine the problem Develop ownership for the problem Brainstorm possible ways of solving the problem	Large group discussion △ teacher ○ student
Participation	Chooses topics for study Gathers resource material Leads discussion Monitors stu- dent participation Listens to students' ideas	Agree upon a plan of action Select appropriate resources Choose role	Large group interactive discussion
Interaction	Facilitates group interaction Encourages individuals and groups Mediates group activity	Establish rules of interaction Contribute ideas Accept, modify and/or build on ideas through consensus Perform chosen roles	Small group interaction
Application	Refocuses ideation Facilitates interaction Listens to participants	Add to plan of action Revise plan of action Use, perform, or do	Purposeful performance of chosen role
Reflection	Initiates project evaluation Diagnoses student progress Plans future application of learning acquired	Evaluate group progress Evaluate their individual contributions Determine future application of learning acquired	A B C

Figure 6.1 Democratic classroom interaction model [from Lynn Nielsen and Judith Finkelstein, "Democratic Classroom Interaction Model," *Social Studies and the Young Learner*, p. 11 (Sept./Oct. 1988)].

III. *Development*: tells how to conduct the day's lesson

Ask the students to list reasons why they might get into a fight with a fellow student. Have the class break up into small groups to compare their answers with the answers they gave in the motivation activity in Part II of this lesson plan. Prepare the list of causes of aggression in a survey format. For example: The major reasons I get angry are when (1) someone lies to me, (2) someone cheats, etc.

Have the members of the class administer the survey to their parents and to three of their friends. Collect the data on a master chart.

IV. *Conclusion*: **tells how to close or evaluate the day's lesson**

Discuss the results of the survey, comparing the answers that students gave with those of their parents. Ask if the causes of aggression are the same for adolescents and adults. Why are they different or the same? Do people control their behavior more or less as they grow older? Is alienation a major cause of conflicts and misbehavior?

(Note to the teacher: Most of the research on juvenile delinquency indicates that a major cause of aggressive behavior is the feeling of alienation of adolescents toward institutions and authority. Feelings of rejection and underrepresentation in the decision-making processes force many youths to strike out and seek to make their presence known in a socially unacceptable manner.)

V. *Materials*: **tells what is needed for the day's lesson**

The only special material needed is a large sheet of tag board to prepare the master chart in the development part of the lesson.

Note: This lesson plan is adapted from an activity that appeared in "Teaching Strategies for Dealing with Violence and Vandalism," by Richard A. Diem, *The Social Studies*, p. 173 (July/August 1982). Reprinted with permission of Helen Dwight Reid Educational Foundation. Heldref Pub., 4000 Albemarle St., N.W., Washington, DC.

THE OLDER LEARNER

As mentioned in Chapter 2, some techniques are used more successfully with older students than younger ones. One of the techniques that is usually reserved for the middle grades is the case study.

Case Study

A case study is a detailed examination of an event or a situation from which students can generalize to similar instances. The case study does not work simply by having the students read the cases; rather, they must analyze issues and make decisions. Hoover and Hoover (1980) provide the following guidelines for conducting a case study:

(1) Identify a basic idea (concept) in need of emphasis. Usually this is in the affective domain, suggesting an area of conflict or a serious disagreement.

(2) If the case is written, the first paragraphs include a brief description of the individual(s) with which one is to identify. Included will be background material (both facts and feelings) and the current situa-

tion. An occasional quote designed to dramatize feelings provides an added touch of realism. (Besides appearing in written form, a case could also be presented in the form of a videotape, film, etc. If nonprint materials are used, it would be helpful for the teacher to prepare a written study guide.)

(3) The next paragraph or two will include a brief description of the opposing individual(s) involved in the situation. Background information and the current issue should likewise be given. An attempt should be made to portray basic feelings and relationships.

(4) Finally, a paragraph or two should be devoted to the basic problem of the case. This will clearly portray clashes, differences of opinion, or issues that are provoking the problem. Immediate facts, feelings, and relationships will dramatize conflict conditions. This is culminated with a final statement or paragraph designed to portray an impending decision.

(5) The case material usually ends with three or four case questions designed to provoke reflective thinking prior to the actual case analysis. They will usually emphasize higher levels of cognition.

(6) An analysis of the case results in a solution to the problem presented in the case. The analysis focuses on such matters as (a) clarification of the issues, (b) exploration of events, (c) evaluation of issues, (d) implications of the findings, and (e) application of the findings.

The following problem, which appears in Oliner (1976, 266 and 267), can be used for a case study.

CASE STUDY

Smithville is a small housing district in the south of Oregon. Ten years ago, the City Council bought ten acres of land in the center of the district for the purpose of developing it into a recreational area at some future data. Meantime, the land was left in its natural state—full of large trees, nature trails, and some wildlife. While some people are happy to leave it as it is, others would like to see it developed into a children's park. The City Council has to make a decision within a month.

Mrs. Green, the mother of two children, ages 4 and 6, argued before the City Council at the last meeting: "I need a safe place where my children can play. They need swings and slides and a place to play ball. Right now, there is no place for young children to play, except on the street." (About 25 percent of the families in Smithville have young children.)

Mr. Johnson, a school teacher, has a different point of view. "Smithville used to be a beautiful place—full of tall trees and greenery. Now it is just full of homes and there is hardly anything green to be seen. We need to protect our environment—and everyone can enjoy the park as it is now."

Mrs. Ray, an elderly widow living on a fixed income, wants to keep the park as it is too: "It would cost thousands of dollars to build a park for young children. This means added taxes which older people, like myself, just can't afford. Let's keep things as they are."

High school students enjoy the park as it is. "Right now, my friends and I can hang around the park and have a good time. If it becomes a place for little kids, where will kids my age go?"

But people who live next to the park are not entirely happy with the kids who "hang around" the park. Joseph Wright's house is right next to the park and he says: "High school kids come to the park at night and make a lot of noise. They leave lots of cans and litter—some of it on my front lawn. A park for small children would be better supervised."

If you were a City Council member, how would you vote?

TOPICS IN SOCIOLOGY

Since sociology is essentially the study of how people behave in groups, a number of relevant topics are described below.

Youth and Older People

The topic of aging needs to be studied in our schools because (1) our society has a rapidly increasing median age and children need to learn about growing older themselves, (2) the study of aging can dispel false beliefs about growing older and allay fears about aging, and (3) the study of aging may assist children in their relationships with their parents and grandparents (Scott, 1986, 116).

Glass (1981) found out that a class of adolescents experienced a positive change in their attitudes toward aspects of aging, and these changed attitudes lasted over a period of time.

These two studies suggest some strategies an educator can use so that his students will perceive the older members of society in a more positive light:

(1) Have students visit a senior citizen center to see these people as active, socializing individuals.

(2) Encourage personal contact between children and older adults who exhibit positive characteristics.

(3) Have children develop empathy for age-related problems. For example, have a student listen to a tape while he wears earplugs.

Religion

The *Abington v. Schempp* Supreme Court decision of 1963 rules that religious indoctrination cannot be conducted within the realm of public education. Justice Tom Clark, in his majority statement, in no way suggested that educators are prevented from mentioning religion:

> It might well be said that one's education is not complete without a study of comparative religion or the history of religion and its relation to the advancement of civilization. It certainly may be said that the Bible is worthy of study for its literary and historic qualities. Nothing we have said here indicates that such study of the Bible or of religion, when presented objectively as a part of a secular program of education, may not be effected consistently with the First Amendment (*Abington v. Schemp*, 374 U.S. 225).

Vanausdall (1979) suggests that educators should teach "about" religion, and this can be done by investigating the following questions:

(1) Does religion have a stabilizing effect on families/society?

(2) What taboos in our culture have a religious basis?

(3) How do urban and rural religious practices and populations differ?

(4) What psychological/social needs might religious identity meet in (a) urban/highly industrialized societies; (b) rural, isolated societies; and (c) tribal societies?

(5) How might one explain the success of the Jews in preserving their unity as a people and a religious group?

Crime and Delinquency

One-half of all persons arrested for crimes covered by uniform crime-reporting indexes are youths under the age of twenty. Young people, more than any other group are likely to be the victims of crime (Bjorklun, 1988). These statistics highlight the necessity that our youth be taught about the causes and results of crime in our society. The following situation is an example of how this might be done [from Eugene Bjorklun, "Teaching about Juvenile Justice," *Social Studies*, pp. 100, 101 (May/June 1988). Reprinted with permission by Heldref Publications].

SCHOOL VANDALISM

One Sunday afternoon, Johnny Jones and Ricky Smith, both age 11, broke into the elementary school they attended, intending to steal a couple of cassette tape recorders. Once inside the building, they decided that stealing the tape recorders was too risky, but they decided to have some fun anyway. They broke a window on the door of the art room and entered. They dumped paint and glue on the floor and smeared red paint all over the walls. Then, they found the door to the audio-visual storage room unlocked. They entered that room and began smashing the equipment, destroying two overhead projectors, a filmstrip projector, and a movie projector. The total amount of damage to the building and equipment was well over $2,000. Unknown to them, while they were engaged in this activity, two girls from the school were playing on the playground. They heard noises in the building, looked in a window and saw Johnny and Ricky, whom they knew, committing the acts of vandalism. The next day, the girls told the principal what they had seen. Johnny and Ricky were called to the office, taken into custody by a police officer whom the principal had called, and their parents were notified (adapted from Hoffman and Moon, 1981).

(1) Have Johnny and Ricky committed any crimes by their actions? If so, what crimes have they committed? If not, what have they done?

(2) Should the boys be released in the custody of their parents until their hearing, or should they be kept in detention until that time?

(3) At the hearing, the judge must be convinced beyond a reasonable doubt that Johnny and Ricky committed the acts of which they are accused. Do you think there is any reasonable doubt about whether or not the boys did those things?

(4) If the judge finds the boys guilty and therefore delinquent, what do you think the judge should do and why?

(5) Should the judge order the boys to help pay for the damage? If so, what do you think would be a reasonable amount? Should their parents have to pay for any of the damage?

(6) There is no mention in the case of the boys' school attendance or behavior record. Do you think that information would have any effect on the judge's decision? Should it have an effect?

Prejudice

Prejudice is defined by Allport (1958, 8) as "an aversive or hostile attitude toward a person who belongs to a group, simply because he [or she] belongs to that group, and is therefore presumed to have the objectionable qualities ascribed to the group."

Children, contrary to popular opinion, express prejudice at an early age. It is learned from (1) media, e.g., movies about cowboys and Indians; (2) home, e.g., parents who forbid a son/daughter from playing with another child of a different race; (3) church, e.g., a religion which advocates disdain toward those who have a different belief; (4) school, e.g., classmates who taunt an unattractive child in the room; and (5) communities, e.g., a neighborhood which expresses disgust when a family from a lower socioeconomic status moves into the area. Byrnes (1988) provides some ways to lessen prejudicial attitudes:

(1) Educators should use activities that increase social contact between various groups.

(2) Educators should use activities that improve self-esteem.

(3) Educators should use strategies that increase cognitive sophistication. This means that children need to be guided away from dogmatism and away from thinking in sharp, dichotomous terms.

(4) Educators need to include activities designed to increase empathy and understanding for members of other groups.

Values Education

A value is a feeling about how a person should or should not behave toward some end-goal. Examples of values include

(1) *Freedom is vital* for citizens.

(2) *Honesty should be exhibited* by everyone.

(3) People should be *treated with equality.*

(4) *Justice needs to be part* of our judicial system.

(5) Classmates should be *treated with courtesy.*

(6) *Violence is not a way* to solve problems.

(7) *National unity is more important* than an individual's rights.

There is always an opposing side to a value. The above seven could be reworded to convey a contrasting value, e.g., some people in the world might agree with number one above if it read "citizens of a country should not have unlimited freedom."

The point is that values exist in every society. Some are almost unanimously agreed upon, while others are topics of sharp disagreement. Whereas some people are very reflective about the values they hold, others give little deliberate thought at all to them.

Youth and adults act based upon values. Rod Farmer (1983) states, therefore, that students need to be able to perceive what values are determining their actions. This is called values education, or teaching strategies intended to enable students to identify values and bring them into focus.

Lavaroni and Togni (1979) have created a values education framework (Figure 6.2). Administrators should be aware that each phase is more complex than its predecessor; thus, Phase I is suitable for a primary student, while Phase IV is for a high school student.

Lavaroni and Togni describe these phases in the following way.

VALUES AWARENESS

Students become increasingly aware of the various beliefs, attitudes, and value indicators that exist in their daily lives. They are asked to collect information from their personal experiences. They are helped to focus on how particular beliefs and behaviors influence interactions between peo-

Phase I. VALUES AWARENESS
1. Identification of value indicators
2. Exploration of alternative value indicators
3. Exploration of possible effects of value choices

Phase II. VALUES CLARIFICATION
1. Clarifying value decisions
2. Clarifying terms
3. Warranting value decisions by:
   a. Stating possible consequences of various value decisions
   b. Estimating probability of consequences of various value decisions
   c. Determining the appropriateness of various consequences

Phase III. VALUES ANALYSIS
1. Identifying factual claims and value claims
2. Assessing the validity of factual claims
3. Providing reasons for various value decisions by
   a. Projecting consequences of value decisions over a wide range of concerns
   b. Rating consequences in terms of desirability/undesirability
   c. Verifying the possibility of consequences
   d. Stating and assessing the values position

Phase IV. VALUES REASONING
1. Identifying value principles inherent in values decisions by:
   a. Applying the Role Exchange Test
   b. Applying the Universal Consequences Test
   c. Applying the New Cases Test

Figure 6.2 A values education framework [from Charles Lavaroni and Richard Togni, "Values Education: A Framework and Exercises," *Social Studies*, p. 135 (May/June 1979)]. Reprinted with permission by Heldref Publications.

ple. The teacher assists the students in perceiving alternative behaviors and identifying some effects of those behaviors.

Example: A teacher leads a discussion concerning group activities by asking, "What happens when you share?"

VALUES CLARIFICATION

Students can become aware of what they value, whether what they value is freely chosen, whether they feel a sense of pride in those choices, and whether there is any consistent application of those choices in their daily lives.

Example: If a student states that something was a "lousy thing," the teacher responds by asking, "What do you mean by 'lousy'?"

VALUES ANALYSIS

Students become more analytical, more precise, and more thorough in their values processing. The student moves toward higher levels of valuing and reasoning.

Example: A teacher has a student look at a consequence of an action from a variety of viewpoints.

VALUES VERIFYING

Students are encouraged to infer basic value principles from a value decision.

Example: A teacher tries to move a student along a continuum by finding out at which of Kohlberg's six stages of moral development the student is (Fenton, 1976).

Controversy in Sociology

Because sociology deals with the behavior of humans within groups, there is a chance that the examination of this behavior in classrooms could meet with opposition. There are some who object to such topics as values clarification and moral reasoning or to such techniques as magic circle or role playing.

Vocal opposition ultimately resulted in the Hatch amendment. This was a 1978 amendment to a 1974 act of Congress that required school officials to obtain written consent from the parent or guardian of a minor before the students could be subjected to questioning or testing of a psychiatric or psychological nature in connection with any federally funded program (Greene and Pasch, 1981, 111). It wasn't until 1984, however, that the United States Department of Education issued regulations to enforce the Hatch amendment.

Today, some school administrators have ordered their teachers not to use strategies such as values clarification because they can lead to embarrassment or an infringement on the privacy of a student (or the student's family).

Despite the factors of embarrassment and invasion of privacy, values education has its supporters. In fact, the revised guidelines of the National Council for the Social Studies states that "social studies education neither can nor should evade questions of values (NCSS, 1979). Values "confusion" can result if values "education" is absent.

Even if students are not taught about values through the written curriculum, they do encounter them in the school's hidden curriculum. Examples of values taught via the unplanned hidden curriculum are (1) admiring peers' dress fashions, (2) assuming students will be honest when taking a test, or (3) placing a low value on violence when separating two scuffling students on the playground.

The rapid advancement of technology affects how students come in contact with values. Electronic technology enables students to see the social realities and dilemmas in the world. Adams encourages schools to take the responsibility for the moral development of students. This doesn't have to result in controversy because "teachers and students do not have to reach a consensus on an issue for moral development to occur" (1988, 82). Some educational researchers assert that the simplest act of discussing a dilemma can lead to moral development. Adams' suggestions for procedures to help students become critical video consumers are

(1) Practice critical viewing.
(2) Discuss programming with children.
(3) Analyze music videos.
(4) Examine advertising messages.
(5) Explore moral dilemmas.
(6) Discuss and document TV programs and commercials.

Students need to see the relevance between social studies content and classroom life. Occasions frequently arise to affect students' behavior by relating it to sociological concepts. Passe (1987, 1988) has described practices that educators often engage in, which prove ineffective in altering students' behavior. Figure 6.3 is derived from his ideas and points out alternative practices that can be effective.

Oliner (1983) has created the following steps, which can be used by educators to develop prosociality in students. People exhibit prosociality if they help others without expecting reciprocal rewards.

1. Develop a Prosocial Vocabulary—Students can define words (see Figure 6.4) or give examples of the motivation that spawns the behavior.

2. Selecting Prosocial Content for Study—Prosocial content should be selected so that it depicts people as they assist others. Figure 6.5 suggests ideas that can be used in a number of areas.

3. Analyzing and Evaluating Prosocial Behavior—Students need the opportunity to inspect the motivations and intentions behind the actions. Figure 6.6 provides an example.

4. Exploring Prosocial Behaviors through Incidental Learnings—The examples below show how prosocial behaviors can be investigated with arranged incidents.

(a) Tell five ways in which your neighbors help you.
(b) Write a short paragraph describing the nicest person you know.

Concept	Common Practices by Teacher in a Classroom Situation	Suggested Alternative Actions by Teacher
cooperation	Teacher establishes rules and punishments for violating these rules.	Teacher must make it clear to the students that special activities like games, skits, and art projects are dependent on the students' behavior; proper actions are rewarded, while improper actions are discouraged.
interdependence and responsibility	Teacher punishes the child who constantly calls out answers, thus decreasing participation opportunities for other members of the class.	Children are often unaware of how their behavior affects others; the concept can be applied to examples in society, such as family chores, traffic laws, and tax collection.
tolerance	Teacher punishes student who teases or ridicules another child who might have a handicap or a different religious belief.	Introduce the concept of tolerance, e.g., reminding students of our forefathers' insistence on the freedom to be different.
conflict resolution	When a quarrel occurs in the room, teacher can be quick to blame someone.	Rather than view conflict as an unfortunate circumstance, view it as an opportunity; e.g., show students how mediators are used in labor disputes, how judges settle arguments, and how compromises are made when purchasing a car.

Figure 6.3 Using sociological concepts to affect student behavior [from Jeff Passe, "Citizenship Education: Its Role in Improving Classroom Behavior," *Social Studies and the Young Learner*, pp. 19–21 (Sept./Oct. 1988)].

Behaviors	Motivations
sharing	sympathy
giving	care
donating	empathy
aiding	compassion
lending	altruism
helping	concern
contributing	respect
bestowing	regard
granting	solicitude
permitting	love
participating	sensitivity
sacrificing	kindliness

Figure 6.4 A vocabulary of prosociality illustrative concepts [from Pearl Oliner, "Putting Compassion and Caring into Social Studies Classrooms," *Social Education*, p. 274 (April 1983)].

(c) Using the yellow pages of your telephone directory, find as many helping agencies and groups as you can.

(d) Name three figures in American history who have helped others.

Using Literature to Teach Sociology

It was discussed in Chapter 3 how children's literature can be used to help children understand historical concepts. The following Assistance Points will help educators understand how literature can also be instrumental in teaching sociological concepts and generalizations. The information in the Assistance Points has been taken from an article by Arlene Gallagher (1988) and from selected issues of *Social Education*. Educators who wish to locate fiction and non-fiction books for students at the elementary, middle, and high school levels can consult the yearly April/May issue of *Social Education*. It contains an annotated bibliography for excellent reading materials that were published in the previous year.

ASSISTANCE POINTS

Questions for Action for the Administrator

1. Assume that a new family has moved into the school district, but one of the children is not being accepted by her classmates. As a supervi-

I. The Family	Helping behaviors of parents, children, siblings, other relatives, and friends towards each other and towards others; prosocial "rules" and expectations in families in different cultures, families of the past, and possible families of the future.
II. The Community	Helping behaviors of students, neighbors, community volunteers and voluntary agencies, individuals, and communities; past community prosocial traditions, possible future community prosocial activities.
III. The State	Historical episodes of groups and individuals within the state who have helped each other, within groups and towards "outsiders." Helping activities of state-level voluntary associations and philanthropies. Prosocial activities and motivations of state officials and employees.
IV. The Nation	Historical episodes of groups and individuals within the nation who have helped each other within groups and across groups. Prosocial activities and motivations of federal officials and employees, national voluntary and philanthropic associations and individuals who work within them. Help to other nations; values and norms for prosocial behaviors in national culture.
V. Other Nations	Same as IV.
VI. Constitutions	Laws and legal procedures which appear to be directed at helping individuals and groups; evolution of helping laws.
VII. International Arena	Helping activities of the United Nations, other government-supported international agencies, voluntary international agencies and groups; historical events in which international efforts have been extended to alleviate famine, rescue war refugees, protect human rights, protect political prisoners, etc.; individuals who have contributed to the formation and day-by-day operation of international helping efforts.

Figure 6.5 Illustrative prosocial content areas for selected topics [from Pearl Oliner, "Putting Compassion and Caring into Social Studies Classrooms," *Social Education*, p. 275 (April 1983)].

sor, what ideas from this chapter might you relay to the classroom teacher to promote harmonious group interaction?

2. Separation of church and state often is an unclear distinction for administrators and school personnel. Two common questions that arise are

(a) How should religious holidays be treated in the classroom?

(b) How does teaching about religion relate to the teaching of values?

What is your stance? You may want to write to the National Council for the Social Studies and request the brochure "Religion in the Public School Curriculum: Questions and Answers," which addresses the above two questions, among others.

3. Administrators need to work with school librarians. To what degree is this done in your building? As an example of how this can be accomplished, ask the librarian at your school to compile a list of books for young people that have a focus on sociology topics. This list can then be distributed to the classroom teachers.

ANALYZING BEHAVIORS

Identify the main elements of the behavior.
  Illustrative questions: What did the (person, agency, group, nation) do? What did the (person, agency, group, nation) have to give up to help? What were the consequences of the behavior? What was the relationship of the actor to the receiver?

ANALYZING INTERNALS

Identify the main elements of the feelings, thoughts, motivations, and other internals.
  Illustrative questions: Why did the (person, agency, group, nation) do this thing? Did (s)he/they expect a reward? What makes you think so? What were the feelings of the receiver before the deed was done? After the deed was done?

Identify the relationships among elements.
  Illustrative questions: How did the (thoughts, feelings, motivations) of the actor and receiver change as a result of the deed? Was there any other way the actor could have expressed his (feeling, thought, intention)? How might the behavior have been different if the actor and receiver were not related?

Identify major points.
  Illustrative questions: What do you think can be learned from this? Would you call this behavior an example of (sharing, helping, giving)? Would you call this an example of "prosocial" behavior? Why or why not?

EVALUATING BEHAVIORS

Identify what needs to be evaluated.
  Illustrative questions: Should we accept this behavior as an example of (sharing, helping, giving)? Was giving the gift a "good" thing to do?

EVALUATING INTERNALS

  Illustrative questions: Some people say the father was motivated by love; others by duty. Which view should we accept?

Identify standards for assessing.
  Illustrative questions: How can we decide whether the behavior was an example of sharing or helping? How can we determine whether the behavior was a "good" thing to do?

  Illustrative questions: How can we know whether a behavior is motivated by love or duty? What are the criteria whereby we can make a judgment? What effect did it have on the receiver?

Propose alternative behaviors.
  Illustrative questions: How could the (person, agency, group, nation) have met the receiver's needs better? Could the needs have been met more efficiently? Whom should the actors have consulted? Why?

Figure 6.6 Analyzing and evaluating prosociality: a teaching strategy [from Pearl Oliner, "Putting Compassion and Caring into Social Studies Classrooms," *Social Education*, p. 276 (April 1983)].

Concept	Title of Book	Author	The Plot or the Ethical Issue in the Story	Level	Publisher	Publication Date
social conscience	Taking Care of Terrific	Lois Lowry	Questions are raised about the rights of bag ladies and the responsibility of the community.	P, I	Houghton Mifflin	1983
cooperation	It's Mine	Leo Lionni	This is an illustrated fable about three quarrelsome frogs who learn to cooperate and share.	P	Knopf	1986
doing good vs. do-gooders	The Diddakoi	Rumer Godden	A young gypsy child loses her grandmother/guardian, and the community holds a hearing to decide the fate of the child.	I	Puffin	1972
good guys and bad	Big Bad Prince	Bill Peet	A bullying bear is magically shrunk in size. The story raises questions about power and its abuse.	P	Houghton Mifflin	1977
moral dilemmas	Doctor DeSoto	William Steig	A mouse dentist does not believe in helping animals dangerous to mice but has to think about this when he encounters a fox with a rotten bicuspid.	P	Farrar, Strauss, and Giroux	1982
a moral community	Molly's Pilgrim	Barbara Cohen	Molly brings her doll dressed as a Russian peasant for the 3rd grade pilgrim display.	P, I	Lothrop, Lee, and Shepard	1983
ridicule	Toby	Marc Talbert	A 10-year-old boy named Toby has a mother who is brain-damaged and a father who is slow. Toby is teased by classmates.	I	Dial	1987

Note: P = Primary Grades and I = Intermediate Grades.

Teaching Sociology with Literature

(See page 170.)

Names and Addresses of Professional Organizations

Following are some addresses for information relating to sociology:

1. Anti-Defamation League of B'nai B'rith
   315 Lexington Avenue
   New York, NY 10016
2. American Civil Liberties Union
   22 East 40th Street
   New York, NY 10016
3. American Sociological Association
   1722 N St., NW
   Washington, DC 20036
   (The ASA publishes the journals *Sociology of Education*, *Contemporary Sociology*, and *Teaching Sociology*.)
4. Gerontological Society
   1411 K St., NW
   Washington, DC 20005
5. The Population Institute
   110 Maryland Ave., NE
   Washington, DC 20002

Research about Sociology: Implications for Educators

Katz (1983) states that children begin to categorize by race and gender by about age three. The concepts of boy, girl, and skin color begin by age six. Racial attitudes begin to strengthen by about age ten or eleven.

Wyner (1978) encourages educators to structure curriculum and teaching to include opportunities for children so that they can interact and identify with adults—adults who can serve as models for a child's self-esteem and values.

REFERENCES

Abington v. Schemp, 374 U.S. 225.

Adams, Dennis and Mary Hamm. "Video Technology and Moral Development," *The Social Studies*, pp. 81–83 (March/April 1988).

Allport, G. W. *The Nature of Prejudice*. New York:Doubleday (1958).

Banks, James A. and Ambrose A. Clegg, Jr. *Teaching Strategies for the Social Studies*, *3rd ed*. White Plains, NY:Longman, Inc. (1985).

Bjorklun, Eugene E. "Teaching about Juvenile Justice," *The Social Studies*, pp. 97–102 (May/June 1988).

Byrnes, Deborah A. "Children and Prejudice," *Social Education*, pp. 267–271 (April/ May 1988).

Crawley, Sharon J. and Leo Mountain. "Opinion Polls and Values Clarification," *The Social Studies*, pp. 271–272 (November/December 1981).

Damico, Sandra Bowman and Christopher Sparks. "Cross-Group Contact Opportunities: Impact on Interpersonal Relationships in Desegregated Middle Schools," *Sociology of Education*, pp. 113–123 (April 1986).

Diem, Richard A. "Teaching Strategies for Dealing with Violence and Vandalism," *The Social Studies*, pp. 172–174 (July/August 1982).

Farmer, Rod. "Values, Social Studies, and Reality," *The Social Studies*, pp. 52–55 (March/April 1983).

Fenton, Edwin. "Moral Education: The Research Findings," *Social Education*, pp. 188–193 (April 1976).

Gallagher, Arlene F. "Children's Literature and the Ethics Dimension," *Social Studies and the Young Learner*, pp. 25–26 (September/October 1988).

Glass, J. Conrad, Jr. "Change Students' Attitudes toward Older Persons," *The Social Studies*, pp. 72–76 (March/April 1981).

Greene, Bert I. and Marvin Pasch. "The Hatch Amendment Regulations: Lessons for the Social Studies," *The Social Studies*, pp. 111–115 (May/June 1986).

Hoffman, Alan J. and Nancy L. Hoffman. "Today's Tarnished Sports Heroes: Implications for Ethics-Based Instruction," *Social Studies and the Young Learner*, pp. 14–18 (September/October 1988).

Hoover, Kenneth H. and Helene M. Hoover. "Exploring Social Issues," *The Social Studies*, pp. 77–79 (March/April 1980).

Jantz, Richard K. and Kenneth Klawitter. "Anthropology and Sociology," in *Elementary School Social Studies: Research as a Guide to Practice*. Bulletin No. 79, edited by Virginia Atwood, Washington, DC:NCSS, pp. 102–118 (1986).

Jarolimek, John. *Social Studies in Elementary Education, 7th edition*. New York:Macmillan (1986).

Katz, P. "Developmental Foundations of Gender and Racial Attitudes," in *The Child's Construction of Social Inequality*. R. Leahy, ed., New York:Academic Press, pp. 41–78 (1983).

Lavaroni, Charles and Richard Togni. "Values Education: A Framework and Exercises," *The Social Studies*, pp. 133–137 (May/June 1979).

National Council for the Social Studies Position Statement. "Revision of the NCSS Social Studies Curriculum Guidelines," *Social Education*, pp. 261–273 (April 1979).

Nielsen, Lynn E. and Judith M. Finkelstein. "Citizenship Education: Looking at Government," *Social Studies and the Young Learner*, pp. 10–13 (September/October 1988).

Oliner, Pearl M. *Teaching Elementary Social Studies*. New York:Harcourt, Brace Jovanovich, Inc. (1976).

Oliner, Pearl M. "Putting Compassion and Caring into Social Studies Classrooms," *Social Education*, pp. 273–276 (April 1983).

Pallas, Aaron et al. "Children Who Do Exceptionally Well in First Grade," *Sociology of Education*, pp. 257–271 (October 1987).

Passe, Jeff. "Improving Classroom Behavior through Social Studies." Paper presented at the 1987 Annual Meeting of the National Council for the Social Studies, Dallas, TX.

Passe, Jeff. "Citizenship Education: Its Role in Improving Classroom Behavior," *Social Studies and the Young Learner*, pp. 19–21 (September/October 1988).

Schuncke, George M. and Suzanne L. Krogh. "Values Concepts of Younger Children," *The Social Studies*, pp. 268–272 (November/December 1982).

Scott, Joan Norman. "Aging Instruction Offers New Challenges for the Social Studies Hour," *The Social Studies*, pp. 116–118 (May/June 1986).

Scully, Angus L. "The Case Method," *The History and Social Science Teacher*, pp. 178–180 (March 1984).

Vanausdall, Jeanette. "Religion Studies in the Public Schools," *The Social Studies*, pp. 251–253 (November/December 1979).

Wyner, Nancy B. "Social and Political Thinking in Children," ERIC document ED160535.

7 | ANTHROPOLOGY: CULTURES NOW AND THEN

Chapter Preview of Key Ideas

★ Anthropology is the study of human culture.

★ There are five aspects to anthropology: (1) cultural anthropology, (2) linguistics, (3) physical anthropology, (4) archaeology, and (5) social anthropology.

★ Anthropology can be interesting to young learners because of its broad nature.

★ Anthropology is pertinent for older learners because it allows them to see the uniqueness of people in the world.

★ There are a number of commercially prepared simulations for the middle grades.

★ Activities about archaeology provide involvement for students.

★ Multicultural education (or multiethnic education) is an effort to develop in students an understanding and appreciation for the various heritages, ethnic groups, and cultures in our country.

Anthropology is the *study of human culture*. Anthropologists not only study human culture from past civilizations, but they also study contemporary human culture. There are five aspects to this social science discipline:

(1) Cultural anthropology—concerned with culture and social groups

(2) Linguistics—concerned with the description, comparison, and historical development of human language

(3) Physical, anthropology—concerned with the physical, biological, and genetic facets of human development

(4) Archaeology—concerned with past cultures by analyzing artifacts

175

(5) Social anthropology—concerned with social systems or structures within a culture

ANTHROPOLOGY AND THE "NEW" SOCIAL STUDIES

Anthropology was one of the social sciences that gained support in the 1960s as the "new" social studies emerged. The National Science Foundation extended support to the *Anthropology Curriculum Project*, which originated with Marion Rice at the University of Georgia. The ACP began in kindergarten and first grade, as these children studied the concept of *culture*. Second graders studied the development of man and his culture, and third graders dealt with cultural change. The cycle was repeated in grades four (culture), five (development of man and his culture), and six (cultural change). The address is

> Anthropology Curriculum Project
> University of Georgia
> Athens, GA 30602

The NSF also supported the project *Man: A Course of Study*, which was a program for grades five and six. MACOS focused on three questions:

(1) What is human about human beings?
(2) How did human beings get that way?
(3) How can they be made more human?

The materials were distributed by

> Curriculum Development Associates
> Washington, DC 20036

Ralph Ojemann and his associates laid the groundwork for *Human Behavior and Potential*, a K–6 program. Materials were distributed by

> Educational Research Council of America
> Cleveland, OH 44113

The *Family of Man*, a program that focused on foreign cultures, was created at the University of Minnesota's Project Social Studies Center and was used with grades K–12. Materials were produced by

> Selective Educational Equipment
> Newton, MA 02195

The *Holt Databank System* emphasized data gathering, data organizing, and data using. The series was published by

Holt, Rinehart and Winston
New York, NY 10017

The *Taba Program in Social Science* was designed for elementary and junior high grades. The program was published by

Addison-Wesley
Menlo Park, CA 94025

Although these projects no longer occupy the prominent place they did in the 1960s, it is still helpful to remember their legacy. Chart 7.1 serves as a guideline to administrators who want to determine if their social studies program properly utilizes anthropology.

TEACHING CONCEPTS AND GENERALIZATIONS

Following are some concepts and generalizations which can be taught to elementary and middle grade students in the area of anthropology:

Concepts

physical characteristics	language	race
culture	traditions	technology
customs	tools	culture traits
artifacts	diffusion	extended families
nuclear families	race	ceremonies
basic human needs	taboos	kinship patterns
subsistence activities	enculturation	acculturation
rites of passage	ethnocentrism	cultural relativity
belief systems	magic	culture shock
cultural universal	fossil	symbols
cultural lag	ethnology	mores
prehistoric conditions	rituals	evolution
borrowed traits	innovation	adaptation
agricultural society	horticultural society	
culture diffusion	nomadic society	
primitive life	ethnic group	

Generalizations

- Food-getting activities are related to a society's level of technology.
- Physical characteristics change with age.
- Every society has kinship patterns.

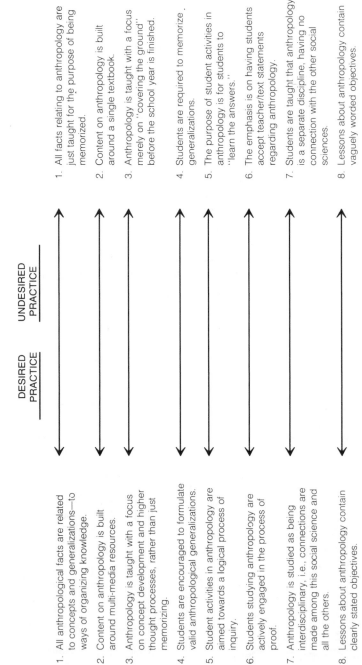

DESIRED PRACTICE ————————— UNDESIRED PRACTICE

Desired Practice:

1. All anthropological facts are related to concepts and generalizations—to ways of organizing knowledge.

2. Content on anthropology is built around multi-media resources.

3. Anthropology is taught with a focus on concept development and higher thought processes, rather than just memorizing.

4. Students are encouraged to formulate valid anthropological generalizations.

5. Student activities in anthropology are aimed towards a logical process of inquiry.

6. Students studying anthropology are actively engaged in the process of proof.

7. Anthropology is studied as being interdisciplinary, i.e., connections are made among this social science and all the others.

8. Lessons about anthropology contain clearly stated objectives.

Undesired Practice:

1. All facts relating to anthropology are just taught for the purpose of being memorized.

2. Content on anthropology is built around a single textbook.

3. Anthropology is taught with a focus merely on "covering the ground" before the school year is finished.

4. Students are required to memorize generalizations.

5. The purpose of student activities in anthropology is for students to "learn the answers."

6. The emphasis is on having students accept teacher/text statements regarding anthropology.

7. Students are taught that anthropology is a separate discipline, having no connection with the other social sciences.

8. Lessons about anthropology contain vaguely worded objectives.

Chart 7.1 Anthropology in the social studies. Educators can scan the continuum to see how frequently they mark the left side of the chart. Those items on the left represent a more desirable approach for the early elementary and middle grades.

- Culture is socially learned.
- The art, music, architecture, sports, food, clothing, and customs of a people produce solidarity.
- Humans have similar needs to be met, but the manner in which these are met differs according to culture.
- Personal traits cause a culture to change more quickly.
- All societies have traditions that help to maintain group identity.
- Cultural change can occur by invention, innovation, or diffusion.

THE YOUNG LEARNER

Walsh (1980) has suggested that the early elementary grades are an especially good time to help young students develop an awareness of and appreciation for cultural differences.

Messick (1983) has prepared a chart showing how the themes of language, arts, and family life can be used to promote an anthropological perspective for the younger student (see Chart 7.2).

The following lesson plan for the early elementary grades depicts how the concepts of *customs* and *traditions* can be taught, along with the generalization "Observing customs and traditions helps solidify family life."

Level	Setting	Activities
Kg	Myself and Others in My World	classroom calendar of "Important Days," which prompts children to share birthdays, elders' memory days, religious holidays, patriotic holidays
		picture-drawing and role-playing "Jobs Parents Do at Home"
		photo-sharing of special events in children's lives with language experience stories written to accompany
		songs and dances related to Important Days events
First	People at Home and at School	rhebus writing on retrieval charts that collect data on "What I Learn" and "How I Learn"
		individual posters "About My Family" that portray family members, their jobs, and favorite things
		individual daily schedule
		films about families from other places

Chart 7.2 Grade level settings and anthropology-related activities.

Level	Setting	Activities
Second	People as Members of Groups	films and picture files to collect data for murals on topics such as "Clothing in Hot Climates," "Ways of Storing Food," "Houses in Different Climates"
		focus on songs, dances, crafts, food from different American ethnic culture each month
		individual picture booklets on "Groups I Belong To" that portray what is learned from each group
Third	People as Members of Communities	visits to ethnic cultural areas of community halls, churches, cemeteries, commercial sections
		films about "old country" of ethnic groups represented in community for data to be used in murals on "Contributions of Different Cultures to Our Community"
		visits to class by community old timers who tell about what different groups brought to community
Fourth	People of a Region	study native artifacts [for that region] and hypothesize about groups' relation to environment
		map settlement patterns of nationalities [in that region]
		visit local museum with individual assignments such as "Getting Light at Night," "Plowing and Planting," or "Going to School"; write illustrated booklet on findings about how these were done in the past

Note: This chart is taken from a similar chart which appeared in "Implementing the Anthropology Strand in Elementary Programs," an article by Rosemary Messick in *Social Studies Review*, pp. 46 and 47 (Fall 1983).

Chart 7.2 (continued). Grade level settings and anthropology-related activities.

EARLY ELEMENTARY LESSON PLAN

Topic: **Family Customs and Traditions**

Grade: **1st**

Date: **December 3, 10:00–10:25**

I. *Purpose*: **tells what a student will learn**

The student will learn the meaning of customs and traditions. The student will also learn that families develop their own customs and traditions in celebrating holidays and other days associated with family life.

II. *Motivation*: **tells how to begin the day's lesson**

Display the American flag, and ask if the children know any special days during the summer when people put the flag up in front of their homes. If the children are not too responsive, show large photos depicting typical Fourth of July activities. Lead the discussion toward the Fourth of July and the significance of the holiday as the nation's birthday.

III. *Development*: **tells how to conduct the day's lesson**

Ask the children to remember what they did on the last Fourth of July. Have them tell about it (picnicking, swimming, watching parades, camping, watching fireworks, and so on).

Continue the discussion of holiday celebration by asking such questions as "Do you like this holiday?" "What do you usually see on this holiday?" "Do you go someplace special on that day? Tell us about it." "Are there special games you play or special foods you eat on the Fourth of July?"

Have the children draw a picture of something they did with their families and friends on the Fourth of July. If they cannot remember or if they did not celebrate the holiday, have them draw something they would *like* to do on the Fourth of July.

Have volunteers share their pictures with their classmates. Display all the pictures on the bulletin board.

IV. *Conclusion*: **tells how to close or evaluate the day's lesson**

Lead the children to a discussion of other holidays celebrated by their families (birthdays, Christmas, Easter, Rosh Hashanah, and so on). Encourage them to tell about what their family does together on those special days.

Write the concepts "customs" and "traditions" on the chalkboard. Have children pronounce the words and say them several times. Explain the meaning of these concepts in terms of the things we do in somewhat the same way each time we celebrate an event.

Encourage children to talk about customs and traditions in their families.

V. *Materials*: **tells what is needed for the day's lesson**

Photographs of Fourth of July activities, drawing materials for the children.

Note: The above lesson plan was adapted from the plan on page 166 of *Social Studies in Elementary Education*, 7th edition, © 1986 by John Jarolimek. Reprinted with permission.

In some ways, anthropology is a unifier, i.e., it touches all aspects of human existence. For this reason, it proves very interesting to young learners. Ideas for activities that can be used with children of this age are presented below:

(1) *Tools*

Challenge students to make a tool to transport some objects (e.g., some crayons) from one desk to another. The only material they are allowed to use is one sheet of 8 1/2" × 11" paper. This shows the unique capability of humans to make and use tools.

(2) *Language*

Present the students with a number of pictographs. Have them use these to prepare a message that North American Indians might have used to communicate with one another. This allows students to compare an early communication system with their own system.

(3) *Food*

Bring rice to class for the students to see. Explain that this is the dominant food item in China. Later, prepare the rice and serve it with chopsticks. This enables students to gain an insight into the culture of a people.

(4) *Homes*

Bring in pictures of different kinds of furniture that are found in homes around the world—past and present. Have students analyze why the appearance is different. For example, why would a four-poster bed be used rather than a straw mat? Why would some people sit at a table while others eat on the floor?

THE OLDER LEARNER

The middle grade child can benefit from activities relating to anthropology. Aware of their own differences at this age, they can identify with the differences that exist among people around this world. Social studies for these students needs to be exciting, interesting, enjoyable, and relevant. Lessons regarding anthropology can be all of these things.

Teaming of students is often done at the middle grade, providing a logical tie to the unifying nature of anthropology. It can be helpful for an administrator to know the steps to follow for student teaming:

(1) Select four or five students for each team. The selection should include one above average, two or three average, and one below average. Also take into account gender and ethnic background. Let each team be a microcosm of the entire class.

(2) Let the teams pick a name, e.g., "Fantastic Four," "Chipmunks," "Brainstormers," etc.

(3) The teacher introduces material by lecture or class discussion.

(4) Give worksheets, allowing students to work together to find answers.

(5) Let them quiz each other and help one another work out any problems a teammate might have. They can discuss as a group or use whatever means they wish to master the material.

(6) After the team's practice session, the students take an individual test or quiz.

(7) The tests are checked, and the individual scores are formed into team scores by the teacher.

(8) The results can be rewarded according to the teacher's preference. Charts can be kept displaying the results, or newsletters can be printed, congratulating the winners (Slavin, 1986).

Teaming of teachers can also be done. One example of how several middle grade teachers can cooperate to integrate a number of curriculum areas appears in Figure 7.1. In this instance, the theme is from social studies—Latin America—and a number of anthropological concepts are taught.

There are a number of topics that enhance cultural understanding in fascinating ways. Daniel Leclerc (1978) asserts that architecture tells "us about the technologies, social structure, religions, political ideologies, life-styles, and self-perceptions of a society" (p. 1). Following is one of the activities he recommends:

> Much of the surviving architecture of ancient civilizations is religious, memorial, or symbolic. If you were an archeologist in the year 2280 A.D. scouring America for clues to our civilization, what would the structures built in our time (underground missile defense bunkers, the St. Lawrence Seaway, rocket launch platforms at Cape Canaveral, etc.) tell you about our culture? (p. 7)

Thomas Turner (1979) explains how to teach with *popular culture*. This term "consists of values, the cultural forms which express these values, and the media through which they are expressed" (p. 1). A few of the ideas used to teach this topic include (1) popular music; (2) television; (3) movies; (4) parties and social gatherings, i.e., the behavior of people at these functions; (5) printed materials, graphics, and maps, e.g., examining billboards, comic books, etc., to find out about the people; (6) fads; and (7) fashions.

There are a number of simulations dealing with anthropology, and these are valuable because they increase culture awareness of students. Some of these simulations appear in Chart 7.3.

Social Studies:	Study culture of Latin America Make salt maps of the topography of Latin America Make dioramas of Inca villages and temples Hold a modern day News Show of Inca life Do map skills activities Make a time line of the history of Latin America
Mathematics:	Make Peruvian rep braids--used for counting
Science:	Make graphs of rainfall of Latin America Make graphs showing altitudes of mountains in Latin America Create a weather show to perform on the Inca News Show
Language Arts:	Do research reports on various aspects of Latin America
Chorus:	Learn Latin American songs Make Latin American instruments (e.g., tambourine) Learn Latin American dances
Art:	make a large wall mural illustrating life in Latin America
Home Economics:	Cook food of Latin America (tortillas, tacos, enchiladas, burritos, etc.)
Culminating Activity:	Hold a Latin American Fair Display all art work, dioramas, piñatas Have shops where the students display and sell their arts and crafts Have entertainment; chorus groups sing festival songs and do Latin American dances Show movies about Latin America Home economics classes cook and sell Latin American food Have a costume contest

Figure 7.1 Interdisciplinary team teaching on the topic of Latin America. [Information in this figure was obtained from a presentation by Bruce Middle School (Jefferson County, Kentucky) teachers at the Fall Conference of the Kentucky Council for the Social Studies (September 5, 1984).]

Name	Grade Level	Number of Players	Time Required	Distributor	Description of Simulation
Bafa' Bafa'	8–12	large group	1–2 hours	Simile II	Investigates the meaning of culture
Culture Contact	7–12	large group	2–4 hours	Games Central	Deals with two dissimilar cultures
Dig 2	7–12	large group	3 weeks	Interact	A simulation in archaeology
Fifties	7–12	large group	3 weeks	Interact	A simulation of the events, personalities, life-styles, and culture of the 1950s
Gateway	6–12	large group	16 hours	Interact	A simulation of immigration issues in past and present
Ghetto	8–12	medium or large group	2–3 hours	Bobbs Merrill	Students confront problems of the urban poor.
Gold Rush	4–8	large group	3 weeks	Interact	Students experience life in a 19th century gold mining camp.
Humanus	7–12	small group	2–5 hours	Simile II	A world catastrophe forces the students to examine their assumptions about human nature and society.
Mahopa	6–9	large group	15–20 hours	Interact	Students develop an understanding of the North American Indian culture.
Mummy's Message	5–12	large group	4–5 hours	Interact	Simulates an archaeological expedition into an Egyptian pyramid
Rafa' Rafa'	4–8	large group	1–2 hours	Simile II	Similar to Bafa' Bafa', but less complicated
Sanga	5–9	large group	5 hours	Interact	Promotes understanding of a West African tribe
Sunshine	4–8	large group	3 hours	Interact	Investigates ways of solving racial problems
Talking Rocks	5–12	small, medium, or large group	2–3 hours	Simile II	Students discover origin of writing and the versatility and utility of written communication.
Time Capsule	5–12	large group	3 weeks	Interact	Students select cultural artifacts to put in a time capsule.
Up Caste Down Caste	5–12	small group	3–4 hours	M. E. Haas	Students investigate the Hindu religion and how the beliefs affect Indian life.

Chart 7.3 Simulations dealing with anthropology.

Middle grade students can study the concept of cultural differences by inquiring where and how we obtained some of the words in our English language. Some examples of words to be searched appear in the list below. All of them are borrowed from other cultures.

English Language Word	Language Origin of Word
parka	Russian
kowtow	Chinese
coyote	Mexican American Spanish
opossum	Algonquin Indian
plaza	Spanish
taboo	Polynesian
whiskey	Gaelic
bagel	Yiddish
cookie	Dutch
khaki	Hindi (India)
kindergarten	German
avenue	French
yam	Senegalese (Africa)

Origami, the fascinating art of creative paper folding, has become a hobby of many Americans. Students can follow directions in such books as *Origami Storybook* by Florence Sakado and experience a traditional Japanese art.

The topic of "the family" is a viable approach by which to compare cultures. Thomas Dynneson (1977) has used the teaching technique of webbing to clearly identify the structure of the family. Each of the terms enclosed by a circle in Figure 7.2 is a concept.

From this conceptual web, an outline is prepared, sequencing all of the concepts (see Figure 7.3) Next, a chart is prepared from the outline, by means of which cross-cultural comparisons can be made between a Norwegian family and a Hopi family (see Chart 7.4).

The last step is then for students to use encyclopedias, textbooks, magazines, filmstrips, etc., to gather information on the items from Chart 7.4, leading to a point-by-point comparison. The class can prepare statements, such as the one that appears below, for each letter item on the chart.

    II. Descendency

        A.

        B. Kinship—Family relationships are traced
           through the female members of a Hopi family,

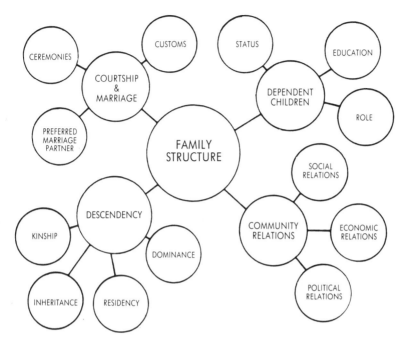

Figure 7.2 The conceptual web [from Thomas Dynneson, "A Cross-Cultural Approach to Learning about the Family," *Social Education*, p. 482 (October 1977)].

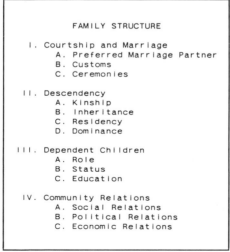

Figure 7.3 Outline derived from a conceptual web. [This outline is taken from Thomas L. Dynneson's article, "A Cross-Cultural Approach to Learning about the Family," *Social Education*, p. 483 (October 1977).]

whereas they are traced through the male
members of a Norwegian family (Dynneson,
1977, 483).

C.

ARCHAEOLOGY

Archaeology is the study of past cultures by analyzing artifacts, or objects, made by humans. Teachers can collect their own supply of artifacts
on their foreign travels. Farmer and Schisgall (1982) gather a number of
artifacts in "culture boxes," with each artifact accompanied by a question,
e.g., "Is the train ticket hand or machine stamped?" "What does the match-
book cover advertise?"

The following plan proposes how to teach a lesson on archaeology to
middle grade students; it addresses the concept of *artifacts*. The generalization focused on is "Cultural values are reflected in very common objects."

Norwegian Family	*Hopi Family*
I. Courtship and Marriage	I. Courtship and Marriage
A. Preferred Marriage Partner	A. Preferred Marriage Partner
B. Customs	B. Customs
C. Ceremonies	C. Ceremonies
II. Descendency	II. Descendency
A. Kinship	A. Kinship
B. Inheritance	B. Inheritance
C. Residency	C. Residency
D. Dominance	D. Dominance
III. Dependent Children	III. Dependent Children
A. Role	A. Role
B. Status	B. Status
C. Education	C. Education
IV. Community Relations	IV. Community Relations
A. Social Relations	A. Social Relations
B. Political Relations	B. Political Relations
C. Economic Relations	C. Economic Relations

Chart 7.4 Comparing family structure. [This information is taken from Thomas L. Dynneson's
article, "A Cross-Cultural Approach to Learning about the Family," *Social Education*, p. 483 (October 1977).]

MIDDLE GRADE LESSON PLAN

Topic: **A New Use for Old Garbage**

Grade: **7th**

Date: **May 14, 1:30–3:00**

I. **Purpose: tells what a student will learn**

    (a) To practice the skills of an archaeologist

    (b) To identify known and unknown materials

    (c) To classify the materials

    (d) To form hypotheses based on physical evidence

    (e) To practice working in groups

    (f) To develop the skills of oral and written reporting

    (g) To use the skills of analysis and application

II. **Motivation: tells how to begin the day's lesson**

Break the class into groups of three to five students and then give each group a numbered bag of clean garbage.

III. **Development: tells how to conduct the day's lesson**

Handout #1: Archaeology Exercise

The year is 2180. As an archaeologist, you have been excavating the Kingston-Bayridge site. Through aerial photographs you have been able to construct a diagram (see Diagram 7.1) showing the outlines of eleven houses and the street on which they were located.

By excavating in the backyards of these houses, you have uncovered the garbage pits for each house. A remarkable vacuum process has kept the garbage well preserved and you are able to identify many of the articles. You have placed the articles from each garbage pit into a bag and have taken them back to the lab. However, because of a mix-up the numbers on the bags were changed. As a result, the numbers on the bags do not match the numbers on the houses. For example, Garbage Bag #1 could belong to any one of the eleven houses.

This is what you have to do:

(1) Look at the articles found in your garbage bag and decide what each is. Classify each of the articles into groups with common characteristics.

(2) Choose a secretary to (a) record what articles were found in the pit, (b) list the articles found in the garbage pit on the blackboard, and (c) hand a list of articles to the teacher to be copied.

(continued)

---

(3) Each person in the group writes a report hypothesizing about the type of people who lived in the house based on the articles found in the garbage pit.

(4) Each group discusses the hypotheses posed by its members and comes to some consensus. Choose a spokesperson who will describe to the rest of the class what was contained in the garbage pit and what kind of people lived in the house.

The eleven spokespersons describe their findings and hypotheses to the class. At this point, the class may challenge the hypotheses and/or add others.

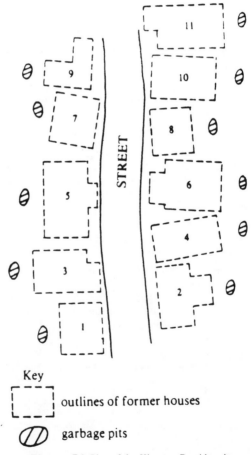

Key

outlines of former houses

garbage pits

Diagram 7.1 Plan of the Kingston-Bayridge site.

After the spokespersons have made their reports, the teacher gathers the lists from the groups' secretaries, runs them off, and distributes them to the students as the following handout.

Handout #2: Archaeologists' Reports

Garbage Bag #11

baseball ticket	*T.V. Guide*
Spiderman comic	Disneyland ticket
Cascade dishwashing detergent	cocoa
Mork & Mindy cards	candy wrappers
Sprite can	baseball cards

Indicate to the students that they still do not know which bag belongs to which house because of the mix-up at the lab. However, a time capsule has been discovered on the street containing eleven "Family Profiles." The family profile will take the format shown in the next handout.

Handout #3: Family Profiles

House #5

This is a family consisting of a husband, wife, and a 12-year-old son in the year 1980. Both parents work, making it necessary to use modern conveniences around the house such as prepared foods and labor-saving appliances. This family likes doing things together. For example, three years ago they visited Disneyland. On Saturdays, Bob, the 12-year-old, has a hot chocolate and joins his father in watching baseball on T.V.

(The teacher should try to incorporate as many articles as possible that are found in the garbage bag describing each family.)

The teacher hands out the "Family Profiles" on a sheet of paper and asks the class to match the "Archaeologists' Reports" with the "Family Profiles."

IV. *Conclusion:* **tells how to close or evaluate the day's lesson**

Review the answers of the students as they matched the "Archaeologists' Reports" with the "Family Profiles." How close were their hypotheses about each family, based on the garbage, to the actual family described in the "Family Profiles"?

V. *Materials*: tells what is needed for the day's lesson

Ten to fifteen bags of "clean" garbage. Using small garbage bags, the teacher should fill them with a number of articles varying from comic books, soap wrappers, bottle caps, and cereal boxes to perfume bottles, newspapers, magazines, and cigarette packages. In addition, small baggies of flour, sugar, bran, salt, and coffee are used—requiring the students to taste them to make an identification.

Handout #1, Handout #2, Handout #3

Note: This lesson was adapted from the material by Ron Hotchkiss, "A New Use for Old Garbage," *The History and Social Science Teacher*, pp. 44–45 (Fall 1981).

If a class actually has access to an area where they can bury some "artifacts," Marilyn Crowder's (1983) article would be of interest. She describes how an English teacher and a social studies teacher conduct an interdisciplinary unit combining language arts and archaeology. Students first receive a lecture on archaeology. They then do library research, hear guest speakers, and view films prior to the actual "dig."

MULTICULTURAL EDUCATION

Many educators view the terms *multicultural education* and *multiethnic education* as being nearly the same (Welton and Mallan, 1988; Michaelis, 1988). Multicultural education began in the 1960s as an effort to develop in students an understanding and appreciation for the diverse heritages, ethnic groups, and cultures in our country. The "melting pot" notion of various groups being homogenized into a single identity has been replaced by the "pluralistic" approach, which perceives the groups as intermingling but retaining their individual differences.

Many teachers have good intentions of broadening students' views about other cultures when they have a class make tepees to study North American Indians or make sugar cube igloos to study the Eskimos. Instead, this can have the opposite effect of creating stereotypes unless teachers point out that these "exotic" samples of a group's culture are not typical of every member of that group. Valerie Pang (1988) explains it very well:

I've since come to realize that multiethnic education . . . should present a balance between our national identity as Americans and our diverse ethnic heritage. Now I try to show students that there's no single "model American." . . . I emphasize that the richness of our country derives from the cultures of all the people who live here, that the various ethnic groups function side by side and together make up the "American culture" [p. 57].

Chart 7.5 represents James Banks's ideas on what a multiethnic studies program should look like.

ASSISTANCE POINTS

Questions for Action for the Administrator

1. Your supervisory experience reminds you that a spiral curriculum has the advantage of presenting increasingly complex material at successive grade levels. Use information from Chapter 2 and this chapter to identify some anthropological concepts you can suggest to teachers during a conference if they want to teach about the topic of "culture."

2. If your teachers are doing what they are supposed to be doing, what materials should they be using to teach about foreign countries? For example, do you notice them using an "artifact box" or a "culture box," which show the life-styles of people in other parts of the world? ˙

3. Assume that you have visited a classroom in which the teacher has been using a conceptual web to teach anthropological material. Explain why each of the following practices could have been used by the teacher:

    (a) A chalkboard with circles containing concepts
    (b) An overhead transparency showing an outline
    (c) A handout listing comparisons of the two examples being studied

Key Terms

It may be helpful for educators to review the meanings of a number of key terms that pertain to anthropology.

Culture: the total patterns of behavior of a group of people

Ethnocentrism: judging another group's actions by the standards of one's own group

Cultural relativity: the belief that each culture is equally important

Subsistence patterns: the ways in which people satisfy their material needs

Enculturation: the method by which humans learn the culture in which they are reared

Acculturation: the process whereby people's culture changes through prolonged contact with another culture

Cultural conflict: conflict that arises when cultures come in contact with each other

Dominant Characteristics	Desirable Characteristics
Focuses on isolated aspects of the histories and cultures of ethnic groups.	Describes the history and cultures of ethnic groups holistically.
Trivializes the histories and cultures of ethnic groups.	Describes the cultures of ethnic groups as dynamic wholes and processes of change.
Presents events, issues, and concepts primarily from Anglocentric and mainstream perspectives and points of view.	Presents events, issues, and concepts from the persepctives and points of view of diverse racial and ethnic groups.
Is Eurocentric—shows the development of America primarily as an extension of Europe into the Americas.	Is multidimensional and geocultural—shows how peoples and cultures came to America from many different parts of the world, including Asia and Africa, and the important roles they played in the development of U.S. society.
Content about ethnic groups is an appendage to the regular or core curriculum.	Content about ethnic groups is an integral part of the regular or core curriculum.
Ethnic minority cultures are described as deprived or pathological.	Ethnic minority cultures are described as different from mainstream Anglo culture but as normal and functional.
Concepts such as institutional racism, class stratification, powerlessness, and the victimization of ethnic and racial groups are given scant attention.	An important focus is on concepts such as institutional racism, class stratification, powerlessness, and the victimization of ethnic and racial groups.
The curriculum is dominated by the assimilationist ideology, Pluralist and radical ideologies are either ignored or depicted as undesirable.	The curriculum reflects a pluralistic ideology, with some attention given to radical ideas and concepts.
Focuses on lower-level knowledge, ethnic heroes, holidays, and recall of factual information.	Focuses on higher-level knowledge, such as concepts, generalizations, and theories.
Emphasizes the mastery of knowledge and cognitive outcomes.	Emphasizes decision making and citizen action. Knowledge formulation, value analysis, and citizen action are important components of the curriculum. Knowledge is synthesized with clarified values in order to make reflective decisions that guide action (Banks with Clegg, 1985).
Encourages acceptance of existing ethnic, class, and racial stratification.	Focuses on social criticism and social change.

Chart 7.5 Dominant and desirable characteristics of multiethnic studies [taken from "The Social Studies, Ethnic Diversity, and Social Change," *Elementary School Journal*, James A Banks, p. 356 (May 1987)].

Culture shock: the experience that a person has when coming in contact with a culture that is dissimilar to the one he or she is used to

Belief: the acceptance of something as being true without positive proof

Artifact: any object made by human skill or work

Diffusion: the flow of ideas, traits, and tools from one culture to another

Innovation: introducing new ideas, traits, and tools into a culture

Culture element or culture trait: the smallest unit of culture. An artifact such as a bowl or the custom of shaking hands when meeting are examples of culture elements.

Culture area: the geographical region where a number of culture traits are found. Western Europe and the Southwest United States are examples of culture areas.

Race: a group of people who share several biological traits, e.g., skin color, hair type, eye shapes, etc.

Ethnic group: individuals who share a common culture identity, values, religious beliefs, etc.

Research about Anthropology: Implications for Educators

David Martin (1985, 608) has summarized research findings and arrived at a number of techniques that might help reduce ethnocentrism in social studies classrooms:

1. Provide opportunities for children to discuss openly why they react positively or negatively toward a particular cultural group.

2. Encourage children to express ways in which their culture may appear strange or bizarre to foreigners.

3. Discuss superordinate ways in which all human groups are similar despite specific differences, e.g., kinship, division of tasks, language, prolonged childhood dependency, belief systems, use of symbols, tool systems.

4. Teach children about the processes by which humans develop stereotypes, and have them identify ways in which they have seen themselves follow those processes.

5. Point out nonstereotypic behaviors of groups being studied.

6. Teach about the positive contributions to human life by groups toward whom ethnocentrism has been expressed.

7. Teach students that wide variations of behavior exist within any culture; thus, stereotyping is bound to be false.

8. Help students to create, explore, and analyze synthetic or model cul-

tures in order to develop the cognitive tools needed to examine and understand other real cultures.

Names of Addresses of Professional Organizations

Following are some addresses for information related to anthropology:

1. American Anthropological Association
   1703 New Hampshire Avenue, N.W.
   Washington, DC 20009
   (The AAA publishes the journals *Anthropology & Education Quarterly* and *American Anthropologist.*)
2. Archaeological Institute of America
   675 Commonwealth Avenue
   Boston, MA 02215
   (The AIA publishes the journals *Archaeology* and *American Journal of Archaeology.*)
3. Smithsonian Associates
   900 Jefferson Drive
   Washington, DC 20560
   (Smithsonian Associates publishes the magazine *Smithsonian.*)
4. Cobblestone Publishing, Inc.
   20 Grove Street
   Peterborough, NH 03458
   (Cobblestone—in cooperation with the American Museum of Natural History in New York City—publishes the magazine *Faces.*)
5. American Museum of Natural History
   Central Park West at 79th St.
   New York, NY 10024
   (The Museum publishes the magazine *Natural History.*)
6. Popular Culture Association
   Pat Browne, Journals Department
   Bowling Green University Popular Press
   Bowling Green, OH 43403
   (The PCA publishes the *Journal of Popular Culture.*)
7. *Current Anthropology*
   Orlie Higgins, Circulation Mgr.
   University of Chicago Press
   Journals Division P.O. Box 37005
   Chicago, IL 60637

REFERENCES

Banks, James A. "The Social Studies, Ethnic Diversity, and Social Change," *Elementary School Journal*, pp. 531–543 (May 1987).

Banks, James A. "Ethnicity: Implications for Curriculum Reform," *The Social Studies*, pp. 3–10 (January/February 1979).

Carroll, Rives Fowlkes. "Schoolyard Archaeology," *The Social Studies*, pp. 69–75 (March/April 1987).

Chilcott, Jack. "Curriculum Models for Teaching Anthropology," *Anthropology and Education Quarterly*, pp. 14–18 (February 1977).

Council on Anthropology and Education. "The Status of Precollegiate Anthropology: Progress or Peril," *Anthropology & Education Quarterly*, pp. 304–311 (Winter 1981).

Crowder, Marilyn. "Digging into the Past," *Southern Social Studies Quarterly*, pp. 14–18 (Fall 1983).

DeCosta, S. B. "Not All Children Are Anglo and Middle Class: A Practical Beginning for the Elementary Teacher," *Theory into Practice*, pp. 155–162 (Spring 1984).

Dickinson, David K. "Creating and Using Formal Occasions in the Classroom," *Anthropology & Education Quarterly*, pp. 47–62 (Spring 1985).

Dynneson, Thomas L. "A Cross-Cultural Approach to Learning about the Family," *Social Education*, pp. 482–483 (October 1977).

Eddy, Elizabeth M. "Theory, Research, and Application in Educational Anthropology," *Anthropology & Education Quarterly*, pp. 83–104 (Summer 1985).

Farmer, Rod and Jane Schisgall. "The Culture Box: Teaching with Artifacts," *Southern Social Studies Quarterly*, pp. 5–9 (Spring 1982).

Green, Janice. "Hello, World!" *Instructor*, pp. 91–94 (October 1979).

Hatch, J. Amos. "Impression Management in Kindergarten Classrooms: An Analysis of Children's Face-Work in Peer Interactions," *Anthropology & Education Quarterly*, pp. 100–115 (June 1987).

Hotchkiss, Ron. "A New Use for Old Garbage," *The History and Social Science Teacher*, pp. 44–45 (Fall 1981).

Hunkins, Francis et al. *Social Studies in the Elementary School*. Columbus, OH:Merrill (1982).

Hussey, Michael. "Principles for Developing a Multi-Cultural Curriculum," *Early Childhood Development and Care*, 10(4):327–332 (1983).

Jarolimek, John. *Social Studies in Elementary Education, 7th edition*. New York:Macmillan (1986).

Lambert, Glenn E. "Teaching the Concept of Ethnocentrism," *Social Education*, pp. 408–409 (May 1978).

Leclerc, Daniel C. "Architecture as a Primary Source for Social Studies," *How to Do It Series* (Series 2, No. 5), Washington, DC:National Council for the Social Studies (1978).

Mahood, Wayne and Lyn Rusick. "Nacirema, Weans, and Bushmen: Studying Cultures," *The Social Studies*, pp. 184–187 (July/August 1981).

Mahood, Wayne. "The Land of Milk and Honey: Simulating the Immigrant Experience," *Social Education*, pp. 22–24 (January 1980).

Martin, David S. "Ethnocentrism Revisited: Another Look at a Persistent Problem," *Social Education*, pp. 604–609 (October 1985).

McCarthy, Gloria and Molly Marso. *Discovering Archaeology*. Buffalo, NY:D.O.K. Publishers (1983).

Messick, Rosemary G. "Implementing the Anthropology Strand in Elementary Programs," *Social Studies Review*, pp. 45–50 (Fall 1983).

Michaelis, John U. *Social Studies for Children, ninth edition*. Englewood Cliffs, NJ: Prentice Hall (1988).

Muessig, Raymond H. and Vincent R. Rogers. "Suggested Methods for Teaching," in *The Study of Anthropology* by Pertti J. Pelto. Columbus, OH:Merrill (1965).

National Council for the Social Studies, Task Force on Ethnic Studies Curriculum Guidelines. *Curriculum Guidelines for Multiethnic Education*. Washington, DC: NCSS (1976).

Oicles, Ellen. "Use of Artifacts in Teaching Culture," *Social Studies Review*, pp. 51–54 (Fall 1983).

Olson, Tazuko N. "Child's Cultural Awareness," *Social Studies*, pp. 25–31 (January/ February 1982).

Onderdonk, Richard. "Piaget and Archaeology," *Archaeology*, p. 80 (November/December 1986).

Owen, Roger C. "Anthropology and a Social Science/Social Studies: One More Plea," *The Social Studies*, pp. 207–211 (September/October 1982).

Pang, Valerie O. "Teaching about Ethnic Heritage: More Than Costumes and Unusual Food," *Learning 88*, pp. 56–57 (January 1988).

Pelto, Pertti J. and Raymond H. Muessig. *The Study and Teaching of Anthropology*. Columbus, OH:Merrill (1980).

Ross, Wayne. "A Bibliography of Teacher and Classroom Resources for Multicultural Education," *Ohio Council for the Social Studies Review*, pp. 31–37 (Spring 1985).

Slavin, Robert E. *Using Student Team Learning, third edition*. Baltimore: Johns Hopkins University, Center for Research on Elementary & Middle Schools (1986).

Turner, Thomas N. "Using Popular Culture in the Social Studies," *How to Do It Series* (Series 2, No. 9), Washington, DC:National Council for the Social Studies (1979).

Van Cleaf, David W. "Student Anthropologists Examine TV Commercials," *The Social Studies*, pp. 130–131 (May/June 1986).

Walsh, Huber M. *Introducing the Young Child to the Social World*. New York:Macmillan (1980).

Welton, David A. and John T. Mallan. *Children and Their World, third edition*. Boston:Houghton Mifflin (1988).

Wieseman, Robert A. "Multicultural Beginnings and Early Learning," *Journal of Instructional Psychology*, pp. 172–176 (December 1986).

Williams, Melvin. "Observations in Pittsburgh Ghetto Schools," *Anthropology & Education Quarterly*, pp. 211–220 (Fall 1981).

8 | ECONOMICS: WHO'S GOT THE BEEF?

Chapter Preview of Key Ideas

★ *Economics is often an unpopular topic for students and teachers. This can be offset by infusing it into other areas of the school curriculum.*

★ *A program, such as the Developmental Economic Education Program, can involve the teachers in a school district.*

★ *Economic education is a component of economics for both early elementary and middle grade students.*

★ *Young children have an incomplete knowledge of economics.*

★ *There are a few basic concepts that young children need to know, e.g., scarcity, needs, wants, goods, and services.*

★ *Young children can learn economics by looking for examples in the community around them.*

★ *Older children can view economics with its implications for the nation and the world.*

★ *Career education is a life-long activity.*

★ *The United States Office of Education has developed career clusters.*

★ *Career awareness for students is followed by career exploration.*

Economics can be considered as the study of "how people in a society use resources to satisfy their needs and wants" (Hunkins et al., 1982, 62). This social science is sometimes called the "dismal science" because of its seemingly inscrutable and uninteresting content. However, the aversion that students and teachers often exhibit toward this area is unwarranted because of the overriding importance of economics to our lives. People are forced daily to make choices about how they will use their resources and how they will match up their needs and wants.

Two areas related to economics will be discussed in this chapter: career education and consumer education. Career education is concerned with jobs because that is how our culture expects citizens to acquire the money to satisfy their needs and wants. Consumer education focuses on how citizens can wisely spend the money they earn from their occupations.

Since economic instruction is sometimes lacking in the elementary grades, one solution is to infuse the teaching of economics into other curricular areas (Hilke, 1983, 33):

> . . . [T]he concepts of money and trade would fit into a math unit. Other examples might include the study of economic articles in magazines and newspapers during reading class; learning vocabulary and how to spell economic words in spelling; division of labor and specialization while creating group projects; and even the concept of supply and demand while waiting in the lunch line.

According to Laughlin (1983), an infusion process that an educator wishes to implement includes the eight steps that appear in Chart 8.1.

Economic education should be a K-12 effort in our schools. The Developmental Economic Education Program (DEEP) addresses this spectrum with its focus on program planning, materials selection and development, teacher in-service, and program evaluation.

DEEP, initiated in 1965, is coordinated at the national level by the Joint Council on Economic Education (JCEE), which provides workshops, conferences, materials, and evaluation instruments to aid school districts.

Don Leet (1985) explains how a school district can establish a DEEP (see Figure 8.1).

TEACHING CONCEPTS AND GENERALIZATIONS

Following are some concepts and generalizations that administrators can relay to teachers. These can be taught to elementary and middle grade students in the area of economics.

Concepts

economic wants	economic needs	demand
mixed economy	scarcity	production
consumption	natural resources	goods
services	supply	distribution

Step 1   Select an economic concept, topic, or problem to infuse into the existing curriculum. When making this selection, care should be given to

A. The grade level and abilities of the students
B. The interests, learning styles, and previous learning experiences of the students
C. The interests, motivation, educational background, and teaching style of the classroom teacher
D. The importance of the economic concept, issue, or topic to the students and/or to the larger community

Step 2   Identify and place economic content within instructional units that lend themselves to the study of selected economic concepts, generalizations, and understandings.

Step 3   Develop at least one economic-related instructional objective to complement the existing instructional objectives.

Step 4   Identify additional specific, inferential, and critical skills to be introduced or developed in order to attain the new instructional objectives which now include economic content.

Step 5   Outline economic knowledge, concepts, generalizations, and understandings to be included in the existing curriculum to supplement and/or enirch the content of the existing instructional unit.

Step 6   Modify teaching procedures and the inclusion of new student learning activities to meet the economic instructional objective.

Step 7   Identify student and teacher resource materials needed to supplement the unit.

Step 8   Develop student evaluation activities to determine whether or not the objectives of the unit have been achieved.

Chart 8.1 Steps to infuse economics into a curriculum.

Step One: *Select a DEEP Steering Committee.*

The committee should consist of ten to twelve members. Early elementa middle, and high school teachers should be represented. The school disti administrator responsible for the program (and designated as the DEEP c ordinator) should chair the committee. At least one principal as well as representative of the local teachers' organization should be on the co mittee.

Step Two: *Determine the district's baseline of economic knowledge.*

Survey the teachers' backgrounds and interest in economics along with evaluation of student knowledge of basic economics concepts. The loc Center for Economic Education can help create the survey instrument. R sults of the survey enable the district to determine what instruction is need and who is most available to carry out the instruction.

Step Three: *Adopt a scope and sequence document.*

This document details which economics concepts should be taught at ea grade level. Give the document to teachers for them to react to.

Step Four: *Create new curriculum strategies.*

Use the finished scope and sequence document to create, select, and pil new curriculum strategies. A pilot program could be implemented for each the following grade divisions: primary, intermediate, middle or junior hig and high school.

Step Five: *Recruit additional teachers.*

New teachers should be brought in to assist in teaching and evaluating th new lessons. It often works best in the elementary grades to combine eco nomics instruction with other activities such as art, music, math, and readin

Step Six: *Conduct a maintenance program.*

Once the K–12 economics curriculum has been developed and impl mented, a maintenance program should be created for the purpose of mor toring students' progress toward economic literacy through an annual tes ing program. Teachers at various schools can be designated as DEEP Si Coordinators, providing a link between local school sites and the DEEP cu riculum established at the district level.

Figure 8.1 The process of establishing a DEEP.

exchange
wages
taxes
bank
entrepreneur
consumers
saving
economic system
allocation
sellers
workers
profits
free trade
labor
recession
mass production
cost of living
salary
life-style
advertising
bonds

division of labor
barter
market
competition
trade-offs
producers
spending habits
inflation
economic growth
rent
employers
prices
tariff
gross national product
industrial revolution
coins
career
human resources
work
merchandise

assembly line
income
money
cost
interdependence
credit
investment
occupation
buyers
unemployment
poverty
monopoly
cottage industry
wealth
job skills
leisure
public service
stocks

Generalizations

- The basic economic problem is one of people trying to satisfy unlimited wants with limited resources.
- The interdependence of people in the world makes exchange and trade a necessity.
- Workers sell their services to employers in return for wages.
- Wise use of leisure time complements happiness in one's career.
- Education helps a person make a career choice.
- Consumer economic wants exert a major influence on production in the marketplace.
- False advertising takes unfair advantage of consumers.

THE YOUNG LEARNER

The young child's knowledge of economics is developing, but it is incomplete. Furth (1980) describes young children, for example, as not understanding the act of making a purchase in a store. They see it as a ritual that adults go through; they don't associate a cause and effect relationship to the exchange.

Darrin (1968) studied 1,000 K–6 students. He concluded that many topics were teachable to the students. However, some topics were too difficult for kindergarten and first grade students, e.g.,

(1) Individual and social implications of unemployment
(2) Law of supply and demand
(3) Changing situations in agriculture
(4) Competition as a foundation of capitalism

Primary age children can be taught many easily understood concepts, of which one of the most essential is *scarcity*. Ask students to think of a time when they were standing in line, waiting for something—only to have the item run out. Perhaps they were waiting for discount tickets to an event or waiting for cans of pop that were being passed out after a ball game on a hot day. Tell them that this feeling of not being able to get something is what scarcity means.

Have the students write down the name of something they would like to have. Directly above that, they should write down something they would like even more. Do this several times to get across the idea that people have unlimited *wants*. Have them look at the list to determine if there is anything which is a *need*, that is, something which they cannot live without.

Ask the students how they get baseball cards. Besides buying them, they also *trade* for them with friends and classmates. Discuss whether a student ever trades several cards to get just one card. Why?

Hands-on experiences can help children understand *money*. They can examine the physical characteristics of size, weight, color, and shape. They can use money to buy items that are brought to class, e.g., a pencil would require fifteen pennies or else one dime and two nickels.

All people are *consumers*, even children. Have the students make a list of all the things they have used or consumed that day, e.g., toothpaste, soap, cereal, water, etc. The things a person consumes are called *goods* (milk and paper) or *services* (a parent driving a child to school and the police officer helping the children cross the street in front of the school).

Ask students to bring in empty boxes of food (oatmeal, breakfast cereal, granola bars, etc.). Have them notice the *price* on each box. If there is only a bar code, then give them an approximate amount to write on the box. Discuss whether the store owner gets to keep all the money indicated by the price. He gets to keep some, which is called a *profit*, but some of it goes to pay the people who work in the store, as well as for other costs.

Our world requires *specialization*, as people are trained to do a particular job. Since most people are not proficient in medicine, they require the services of a doctor. Similarly, if they do not know how to repair a car, they must go to a specialist who is trained to fix automobiles. Ask students for examples of when a person must rely on someone else who has special skills or knowledge.

Related to specialization is *division of labor*. Ask students if they know how a television is built. Does one person build the entire set? Showing students pictures of a factory can help them understand how an assembly line operates.

The following lesson plan illustrates how an educator can develop the concept of "division of labor" with a class of young children.

EARLY ELEMENTARY LESSON PLAN

Topic: **Division of Labor**

Grade: **3rd**

Date: **September 28, 2:00–2:30**

I. *Purpose*: **tells what a student will learn**

Students will understand the term *division of labor* and give examples of it.

II. *Motivation*: **tells how to begin the day's lesson**

Have children discuss jobs they know about in their family or neighborhood by responding to these questions:

Do you have a job at home? What do you do?
What is the difference between your job and the jobs of grown-ups?

Explain that in the upcoming lesson they are going to learn about different kinds of jobs in the community.

III. *Development*: **tells how to conduct the day's lesson**

Put the following chart on the chalkboard.

Name of job	Reasons for the job
1. _____	_____
2. _____	_____
3. _____	_____

Ask each child to think of jobs and reasons to write on the lines. Go around the class and obtain an answer from each child, writing them on the chalkboard. Have children discuss the need for a variety of jobs by responding to these questions:

- Why is it that we have so many different jobs in our community?
- Why couldn't each family do all these jobs itself?
- Why do you suppose people in a community divide the work the way they do?
- Do people who have these jobs have special skills? What do you mean?
- Do you think people can do their jobs better when each person has a special job? Why do you think so?

Tell the children that when people divide work so that each one does something special, we call that division of labor. Write this term on the chalkboard. Discuss this term by having the class respond to these questions:

- Does anyone know another word for labor? (Children could suggest *work* as a synonym for labor.)
- Can anyone tell us in his or her own words what division of labor means? (Children could respond that "Division of labor means dividing the work.")

IV. *Conclusion*: **tells how to close or evaluate the day's lesson**

Have the students tell in their own words how they see division of labor in these places:

in their school	in a hospital
at the shopping center	in their families
in the supermarket	at the airport

V. *Materials*: **tells what is needed for the day's lesson**

No special materials are needed.

Note: This lesson plan is adapted from John Jarolimek, *Social Studies in Elementary Education, seventh edition*, Macmillan, pp. 158 and 159 (1986).

Yeargan and Hatcher (1985) describe the activities of a third grade class as they studied the concepts of *profits* and *producers*. The class actually visited a neighborhood bakery to observe how a product was made. They determined (through a school survey) that chocolate cupcakes were in demand by other students, at which time they began to make and sell them. Other ideas for teaching economics through community involvement are set out by Mark Schug (1984).

A popular program for late primary and early intermediate students has been devised by Marilyn Kourilsky (1978). The Mini-Society Program allows students in grades 3–6 to create their own microcosmic version of an adult economy. Students buy and sell goods, such as pencils, pens, and erasers, using printed money. They also offer services such as banking, piano lessons, and hair styling. Concepts such as *competition* and *inflation* are also experienced by the students.

If an administrator wants to check the economic knowledge of young children, the *Primary Test of Economic Understanding* (PTEU) can be used. It was developed by Don Davison and John Kilgore at the University of Iowa.

THE OLDER LEARNER

By the time a child reaches the intermediate grades, he is able to think beyond personal decision making in economics and is able to relate decision making to the society at large. Middle grade or junior high students are interested in economic problems of the nation and the world; e.g., How should our tax money be spent? What implications does the unemployment problem have on the economy?

Armento and Fiores (1986) have organized learning tasks based upon psychological processes. Chart 8.2 presents sequential levels of economic instruction. The fourth level (Formal Concept Refinement Phase) applies to students in the intermediate grades.

Schug (1986) suggests that the questions from Chart 8.3 can be key points in the curriculum when teaching economics to older students.

A popular simulation game for middle and high school students is "The Stock Market Game." It is a ten-week game designed to introduce students to the American economy and the world of finance and investing. The simulation sharpens study skills by placing students in decision-making roles which require research, judgment, analysis, mathematical ability, and interpersonal cooperation.

"The Stock Market Game" is played with imaginary funds as students follow stock prices in the newspaper. Competing teams trade on the New York and American Stock Exchanges in order to develop a portfolio showing the highest gain on the original investment. Further information on "The Stock Market Game" can be obtained by contacting a local Center on Economic Education.

Another popular resource is "Trade-Offs," a television series designed to teach basic economic concepts to students in grades 5–8. There are fifteen twenty-minute films (also available on videotape). Information on "Trade-Offs" is available from the Joint Council on Economic Education, 2 Park Avenue, New York, NY 10016. The series is often run on public television, so it might be obtained from the state network.

A standardized test is available to test the economic knowledge of older students. The *Basic Economics Test* was developed at Illinois State Univer-

Informal, Early Childhood Phase

As young children engage in economic experiences, they can indicate their understanding by

- role-playing or enacting the main ideas of the experience
- drawing pictures and describing the ideas in their own words
- grouping experiences together and giving the groupings names or labels
- identifying examples of particular ideas

Formal, Concept Introduction Phase

When an economic concept is first formally introduced to learners in an instructional setting, the learners can indicate their understanding by

- describing the concept in their own words
- indicating recognition of the concept when presented in another context
- distinguishing examples from nonexamples of the concept
- using labels (names; synonymous, developmentally appropriate words) for particular concepts. For example, young children might use the term "trade-offs" as opposed to the term "opportunity cost."

Formal, Concept Development Phase

A concept is developed as students examine a range of examples which illustrate the core idea. As these examples become more sophisticated in depth and breadth, students should be able to demonstrate their understanding by

- distinguishing between closely related concepts
- grouping concepts to illustrate their hierarchical arrangement (superordinate, subordinate, coordinate organization)
- comparing and contrasting examples
- identifying new examples of the concept
- explaining new situations by applying concept

Formal Concept Refinement Phase

As students examine examples illustrating the breadth, depth, and scope of conceptual knowledge, they continue to reorganize and refine their knowledge. Students should be able to engage in the following constructive behaviors at this stage of learning:

- defining the concept and evaluating examples in terms of their correspondence with the concept definition
- classifying concepts to illustrate relations, causal and hierarchical patterns
- predicting cause–effect relationships in new examples
- analyzing situations by applying conceptual knowledge
- synthesizing knowledge through the development of a new mode of expression (play, essay, paper, etc.)
- applying knowledge to the assessment of problems and social issues
- evaluating knowledge and the uses one makes of that knowledge

Chart 8.2 Concept construction phases for economics [taken from "Learning about the Economic World," by Beverly Armento and Sharon Flores in *Elementary School Social Studies: Research as a Guide to Practice*. Bulletin No. 79, edited by Virginia Atwood, Washington, DC: NCSS, p. 95 (1986)].

- What is the role of specialization in our state? regions? nation? world?
- How did inventions, technology, and assembly lines change life in our country?
- How were the American colonies specialized?
- How was mass production important for American economic growth?
- How did inventions change American life?
- What were some characteristics of the American entrepreneur?
- What is a market system?
- What is a monopoly? a competitive market?
- What is the role of government in the economy?
- How does the United States today depend on other countries?
- How do people in other parts of the world use their economic resources?

Chart 8.3 Key economics questions for intermediate grades.

sity by John Chizmar. Norm data were gathered from students in grades 4–6.

CAREER EDUCATION

There is no commonly accepted definition of career education. The many definitions that can be found seem to contain five principles:

(1) Career education is a life-long activity (preschool through adulthood).
(2) Career education must take place in both the school and the nonschool arenas.
(3) Career education must help the student prepare for work.
(4) Career education should result in a sense of satisfaction for the student.
(5) Career education should be integrated with the rest of the curriculum.

Since there are about 30,000 different job titles in our nation, it is not possible for a school district to teach about all of them. Rather, it is more manageable to teach about groups of jobs. The United States Office of Education has established fifteen career clusters:

(1) Agri-business and natural resources
(2) Business and office work
(3) Communication and media
(4) Construction
(5) Consumer and homemaking
(6) Environment
(7) Fine arts and humanities
(8) Health
(9) Hospitality and recreation
(10) Manufacturing
(11) Marine science
(12) Marketing and distribution
(13) Personal services
(14) Public service
(15) Transportation

Students need to be taught about careers in all of these clusters. However, the approach must be different, depending upon the age of the student. Career "awareness" is appropriate in the elementary grades. Students acquire information about the various jobs in our society, in addition to developing an awareness of their own interests and abilities. Some activities to accomplish this "awareness" might be as follows:

(1) Take field trips to see people in the community at work.
(2) Have students match the picture of a worker with the tool that she uses.
(3) Invite a worker into the classroom to talk about his or her job. Inviting a female truck driver would be a good way to combat sex-role stereotyping.
(4) Commend students on their punctuality as an effort to reinforce this quality (which is important to keeping a job).
(5) Put together a bulletin board or collage from pictures of their parents' occupations.
(6) Students can role-play certain activities, such as an auto mechanic working on a car.
(7) Make a diorama of parts of the city that interest the students. Discuss what people do there.

(8) Look through the *Yellow Pages* to seek out the many jobs available in the community.

(9) Ask the class to describe in writing or in art what they would like to be. "Career fantasy" is described by Mazza and Mazza (1982). It allows a child to be anything he or she wants to be without economic, social, or intellectual restraints.

At the middle school or junior high level, "career exploration" is the focus. This means that students "are encouraged to visualize themselves in various work settings and their consequent life-styles and to test the meaning of their various work values" (Hoyt et al., 1978, 20). Some activities appropriate for this level include

(1) Students sell snacks, school supplies, etc., in a classroom store to learn about a retail business.

(2) Analyze newspaper ads for discussion of jobs available for people with certain skills.

(3) Play the "What's My Line" game, trying to guess the occupation of the guests.

(4) Interview workers in the community, comparing information such as "How much training does it require?" "Does the job require traveling?" "Does the job require any mechanical aptitudes?"

(5) Students prepare a research report on a particular career that interests them and then create a symbol to represent that career.

"Career day" always has appeal for school children. Rubinton (1985) explains how a Brooklyn, New York college and a school district cooperated to carry out a career education venture: Career Exploration for Youth (CEY). The project has four components:

(1) *Children's Program*
Hands-on career courses were offered to middle grade students. Instructors were recruited from the local community college as well as from local junior high schools and high schools. Course titles had fascinating names like "The Business of Sports," "Things That Go Bleep," "At Your Service," etc. All of the fifteen career clusters were represented with a course.

(2) *Parents' Program*
The parents of the children enrolled in the CEY program were also involved in career education as they were registered in a course or a workshop on career decision making and career development.

(3) *School Personnel Program*
The teachers and other school personnel were offered a course dealing with how to establish career education programs.

(4) *Recreation Program*
The students were offered supervised instruction by the local community college. Choices included such activities as tennis, creative crafts, and aerobic dance. The recreation feature of CEY was important in motivating the students to commit their Saturdays to an educational experience and to complement their career education choice.

Children's Literature

Children's literature provides an avenue for students to learn concepts and generalizations about career education. Westerberger (1982) says that there are a number of good books for children which can tie together the elements of a story (characters, theme, and plot) with the following elements of career education:

(1) *Economic Awareness*
Henry (in *Henry Huggins*) learned about the value of money when he sold night crawlers he had caught.

(2) *Self-Awareness*
The main character in *A Penny's Worth of Character* accepts money from a storekeeper he has deceived but later regains his self-respect.

(3) *Competency Skills*
In *Charlie Needs a Cloak*, children learn that a person must have certain competency skills in order to obtain the necessities of life.

(4) *Decision Making*
The main character in *Shadow of a Bull* is forced to decide whether he should follow his own career interests or follow his father as a bullfighter.

To demonstrate how a book can be the basis for a lesson on career education and economics, review the following plan, which is designed for a middle grade class.

MIDDLE GRADE LESSON PLAN

Topic: **Studying Social and Economic Concepts**
Grade: **8th**
Date: **October 15, 1:00–2:00**

I.   *Purpose*: tells what a student will learn

Students will examine roles of men and women to understand how strict adherence to traditional roles imposes economic, social, and emotional limits.

Students will follow an interdisciplinary, integrated approach, relating literature, economics, and history.

II. *Motivation*: tells how to begin the day's lesson

The students should previously be assigned the short story "The Story of X," describing a couple's attempt to raise a child free from sex-role stereotypes. The story alerts students to many stereotypes and biases that exist in our society. It is also a vehicle for discussing sex-role expectations under which students feel they are being brought up.

III. *Development*: tells how to conduct the day's lesson

Prior to this lesson the class will read *Rachel's Legacy* by Hila Colman. Students can relate the concepts of economics, history, linguistics, and sociology to their own lives as well as to the characters in the book.

The novel is a story of a Jewish immigrant mother and her three daughters. One daughter fits the stereotype of the "traditional female"; the second rebels against all of her mother's values, customs, and expectations; the third, Rachel, is very independent, the opposite of the "traditional" type. One sister tells Rachel that she "should have been a man."

Rachel begins as a seamstress in a garment factory and attends night school; she is a hard-working, goal-oriented woman. Eventually, she opens a factory with her cousin and brother-in-law; however, it is Rachel who makes all the major decisions. Discussion of the story can revolve around the following concepts:

Economic wants. Because the mother's economic wants are basic and the children's are unlimited (including cultural experiences, better education, and protection of individual rights), conflicts result.

Productive resources. As a factory manager, Rachel must have a complete understanding of natural resources, capital goods, and human resources. Rachel is concerned not only about impending strikes of the workers, but also about their rights, which she is determined to protect despite her cousin's desire to maximize profits at any expense.

Economic incentive. The profit motive and self-interest bring Rachel into conflict with her partners; although she too wants to make a profit, she feels the profit should be shared with her workers.

Markets, supply, and demand. After analyzing the market, Rachel convinces her partners to start their garment business making only girls' white dresses, which are always in demand for special occasions. They market them directly to the stores, eliminating the middle person.

Saving and investment. Rachel realizes that her husband does not have a good grasp of economic concepts. In her will, she stipulates that he should sell the business and set the money aside for their daughter's future. He does not sell, however, and he and his daughter lose all their material wealth. His daughter Ellie feels that she nevertheless still has a legacy—not a financial one, but one of independence, goal-setting, and desire, which she inherited from her mother Rachel.

IV. *Conclusion*: **tells how to close or evaluate the day's lesson**

Ask the class to assume the role of Rachel and write a letter applying for a job as a factory manager in the 1980s. The student should refer to and extol the characteristics that Rachel has exhibited in the story.

V. *Materials*: **tells what is needed for the day's lesson**

Books ("The Story of X"; *Rachel's Legacy*)

Note: The above lesson plan is adapted from "Studying Social and Economic Concepts," by Christy Hammer in *Social Education*, pp. 280–281 (April/May 1987).

ASSISTANCE POINTS

Questions for Action for the Administrator

1. After reading this chapter, you decide that you need to strengthen student performance in economics. Each state has a Council on Economic Education. Contact the state director and have a representative send materials, which can be piloted in a few classrooms in your district. You can use the steps shown in Figure 8.1 to establish the economics pilot program.

2. Encourage the middle grade teachers in your district to write to corporations, asking them to send a copy of their company's annual report. Students can use the information to study the products they manufacture, as well as some economic terms, e.g., profit, stock, cost per share, etc. In addition, what would you expect to see in the lesson plans of teachers that would indicate that they are also incorporating elements of career education into these activities?

3. Canvas the primary grade teachers in your district to see how many of the concepts in this chapter they currently teach. Some teachers neglect economic concepts because they feel they don't have enough knowledge to teach them. Is this the case with the teachers you canvas?

4. Suppose that a curriculum audit revealed that your district's social studies objectives were not clear or valid. Write a few objectives that,

in your opinion, would illustrate that students have a basic understanding of how our economic system operates.

Names and Addresses of Professional Organizations

The following addresses can be helpful in supplying information or materials about economics:

1. Foundation for Teaching Economics
550 Kearney Street
Suite 1000
San Francisco, CA 94108
2. Joint Council on Economic Education
2 Park Avenue
New York, NY 10016
3. National Center for Economic Education for Children
Lesley College
35 Mellen Street
Cambridge, MA 02138
(The NCEEC publishes the pamphlet *The Elementary Economist.*)
4. Consumers Union
256 Washington St.
Mt. Vernon, NY 10553
5. United Auto Workers Education Dept.
Solidarity House
8000 East Jefferson
Detroit, MI 48214
6. AFL-CIO Education Dept.
815 16th Street N.W.
Washington, DC 20006

Some companies provide materials for educators, such as the following:

7. Procter & Gamble Co.
P.O. Box 599
Cincinnati, OH 45201
8. World Research, Inc.
11722 Sorrento Valley Rd.
San Diego, CA 92121
9. Federal Reserve Bank
Public Information Dept.
P.O. Box 7702
San Francisco, CA 94120

Research about Economics: Implications for Educators

Schug and Birkey (1985) interviewed students at preschool/kindergarten, grade 1, and grade 3. One conclusion was that these children valued money only inasmuch as it could be *used*. In other words, they didn't understand the value behind paper money; rather, they saw the bills as valuable if they could be used to purchase things.

Lizelle Peterson (1985) trained eight- and nine-year-olds to identify deceptive television ad techniques (phrases such as "You'll love it." or "It's the best.") and legitimate product information. This activity demonstrated that children of this age are capable of learning about consumer education.

REFERENCES

Armento, Beverly and Sharon Flores. "Learning about the Economic World," in *Elementary School Social Studies: Research as a Guide to Practice*. Bulletin No. 79, Virginia Atwood, ed. Washington, DC:National Council for the Social Studies, pp. 85–101 (1986).

Armento, Beverly J. "Ideas for Teaching Economics Derived from Learning Theory," *Theory into Practice*, pp. 176–182 (Summer 1987).

Banaszak, Ronald A. and Elmer U. Clawson. *Strategies for Teaching Economics: Junior High School Level*. NY:Joint Council on Economic Education (1981).

Cleary, Beverly. *Henry Huggins*. NY:William Morrow (1950).

Colman, Hila. *Rachel's Legacy*. NY:William Morrow (1978).

Darrin, G. "Economics in the Elementary School Curriculum: Study of the District of Columbia Laboratory Schools," Doctoral dissertation, College Park, MD:University of Maryland (1968).

Davison, Donald G. and John H. Kilgore. *Primary Test of Economic Understanding: Examiners's Manual*. Iowa City, IA:College of Business Administration, The University of Iowa (1971).

Davison, Donald G. *Strategies for Teaching Economics: Primary Level*. NY:Joint Council for Economic Education (1977).

de Paola, Tomie. *Charlie Needs a Cloak*. Englewood Cliffs, NJ:Prentice Hall (1973).

Fox, Karen F. "What Children Bring to School: The Beginnings of Economic Education," *Social Education*, pp. 478–481 (October 1978).

Furth, Hans. *The World of Grown Ups: Children's Conception of Society*. NY:Elsevier North Holland, Inc. (1980).

Gould, Lois. "The Story of X," in *Stories for Free Children*. Letty Cottin Pogrebin, ed. NY:McGraw-Hill, pp. 13–16 (1982).

Hammer, Christy. "Studying Social and Economic Concepts," *Social Education*, pp. 280–281 (April/May 1987).

Hansen, W. Lee et al. *Master Curriculum Guide in Economics for the Nation's Schools: A Framework for Teaching Economic Concepts*. NY:Joint Council on Economic Education (1977).

Hendricks, Robert H. et al. *Learning Economics through Children's Stories, fifth edition.* NY:Joint Council on Economic Education (1986).

Highsmith, Robert J. "Resources in Economic Education," *Social Studies Review*, pp. 28–34 (Winter 1983).

Hilke, Eileen. "Infusing Economics into the Existing Curriculum," *Sourthern Social Studies Quarterly*, pp. 33–39 (Spring 1988).

Hoyt, Kenneth B. et al. *Career Education and the Elementary School Teacher.* Salt Lake City, UT:Olympus Publishing Co. (1973).

Hunkins, Francis et al. *Social Studies in the Elementary Schools.* Columbus, OH: Merrill (1982).

Jarolimek, John. *Social Studies in Elementary Education, seventh edition.* NY:Macmillan (1986).

Kourilsky, Marilyn. *Strategies for Teaching Economics: Intermediate Level.* NY:Joint Council on Economic Education (1978).

Laughlin, Margaret. "Infusion—No Addition: Infusing Economics into the Curriculum," *Social Studies Review*, pp. 29–34 (Fall 1983).

Lawson, L. D. and M. G. O'Donnell. "Identifying Factors That Influence the Learning of Economics," *Journal of Economic Education*, pp. 177–185 (Summer 1986).

Leet, Don R. "The Development Economic Education Program (DEEP): A Strategy for Achieving Economic Literacy," *Social Studies Review*, pp. 8–12 (Spring 1985).

Mazza, Nicholas and Janice Mazza. "Elementary School Children and Career Fantasy," *Viewpoints in Teaching and Learning*, pp. 6–14 (Spring 1982).

Peterson, Lizelle. "Preventive Consumer Education in Children's Judgments of Televised Advertisements," *Education and Treatment of Children*, pp. 199–219 (Summer 1985).

Rubinton, Natalie. "Career Exploration for Middle School Youth: A University–School Cooperative," *Vocational Guidance Quarterly*, pp. 249–255 (March 1985).

Schug, Mark. "The Development of Economic Thinking in Children and Adolescents," *Social Education*, pp. 141–145 (February 1983).

Schug, Mark. "Approaches for Teaching Community Economics," in *Community Study: Application and Opportunities.* Bulletin No. 73, Mark Schug and Robert Beery, eds. Washington, DC:National Council for the Social Studies, pp. 29– 40 (1984).

Schug, Mark and J. Birkey. "The Development of Children's Economic Reasoning," *Theory and Research in Education*, 13:31–42 (1985).

Schug, Mark C. *Economics for Kids.* Washington, DC:National Education Association and the Joint Council on Economic Education (1986).

Stuart, Jesse. *A Penny's Worth of Character.* NY:McGraw-Hill (1954).

Symmes, S. Stowell (ed.) *Economic Education: Links to the Social Studies.* Bulletin No. 65. Washington, DC:National Council for the Social Studies (1981).

Westerberger, Virginia and Daryl Sander. "Career Education and Children's Literature," *Social Studies*, pp. 4–7 (January/February 1982).

Wojciechowska, Maia. *Shadow of a Bull.* NY:Atheneum (1964).

Yeargan, H. and B. Hatcher. "The Cupcake Factory: Helping Elementary Students Understand Economics," *Social Studies*, pp. 82–84 (March/April 1985).

9 | SPECIAL NEEDS: DON'T FORGET THE STUDENTS

Chapter Preview of Key Ideas

★ *Teachers address students' special needs by giving attention to all students, not just a few students in a special category.*

★ *Every student in the classroom is exceptional in some aspect.*

★ *Handicapped students' education is ensured by federal law PL 94-142.*

★ *Mainstreaming is the practice of placing handicapped students in regular classrooms.*

★ *Individual education plans (IEPs) are a source for teachers to provide social studies education.*

★ *Social studies activities for gifted and talented students should be based on more factors than just high scores on an IQ test.*

★ *Individualized instruction means that a lesson is personally meaningful to each student.*

★ *Thinking skills involve several areas: (1) general thinking strategies, (2) critical thinking, and (3) microthinking skills.*

★ *Teachers use questioning strategies to reach the various needs of students.*

The focus of this chapter is on "special needs." This term should not suggest that the chapter is limited to the needs of just a few special students; rather, it indicates students' needs that require special attention by the educator. Therefore, the chapter discusses such topics as individualization of instruction, thinking skills, learning styles, questioning techniques, and education for exceptional students who span the range from gifted to handicapped. It is important for an educator to approach special needs with the feeling that all students in a class should receive special attention from the teacher. In other words, it is just as important to be concerned with learning styles of slow learning students as with learning styles of the more academically able. Similarly, a teacher should apply the proper questioning techniques with each student in a classroom.

EXCEPTIONAL STUDENTS

While every child needs to be considered important and exceptional in certain aspects, the term is generally associated with that segment of the population who fall markedly above or below grade-level norms. Kirk and Gallagher (1983) define the atypical, exceptional child as one who

> . . . deviates from the average or normal child (1) in mental characteristics, (2) in sensory abilities, (3) in neuromotor or physical characteristics, (4) in social behavior, (5) in communication abilities, or (6) in multiple handicaps. Such deviation must be of such an extent that the child requires a modification of school practices, or special educational services, to develop to maximum capacity (p. 4).

HANDICAPPED STUDENTS

Two pieces of legislation in the 1970s had immense impact for the education of handicapped students. Section 504 of the Vocational Rehabilitation Act of 1973 was intended to remove discriminatory practices against the handicapped. Public Law 94-142, passed into law in 1975, provided for free, appropriate public education—in the least restrictive environment—for every handicapped person between the ages of three and twenty-one. The inclusion of handicapped students in a regular classroom is known as "mainstreaming," which involves the classroom teacher in the education of the student. Some of the handicapping conditions include learning disabled, speech impaired, mentally retarded, emotionally disturbed, hearing impaired, orthopedically impaired, multihandicapped, visually impaired, and other health impaired. The best arrangement for providing instruction to the handicapped child is shown in Diagram 9.1, whereby a number of school personnel assist the classroom teacher.

INDIVIDUALIZED EDUCATION PROGRAM

One of the main provisions of PL 94-142 is to create an individualized Education Program (IEP) for each mainstreamed student. The IEP must

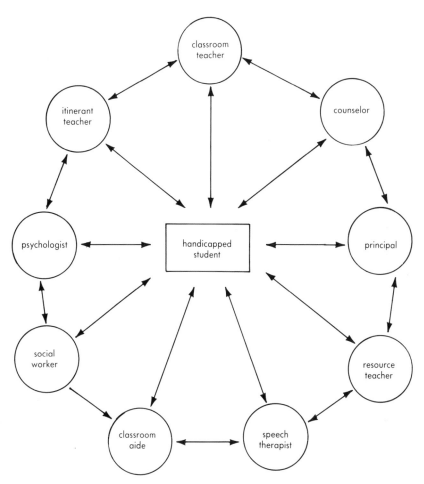

Diagram 9.1 Involvement by school personnel in mainstreaming.

be prepared at least once a year with the cooperation of the pertinent school personnel and the parents of the students. It is stated in long-range goals rather than in short-term lesson plans; however, the goals are very important as teachers construct their daily plans for the student. A sample blank form of an IEP is shown in Figure 9.1.

PLANS DERIVED FROM IEPs

Whereas lesson plans for a regular classroom are generally made for use with the entire class, lesson plans for a handicapped child cannot be carried out in the same way. Wood and Miederhoff (1988) state that lesson

Yorktown Central School District

198_-8_ Data

Student's Name _____ Last _____ First _____

IEP Year 198_-8_
Originating Teacher: _____
School: _____

Home District: _____ Date of Birth ___/___/___
Name of Parent or Guardian: _____ Home Phone: _____
Home Address: _____

Check Res. Room ☐ Spec. Class ☐ Itin. ☐ Res. Room ☐ Spec. Class ☐ Itin. ☐

Zip _____

EDUCATIONAL TESTING DATA

	Test Name	Score	Date Given
Reading Scores: Incoming			
Math Scores: Incoming			

Instructional Level of Materials Used
Incoming (Spring) READING _____
Incoming (Spring) MATH _____

I.Q. Test Data: _____ Test Name _____
Verbal _____ Performance _____ Full Scale _____
I.Q. _____ I.Q. _____ I.Q. _____
Given By: _____ Date: _____

Retest Data: _____ Test Name _____
Verbal _____ Performance _____ Full Scale _____
I.Q. _____ I.Q. _____ I.Q. _____
Given By: _____ Date: _____

Other Test Data: | Test Name | Score | Date Given |

	Test	Score	Date
Math Scores: End of Year			
Reading Scores: End of Year			

Instructional Level of Materials Used
End of year READING _____
End of year MATH _____

MEETING DATA

SPECIAL STRENGTHS
(NOTE: Include comments for both)

WEAKNESSES
Academic and Personal/Social Areas)

Spring Meeting, 19___ :
Date: _____
Location: _____
Attending: _____ Title or Relation

Early Fall Meeting, 19___ :
Date: _____
Location: _____
Attending: _____ Title or Relation

Spring (Final) Meeting, 19___ :
Date: _____
Location: _____
Attending: _____ Title or Relation

Recommended Placement for the Fall: _____

Other student information: _____

Describe extent to which student will be participating in regular school programs: _____

Relevant medical information: _____

(Student's File Copy)

Figure 9.1 Individualized education plan [taken from *Mainstreaming in the Social Studies*, NCSS Bulletin No. 62, by John and Myra Herlihy, eds., pp. 28, 29].

plans must be adapted in three ways before they are suitable for the mainstreamed student:

(1) *Adapt the Teaching Mode*
Select the most appropriate method of teaching from the four major categories: (a) expository mode, e.g., lecture; (b) inquiry mode, e.g., asking questions; (c) demonstration mode, e.g., modeling; and (d) activity mode, e.g., role-playing.

(2) *Adapt the Media*
Choose the proper media (bulletin board, cassette tapes, etc.) that compensate for the particular learning difficulty of the student.

(3) *Adapt the Content Format*
Adjust the difficulty of the content as it appears in textbooks, worksheets, blackboard materials, demonstrations, etc. This can be done by breaking a large task down into several smaller segments.

Although the special education teacher or the resource room teacher assumes much of the responsibility for educating the handicapped student, the regular classroom teacher is also required to provide instruction to the student. What can an administrator recommend to a social studies classroom teacher to address the various needs of mainstreamed students?

Students with Visual Impairments

Visual impairments range from partially sighted to blind. Following are some teaching suggestions for this range:

(1) Use auditory substitutes for reading. Put readings on tapes.

(2) Use braille textbooks and readings.

(3) Prepare assignments on large-print typewriters.

(4) Call students by name when responding to raised hands.

(5) Seat partially sighted students near the blackboard.

(6) Team visually impaired students with sighted partners on field trips and studies of the local community.

(7) Use interviewing as a data-gathering technique.

(8) Use class discussion frequently.

(9) Read aloud all statements as they are being written on the blackboard.

(10) Limit the amount of reading required of partially sighted students. Vary the use of audio tapes with large-print materials to reduce fatigue.

(11) Reduce extraneous classroom noise. Partially sighted and blind students rely on listening as an important avenue of learning.

(12) Provide students with tactile charts, graphs, and diagrams where possible. When using charts, graphs, or diagrams for which no tactile equivalents are available, make certain to describe each thoroughly.

(13) Allow students using braille more time for note taking.

(14) Provide braille or taped tests. Visually impaired students will likely require additional time to answer tests.

(15) Provide adequate shelving in the classroom for each visually impaired student. Braille and large print books require more desk space than most reading materials. Students will need to organize their materials carefully so that they have easy access to them. Allow visually impaired students more time to get ready for the lesson.

(16) Keep all classroom doors either completely opened or completely closed. Partially opened doors are dangerous to visually impaired students.

(17) When the physical arrangement of the classroom is changed, orient the student to the changes (Curtis, 1982, 12–13).

Students with Mental Retardation

Mental retardation encompasses several categories. Mildly retarded (educable) is associated with IQs between 52–67. Moderately retarded (trainable) is associated with IQs between 36–51. Severely retarded (custodial) involves students with IQs of 35 or below. Following are some social studies classroom teaching suggestions for mentally retarded students:

(1) Use concrete examples when introducing new ideas.

(2) Provide students with opportunities to generalize learning from the classroom to the world outside.

(3) Help students to see analogous situations.

(4) Help students to understand why the particular learning is important to them.

(5) Provide for frequent reviews of knowledge and for numerous opportunities to practice skills.

(6) Create opportunities for verbal expression.

(7) Use interesting materials written at the students' reading levels.

(8) Use group experiences as much as possible.

(9) Use visual aids to supplement verbal instruction.

(10) Praise work that is well done.

(11) Allow the mentally handicapped students to work on shorter and less difficult assignments than the other students (Curtis, 1982, 14).

Students with Physical Motor Impairments

Some of the most common physical disabilities include cerebral palsy, epilepsy, spina bifida, amputation, and muscular dystrophy.

Some teaching suggestions follow:

(1) Eliminate physical barriers in the classroom and school to permit student movement to all areas of the classroom and to areas such as the library.

(2) Use nondisabled student aides for note taking, library research, etc.

(3) Shorten or modify activities for physically impaired students to prevent failure.

(4) Arrange for special equipment such as electric typewriters, language boards, page turners, pencil holders, and stand-up tables.

(5) Allow students with difficult speech adequate time to comment or to respond to questions. Do not avoid asking these students questions because you think it will cause them to be embarrassed.

(6) Assign nondisabled students to assist where needed on trips into the community (Curtis, 1982, 14–15).

Students with Hearing Impairments

Hearing impairments extend from mild to deaf. Following are some teaching suggestions for this range:

(1) Seat student at the front of the classroom where the teacher's face can be easily observed.

(2) The teacher and members of the class should face the hearing-impaired student when they are speaking.

(3) Teacher and students should talk at the normal rate, neither too fast nor too slow.

(4) During the presentation of the lesson, the teacher should not walk and talk at the same time.

(5) Encourage nondisabled students to speak in sentences; single words are difficult to lip-read.

(6) Reduce environmental noise as much as possible; such noise masks speech sounds.

(7) Use visual aids freely.

(8) Write all assignments on the blackboard; do not give verbal instructions only.

(9) Provide the hearing-impaired students with an outline of the class discussion and lesson ahead of time.

(10) Notes on a discussion can be taken by a nonhandicapped student.

(11) Provide simplified reading materials.

(12) Provide exercises for vocabulary building (Curtis, 1982, 15).

The following plan reveals how a lesson can be arranged for use with hearing-impaired students. It is an example of induction teaching and contains some of the suggestions mentioned earlier by Curtis (1982) and Wood and Miederhoff (1988).

MIDDLE GRADE LESSON PLAN

Topic: **Culture Borrowing**

Grade: **6th**

Date: **October 5, 1:45–2:30**

I. *Purpose*: **tells what a student will learn**

At the end of the lesson, the students will be able to identify the culture origin of three commonplace substances, e.g., glass, coffee, and cotton.

After experiencing this lesson on culture borrowing, students will be able to identify, verbally or in written form, three aspects of their lives that have been directly influenced by other cultures.

At the end of this lesson, students will be able to speculate on possible ways the above aspects found their way into our culture.

II. *Motivation*: **tells how to begin the day's lesson**

Review with the class the unit they have just concluded regarding three fairly isolated cultures. Then tell them that they are going to look at what happens when cultures make contact with each other.

III. *Development*: **tells how to conduct the day's lesson**

The teacher presents a display to the class of the following items: calendar, drinking glass, cotton shirt, loose tea, coffee beans, paper, telephone, and light bulb (using real objects, not pictures). Criterial attributes of the concept of "cultural borrowing" are embedded in the examples; some of the items are nonexamples.

Students analyze the items and identify (induce) elements they have in common (criterial attributes). The teacher also asks students to determine what the items do not have in common. The students are then asked to consider the origin of the items.

Students group examples according to criterial attributes, i.e., they put the calendar, drinking glass, shirt, tea, coffee, and paper in one group; they put the light bulb and telephone in another group.

The students label the first group of items "Borrowed from Other Cultures" and the second group "From Our Culture." The teacher shows on a map the place of origin of the borrowed items.

Students generate additional examples and nonexamples. Some aspects from their own life-styles that have been borrowed from other cultures could be pizza, chow mein, and Beatles' music.

IV. *Conclusion*: **tells how to close or evaluate the day's lesson**

The teacher asks the following questions:

(1) What is there in your own daily life that has been borrowed from another culture?

(2) Can you identify the cultural origins of glass, cotton, and coffee?

(3) How do you think some of these items found their way into our culture?

Given a list of "borrowed items," a symbol for each time, and a mimeographed copy of a world map with countries delineated, the student will draw the symbol of the "borrowed item" on the map in the country of its origin.

There will be a brief review of the items used in day-to-day life that have been borrowed from other cultures and the ways in which these items found their way into our culture.

V. *Materials*: **tells what is needed for the day's lesson**

Calendar, drinking glass, cotton shirt, loose tea, coffee beans, paper, telephone, light bulb; mimeographed copies of world map.

Adaptations for Hearing-Impaired Students:

(a) When speaking to the class

(1) Speak in a voice that is natural in pace and volume. Do not over-enunciate words; this complicates lipreading.

(2) Always face the class when speaking. Do not speak while writing on the board or pointing out things on the map.

(3) Do not pace while speaking to the class; this also complicates lipreading.

(4) Repeat all questions asked by other class members.

(b) Visual aids

(1) It is helpful to list key words on the board. For example, in the above lesson, it would be helpful to list the borrowed items and their countries of origin on the board after showing them on the map.

(2) Provide a script or outline of unsubtitled filmstrips or movies to hearing-impaired students. They can derive much more meaning from these visual aids if they know the context or subject matter to be covered.

(c) Group work

Since receiving information while in a group is more difficult for hearing-impaired students than receiving information by interacting with someone on a one-to-one basis, keep the groups small. This adaptation applies to Part III: Development (above).

(d) General

(1) Consult with hearing-impaired students periodically to make sure that the adaptations are adequate and that the students are getting all the necessary information.

(2) Don't make it obvious to the whole class that you are making adaptations for your hearing-impaired students. Your subtlety and tact in this area will do much to help the student feel more comfortable and part of the class.

(e) Delivery systems

(1) Itinerant teachers of the hearing impaired

(2) Resource room and resource teachers

(3) Preplanning with ancillary team and generation of IEP, and timetable of support materials and services throughout the year

Note: The above plan is adapted from the plan created by Michele M. Paoletti and which appeared in Mainstreaming in the Social Studies, edited by John Herlihy and Myra Herlihy. NCSS Bulletin 62, pp. 56–57 (1980).

GIFTED AND TALENTED STUDENTS

Gifted and talented students are not covered by federal legislation as are the handicapped, but they nevertheless need to be attended to with the same degree of importance. Giftedness can be defined not only by the criterion of performance on IQ tests, but also by talent in the areas of leadership, specific academics, performing, visual arts, and creativity. Terman and Merrill classify students with IQs equal to or greater than 120 as gifted; this includes about 13 percent of the population.

One model for organizing instruction for the gifted has been devised by Renzulli (1977). This model, called the Enrichment Triad Model, is illustrated in Diagram 9.2.

Type I activities are exploratory, i.e., they provoke curiosity, stimulate interest, or identify contradictions. Speakers, field trips, films, pictures, interest centers, etc., can provide the motivation in this category. Type II

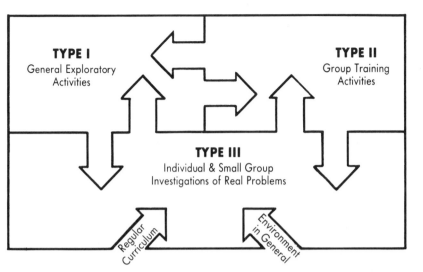

Diagram 9.2 The enrichment triad model [from *The Enrichment Triad Model*, Joseph Renzulli, Creative Learning Press, Mansfield Center, CT, p. 14 (1977)].

activities provide group training activities, e.g., higher level thinking strategies, brainstorming, research skills, or creative writing. Type III activities call for investigation of real problems, whereby students work individually or in small groups to devise a product or a solution to the question.

Some general suggestions for teaching gifted children have been supplied by Jarolimek (1986):

(1) Provide a generous amount of challenging reading material that will allow them to read for informational purposes.

(2) Plan learning activities that call for problem solving, making logical associations, making logical deductions, and making generalizations.

(3) Give them many opportunities to plan their own work; allow for a considerable amount of individual initiative, commensurate with their degree of maturity.

(4) Provide for individual study and research. This should include use of the library and references, as well as note keeping, outlining, summarizing, and reporting.

(5) Expect and encourage much originality in self-expression—in discussions, dramatizations, projects, and activities.

(6) Recognize that they have less need for extended firsthand and con-

crete experiences than do slow learning or average learning children because they are able to work with abstractions more easily, see associations and relationships more quickly, and have quicker reaction times.

(7) Encourage these children to develop self-evaluative skills; they are generally capable of effectively evaluating their own work.

(8) Give them many opportunities for leadership responsibilities. Provide occasions for gifted children to use their talents in helping slower learning children on a tutorial basis. In some schools children of the intermediate grades with high intellectual abilities also work with primary-grade children.

(9) Remember that gifted children have many of the common needs of all children. Although it is true that they are ordinarily accelerated in other aspects of their development as well, their physical growth, muscular coordination, social development, and emotional stability cannot be equated with their rate of growth in mental development.

(10) The complete acceptance by the teacher of the high intellectual abilities of gifted children is essential to planning an effective program for them. The teacher who sees gifted children as a threat becomes defensive and is unable to work with them satisfactorily (pp. 131–132).

INDIVIDUALIZING INSTRUCTION

Contrary to what is implied by the name, "individualizing instruction" does not require that a teacher work one-on-one with a student; this practice is called tutoring. Individualizing instruction simply means that a teacher makes a lesson personally meaningful for the child. Since it is impossible for a teacher to work with every student in the classroom on a one-to-one basis all the time, social studies instruction usually takes on the form of group work. Using group work with one-to-one attention in order to individualize instruction is not a problem, as long as the group lesson attends to the needs of all the students.

Jarolimek (1986, 111–125) presents four approaches that can be used by a teacher to individualize instruction. The first is management approaches, which includes the following aspects:

(1) Room environment—arranging the classroom so that students can conveniently move around in it and locate resources in it

(2) Learner groups—frequently establish temporary, task-oriented groups, sometimes called student teaming (four- or five-member teams). The jigsaw method is characterized by each member of a

learning group completing a portion of the larger assignment. Unlike reading groups, these cooperative learning groups should often be formed with students of unequal abilities. Varied interests and abilities enable a group to complete a social studies project.

(3) Scheduling—allow students to work at their own pace. Some students might need a longer period of time to complete an assignment.

The second approach described by Jarolimek is multimedia approaches. This includes:

(1) Social studies reading materials
(2) Social studies learning kits and packages, which contain a pretest, a listing of the skill activities to be done by the student, and an evaluatory procedure after the work is completed
(3) Learning centers—an area of the classroom set aside for social studies activities and resources, with directions telling the pupils what to do

The third approach to individualizing instruction is performance-based approaches, exemplified by the following:

(1) Learner contracts—laying out work that the student agrees to do (see Figure 9.2 for an example)
(2) Special assignment—a project to accommodate the special interests or talents of a student

---

AN AGREEMENT

As my contribution to the unit, OUR TOWN, I agree to do the project or projects checked:

_____ 1. Interview a person who has lived here a long time.

_____ 2. Conduct a survey of old buildings in our town.

_____ 3. Write a true story about our town.

_____ 4. Write a short play about our town.

_____ 5. Work on a mural with _____
(Name other children)

_____ 6. Paint a picture of something in our town.

_____ 7. Prepare a TV program script about our town.

_____ 8. Do an original activity of my own: _____

_____

Today's date: _____   _____
                                                Student
Due date: _____   _____
                                                Teacher

Figure 9.2 A sample learning contract [taken from p. 122 of *Social Studies in Elementary Education, 7th ed.*, by John Jarolimek, Macmillan, NY (1986)]. Reprinted with permission of Macmillan.

(3) Individualized education program—for mainstreamed students
(4) Mastery learning based on behavioral objectives—using performance-based procedures (e.g., minimum competency tests) to determine if students have mastered specific objectives—but adjusting the time conditions or teaching method for certain students

The fourth approach by Jarolimek is creative or activity-based approaches, which enables a student to express herself individually, e.g., constructing a relief map, performing a folk music selection, making popsicle stick puppets, or reenacting the signing of the Declaration of Independence.

From the preceding paragraphs, it can be determined that several student attributes must be considered by a teacher when individualizing: interests, abilities, and talents. There is one other consideration: the learning style of the student.

Learning Style

Each student has a preferred way (or style) of learning made up of cognitive, affective, and physiological factors. Rita and Kenneth Dunn (1978) have separated "style" into eighteen components:

Environmental

1. Sound (noisy or quiet)
2. Light (bright or dark)
3. Temperature (warm or cool)
4. Design (hard chair or easy chair; sit at desk or lie on floor)

Emotional

5. Motivation (self-motivator or needs encouragement)
6. Persistence (work for long periods or short periods)
7. Responsibility (follows through on task or needs supervision)
8. Structure (refers to how well a student is able to work within specific rules established for completing an assignment)

Sociological

9. Self-oriented
10. Colleague-oriented
11. Authority-oriented
12. Pair-oriented
13. Team-oriented
14. Varied

Physical

15. Perceptual (visual, auditory, kinesthetic)
16. Intake (proper nourishment, health, etc.)
17. Time (morning or night)
18. Mobility (stationary or moving about)

The Dunns have concluded that students can single out their own learning styles and that a student who is taught in a manner consistent with her preferred learning style will perform better than when taught through a less desirable learning style. The 100-item Learning Style Inventory (LSI) can be self-administered by intermediate or middle grade students. Observation by an educator can determine the dominant learning style for primary students who are too young to complete the LSI. A primary version of the LSI is now available by contacting the following address:

Center for the Study of Learning and Teaching Styles
St. John's University
Grand Central Parkway and Utopia Parkway
New York, NY 11439

Other authorities have designed instruments to measure learning styles. The Transaction Ability Inventory (Gregorc, 1979) is designed for junior high students (and older). It looks at concrete vs. abstract and random vs. sequential styles of learning.

Kolb's (1984) Experiential Learning Model identifies four major learning styles: convergent, divergent, assimilation, and accommodative.

Much attention has been given in recent years to left-brain/right-brain learning. Some researchers (Springer and Deutsch, 1981) have made distinctions between the functions of the two halves of the brain, maintaining that students with a leftward bias favor the right hemisphere, while those with a rightward bias favor the left hemisphere.

Since there is still speculation as to how valid the learning influences of the two halves of the brain are, social studies educators should arrange instruction so as to have a flexible learning environment in the classroom—providing alternatives for students who do not seem to respond to a particular mode of instruction. For example, communicate both verbally (left brain) and nonverbally (right brain) with the students. Establish some activities that require a student to proceed analytically (left brain) in a step-by-step fashion and some activities that require a student to perceive synthetically (right brain), i.e., to see the "whole picture."

THINKING SKILLS

Nearly all school districts would claim that one of their philosophical goals is to teach their students to be thinking individuals. When it comes down to specifying what is meant by "thinking skills," the definitions can be somewhat elusive. We need to view "thinking" as a comprehensive term with many components. Presseisen (1986) discusses a number of current researchers and their approaches to teaching thinking:

(1) Robert Sternberg emphasizes information processing.

(2) Robert Ennis emphasizes critical thinking.

(3) Matthew Lipman stresses philosophy and reasoning.

(4) Edward deBono underscores direct teaching of creativity as a base for thinking.

(5) David Perkins accentuates product development from creative thinking.

(6) Reuven Feuerstein underlines the importance of the teacher in thinking instruction.

(7) Arthur Whimbey advocates a holistic orientation to learning and students' explanations of their own thinking.

(8) Raymond Nickerson stresses basic abilities that comprise thinking.

(9) Barry Beyer focuses on the processes that are important in teaching thinking.

Teaching pupils how to think fulfills a need that every student has. Barry Beyer has written extensively in the area of social studies and thinking. His components of this broad term are shown in Chart 9.1. Notice that Beyer does not list "creative thinking" as a discrete operation because it is actually performed along with many of the other thinking operations.

Shown below are examples of how to teach some of the skills shown in the chart.

Problem solving: Present a sixth grade class with pairs of cities. Ask them to determine the route that would

1. General thinking strategies
   A. Problem solving
      (1) Recognize a problem
      (2) Represent the problem
      (3) Devise/choose solution plan
      (4) Execute the plan
      (5) Evaluate the solution
   B. Decision making
      (1) Define the goal
      (2) Identify alternatives
      (3) Analyze alternatives
      (4) Rank alternatives
      (5) Judge highest ranked alternatives
      (6) Choose "best" alternatives
   C. Conceptualizing
      (1) Identify examples
      (2) Identify common attributes
      (3) Classify attributes
      (4) Interrelate categories of attributes
      (5) Identify additional examples/nonexamples
      (6) Modify concept attributes/structure

2. Critical thinking skills
   A. Distinguishing between verifiable facts and value claims
   B. Distinguishing relevant from irrelevant information, claims, or reasons
   C. Determining the factual accuracy of a statement
   D. Determining the credibility of a source
   E. Identifying ambiguous claims or arguments
   F. Identifying unstated assumptions
   G. Detecting bias
   H. Identifying logical fallacies
   I. Recognizing logical inconsistencies in a line of reasoning
   J. Determining the strength of an argument or a claim

3. Microthinking skills
   A. Information processing
      (1) Recall
      (2) Translation
      (3) Interpretation
      (4) Extrapolation
      (5) Application
      (6) Analysis (compare, contrast, classify, seriate, etc.)
      (7) Synthesis
      (8) Evaluation
   B. Reasoning
      (1) Inductive
      (2) Deductive
      (3) Analogical

Chart 9.1 Cognitive or thinking operations. [This chart is derived from p. 27 of Barry Beyer, *Practical Strategies for the Teaching of Thinking*, Allyn & Bacon, Boston, MA (1987)]. Reprinted with permission.

satisfy both of the following conditions: (1) least expensive travel costs and (2) shortest time for the trip.

Decision making: The second grade class feels that they do not get enough time at the interest centers in the room. Encourage them to decide on a way to arrange a schedule so that everyone will get a turn during the week.

Critical thinking: Present students with an advertisement for a product or service from a newspaper. Students should pick out ambiguous claims.

Critical thinking: Use a political cartoon, such as the

Affixing blame for our economic problems.

Figure 9.3 Cartoon [Paul Conrad © 1982, Los Angeles Times. Reprinted with permission, Los Angeles Times Syndicate].

one in Figure 9.3, to have students determine if the impression is accurate that our economic problems trace back to previous generations, identify some unstated assumptions about the need not to accept responsibility for one's actions, and conclude what the logical result will be if the line of reasoning in the cartoon is accepted.

The following lesson plan demonstrates how the thinking strategy of "conceptualizing" can be taught. The students are asked to (1) identify examples of things children can do, (2) identify common attributes of these examples, (3) classify these attributes, (4) interrelate categories of these attributes, and (5) identify additional examples/nonexamples.

EARLY ELEMENTARY LESSON PLAN

Topic: **Things We Have Learned to Do: Alike and Different**

Grade: **2nd**

Date: **November 15, 10:30–11:00**

I. *Purpose*: **tells what a student will learn**

Students will (1) classify a set of student-drawn pictures into at least two different groups, (2) state at least one attribute common to the pictures in each group, (3) tell at least one way in which the pictures in one group are different from those in the other group, (4) identify a label for each group that reflects what the pictures in the group have in common, and (5) tell one thing that all the pictures have in common.

II. *Motivation*: **tells how to begin the day's lesson**

The teacher should ask the children to think for a minute about a pet that has been trained to do something (e.g., a dog that sits up for food, a parakeet that talks). This could be a pet they own or one owned by somebody else that they have heard about. Give time for some of the students to discuss the pets.

III. *Development*: **tells how to conduct the day's lesson**

Ask the students to draw a picture showing something they know how to do (e.g., brush their teeth). Pass out the necessary materials for this and provide time for students to complete their pictures.

Ask some of the students to show the pictures to the class and briefly describe what they show. Then select about seven pictures and use masking tape to affix them to the chalkboard. Point to each picture and reiterate what it shows.

Ask students to think of ways in which some of the pictures are alike and to explain their reasoning. Aim at forming at least two different groups of pictures. As a group of pictures is identified, move the pictures from their original location and reaffix and cluster them.

Ask students to think of a name for each group, and print it above each cluster of pictures. Use prompting questions as needed.

Ask if students can think of a name that will apply to *all* the pictures. Print it above the group names. Emphasize the main concept label (things we have learned to do) and the subgroup labels (at home, at school). Also, point out how each picture illustrates the concept.

IV. *Conclusion*: **tells how to close or evaluate the day's lesson**

Provide additional practice by calling on several students and having each tell in which category his or her picture belongs and why.

V. *Materials*: **tells what is needed for the day's lesson**

Drawing supplies.

Note: This plan is adapted from a lesson plan appearing on pp. 220–221 of *Elementary and Middle School Social Studies* by David Naylor and Richard Diem. New York:Random House (1987).

HOW TO TEACH THINKING SKILLS

Beyer (1983) suggests that thinking skills should be taught with the following four principles in mind:

(1) Skills should be taught systematically. Instruction should proceed through the stages of readiness, introduction, reinforcement, and extension.

(2) Instruction should be direct. The teacher should initially describe an example of the skill or have the students actually do it, followed by explaining the specific steps and rules for executing the skill. Next, the teacher should demonstrate how the skill works with the content being studied, after which he gives the students an opportunity to apply the skill procedures to similar data. Finally, the students are asked to state and explain the basic components of the skill as they have used them.

(3) Instruction should be integrated. A thinking skill should not be taught in isolation but should be integrated with the subject matter and other skills.

(4) Instruction should be developmental. The teaching of thinking skills

should advance in complexity along with the movement of the child from grade to grade.

QUESTIONING

Oral questions directed by a teacher toward students in the class have the potential for arousing the curiosity of each pupil and drawing each pupil into the lesson; however, the questions must be skillfully phrased and delivered.

Selecting Questions

It is important to select the right question. All of the following questions about George Washington could be asked, but which one is most appropriate?

- What years did George Washington serve as President of the United States?
- What background did George Washington have to qualify him to be president of the United States?
- How did George Washington perform differently as president of the United States in his second term compared with his first term?

The first of the three questions merely asks for information that a student can look up in the appendix of a textbook. The second question requires that a student have read something about Washington's life prior to 1789. The third demands that a student analytically examine the actions of Washington.

Probably the most often used system to select questions is based upon the categories developed by Benjamin Bloom and others (1956). His hierarchy extends from simple (knowledge) to complex (evaluation):

(a) *Knowledge* (recall or memory of information)
Example: What is the capital of Egypt?

(b) *Comprehension* (understanding of information)
Example: What are some reasons for Egypt's success in growing cotton?

(c) *Application* (using information in a new situation)
Example: Since you have had practice in using bar graphs, what is the value of Egypt's cotton exports shown on this graph?

(d) *Analysis* (breaking down a situation into component parts)
Example: What are some reasons why the growing of cotton is an important part of the Egyptian economy?

(e) *Synthesis* (putting together elements to form a whole)
   Example: What do you think would happen to Egypt's agriculture if it had more rainfall throughout the country?
(f) *Evaluation* (making judgments)
   Example: What region of Egypt do you consider to be the most essential to its agricultural production?

Phrasing Questions

The following tips can help in the proper wording of a question:

(1) Be succinct. Avoid long, involuted questions.
(2) Be clear. Phrase the question so that the student has a definite notion of what you intend.
(3) Avoid multiple questions. Ask one question, get an answer, and proceed to the next question. Don't piggyback several questions as one, for this confuses students.
(4) Ask the question and then call on a student, not vice versa. By asking the question first, all students in the class realize they could be called upon to answer.
(5) Be cautious about dead-end questions (ones that result in a "Yes" or "No" answer). Phrase questions so that a student must give a lengthier, more thoughtful response.
(6) After phrasing a question, wait four or five seconds before calling on a student. This allows the pupils time to formulate a response.

An administrator who is asked for help in selecting and phrasing questions (from Bloom's taxonomy) representing the range from simple to complex might concentrate on key words shown in Chart 9.2.

Educators can use questioning as an avenue to reach the individual needs of pupils. A teacher should appraise his own behavior to make sure that (1) questions are asked covering a variety of thinking levels; (2) follow-up, or probing, is done to seek clarification of a student's answer; and (3) an atmosphere is created in the room to encourage students to respond to questions that are asked.

ASSISTANCE POINTS

Questions for Action for the Administrator

1. Look at Diagram 9.1. As an administrator, what is your responsibility in the education of a student who is mainstreamed?

Knowledge		
define	list	name
identify	state	tell
Comprehension		
explain	predict	distinguish
give an example of	rearrange	rephrase
Application		
apply	build	construct
plan	develop	demonstrate
Analysis		
analyze	classify	compare
contrast	detect	categorize
Synthesis		
create	develop	put together
formulate	propose	make up
Evaluation		
select	judge	decide
what do you consider	evaluate	choose

Chart 9.2 Key words in asking questions.

2. What are some critical thinking skills which can be accomplished by all exceptional students who are either gifted or handicapped?

3. Assume some of the teachers have come to you to request some information on learning styles. To fulfill their request, obtain one of the learning style inventories, e.g., Dunn's "Learning Style Inventory." Prepare an in-service session on its use for your teachers.

4. Assume that a student has been referred because of visual impairment and has had an IEP prepared by the appropriate people. What would you look for during a social studies lesson which would indicate that the teacher is trying to take into account that student's needs?

Names and Addresses of Professional Organizations

Below are some addresses and resources that can be of help to an educator who needs assistance in meeting the special needs of students:

1. The Council for Exceptional Children
   1920 Association Drive
   Reston, VA 22091-1589
   (The CEC publishes *Exceptional Children, Journal of the Division for Early Childhood*, and *Teaching Exceptional Children*.)

2. The Creative Education Foundation, Inc.
   1050 Union Road
   Buffalo, NY 14224
   (This organization publishes the *Journal of Creative Behavior*.)

3. PRO-ED
   8700 School Creek Blvd.
   Austin, TX 78758-6897
   (This organization publishes *Journal of Special Education, Journal of Learning Disabilities, Remedial and Special Education, Topics in Early Childhood Special Education, Academic Therapy*, and *Focus on Autistic Behavior*.)

4. American Printing House for the Blind
   1839 Frankfort Avenue
   Louisville, KY 40206
   (The APHB has "talking books," taped versions of social studies texts, plastic landform models, large raised relief maps of each continent, etc.)

5. Captioned Films for the Deaf
   Special Office for Materials Distribution
   Indiana University Audiovisual Center
   Bloomington, IN 47401

6. Philosophy for Children
   c/o Matthew Lipman
   Montclair State University
   Upper Montclair, NJ 07043
   (This program for gifted students develops logical reasoning skills for grades K–12.)

7. National Association for Gifted Children
   4175 Lovell Rd.
   Circle Pines, MN 55014
   (The NAGC publishes the journal *Gifted Child Quarterly*.)

Research about Special Needs: Implications for Educators

Breiter (1987) surveyed school districts in the state of Iowa to determine some of the characteristics of Talented and Gifted (TAG) programs. The most numerous activities for elementary grades are listed below with the most often reported appearing at the top of the list:

Individual independent study (e.g., The Bermuda Triangle, The White House, Aztecs, Social Concerns, Everglades or Neverglades)

Units (e.g., Money and Banking, Flight, Family Roots, Transportation of the Future, Juvenile Law)

History Day participation

Group project/study (e.g., Statue of Liberty, Pioneer Life, Election, Presidents, Seven Wonders of the World)

Miscellaneous

Omnibus units, which rely on trained volunteers (e.g., The Ancients, Anthropology, Famous Cities, The Law, City Planning)

Classes/courses for GT students

Create-a-country

Community exploration, local history

Problem solving

Writing trivia games

Biographical studies

Study and/or research skills

Simulations

Current events

Field trips

Developing a fair (e.g., medieval fair)

Expansion/extension of regular social studies units

Historical research

Minicourses

Oral history

Self-concept/social relationships

Computer work

REFERENCES

Beyer, Barry K. "Critical Thinking: What Is It?" *Social Education*, pp. 270–276 (April 1985).

Beyer, Barry K. *Practical Strategies for the Teaching of Thinking*. Boston, MA:Allyn and Bacon (1987).

Bloom, Benjamin et al. *Taxonomy of Educational Objectives, Handbook I: Cognitive Domain*. New York:David McKay (1956).

Brandhorst, Allan and Fred Splittgerber. "Social Studies and the Development of Thinking: The State of the Art," *Southern Social Studies Quarterly*, pp. 20–42 (Fall 1987).

Branson, Margaret S. "Critical Thinking Skills: A Continuum for Grades 3–12 in History/Social Science," *Social Studies Review*, pp. 24–32 (Winter 1986).

Breiter, Joan. "What's Happening for Gifted Children in the Social Studies," *Southern Social Studies Quarterly*, pp. 43–54 (Spring 1987).

Cornbleth, Catherine. "Using Questions in Social Studies," *How to Do It*, Notebook Series 2, No. 4. Washington, DC:National Council for the Social Studies (1977).

Costa, Arthur L. and Robert Marzano. "Teaching the Language of Thinking," *Educational Leadership*, pp. 29–33 (October 1987).

Curtis, Charles K. "Teaching Disabled Students in the Regular Social Studies Classroom," *The History and Social Science Teacher*, pp. 9–16 (Fall 1982).

Davis, Anita Price. "Individualizing Instruction in the Social Studies through Learning Centers and Contracts," *How to Do It*, Notebook Series 2, No. 11. Washington, DC:National Council for the Social Studies (1980).

deBono, Edward. "The Direct Teaching of Thinking as a Skill," *Kappan*, pp. 703–708 (June 1983).

Dunn, Rita and Kenneth Dunn. *Teaching Students through Their Individual Learning Styles*. Reston, VA:Reston Publishing (1978).

Ellis, Julia L. "Enriching Social Studies for Gifted Students or All Students: A Four-Component Framework," *The History and Social Science Teacher*, pp. 38–43 (Fall 1982).

Ennis, Robert H. "Critical Thinking and the Curriculum," *National Forum*, pp. 28–31 (Winter 1985).

Epstein, Charlotte. *Special Children in Regular Classrooms*. Reston, VA:Reston Publishing Co., Inc. (1984).

Feuerstein, Reuven. *Instrumental Enrichment*. Baltimore:University Park Press (1980).

Gregorc, Anthony F. "Learning/Teaching Styles: Their Nature and Effects," in *Student Learning Styles: Diagnosing and Prescribing Programs*. James W. Keefe, ed. Reston, VA:National Association of Secondary School Principals, pp. 19–26 (1979).

Heiman, Marcia and Joshua Slomianko. *Critical Thinking Skills*. Washington, DC:National Education Association (1985).

Herlihy, John G. and Myra T. Herlihy, eds. *Mainstreaming in the Social Studies*. Bulletin No. 62. Washington, DC:National Council for the Social Studies (1980).

Jarolimek, John. *Social Studies in Elementary Education, seventh edition*. New York: Macmillan (1986).

Keefe, James W. *Learning Style: Theory and Practice*. Reston, VA:National Association of Secondary School Principals (1987).

Kirk, Samuel and James J. Gallagher. *Educating Exceptional Children, 4th edition*. Boston, MA:Houghton Mifflin Co. (1983).

Kolb, David. *Experiential Learning: Experience as the Source of Learning and Development*. Englewood Cliffs, NJ:Prentice-Hall (1984).

Kneedler, Peter. "Testing Critical Thinking at Grade Eight," *Social Studies Review*, pp. 78–88 (Winter 1986).

Lipman, Matthew. "Philosophy for Children and Critical Thinking," *National Forum*, pp. 18–23 (Winter 1985).

Moskowitz, Fern C. "Strategies for Mainstreamed Students," *Academic Therapy*, pp. 541–547 (May 1988).

Naylor, David T. and Richard Diem. *Elementary and Middle School Social Studies*. New York:Random House (1987).

Nickerson, Raymond S. et al. *The Teaching of Thinking*. Hillsdale, NJ:Lawrence Erlbaum Associates (1985).

Ochoa, Anna S. and Susan K. Shuster. *Social Studies in the Mainstreamed Classroom*. Boulder, CO:ERIC Clearinghouse for Social Studies/Social Science Education, Social Science Education Consortium, Inc. (1980).

Paoletti, Michele M. "Culture Borrowing Lesson Plan," in *Mainstreaming in the Social Studies*. Bulletin No. 62. Washington, DC:National Council for the Social Studies, pp. 56, 57 (1980).

Paul, Richard W. "Critical Thinking and Social Studies," *Teaching K-8*, pp. 53–55 (October 1988).

Perkins, David N. "Creativity by Design," *Educational Leadership*, pp. 18–25 (September 1984).

Presseisen, Barbara Z. *Thinking Skills: Research and Practice*. Washington, DC:National Education Association (1986).

Priddy, Deborah R. "Mainstreaming Students with Disabilities," *Social Studies Review*, pp. 45–50 (Spring 1982).

Reyes, Donald J. "Critical Thinking in Elementary Social Studies Text Series," *The Social Studies*, pp. 151–154 (July/August 1986).

Renzulli, Joseph S. *The Enrichment Triad Model*. Mansfield, CT:Creative Learning Press (1977).

Ross, E. Wayne and Lynne M. Hannay. "Reconsidering Reflective Inquiry: The Role of Critical Theory in the Teaching of Social Studies," *Southern Social Studies Quarterly*, pp. 2–19 (Fall 1987).

Sanford, Howard. "Organizing and Presenting Social Studies Content in a Mainstreamed Class," in *Mainstreaming in the Social Studies*. Bulletin No. 62, edited by John Herlihy and Myra Herlihy. Washington, DC:National Council for the Social Studies, pp. 43–50 (1980).

Shaw, Terry, ed. *Teaching Handicapped Students Social Studies: A Resource Handbook for K-12 Teachers*. Washington, DC:National Education Association (1981).

Simms, Rochelle B. "Mildly Handicapped Students in the Social Studies Class: Facilitating Learning," *The Social Studies*, pp. 265–267 (November/December 1984).

Sisk, Dorothy. *Creative Teaching of the Gifted*. NY:McGraw-Hill (1987).

Springer, S. and G. Deutsch. *Left Brain, Right Brain*. San Francisco:W. H. Freeman (1981).

Sternberg, Robert J. "How Can We Teach Intelligence?" *Educational Leadership*, pp. 38–48 (September 1984).

Stiggins, Richard et al. *Measuring Thinking Skills in the Classroom, revised edition*. Washington, DC:National Education Association (1988).

Talbot, Jan. "The Assessment of Critical Thinking in History/Social Science through Writing," *Social Studies Review*, pp. 33–41 (Winter 1986).

Tannenbaum, Abraham J. *Gifted Children: Psychological and Educational Perspectives*. NY:Macmillan (1983).

Terman, L. M. and M. A. Merrill. *Stanford-Binet Intelligence Scales*. Boston, MA: Houghton Mifflin (1973).

Tuttle, Frederick, Jr. et al. *Program Design and Development for Gifted and Talented Students, 3rd edition*. Washington, DC:National Education Association (1988).

Walsh, Debbie and Richard W. Paul. *The Goal of Critical Thinking*. Washington, DC: American Federation of Teachers (1986).

Whimbey, Arthur and Jack Lochhead. *Problem Solving and Comprehension, 3rd edition*. Philadelphia:The Franklin Institute Press (1982).

Wilen, William W. *Questioning Skills, for Teachers, 2nd edition*. Washington, DC:National Education Association (1986).

Wood, Judy W. and Jennifer W. Miederhoff. "Adapting Lesson Plans for the Mainstreamed Student," *The Clearing House*, pp. 269–276 (February 1988).

Wright, Jill D. *Teaching the Gifted and Talented in the Middle School*. Washington, DC:National Education Association (1983).

10 | INSTRUCTIONAL MATERIALS: TEXTBOOKS TO TECHNOLOGY

Chapter Preview of Key Ideas

★ *Materials include print and nonprint items.*

★ *Textbooks are still the dominant form of instructional material in classrooms.*

★ *Textbooks need to be chosen according to established criteria.*

★ *Innovations in technology have resulted in accompanying changes in the materials that are available to social studies educators.*

★ *Computers are used for instruction and for management.*

★ *Computers allow students to interact with the software.*

★ *Resource persons bring the community into the classroom.*

★ *Television is a commonly found piece of equipment with the potential for reaching large numbers of students.*

★ *Graphics includes tables, graphs, charts, figures, diagrams, and cartoons.*

★ *Creative uses should be found for other frequently used audiovisual materials (e.g., films, slides, and transparencies).*

Social studies needs materials just as a home needs furniture, for without materials, social studies would not be usable by the students. There are a variety of materials that can be used in the classroom: textbooks, computers, resource persons, television, and other audiovisual or technological equipment. "The information revolution is changing the nature of what knowledge needs to be learned, who needs to learn it, who will provide it, and how it will be provided" (Rottman, 1987, 13).

247

TEXTBOOKS

Textbooks are omnipresent in the classroom. Survey results (Weis, 1978) show that in grades 4–12, 90 percent of the social studies classes use a textbook; in K–3 the figure is 65 percent. There are pitfalls in this widespread use, however. Elliott et al. (1985) identified six major problems with ten social studies series that they analyzed:

(1) The series were basals in name only, lacking grade-to-grade integration.

(2) The study of the United States was dominant, slighting international and cross-cultural understanding.

(3) Most series were similar in content, methodology, and scope and sequence.

(4) Many topics were covered superficially.

(5) Representations of women and minorities were unrealistic.

(6) Skill strands emphasized map and globe skills while other higher order thinking skills were relegated to occasional appearances in chapter and unit review exercises (pp. 23 and 24).

A local school district needs to evaluate textbooks carefully before making a selection. Textbook adoption committees should be created so that the views of teachers and administrators are taken into consideration. A textbook evaluation form should be used so that each member of the evaluation committee applies the same criteria. Administrators in the district should make every attempt to provide release time for the committee to do their work. Members "should not be forced to evaluate textbooks between their classes, late in the evening, or while they are supervising a lunchroom" (Farr and Tulley, 1985, 471).

Figure 10.1 (a checklist) shows how a social studies textbook can be evaluated using nine basic categories. The evaluator places a mark in the "Yes" column if the criterion is satisfied or in the "No" column if there is a serious deficiency. There is no point weighting each of the individual criteria, so the committee needs to judge the merit of the textbook by examining the total "Yes vs. No" relationships on the document.

Figure 10.1, Part VI lists as one of its considerations "The readability of the text is on an appropriate level for the students." Quite often a readability measure is applied to determine how readable a textbook is. One such measure is the Fry Graph, which appears in Figure 10.2. Essentially, it uses two factors of (1) number of sentences and (2) number of syllables in order to determine the difficulty of the book. An administrator can suggest the Fry Graph if a teacher wants a general idea of whether a book is going to be too difficult or too easy for a class.

		Yes	No

I. Scope and Sequence
    A. The text reflects a multidisciplinary or interdisiplinary view, i.e., it includes the disciplines of

		Yes	No
1. History	1		
2. Geography	2		
3. Political Science	3		
4. Economics	4		
5. Sociology	5		
6. Anthropology	6		
B. The text includes many of the topics that are in the local curriculum guide	B		

II. Written Material

		Yes	No
A. The text lists the authors and supplies some information about them	A		
B. The text uses a descriptive approach more than a "storybook" approach.	B		
C. The text is up-to-date (recent copyright).	C		
D. The text seems unbiased and fair in its treatment of issues	D		
F. The written material avoids sexual stereotypes.	E		
F. The written material reflects our multicultural society.	F		

III. Visual Material (Maps, Charts, Graphs, etc.)

		Yes	No
A. The text includes a sufficient number of maps and globes.	A		
B. The text presents a well-sequenced program of map and globe skills.	B		
C. The text uses ample color illustrations.	C		
D. The text's illustrations include a variety of photos and sketches.	D		
E. The photos appear sufficient in number, size, and clarity.	E		
F. Questions and captions accompany the pictures.	F		
G. The visual material avoids sexual bias and stereotypes.	G		
H. The visual material reflects our multicultural society.	H		
I. Graphs and charts are adequately represented.	I		

IV. Pupil Activities and Materials

		Yes	No
A. The text includes a variety of activities (e.g., objective questions, subjective questions, experiments, projects, etc.) located throughout the unit or chapter.	A		
B. These activities seem to extend and supplement the chapter or unit rather than merely ask the students to repeat information.	B		
C. A student workbook is available.	C		
D. Higher level questions, as well as lower level questions, are asked.	D		
E. Activities are provided to accommodate various abilities of students.	E		
F. Accompanying audiovisual materials are available for the students to use.	F		

Figure 10.1 Social studies textbook evaluation checklist.

249

		Yes	No
V. Philosophy			
A. The text's philosophy, or approach to teaching social studies, seems to fit that of the teacher.	A		
VI. Grade Placement			
A. The text's physical appearance would be appealing to the students.	A		
B. The text is of the appropriate size for the students.	B		
C. The books are durable with good binding.	C		
D. The readability of the text is on an appropriate level for the students.	D		
E. The style of writing would interest the students.	E		
F. The organization of the text is clear to the students, i.e., chapter titles, unit titles, subheadings, etc., are present.	F		
G. Study aids are present for the students:	G		
1. Glossary.	1		
2. Appendices.	1		
3. Difficult words in italics or bold print.	3		
4. Noted in margin are supplied to point out important ideas.	4		
VII. Teacher's Manual (TM)			
A. The location of the TM is convenient, i.e., in a separate book, interspersed with student pages, etc.	A		
B. Suggestions are provided for working with students of various abilities.	B		
C. Suggestions are given for preparing unit or lesson plans.	C		
D. Bibliographies suggesting additional written materials are present.	D		
E. Lists suggesting additional nonwritten materials are present.	E		
F. The TM includes reproductions of pages in the student's text.	F		
G. The TM is clear in format and is an effective guide for the instructional program.	G		
H. The TM allows the classroom teacher flexibility in deviating from the suggested procedures.	H		
I. Duplicating masters are available.	I		
J. Ideas for evaluating the students are available.	J		
VIII. Evaluation			
A. A test booklet is available.	A		
B. Suggestions for evaluating students are varied, e.g., essay items, multiple choice items, matching items, activities, etc.	B		

Figure 10.1 (continued). Social studies textbook evaluation checklist.

IX. Cost

A. Student edition.
B. Teacher's manual.
C. Student's workbook.
D. Test booklet.
E. Duplicating masters.
F. Accompanying kits.
G. Accompanying posters.
H. TM to test booklet.
I. TM to student workbook.
J. TM to duplicating masters.
K. TM to accompanying kits.
L. TM to accompanying posters.

	Yes	No
A		
B		
C		
D		
E		
F		
G		
H		
I		
J		
K		
L		

Figure 10.1 (continued). Social studies textbook evaluation checklist.

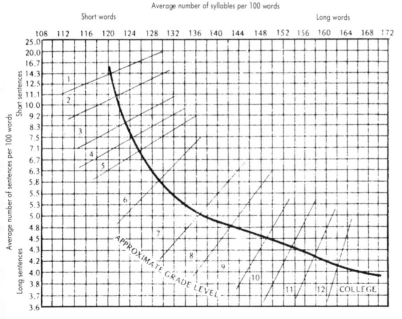

Figure 10.2 Fry readability graph [from Edward Fry, "A Readability Formula that Saves Time," *Journal of Reading*, Vol. 2, p. 577 (April 1968)].

251

COMPUTERS

More than any other subject in the curriculum, social studies relies upon vast quantities of information. Since it is impossible for an individual in the 1990s to locate and acquire all of the available information in ways that were once used, it is imperative that computers be utilized. Chart 10.1 displays some of the terminology that educators employ regarding computers.

Computers in the school can be used for instruction or for management. Depending on the budget, microcomputers can be placed either in each classroom or in a separate room so that teachers use them on a fixed schedule. Schug and Beery (1987, 340–343) present some popular approaches for locating computers in a school building.

(1) *Individual Classroom*

This is the ideal setting for a school district, whereby computers are placed in each classroom with a ratio of one machine for one to three pupils. Because of the high cost, this is usually not done; instead, one or two machines are placed in a room. This arrangement provides for the maximum flexibility in allowing students to use the computer.

(2) *Classroom Sets*

A school sometimes buys a set of fifteen to twenty computers. These are then placed on carts so that they can be moved from one classroom to another.

(3) *Computer Labs*

Some schools place about fifteen to twenty computers in a specified

---

Central processing unit (CPU) — the part of the computer that interprets information and executes instructions.

Disk — a recordlike magnetic storage device.

Hardware — the machinery of the computer.

Memory — the amount of words and numerical data that a computer can store (expressed by the symbol ''K'')

Microcomputer — a small computer.

Peripherals — equipment that accompanies the software and hardware, e.g., printer, a joy stick, a light pen, a mouse, a touch pad, etc.

Program — a set of instructions that tells the computer what to do.

Software — also called the program, which consists of directions written in a computer language.

Terminal — hardware which allows a person to interact with the computer, usually comprised of a monitor, keyboard, and disk drive.

Chart 10.1 Computer vocabulary.

room. Teachers then bring their classes to this room at certain times during the week. This arrangement makes it easier to care for the hardware, but its disadvantage lies in the limited flexibility for student use.

(4) *Resource Centers*
   This approach requires that a few computers be placed in a room such as the library, media center, etc. Students use the machines on a first-come, first-served basis.

Computer literacy needs to begin in the primary grades. Young children are able to acquire the basic skills to operate the computer, interact with software programs, and learn computer languages, such as Logo. Students need to go beyond this entry level by performing in the four basic approaches to computer-assisted instruction (CAI): drill and practice, tutorial lessons, simulations, and data bases.

Drill and practice programs present a series of questions to which students respond. The purpose is to have students review previously studied material, master skills, or memorize facts so that the computer gives feedback to the student after an answer is entered.

An example of a drill and practice program is "Regions of the United States" (distributed by Educational Activities, Inc., P.O. Box 392, Freeport, NY 11520). This program—designed for middle grade students and older—reviews the states and then asks students to identify the states and spell their names correctly. It also teaches the major cities, landforms, products, and climates of the regions of the United States.

Tutorial programs present new material to students in a step-by-step manner. Pauses a.e situated so that students are given a chance to demonstrate that they are learning the ideas being presented.

An example of a tutorial program is "Kids on Keys" (distributed by Spinnaker Software, One Kendall Square, Cambridge, MA 02139). This program—designed for early elementary students—helps pupils learn numbers, letters, and simple words while they become familiar with the keyboard.

Simulations enable the students to experience a situation that would be too dangerous or impractical in real life. The computer allows pupils to exert control over variables in such a way that decision-making and problem-solving skills are exercised.

"Oregon Trail" (distributed by Minnesota Educational Computing Consortium, 3490 Lexington Avenue North, St. Paul, MN 55126) is an example of a simulation for grades 3–6. Students travel west as pioneers in the 1800s. Along the way, they must purchase supplies, plan their route, and hunt for food.

A data base is a collection of information stored in a computer. Information which used to take hours, days, or even longer to accumulate is now available within seconds or minutes. Students can create their data bases (e.g., information on major cities, population, etc.) and store the information on their own disks, or they can use programs that contain commercially prepared data bases.

"Scholastic PFS: World Geography, Cultures, and Economic Databases" (distributed by Scholastic Software, 730 Broadway, New York, NY 10003) is for middle grade students and older. The program consists of three units, each one containing a separate data file on 100 countries, such as characteristics of the land, natural resources, religion, language, national budgets, and trade.

In addition to being used for social studies instruction, as described above, computers can be used for management purposes. Attendance can be recorded, grades can be maintained through electronic grade books, inventories of school equipment can be kept, crossword puzzles can be designed, correspondence can be written on word processing programs, graphics can be created, and tests can be assembled.

An example of a grade keeper is "Grade Averaging" (distributed by Educational Record Sales, 157 Chambers St., New York, NY 10007). It lays out a gradebook format and provides formulas to automatically compute total points, percentages, and averages.

"Crossword Magic" (distributed by Mindscape, P.O. Box 8334, Chicago, IL 60680) is a program teachers can use to design crossword puzzles.

"Print Shop" (distributed by Broderbund, 17 Paul Dr., San Rafeal, CA 94903) is a graphics program whereby the user can create signs, posters, letterheads, banners, etc. A variety of fonts, borders, and designs are possible.

"Joe Spreadsheet" (distributed by Scholastic, Inc., P.O. Box 7502, 2931 E. McCarty St., Jefferson City, MO 65102) is a program that allows an educator to arrange and manipulate information, organizing it to express new relationships. "Joe Spreadsheet" enables an administrator or teacher to sort data, perform calculations, and prepare graphs.

In 1985 California initiated the Technology in the Curriculum (TIC) Project for History-Social Science, which was a curriculum reform attempt "to help teachers make effective use of technology to improve instruction and learning in classrooms" (Eckenrod and Rockman, 1988, 361). The History-Social Science Resource Guide was distributed to 7,000 public schools in California; it contained descriptions of computer and video programs that could be matched with social studies curriculum at a particular grade level. The following lesson plan is adapted from one that was created at a TIC workshop.

MIDDLE GRADE LESSON PLAN

Topic: **Westward Movement**

Grade: **8th**

Date: **February 7, 1:00–2:30**

I. *Purpose*: **tells what a student will learn**

The student will accomplish the following:

(a) Learn to use geographic concepts and processes, including placename location, use of latitude and longitude, and identification of landforms.

(b) Learn about explorers and settlers of the West.

(c) Plan, collect, and use researched data.

(d) Work in decision-making groups effectively.

(e) Have empathy for the struggles of pioneer families.

II. *Motivation*: **tells how to begin the day's lesson**

Read to the class a few pages of *Little House on the Prairie*, by Laura Ingalls Wilder, to give them an idea of the hardships that early settlers faced.

Discuss with the class the following questions:

(a) Where is Oregon located on a map of the United States?

(b) Where did the Oregon Trail begin?

(c) Through what states did the Oregon Trail pass?

(d) About how many miles long was the trail?

(e) Why did people travel to the Oregon Territory?

(f) What kind of transportation was used for the trip?

(g) What kind of dangers would exist on the trip?

III. *Development*: **tells how to conduct the day's lesson**

Explain to the class that they will be using a program called "Oregon Trail." This is a simulation whereby they will need to make budgeting decisions prior to the trip and then resolve additional problems as they attempt to survive the trip.

Do a large class demonstration of part of the simulation. Then have the students work in teams of three to plan and make the trip. One can be the geographer, keeping the map record; one can be the diarist; one can be the treasurer. Each team should complete handouts 1 and 2 as they work through the simulation.

Handout #1: Oregon Trail Diary

Mileage Covered	Events Occurring	Results

Handout #2: Oregon Trail Treasurer's Report

Original Amount	Money Spent	Losses Along the Way	Money Spent at Forts

Final Balance: _____

IV. *Conclusion*: tells how to close or evaluate the day's lesson

After all teams have completed the program, they should compare their experiences.

V. *Materials*: tells what is needed for the day's lesson

Software: "Oregon Trail," MECC; Apple computers; monitors; copies of handouts for each student; copy of *Little House on the Prairie.*

Note: This lesson plan is adapted from ideas presented in "Using Technology to Teach the Westward Movement: A Model Unit/Lesson Plan," which appeared in *Social Studies Review* (Spring 1986), by Beverly Hamilton and Beverly Saylor.

Computer software must be selected with care. Chart 10.2 shows a number of guidelines formulated by the National Council for the Social Studies to help administrators select the appropriate software for their schools.

Nicholas Deluca adds another thought with regard to acquisition of computers in a school district. He feels it is imperative "that local boards of education develop a long-term commitment to the use of computers in the social studies classroom (Deluca, 1983, 334). One way to accomplish this is for teachers and other school personnel to present first-rate proposals to the administration addressing the following topics:

(1) Specifically, how will the computers be used?

(2) How will computers promote instruction and learning?

(3) What will be the training needs of the staff?

(4) What will be the training costs?

(5) How will software be evaluated and acquired?

(6) What will be the costs for software acquisition?

(7) What will be the plan for evaluating and acquiring hardware?

What trends can a curriculum leader expect to witness in the future, as computers assume a more important role in social studies? Charles White (1988) sees a number of emergences:

1) There will be more emphasis on higher level thinking tasks as software is created for students.

2) There will be greater integration of computer software into the social studies curriculum—going beyond programs dealing only with isolated topics.

3) There will be an expansion of interactive video, allowing pupils to respond to stimuli shown on the monitor.

The guidelines are organized around three areas—*Knowledge, Skills,* and *Values*—each of which contains organizational descriptors. A checklist has been included to help evaluators monitor the extent of emphasis a courseware package places on each criterion. The checklist contains four headings—Strong Emphasis (SE), Moderate Emphasis (ME), Inadequate Emphasis (IE), and Not Applicable (NA). When using the checklist, it is important to realize that the breadth of criteria in this document and the variety of courseware on the market preclude a single courseware package from meeting all the standards in these guidelines.

KNOWLEDGE

Social studies educators at all levels have rejected curricula based exclusively on the behavioral and social sciences. Instead, they have adopted a broad based curriculum that not only addresses the concerns of those academic disciplines but concentrates on the personal and social concerns of the student, as well as the multicultural and normative concerns of society.

SE	ME	IE	NA		
					SIGNIFICANT CHARACTERISTICS
				1.01	*Validity* Does the courseware emphasize currently valid knowledge from one or more of the social sciences?*
				1.02	*Accuracy* Does the courseware present a true and comprehensive body of content, free of distortion by omission?
				1.03	*Reality Oriented* Does the courseware's content deal with the realities of today's world in terms of its flaws, strengths, dangers, and promises?
				1.04	*Significance of Past and Present* Does the courseware deal with important concepts, principles, and theories of modern society? Does it present significant ideas that convey the excitement of the past, present, and future?
				1.05	*Bias* Does the courseware avoid bias and/or stereotyping with regard to gender, ethnicity, racial background, religious application, or cultural group? When unfamiliar customs and institutions or different ethnic groups and cultures are dealt with, are they presented in an unbiased and objective manner?
					CONTENT EMPHASIS
				1.11	*Issue Analysis* Does the courseware engage students in analyzing and attempting to resolve social issues? Is a data base provided, and does it contain information of sufficient depth and breadth for students to make realistic decisions? If not, can the data base be expanded by the teacher or student?

*History is included in this classification.

Chart 10.2 Social studies microcomputer courseware evaluation guidelines [taken from *Social Education*, pp. 574–576 (November/December 1984)].

SE	ME	IE	NA

1.12   *Pervasive and Enduring Issues*
Does the courseware focus on problems and/or issues that are socially significant? Do the materials demonstrate the reciprocal relationships among the social sciences, social issues, and action?

1.13   *Global Perspectives*
Does the courseware help students develop a global perspective? Are students assisted in recognizing the local, national, and global implications of the problems being examined and their possible solutions?

1.14   *Development of Society*
Does the courseware develop knowledge and insights into the historical development of human society? Do the facts, concepts, principles, and processes presented offer direction in organizing a study of human behavior? Does it help students understand how modern societies develop, the role of central institutions, and values of national societies and those of the world community?

1.15   *Multiculturalism*
Does the courseware help develop an understanding of the diversity of cultures and institutional arrangements within American society and in other societies within the global community? Does it provide a rational explanation for customs and other distinctive aspects of daily life arrangements that are explored? Does it contribute to the students' acceptance of the legitimacy of their own cultural identity as well as that of others?

1.16   *Personal/Social Growth*
Does the courseware help students understand their own development and capabilities, as influenced by their families, peer groups, ethnic groups, media, and the society at large?

SKILLS

Social studies education should provide students with the opportunities to develop, practice, and use a variety of thought processes and skills. Students should have opportunities to probe, to extract knowledge from experience, to think, and to communicate their findings and conclusions, both orally and in writing. They should learn how to learn—to develop self-direction in gaining meaningful knowledge and employing it effectively. The social studies program should develop the student's ability to make rational decisions. In order to accomplish this, it is essential that students acquire skills in critical thinking, inquiry, information processing, and problem solving.

Chart 10.2 (continued). Social studies microcomputer courseware evaluation guidelines [taken from *Social Education*, pp. 574–576 (November/December 1984)].

SE	ME	IE	NA	

INTELLECTUAL SKILLS

2.01 *Inquiry and Problem Solving*

Does the courseware pose problems which require students to use the methods of inquiry? Specifically, are students given practice in identifying and defining problems, formulating and testing hypotheses, and arriving at valid generalizations?

2.02 *Critical Thinking*

Does the courseware foster the development of critical thinking skills of distinguishing between fact and opinion, detecting slant and bias, determining cause and effect, and evaluating the reliability of sources?

2.03 *Higher Cognitive Levels*

Does the courseware help students develop and/or reinforce the thought processes of analysis, synthesis, and evaluation? Do students encounter material that helps develop their understanding of the relationship between elements and how these elements fit together as a whole? Are students given opportunities to use information to construct a new communication? Are students asked to make judgments based on appropriate criteria?

2.04 *Divergent Thinking*

Does the courseware encourage divergent thinking which allows students to provide a variety of answers for difficult questions?

2.05 *Concept Formation*

Does the courseware present a broad range of illustrations, models, and examples which are appropriate for helping students image, dissect, conceptualize, define, or recognize relationships between patterns or concepts?

DECISION-MAKING SKILLS

2.11 *Processes*

Does the courseware develop decision-making skills of identifying alternatives, establishing criteria to evaluate the alternatives, evaluating the alternatives in light of criteria, and making the decisions? Are students given the opportunity to retest, reinterpret, and reorganize their beliefs about facts and values?

2.12 *Learning Environment*

Does the courseware and its accompanying materials create a social environment populated by believable characters confronting difficult circumstances and choices?

2.13 *Choices*

Does the courseware require the student to make

Chart 10.2 (continued). Social studies microcomputer courseware evaluation guidelines [taken from *Social Education*, pp. 574–576 (November/December 1984)].

SE	ME	IE	NA

choices, and are those choices then used as data for reflection?

2.14 *Information Base*
Does the courseware's data match the kind of data that would be accessible by citizens outside the instructional context? Is the courseware flexible enough to allow the alteration and addition of information, so that students can practice making decisions under a variety of factual and value circumstances?

2.15 *Consequences*
Does the courseware confront students with realistic consequences (for themselves and for others) of decisions they are required to make in using the courseware?

2.16 *Assessment*
Does the courseware and its accompanying materials assist the teacher and the student to assess the latter's skills and abilities in decision making?

2.17 *Degree of Certainty*
Does the courseware provide experiences in making decisions under conditions of uncertainty? Does the courseware help the student recall the basis on which decisions were made and to make revised decisions informed by new understandings?

INFORMATION PROCESSING SKILLS

2.21 *Orientation Skills*
Does the courseware foster the development of map and globe skills?

2.22 *Chronology and Time Skills*
Does the courseware provides students practice in interpreting chronology and applying time skills, i.e., sequencing events and trends, and identifying and using measures of time correctly?

2.23 *Graphic Data Skills*
Does the courseware help students develop skills of reading and interpreting, constructing, and drawing inferences from graphs, tables, and charts?

2.24 *Gathering and Processing Data*
Does the courseware provide opportunities for students to develop skills in locating, organizing, interpreting, and presenting data?

2.25 *Content Reading Skills*
Does the courseware facilitate the development of the student's word attack skills and the ability to read on the literal, interpretative, and applied levels?

2.26 *Communication Skills*
Does the courseware or its accompanying materials

Chart 10.2 (continued). Social studies microcomputer courseware evaluation guidelines [taken from *Social Education*, pp. 574–576 (November/December 1984)].

SE	ME	IE	NA

INFORMATION PROCESSING SKILLS (continued)

2.26 *Communication Skills (continued)*
foster adequately developed communication skills and provide opportunities for communicating effectively orally and in writing?

COOPERATION AND PARTICIPATION SKILLS

2.31 *Interaction*
Do the courseware and its accompanying materials require groups of students to work together? Do the learning tasks require a division of labor? Does successful completion of the tasks require shared information?

2.32 *Cooperation*
Do the courseware and its accompanying materials reinforce the importance of, and provide support for, cooperation in resolving conflicts over contradictory facts and values?

2.33 *Social/Political Participation*
Does interaction with the courseware and its accompanying materials enhance the student's ability to participate effectively in the social and political processes of his/her school and community?

2.34 *Follow-Up Activities*
Does the courseware or its accompanying material offer suggestions for activities that follow logically from the use of the courseware? Does the courseware allow students to experience vicariously the positive and negative consequences, the costs and benefits, the frustrations and satisfactions of taking action?

VALUES

The cultural pluralism characterizing American society makes value conflicts inevitable. These conflicts are particularly evident in debates about solutions to complex social problems confronting our society. Effective participation in resolving these problems requires people who have rationally developed their own value system and are proficient at making defensible value decisions.

Social studies education should provide ample opportunities for students to rationally examine value issues in a nonindoctrinating environment. Additionally, it should promote the reflective examination of value dilemmas that underlie the personal and social issues that students confront in their everyday lives.

SE	ME	IE	NA

SOCIETAL ORIENTATION

3.01 *Influence of Values on Behavior*
Does the courseware help students develop an

Chart 10.2 (continued). Social studies microcomputer courseware evaluation guidelines [taken from *Social Education*, pp. 574–576 (November/December 1984)].

SE	ME	IE	NA	
				understanding and appreciation of the influence of beliefs and values on human behavior patterns?

3.02 *Procedural Values*
Does the courseware help the student identify and develop an appreciation for values that underlie substantive beliefs and procedural guarantees expressed in this nation's fundamental documents?

VALUING PROCESSES

3.11 *Beliefs*
Does the courseware require the student to identify his or her own beliefs, to make choices based on those beliefs, and to understand the consequences of the choices made?

3.12 *Conjoint Reflection*
Does the courseware require conjoint reflection on feelings, behaviors, and beliefs?

3.13 *Defensible Judgments*
Does the courseware support a process of value analysis by which learners can make rational, defensible value judgments?

3.14 *Feedback*
Does the courseware track the process students use in making value judgments and provide useful feedback with respect to its quality and improvement?

Chart 10.2 (continued). Social studies microcomputer courseware evaluation guidelines [taken from *Social Education*, pp. 574–576 (November/December 1984)].

(4) There will be a dramatic expansion of access to data through the use of telephones and modems.

(5) There will be an increase in the amount of data that is placed on CD-ROM discs and is made available in the school library.

RESOURCE PERSONS

A lesson or a unit is often enhanced when a knowledgeable person from the community comes into the school to share her expertise with a group of students. A card file of these resource persons should be kept in every school so that a teacher can quickly locate and invite an individual to the school. Resource persons can be selected based upon such features as special experiences, travel background, career training, cultural information, or unique talents.

Examples of resource persons are:

travel agents	authors
airport employees	bankers
lawyers	merchants
exchange students	travelers
people with interesting	police officers
hobbies	city officials
construction workers	

However, resource persons need to be selected with care. Such people should be good communicators in front of groups, they should be able to relate to young people, and they should have a clear idea of the purpose of their visit to the school.

TELEVISION

Television is a powerful force in our society. By the time a student has completed high school, he has spent more hours in front of a TV than he has spent in a classroom. Commercial or public television has a worthwhile function in schools if they are used to achieve purposes that the teacher and other traditional materials cannot perform as effectively.

Advantages of television include (1) high motivation of pupils and (2) presentation of information that cannot otherwise be easily obtained. Outstanding documentaries (e.g., "JFK—A Time Remembered"), news programs (e.g., coverage of shuttle launches), and historical fiction (e.g., "Christopher Columbus") can be used to enrich social studies.

In many areas public television operates excellent programs during the day for early elementary and middle grade students. One such example is Kentucky Educational Television (KET), which has cooperated with the Kentucky Department of Education to televise the results of the Kentucky student Mock Election Program.

In view of the fact that Kentucky lies along the New Madrid Fault, KET assisted with the generation of awareness about what safety precautions to take during an earthquake. KET aired shows to help vieweres prepare for the earthquake that scientists predict will occur before the 21st century.

Commonly found series on educational TV throughout the country include "Trade-Offs" (deals with economic principles and understanding for grades 4–6); "It's a Rainbow World" (K–1 students learn about self-concept, family relationships, personal safety, etc.); "We Live Next Door" (K–3 neighborhood studies designed to teach citizenship); and "Truly American" (presents biographies of prominent Americans for grades 4–8).

GRAPHICS

Graphs, tables, charts, figures, diagrams, and cartoons are instances of the term *graphics*, which means laying out data in pictorial or symbolic fashion. Information shown in graphic form enables students to understand large quantities of data because they are condensed in a small space. However, students need to be taught how to read and interpret graphic representations; furthermore, they should be taught how to prepare them. The following plan shows how a lesson on picture and bar graphs can be taught to third grade students.

EARLY ELEMENTARY LESSON PLAN

Topic: **Picture and Bar Graphs**

Grade: **3rd**

Date: **April 14, 1:30–2:15**

I. *Purpose*: **tells what a student will learn**

Students will be able to read different types of graphs and construct their own graphs.

II. *Motivation*: **tells how to begin the day's lesson**

The teacher will show the students four different types of graphs (picture, bar, circle, and line). She will say that all of these are ways to show the number or amount of something. Each student will then be given a newspaper or a news magazine so that he can look for examples of these graphs. When the students have had a few minutes to locate them, the teacher will remind the class that graphs are encountered frequently in our daily lives.

III. *Development*: **tells how to conduct the day's activities**

The teacher will explain to the class that today they will be working with two of the four kinds of graphs: picture and bar. She should point out the contents on a sample picture graph, which shows information gathered from a fictional group of ten year olds (see Figure 10.3).

The teacher should ask questions to enable the students to gain meaning from the graph, e.g.,

(1) What is the title of this graph?

(2) How many shows are represented on the graph? Name them.

Name of
Program

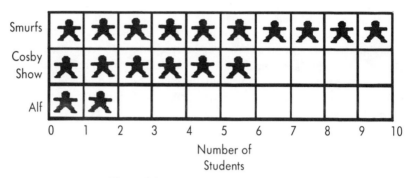

Number of
Students

Figure 10.3 Popularity of TV programs.

(3) What is the most popular show? How many students chose it?

(4) What is the next most popular show? How many students chose it?

(5) What is the least popular show? How many chose it?

(6) How many more students chose *Smurfs* than *Alf*?

The teacher will explain to the group that the same information on this picture graph can be shown by using another kind of graph: a bar graph. At this time she should display Figure 10.4. Students should be asked the same questions as above. They should realize that the picture symbols have been replaced by shaded rectangles, but this does not change the total number for each of the three TV shows.

Name of
Program

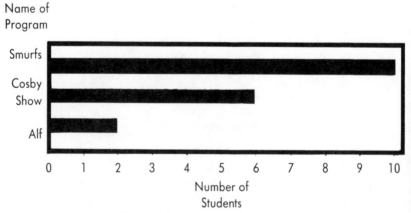

Number of
Students

Figure 10.4 Popularity of TV programs.

IV. *Conclusion*: **tells how to close or evaluate the day's lesson**

The teacher will tell the students they are now going to have a chance to make their own graphs. Each student will be given a slip of paper on which he should write the answer to the following question: "What show do you most enjoy watching: *Alf, Cosby Show*, or *Smurfs?*" As several students collect the slips and read the answers, the teacher should write the results on the chalkboard.

Each student is given two sheets of graph paper. The teacher should help them make a picture graph first and then a bar graph, using the data on the chalkboard. Students should be reminded to write the names of the three shows on the left side of the graph and to write numbers (beginning with zero) along the bottom line of the graph. The biggest number on this line · should be equal to the biggest number on the chalkboard.

The symbols they use should be easy to draw, i.e., a small stick figure of a person drawn in a graph square. To finish up, three labels should be selected: one for the vertical axis, one for the horizontal axis, and one for the title of the graph.

After the teacher has circulated around the room to check for accuracy, the students should now make their bar graph. They can begin by making the vertical and horizontal lines just like the picture graph. Instead of drawing stick figures, however, they should shade in enough graph squares to match the total for each of the three TV shows. The teacher should again circulate to be sure students are doing the work correctly.

To wrap up the lesson, the students should use their graphs to answer the following questions:

(1) What show does our class like the most?

(2) How many more students like it than the show in second place? than the show in third place?

(3) About how many times longer is the longest bar compared to the shortest bar?

(4) What might be another title we could give to our graph?

(5) Do you think our graphs would be different or the same if we used a third grade class in New York City?

V. *Materials*: **tells what is needed for the day's lesson**

Teacher-prepared picture and bar graphs; slips of paper; graph paper; rulers; pencils; newspapers; news magazines.

Note: This lesson by Kent Freeland and Samrie Brewer appeared in "Graphs for Early Elementary Social Studies," *Ohio Council for the Social Studies Review*, pp. 32–34 (Spring 1989).

OTHER EQUIPMENT AND MATERIALS

Audiovisual aids which haven't already been discussed consist of

films	filmstrips
audio tapes	records
slides	transparencies
videotapes	posters
pictures	

These items are nonreading in nature, i.e., they rely primarily on sight and sound rather than on the printed words.

No teacher would want to be criticized for showing a film just to fill up time. A supervisor or principal might want to suggest the following tips on showing a film or videotape:

(1) Have you tried turning the sound off? Students can sharpen their observational qualities if they are asked to tell what the film is about by relying only on the visual presentation.

(2) Have you tried showing just part of the film or videotape? If a film or videotape is long or if parts are not relevant, it is wise to show only that portion which pertains to the objectives of the lesson.

(3) Have you tried stopping the film or videotape at selected points? No one says that they must be viewed nonstop. There are times when a teacher should stop the action to discuss events that just occurred on the film or tape.

Filmstrips and slides have the benefit of depicting images on a wide variety of topics; they also have the advantage of being relatively inexpensive when compared to films or videotapes. Curriculum leaders should encourage teachers to think about these alternatives if money is a consideration.

Audio tapes and records require good listening skills by the students. Teachers should be encouraged to provide an outline to the pupils of the audio presentation, have the students take notes as they listen, or stop the play periodically to review what has been said.

Transparencies, pictures, and posters all depend upon symbolic interpretation, and this means that the teacher needs to follow the correct procedures to enable students to gain meaning from these visual resources. Using Bloom's taxonomy (see Chapter 9), the teacher should phrase questions so that the students are able to extract not only "knowledge" (e.g., "What does the woman have in her hand in this transparency?"), but also higher forms of learning (e.g., "How does the tool this woman is using compare with the tools that we use to do the same task?").

Administrators need to caution their teachers to preview AV materials before using them in the classroom. The checklist in Figure 10.5 will assist an educator in obtaining a comprehensive assortment of instructional resources.

ASSISTANCE POINTS

Questions for Action for the Administrator

1. Identify an area from this chapter that you consider to be a strength of your school/district, e.g., computer hardware. Then identify an area that needs improvement. What could you be doing to deal more effectively with it?

2. Textbooks are the most frequently used materials in the classroom. How can administrators help teachers select them wisely?

3. Select some computer software catalogs for your teachers to order from. When the software arrives, evaluate them, using the guidelines in Chart 10.2.

4. Suggest that some of your teachers compile a directory for resource persons in the area. This project might be done as part of the requirements for a university course they are taking.

5. What resources are available in your community to meet the needs of at-risk students?

Research about Materials: Implications for Educators

The following study by Capper and Copple (1985) summarizes how computers are used in schools:

1. Boys use the computers more than girls.

2. Lower ability students tend to use the computer for drill and practice.

3. Higher ability students use the computer to deal with problem-solving activities.

4. Average ability students are much less apt to use the computer than are higher or lower ability students.

Names and Addresses of Professional Organizations

On page 271 are some addresses to which social studies administrators can write if they want more information about materials and equipment.

	Present in All Classrooms		Not Present in These Classrooms
1. Computer	yes	no	
2. Computer printer	yes	no	
3. Computer software	yes	no	
4. Chalkboard	yes	no	
5. Bulletin board	yes	no	
6. Wall map	yes	no	
7. Globe	yes	no	
8. Set of encyclopedias	yes	no	
9. Access to 16 mm film projector with screen	yes	no	
10. Television	yes	no	
11. A textbook for each pupil	yes	no	
12. Almanac	yes	no	
13. Dictionaries	yes	no	
14. Access to overhead projector with screen	yes	no	
15. Access to videotape camera	yes	no	
16. Access to videotape playback machine	yes	no	
17. Access to instamatic or quick developing camera	yes	no	
18. Access to slide projector with screen	yes	no	
19. Atlas	yes	no	
20. Classroom newspaper (*Weekly Reader*, etc.), local newspaper, or weekly news magazine	yes	no	
21. Access to audio cassette tape recorder	yes	no	
22. Access to record player	yes	no	
23. Access to filmstrip projector	yes	no	
24. Access to photocopying machine			
25. Access to ditto or mimeograph machine	yes	no	
26. Access to thermofax machine	yes	no	
27. List of community speakers	yes	no	
28. List of community field trip sites	yes	no	
29. List of school district (or other rental source) films, transparencies, slides, filmstrips, kits, games, videocassettes, audio tapes, and records	yes	no	

Figure 10.5 Principal's checklist for social studies material.

1. Social Studies School Service
   10200 Jefferson Boulevard, Room 1
   P.O. Box 802
   Culver City, CA 90232-0802
   (SSSS publishes catalogs and sells K-12 items.)
2. International Council for Computers in Education
   University of Oregon
   1787 Agate St.
   Eugene, OR 97403-1923
   (ICCE publishes the journal *The Computing Teacher.*)
3. *Classroom Computer Learning*
   5615 W. Cermak Rd.
   Cicero, IL 60650
4. *Popular Computing*
   Box 272
   Calabasas, CA 91302
5. Association for Educational Communications & Technology
   1126 16th St., NW
   Washington, DC 20036
   (AECT publishes the journal *Tech Trends.*)
6. *Electronic Learning*
   902 Sylvan Ave.
   Englewood Cliffs, NJ 07632
7. *Ed Tech*
   720 Palisade Avenue
   Englewood Cliffs, NJ 07632
8. *T.H.E. Journal*
   Technological Horizons in Education
   P.O. Box 15126
   Santa Ana, CA 92705-0126
   (This journal publishes capsule descriptions of new developments in educational technology.)
9. *Microcomputer and Software Information for Teachers*
   Northwest Regional Educational Library
   300 W. Sixth Ave.
   Portland, OR 97204
10. Educational Products Information Exchange
    P.O. Box 620
    Stony Brook, NY 11790
    (EPIE distributes evaluations of materials.)
11. Minnesota Educational Computing Consortium

3490 Lexington Avenue North
St. Paul, MN 55126
(MECC coordinates computing activities and develops and markets software.)

12. Vital Information, Inc.
7899 Mastin Dr.
Overland Park, KS 66204
(Vital information publishes a handbook entitled *Educator's Handbook and Software Directory*.)

13. TALMIS
115 North Oak Park Ave.
Oak Park, IL 60301
(TALMIS publishes a directory entitled *Sources for Courses*.)

14. *Electronic Education*
1311 Executive Center Dr.
Suite 220
Tallahassee, FL 32301

15. Education News Service
P.O. Box 1789
Carmichael, CA 95609
(ENS produces a newsletter covering new technology for educators.)

16. Peter Li, Inc.
2451 East River Road
Dayton, OH 45439
(Publishes *Classroom Computer Learning*.)

17. *Educator's Guide to Free Social Studies Materials*
Educators' Progress Service, Inc.
Randolph, WI 53956

18. *Free and Inexpensive Teaching Aids*
Box 369
Riverside, CA 92502

19. *Selected Free Materials for Classroom Teachers, 5th ed.*
Fearon Publishers
6 Davis Drive
Belmont, CA 94002

20. *Curriculum Product News*
P.O. Box 5250
Pittsfield, MA 01203-5250
(CPN provides capsule information on K-12 materials/equipment and the addresses where they can be ordered.)

REFERENCES

Becker, Henry Jay. *Instructional Use of School Computers: Reports from the 1985 National Survey*. Baltimore:Johns Hopkins University, Issue 2 (1986).

Capper, J. and C. Copple. "Computer Use in Education: Research Review and Instructional Implications," *The Research into Practice Digest*, 1(3) (1985).

Cuban, Larry. *Teachers and Machines*. Wolfeboro, NH:Teachers College Press (1986).

Deluca, Nicholas M. "Social Studies Teachers and Computer Technology: An Administrator's Perspective," *Social Education*, pp. 333–334 (May 1983).

Diem, Richard A. "Computers in the Social Studies Classroom," *How To Do It Series*, Washington, DC:National Council for the Social Studies, Series 2, No. 14 (1981).

Eckenrod, James S. and Saul Rockman. "Connections between Television and the Social Studies Curriculum," *Social Education*, pp. 357–362 (September 1988).

Elliot, David L. et al. "Do Textbooks Belong in Elementary Social Studies?" *Educational Leadership*, pp. 22–24 (April 1985).

Farr, Roger and Michael A. Tulley. "Do Adoption Committees Perpetuate Mediocre Textbooks?" *Kappan*, pp. 467–471 (March 1985).

Freeland, Kent and Samrie Brewer. "Graphs for Early Elementary Social Studies," *Ohio Council for the Social Studies Review*, pp. 32–36 (Spring 1989).

Haas, Mary E. "Evaluating Sponsored Materials," *How to Do It in the Social Studies Classroom*, Washington, DC:National Council for the Social Studies, Series 4, No. 3 (n.d.).

Hamilton, Beverly and Beverly Saylor. "Using Technology to Teach the Westward Movement: A Mode Unit/Lesson Plan," *Social Studies Review*, pp. 70–77 (Spring 1986).

Hamm, Mary and Dennis Adams. "Video Demands New Thinking Skills," *School Administrator*, pp. 13–16 (April 1988).

Hunter, Beverly. "Knowledge-Creative Learning with Data Bases," *Social Education*, pp. 38–43 (January 1987).

Marchionini, Gary. "Hypermedia and Learning: Freedom and Chaos," *Educational Technology*, pp. 8–12 (November 1988).

Mason, John L. "Educational Technology in Schools and in Business: A Personal Experience," *Educational Horizons*, pp. 154–157 (Summer 1988).

O'Connor, Richard J. "Emerging Developments in the Use of Television as a Teaching Tool," *American Middle School Education*, pp. 35–40 (Fall 1988).

Patton, William E. (ed.). *Improving the Use of Social Studies Textbooks*. Bulletin No. 63. Washington, DC:National Council for the Social Studies (1980).

Rottman, Clara Thoren. "How Video Is Reshaping Learning and the Learner," *School Administrator*, pp. 13, 14 (April 1987).

Schug, Mark C. and Robert Beery. *Teaching Social Studies in the Elementary School*. Glenview, IL:Scott, Foresman and Co. (1987).

Strohmer, Joanne C. "Are We Using Technology to Train Pigeons or Thinkers?" *Principal*, pp. 6, 7 (November 1987).

"State-Mandated Computer Instruction," in *Education Week*, Data from Quality Education Data, Inc., p. 3 (November 30, 1988).

"Task Force on Technology," in *Time for Results, The Governors' 1991 Report on Education*. Washington, DC:National Governors' Association (1986).

The National Task Force on Educational Technology. "Transforming American Education: Reducing the Risk to the Nation, a Report to the Secretary of Education," Washington, DC (April 1986).

Weis, Iris R. *Report of the 1977 National Survey of Science, Mathematics, and Social Studies Education*. Report to the National Science Foundation. Research Triangle Park, North Carolina: Center for Educational Research and Evaluation (1978).

White, Charles S. "Computers in Social Studies Classrooms," *Viewpoints: The Indiana Council for the Social Studies Newsletter*, ERIC Digest EDO-SO88-5, pp. 35–36 (November/December 1988).

White, Charles S. "Teachers Using Technology," *Social Education*, pp. 44–47 (January 1987).

Woodward, Arthur et al. "Beyond Textbooks in Elementary Social Studies," *Social Education*, pp. 50–53 (January 1986).

11 | MORE SOCIAL STUDIES: ACROSS THE SOCIAL SCIENCES

Chapter Preview of Key Ideas

★ Some topics in social studies overlap several social science disciplines.

★ Psychology looks at human behavior.

★ Philosophy is the study of wisdom and knowledge.

★ Science and society deals with social issues and technology, e.g., land use, water use, air use, noise, and energy.

★ International education focuses on the interconnectedness among people in the world.

★ Peace education develops alternatives to war.

★ Future studies prepares students for life in the future.

★ Women's studies educates students to the place of women in society.

★ Topics in this chapter can be taught by using such vehicles as current events, field trips, reading in the social studies, and writing in the social studies.

Chapters 3 through 8 of this book discussed the six major social sciences, which comprise the essence of social studies. The curricular area of social studies, however, goes beyond these six; it covers topics that sometimes are mandated by state legislatures and state boards of education (e.g., character education); that sometimes span several of the social sciences (e.g., pollution); and that sometimes interface with other components of the school curriculum (e.g., conservation). In other words, social studies tends to be an area of instruction that integrates with other subjects.

The topics that "go beyond the social sciences" and will be discussed in this chapter are

> psychology
> philosophy
> science and society
> environmental education and energy education
> international education
> peace education
> future studies
> women's studies

Four strategies will also be discussed in this chapter. They are not considered topics; instead, they are ways in which the above eight topics—along with others—can be taught. These four strategies are (1) current events and controversial topics, (2) field trips, (3) reading in the social studies, and (4) writing in the social studies.

PSYCHOLOGY

Psychology intends to answer the question, "Why do humans act and think the way they do?" Smiley (1983) asserts that this is a valid aspect of social studies because it enables students to analyze themselves as human beings in the following ways:

(1) Psychology helps students develop an awareness of individual identity. Students come to realize that they learn because of individual abilities that they have (e.g., through the senses of sight, touch, and hearing).

(2) Psychology helps students create a positive self-concept when they partake in group processes.

(3) Psychology helps students strive for self-actualization, when they complete a project with a sense of pride and satisfaction.

(4) Psychology helps students develop and clarify value systems, when they understand the beliefs that shape their actions.

PHILOSOPHY

Philosophy is the study of wisdom and knowledge. It is an area of human activity that encourages students to raise questions. According to Hunkins (1982), there are three basic questions to answer in philosophy. (1) What is real? This question allows students to reach an awareness of the reality of their world. (2) What is true? This question allows students to make true statements about reality. (3) What is good? This question enables students to arrive at fair or right decisions.

In a sense, philosophy underlies the social sciences because it enables students to

- discover alternatives
- discover consistency
- support their conclusions with defensible reasons
- heighten their creativity
- discover part–whole relationships
- discover situations that need investigation (Lipman et al., 1977)

SCIENCE AND SOCIETY

This broad term refers to the increasingly popular effort to teach students how science and society interact. Science, Technology, & Society is a national network which has been established to accomplish the following goals:

(1) Relate science and technology to social issues.

(2) Integrate knowledge from different subject areas and disciplines.

(3) Examine differing viewpoints and alternatives.

(4) Assess technological impacts in light of ethical principles and moral standards.

(5) Develop problem-solving and decision-making skills.

(6) Encourage students to participate in the community as active citizens.

A number of areas can be included in this category, for example, environmental education, energy education, the world's population crisis, and food production. The National Council for the Social Studies has prepared guidelines for teaching science-related social issues. They appear in Chart 11.1.

Environmental and Energy Education

In 1975 the National Council for the Social Studies moved to include environmental education in schools' social studies programs. Maxim (1983) provides two major objectives of environmental education:

(1) To acquire basic understandings about the environment and about the causes and dangers inherent in our abuse of the environment

(2) To develop positive attitudes toward and a respect for the quality of the environment (p. 398)

1. **Choosing a Topic and Evaluating Existing Material**

Considerations for topic choice include
   a. Teacher expertise and ability.
   b. Resources available, including other teachers and experts in the field, for teachers and students.
   c. Student interest, concerns, grade level, cognitive ability, and subject matter levels.
   d. Compatibility of topic with existing course of study or on-going educational activity.
   e. General appropriateness of topic and its lasting importance and contribution toward general education.
   f. Whether this topic would contribute to an overload of gloom and doom. Can solutions be offered? Can the issue be resolved by a free society acting together?
   g. Topics provide opportunities for an accurate meld of science and social studies approaches to the particular topic.
   h. Relevance of topic to students' immediate lives or lives in the imaginable future. Processes of problem solving and ethical decision making are learned while studying a personally relevant issue and then generalized to more complex and profound issues as the student matures and becomes more comfortable dealing with science-related issues.

1.1 Teachers attempting to introduce science-related issues into their classes must be aware of the attitudes and sensitivities toward the topic in the community.

1.2 Information presented must be *balanced* so that all points of view are presented in such a way that they have approximately equal impact. For example, can an article offer as flashy bait as a well-financed film?

1.3 Teachers discuss their plans to teach about a science-related social issue with their director of instruction and/or principal before beginning. Since these issues are very sensitive, it is best to discuss the matter with school personnel ahead of time.

1.4 The topic chosen must be illustrative of some general aspect of the interrelation between science and society. Examples of general aspects of the science/society interrelation include:
   a. Scientific information is a determinant of government social policy, e.g., the Supreme Court school integration decision was based on social science information indicating the psychological harm done to black students by segregated school systems.
   b. Government policy is a determinant of the direction of scientific research, especially through its funding procedures, e.g., emphasis on cancer-cure research.
   c. Application of scientific information (technology) is a cause of social change, most of which is indirect, unplanned, and unexpected, e.g., the use of antibiotics and insecticides as a cause of population growth in developing "third world" countries.
   d. Application of scientific information affects personal freedom of choice, e.g., birth control methods, especially the "pill," made childbearing a matter of choice; conversely, behavior control methods used by public institutions can limit personal freedom.
   e. The effect of social values on scientific research, e.g., the development of birth control methods, cancer research stressing cure rather than prevention.
   f. Individual and societal responses to rapid change and enlarged area of choice, described in Toffler's *Future Shock* need to be considered and discussed.
   g. The nature of human values and the nature of human beings from which those values spring, e.g., the biological nature of mankind and the environments which

Chart 11.1 Guidelines for teaching science-related social issues. (These Guidelines are from *Social Education*, pp. 259–261, April 1983.)

allow the fullest development of human potential. This topic of human nature represents a vital touch point between the social and the natural sciences. Social psychological research sheds light on situational and cultural antecedents of social behavior.

h. The social responsibilities of scientists in influencing the use to which their discoveries are put.

i. Ethical issues in scientific research involving human beings, e.g., responsibilities of experimenter in providing "informed consent" of subjects.

j. Areas of personal decision making regarding the use or nonuse of a particular new product or technology, e.g., to know the possible negative side effects of certain medicines or cosmetics. What are the responsibilities of industry, government, and the consumer in providing/obtaining the information necessary for making a wise decision?

1.5 Materials chosen must be well written or, in the case of audiovisual materials, well produced in order that they meet your objectives. Some audiovisual materials, for example, are interesting and/or artistically and technically well done but do not clearly present the information.

1.6 The process of decision making or problem solving, whichever is relevant to the topic chosen, must be emphasized over facts.

1.7 Concepts and principles must be emphasized over facts; facts as related in concepts and principles and the construction of the latter need to be taught.

2. **Gathering Information**

Teachers help students
a. Locate information in the physical and biological sciences.
b. Read and acquire information from scientific reports.
c. Develop basic science vocabulary and concepts.
d. Locate social science information.
e. Develop basic social science vocabulary and concepts.
f. Collect their own raw data using surveys, observations, interviews, and other means of collecting data from primary sources.
g. Learn through careful analytic viewing and listening to television, radio, films, filmstrips, and other media, as well as through reading of books and publications written at the layperson's level.

3. **Processing Information**

Teachers help students process information by increasing their competency in
a. Observing, especially the making of controlled observations.
b. Classifying information.
c. Using numbers and finding averages.
d. Identifying movement and direction, rates of change over time, and trends.
e. Extrapolating information, reading and constructing maps, graphs, tables, charts.
f. Constructing inferences based upon observations.
g. Making generalizations supported by informational findings.
h. Use of concept formation on inquiry strategies.

4. **Evaluating Information**

4.1 Teachers help students determine the usefulness of informational documents when they
a. Identify the author and publications.

Chart 11.1 (continued). Guidelines for teaching science-related social issues. (These Guidelines are from *Social Education*, pp. 259–261, April 1983.)

279

b. Determine the area of expertise of the author.

c. Detect bias and state possible reasons for bias in interpreting facts given in an article or presented in a film.

d. Determine the audience for the print or nonprint information.

e. Learn some of the techniques for checking the reliability of an information source.

4.2 Better, more usable programs result when students can

a. Compare data from one source to another source.

b. Separate facts from interpretations in an article.

c. Find facts that support conclusions the author makes.

4.3 A good informational source's facts

a. State the methods used for obtaining them.

b. Deal directly with the problem under consideration.

c. Fit the conclusions drawn or support the hypotheses with the facts.

4.4 The use of primary sources of information needs to be encouraged whenever possible.

5. Problem Solving

5.1 Teachers help students define the problem under study carefully, noting the variables:

a. The parties involved or affected (individuals and groups).

b. The causes of the problem, such as new technology for which there is no precedent; no legal, political, social, or ethical framework.

c. Interaction of causes and factors contributing to the friction or creating the problem.

d. Nature of the problem—moral, political, social, etc.

5.2 Teachers help students determine what information is necessary in order to deal with the problem and help them locate and evaluate this information.

5.3 Teachers help students apply their information to the problem. The information should

a. Specifically apply to the problem area affected.

b. Explicate or define further the causes and factors as identified in 5.1 a and b. If the information does not apply, the student should return to the information-gathering steps and begin again.

c. Note and explain new or additionally discovered factors.

d. Make clear the interaction of factors.

e. Be analyzed to ascertain that the nature of the problem is correctly identified.

f. Suggest solutions that apply. That is, political problems require political solutions; ethical problems may require individual ethical choices.

g. In some cases, lend itself to use in simulations and games or to graphically prepared data so that students can begin to predict possible results of different solutions.

h. Evaluate consequences of each possible outcome in terms of *clearly stated and ranked* values of the person or group.

i. Make recommendations or draw conclusions, based on previous steps a–h.

5.4 Teachers provide opportunities for students to use various valuing, decision-making

Chart 11.1 (continued). Guidelines for teaching science-related social issues. (These Guidelines are from *Social Education*, pp. 259–261, April 1983.)

280

models in hypothetical situations. Examples of decision-making models are (1) Brady's ethical decision-making model, (2) Fletcher's Guidelines for making ethical decisions, (3) Kurtz's Guidelines for evaluating moral issues, (4) Kohlberg's moral reasoning, (5) Rath's value clarification, and (6) Oliver's jurisprudential inquiry.

6. **Evaluating and Testing**
   Teacher evaluations need to provide
   a. A valid means ascertaining whether or not stated goals and objectives have been met.
   b. For continuous feedback and modification as needed after the unit is underway.
   c. An opportunity for differing student views as long as these views are supported by facts. No one particular point of view needs to prevail.

Chart 11.1 (continued). Guidelines for teaching science-related social issues. (These Guidelines are from *Social Education*, pp. 259–261, April 1983.)

The term *environment* encircles a number of concerns of human beings as they deal with the physical world in which they live.

LAND USE

Concepts such as recycling and reforestation are brought into play. Activities to bring attention to the proper use of the land could include having early elementary students pick up litter from the playground or having middle grade students list and discuss ways that farmland is used, aside from crop production, e.g., shopping centers, interstate highways, and golf courses.

WATER USE

Concepts such as ecosystem and resources can be introduced. Activities dealing with water use include asking early elementary students to have their families store a container of ice water in the refrigerator rather than running the tap water until it gets cold. Middle grade students can take samples of local water and analyze it for visible signs of pollution. These samples can also be sent to local laboratories to be tested for chemical impurities.

AIR USE

Concepts such as pollution and industrialization can be taught. An early elementary activity could be having students locate instances where manufacturing causes air pollution. Middle grade students could write to industries to inquire about how they have curbed their air pollutants in recent years.

NOISE

Concepts such as decibel rating and quality of life can be taught. One activity might be to have early elementary students record on tape the sounds in their neighborhood. Middle grade students could investigate the effects of excessively loud noises on a person's health.

ENERGY

Relevant concepts include conservation and waste disposal. Young children could take a field trip to a power generating plant. One such site is the Rockport Generating Plant in Spencer County, Indiana, which has built an information center to accommodate school children and demonstrate how coal is transformed into electrical energy.

Middle grade students could construct a data retrieval chart that would record the dominant forms of energy that societies have used throughout the centuries.

The evaluation checklist that appears in Chart 11.2 can be a valuable reference aid for a curriculum supervisor who wants to weigh the district's ideas against established standards. The checklist was prepared in accordance with energy education guidelines that were created by the National Council for the Social Studies.

INTERNATIONAL EDUCATION

International studies, or global education, can be defined as the cultivation of a world perspective, so a student can see the interconnectedness throughout the world. Kniep (1986) has noted that knowing the content of global education is more important than knowing its definition. He identifies four elements as being essential:

(1) *Studying Human Values*
There are universal values (e.g., life, liberty, and equality) as well as diverse values (e.g., unique housing, food, clothing, etc.).

(2) *Studying Global Systems*
The interdependent nature of our world focuses on global economic, political, ecological, and technological systems.

(3) *Studying Global Issues and Problems*
Examples of these international topics include peace and security systems, development issues, environmental issues, and human rights issues.

(4) *Studying Global History*
Students need to have a broad historic vista that goes beyond the

Rating			
Strongly	Moderately	Hardly at All	Specific Guidelines
			1.1 Does the program explicitly state and justify goals which are consistent with the General Social Studies Curriculum Guidelines in that it fosters the *Ideal Society* and the *Socially Educated Person?*
			1.2a Does the program encourage public/citizen competency by providing tools, skills,and commitments required for active participation in energy policy issues in the public arena?
			1.2b Does the program encourage personal life-style competency by providing the commitment and know-how to deal with changing energy realities in one's own consumption patterns in shared communities where others have needs and interests?
			1.3 Does the program preserve the fundamental rights and integrity of the person and foster the development of children and youth into rational participants in a free society?
			2.1 Does the program incorporate flexibility to relate to individual students' entry experience, knowledge, values, and competencies?
			2.2 Does the program result in outcomes that are significant for the learner?
			2.3 Does the program build upon the interests and needs of the student as opposed to the program sponsor?
			3.1 Does the program draw upon a wide variety of relevant disciplines in the social, natural, and physical sciences, using concepts, principles, and systems as they are appropriate to the issue under examination?
			3.2 Does the program reflect the complexity of energy issues by stressing relationships (systems) which show the connectedness, mutuality, and reciprocity of energy flows within natural systems and society?
			3.3 Does the program use information as instrumental content for students to manipulate in their development of concepts, principles, and systems?
			3.4 Does the program reflect the ethics of handling knowledge by cherishing truthfulness, defending the freedom of inquiry and debate, and proclaiming the advantages, disadvantages, quandaries, and consequences of various energy technologies?
			4.1 Does the program provide for the active involvement of students in setting objectives and designing activities?
			4.2 Does the program build upon the entry skills, atti-

Chart 11.2 Energy education evaluation checklist [taken from Kathleen Lane, "Energy Education Evaluation Checklist," *Indiana Social Studies Quarterly*, pp. 61–63 (Winter 1982–83)].

Rating			
Strongly	Moderately	Hardly at All	Specific Guidelines
			tudes, knowledge, and experience of students, helping them to conceptualize their experience while providing new experiences and problems for exploration?
			4.3 Does the program provide for multiple learning activities recognizing a variety of learning stages?
			4.4 Does the program foster reflective inquiry skills and problem-solving dispositions by engaging students actively in raising their own questions?
			5.1 Does the program build upon existing courses and program strengths?
			5.2 Do the program instructional materials, guides, and learning opportunities include the maximum possible participation of the community of educators and learners to be served?
			5.3 Does the program introduce energy education so as to promote rationality of choice, user competency, and a sense of efficacy and ownership within the educational community who chose to engage in energy education?
			5.4 Does the program follow a developmental model (developing existing skills and interests), rather than a deficit model?
			5.5 Does the program make available viewpoints other than those of the sponsors?
			5.6 Does the program include training time and resources for teachers and others to invest themselves in energy education, developing the required knowledge and skills, discerning the complex nature of energy realities, exploring various energy education approaches, and choosing appropriate energy units?
			5.7 Does the program introduce energy education in a way that builds and sustains support within the social studies from teachers, students, and community members?

Chart 11.2 (continued). Energy education evaluation checklist [taken from Kathleen Lane, "Energy Education Evaluation Checklist," *Indiana Social Studies Quarterly*, pp. 61–63 (Winter 1982–83)].

history of Western culture. They need to be "grounded in the knowledge that contact and exchange among civilizations has been more or less continuous for the last 2,000 years" (Kniep, 1986, 444).

The following lesson plan in part touches upon points one and two above—studying human values and studying global systems. "Globingo" asks students to think about examples of values such as clothing and food and of global systems such as economics and technology.

MIDDLE GRADE LESSON PLAN

Topic: **Globingo**

Grade: **8th**

Date: **October 5, 1:10–2:00**

I. *Purpose*: **tells what a student will learn**

Students will discover how class members are connected to the rest of the world and will speculate about further "global connections."

II. *Motivation*: **tells how to begin the day's lesson**

Ask the class to think whether or not they have "international connections." Ask them to give some examples; they might supply such answers as "travel to another country," "doing business with a foreign company," "hosting a foreign exchange student," or "meeting a person from another part of the world." Tell them that the lesson today will show them that, even if they have never left the United States, they can have an "international connection."

III. *Development*: **tells how to conduct the day's lesson**

Distribute copies of the handout to all the students. Explain that the object of "Globingo" is to fill in as many squares as possible with the names of classmates who fit those squares. As soon as one row—horizontal, vertical, or diagonal—has been completely filled in, the student has scored a "globingo."

Handout: Globingo

Find someone who:

A. has traveled to some foreign country	B. has a pen pal in another country	C. is learning a foreign language	D. has a relative in another country
E. has helped a visitor from another country	F. enjoys a music group from another country	G. is wearing something that was made in another country	H. enjoys eating food from other countries

I. can name a famous sports star from another country	J. has a family car that was made in another country	K. has talked to someone who has lived in another country	L. lives in a home where more than one language is spoken
M. saw a story about another country in the newspaper recently	N. learned something about another country on TV recently	O. owns a TV or other appliance made in another country	P. has a parent or other relative who was born in another country

A	B	C	D
_____ name _____ country	_____ name _____ country	_____ name _____ country	_____ name _____ country
E	**F**	**G**	**H**
_____ name _____ country	_____ name _____ country	_____ name _____ country	_____ name _____ country
I	**J**	**K**	**L**
_____ name _____ country	_____ name _____ country	_____ name _____ country	_____ name _____ country

M	N	O	P
name	name	name	name
country	country	country	country

Point out that the code key on the handout explains the letter-coded spaces on the game sheet. Emphasize that the name of the relevant country, as well as the student's name, should be recorded in each square. Explain that each student may sign another classmate's sheet only once, even if more than one square could apply to that student. (This rule encourages the maximum possible interaction among students.)

Allow fifteen to twenty minutes for students to walk around the classroom looking for classmates who fit the various squares. It is important during this period that students ask one another questions rather than passively hand around the game sheets. Students should "dig" for the information they need. They should continue to try to fill out their game sheets even after they have scored one or more "globingos." Try to keep the game going until every student has scored.

IV. *Conclusion*: **tells how to close or evaluate the day's lesson**

Ask students what they learned about one another in the process of filling in their "globingo" squares. What was the most surprising thing they learned about any of their classmates? Were they amazed how many international connections the class has?

On a large map of the world, help students locate all the nations identified in this activity. This can be done by cutting apart the squares on the game sheets and pinning them to the appropriate locations on a world map.

Probe students to explain the reasons for all the connections they found in this activity. What caused these connections? In what ways do we learn more about the rest of the world? In what ways do we learn more about the rest of the world? Television? Travel? Newspapers? Trading among nations?

V. *Materials*: **tells what is needed for the day's lesson**

"Globingo" handout and large map of the world.

Note: This lesson was adapted from the plan by Jacquelyn Johnson and John Benegar, "Global Issues in the Intermediate School," *Social Education*, pp. 132, 133 (February 1983).

The need for learning about people in other parts of the world has been addressed by a number of education organizations. School officials should consult the position statements of the following groups to see what their policy resolutions are:

- American Association of School Administrators
- American Federation of Teachers
- National Association of Elementary School Principals
- Association for Supervision and Curriculum Development
- Council of Chief State School Officers
- National Association of Secondary School Principals
- National Association of State Boards of Education
- National Education Association
- National Council for the Social Studies
- National PTA
- National School Boards Association

Although global education has worthwhile aims, it does not go without its detractors. "In the minds of some critics, the emphasis on global issues somehow detracts from the development in students of a One Hundred Percent Americanism. And the study of the interdependency of nations diminishes our faith in our own sovereignty" (Wronski, 1988, 147).

The attacks contain allegations that global education materials promote a one-world ambition, represent a political left agenda, and overemphasize the redistribution of world wealth. It is not intended that the three items in the previous sentence should be part of a global education program, for they promote a particular political or economic point of view. Instead, its purpose is to—as John Goodland (1986) states—put the learner at the world's center. In light of the fact that the United States accounts for less than 5 percent of the world's population, it is imperative that students understand the other 95 percent.

PEACE EDUCATION

Peace education "includes the development of knowledge, insight, and skills as well as the building up of opinions and attitudes, beginning with norms and values embedded in peace, and directed towards the realisation of a human and peaceful world" (Vriens and Aspeslagh, 1985, 11).

Administrators might follow the route the Milwaukee Public Schools took in establishing a peace studies curriculum. It began when a member of the Milwaukee Board of School Directors agreed to a request to introduce a peace studies resolution at a future meeting of the school board. The board later referred the resolution to both the superintendent and the instruction committee of the school board for further consideration. When the resolution was brought before a public hearing, a determined group of people urged that peace studies be interdisciplinary, comprehensive, and available to students at all age and grade levels. The board supported this and established a Peace Studies Task Force.

The task force devised three foci for the Peace Studies curriculum:

(1) Creating an environment
(2) Creative resolution of conflict
(3) Global awareness education

This lengthy process—from initially contacting the board of school directors until the board's acceptance of the Task Force's final report—took nearly two years.

When thinking about a peace education program, administrators need to know that students tend to think of "peace" in terms of "war"—that peace is the absence of war. Therefore, special attention should be given to identifying aspects of peace, e.g., examples of people who have brought about compromises (Anwar el-Sadat), who have brought help to the world (Mother Teresa), and who have striven for justice and human rights (Ghandi). Students should be presented with examples of institutions that have benefited humanity (Nobel Peace Prize Commission) and have provided aid to the oppressed (Amnesty International) (Haas, 1985, 256).

FUTURE STUDIES

A student who is in first grade in 1989 will graduate from high school in the year 2000; therefore, today's students need to be concerned about the future. Today's students already have glimpses of the future; for if they have been to EPCOT Center in Florida, they might have experienced a display of crops that are grown in a controlled environment. Watching movies such as "Star Wars" reveals what flight may be like in years to come. With knowledge increasing at an exponential rate, who knows when today's fantasy will become tomorrow's reality?

Future studies in the school is the development of a student's ability to prepare for life in the future. Some commonly used activities which administrators can recommend to classroom teachers include:

(1) *Future Wheel*
    This is an activity that is used to predict negative and positive consequences of a particular idea or event. Results of these consequences are then identified through several levels.

(2) *Cross-Impact Matrix*
   This is a method of forecasting, which uses a grid arrangement to help show the interrelationships among issues, occurrences, or trends.
(3) *Trend Extrapolation Forecasting*
   This is a technique that enables students to become aware of current trends and how they might affect our future lives.
(4) *Scenario*
   In this activity, students write a description of a future situation—incorporating causal explanations of how this situation came to be.

LaConte (1983) discusses several school systems that have instituted future studies into their curricula. One of these is the Riley Elementary School in San Bernardino, California. The principal recruited staff members who were interested in future studies and set up a summer in-service for them, with instruction for students to commence that fall. The program is a two-year sequence, with each of the following topics allotted two months:

* outer space
* earth science
* world interdependence
* oceanography
* technology
* economics
* feeding the world
* energy

LaConte (1983, 44) lists four elements that are common to all future studies programs: (1) all of them treat the study of the future as an investigation of alternatives, i.e., determining what might happen; (2) the emphasis is always on process, not content, i.e., problem solving, critical thinking, decision making, and investigation; (3) all of them view future studies as a form of values clarification, i.e., finding out why they prefer one future to another; and (4) there is a constant concern with the development of a sense of consequence, i.e., "if-then" possibilities.

WOMEN'S STUDIES

Women's studies is learning about women as well as doing whatever is necessary to eliminate sexism from society (Kaltsounis, 1987, 303). One of the most successful forces in this effort is the National Women's History Project, which was formed in 1980. It was instrumental in petitioning the U.S. Congress to proclaim March as "Women's History Month."

Some ideas for administrators include

(1) Convene a planning group early in the year to celebrate "Women's History Month" and "Women's History Week." The group should be comprised of the community as well as various groups involved with the school.

(2) Encourage teachers to use nonsexist terminology, e.g., fire fighter, not fireman; police officer, not policeman; mail carrier, not mailman.

(3) Locate lists and sources of biographies of women. Teachers can have their students read these books about women who are influential, e.g., Winnie Mandela, Margaret Thatcher, Sandra Day O'Connor, Jane Addams.

(4) Get the cooperation of media (newspapers, radio stations, etc.) to print or broadcast oral histories which have been written by elementary/middle grade students about women from the local community.

So far this chapter has discussed some content areas. The rest of the chapter will discuss some strategies that can be used to teach these and other content areas. The techniques are (1) current events, (2) field trips, (3) reading in the social studies, and (4) writing in the social studies.

CURRENT EVENTS

This technique is sometimes called "current affairs" or "current issues." Its purpose is to serve as a vehicle to help students learn how to make sense of the happenings and situations in the world around them. Jarolimek (1986, 207–208) lists three ways of working current events into the school curriculum:

(1) Allot a certain period of time each day or each week—separate from the regular social studies class period—to discuss current events.

(2) Discuss relevant news items that relate to the lesson for that day during the regular social studies class period.

(3) Alternate units on current news events with units that are regularly required.

Even young children who cannot read accounts of news events need to be exposed to current events. Following are some ideas that can be used with both younger and older students.

Younger Students

(1) Convert an interest center into one that focuses on a country that is in the news. Bring in pictures and objects that students can look at.

(2) Students can watch news programs on television and discuss them in class the next day. The teacher could also tape a telecast and replay it in the classroom. Students could be asked to decide how these events affect their lives.

(3) Students can prepare a bulletin board, posting pictures and even three-dimensional objects on the display. It is a good idea to use a world map as part of the bulletin board.

Older Students

(1) After students have followed a news story for several days, have them write a headline which they believe might appear in tomorrow's paper.

(2) Have students conduct mock news broadcasts for which they have to synthesize the important happenings and write their accounts of them.

(3) Students can keep a scrapbook for following news events over a period of time. They should look for relationships that indicate how certain happenings lead to future events.

Passe (1988) has discovered that internal factors of teachers are related to curricular decision making. A specific example of this occurred in his study when he found that "[t]eachers who keep up with the news on a regular basis seem more likely to use the knowledge gained from that activity in the classroom than teachers who are not so aware of current affairs" (p. 86). School administrators might want to include current events questions when interviewing applicants for teaching jobs and then encourage teachers to maintain reading and viewing habits related to current events after they employ a person.

A number of news materials are available for classroom use; local newspapers are an excellent source. Many city newspapers are involved with the Newspaper in Education (NIE) program. Information about this can be obtained from

ANPA Foundation
P.O. Box 17407
Dulles International Airport
Washington, DC 20041

Other commercial programs include

USA Today
P.O. Box 500-CL
Washington, DC 20044

U.S. News and World Report
9300 N Street
Room 264
Washington, DC 20037

Newsweek
Newsweek Education Division
444 Madison Ave.
New York, NY 10022

Time
Education Program
10 N. Main St.
Yardley, PA 19067

World Newsmap of the Week
P.O. Box 310
Highwood, IL 60040

World News of the Week
100 Subscription Processing Center
South Milwaukee, WI 53172

Scholastic News
902 Sylvan Ave.
Englewood Cliffs, NJ 07632

Weekly Reader
4343 Equity Drive
P.O. Box 16730
Columbus, OH 43216

When using current events or teaching other topics such as apartheid, crime, poverty, population growth, world hunger, etc., there is always the potential for touching upon conflicting value patterns of students or community members. Shermis (1983) affords school administrators some guidelines as to how they can handle controversy with more confidence:

(1) Be prepared to defend one's choice of topic and procedures with a full rationale.
(2) Before beginning, get help from the profession, e.g., "Position Statement on the Freedom to Teach and the Freedom to Learn" by the National Council for the Social Studies.
(3) Discriminate between indoctrination and guidance.
(4) Have access to a large amount of data to support your stance.

FIELD TRIPS

These study trips are excellent ways of utilizing community resources. Administrators need to make sure that teachers follow appropriate procedures when they intend to take their class to one of these sites. Some suggestions include

(1) The purpose of the field trip should be clear. Ideally, the teacher should have visited the site prior to the trip.

(2) Teachers need to seek administrative permission for the trip.

(3) Transportation must be arranged.

(4) Parents need to sign permission forms.

(5) Volunteers should be secured to accompany the students.

(6) Follow-up activities should be carried out by the teacher and the class, e.g., writing thank you notes to the place visited and summarizing the learning benefits of the field trip.

READING IN THE SOCIAL STUDIES

Since reading is probably the most critical ability for a student's success in school, it is paramount that teachers are sensitive to this process in social studies instruction. Some recommendations for addressing the range of reading abilities in a classroom require resources, time, or skills that are available on a limited basis: (1) use multiple texts, (2) rewrite the material at a simpler level, (3) use a nonreading approach to social studies, and (4) secure simpler nontext materials for slower readers (Jarolimek, 1986, 229).

Reading in the content area of social studies implies some prereading considerations to set the stage. Here are some suggestions:

(1) *Scanning*
Students should have a chance to scan new material. The teacher can have the students page quickly through the chapter, noticing the chapter title, subtitles, section headings, and picture illustrations. This gives the students an idea of what the chapter is about.

(2) *Vocabulary*
Identify words in the material to be read that will cause difficulty for the students. Social studies is infused with technical terms (plateau, legislature, century), words with multiple meanings (bill, party, mouth), and figurative words (iron curtain, Sunbelt, hot line).

(3) *Establish Purpose*
Students need to know why they are reading the material. This can be

done simply by displaying an object that relates to the assignment they are to read and leading a short discussion about it. Another technique is a structured overview, an example of which is shown in Figure 11.1. Key concepts are extracted from a passage and arranged to show connections. A structured overview is similar to an outline, but it is more graphic.

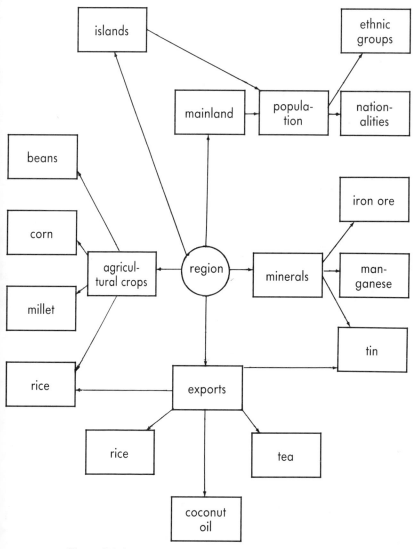

Figure 11.1 Structured overview on the region of Southeast Asia.

(4) *Previewing*

A technique such as SQ3R can be taught to the students. First, students survey the material, which can be done by looking at boldfaced headings. Second, they create questions about what they think they will learn from the material. Third, they will read the material. Fourth, they will recite and discuss answers to the earlier questions. Fifth, they will review the material.

Once the prereading has been done, students are ready to tackle the reading assignment. Teachers should consider some of the following ideas:

(1) Have students use the topic sentence as an aid to understanding a paragraph.

(2) Have students use the illustrations in the book and the captions which accompany the illustrations to gain meaning from the page.

(3) Have students utilize comprehension skills, such as using context clues, applying word-attack skills, finding main ideas and supporting details, summarizing information, identifying relationships among ideas, making inferences from the information just read, and distinguishing between fact and opinion.

(4) Prepare a study guide for the students to use. Its purpose is to assist the students to "read to learn." An example of one study guide format is to have the students answer a series of questions which are constructed on varying levels, i.e., literal, interpretive, and applied.

WRITING IN THE SOCIAL STUDIES

Students don't write enough in social studies. There is, however, a plentiful supply of activities they can engage in, e.g.,

(1) Write book reviews

(2) Take notes while listening to a speaker

(3) Write explanations of events or exhibits or after a field trip

(4) Create "news" stories about historical events

(5) Maintain class diary (Jarolimek, 1986, 260–261)

Writing needs to be thought of as a process by which a student discovers what he knows about a topic. The process is characterized by four stages: (1) prewrite, which involves selecting a topic, gathering data, and organizing ideas; (2) draft, which is making a rough copy; (3) revise, which necessitates making appropriate changes in the rough copy; and (4) complete final copy.

An example appears in the following lesson plan of how an early elementary child can do writing in the social studies about a famous American woman.

EARLY ELEMENTARY GRADE LESSON PLAN

Topic: **Writing about Rosa Parks**

Grade: **4th**

Date: **April 12, 10:00–10:40**

I. *Purpose*: **tells what a student will learn**

After completing the skills lesson, the students will be able to (1) formulate appropriate questions for the writing of a report on a particular topic, (2) write paragraphs that are based on main ideas, and (3) revise the paragraphs into a final copy.

II. *Motivation*: **tells how to begin the day's lesson**

Inform the class that today they will begin work on "Famous American Women," which was announced last week. By this time, each of them has had a chance to select a woman as the subject of the report he will write. Ask several of the students to give the names of the women they have chosen.

III. *Development*: **tells how to conduct the day's lesson**

Tell the class that they will work together this class period to carry out some of the steps in writing a good report. Put the following stages on the board:

(1) Prewrite

(2) Draft

(3) Revise

(4) Final copy

Remind them that they will need to do all of these stages during the next two weeks; however, today the class will work on stages 1 and 2 together.

The first step in prewriting is to select a topic. The person chosen for today's lesson is Rosa Parks. Since the report will be read by the fifth grade class next door, the next step is to decide what kind of information fifth graders would be interested in knowing. To complete the prewriting and drafting steps, the class will need to come up with some questions that they want to answer.

Handout: Rosa Parks

Rosa Parks finished her day's work in Montgomery, Alabama. She got on a bus and paid her fare. Then, she sat in a seat toward the front of the bus.

In 1955, many southeastern cities had laws that black people had to follow. Blacks could not sit at the front of a public bus. They also had to give up their seats to white people if the bus was crowded. That night, a white man asked Rosa Parks for her seat. She said no. She knew that she was being treated unfairly.

Rosa Parks was arrested and fined $10. Thousands of black people in Montgomery then refused to ride the buses. The bus companies began to lose money. The protest movement was led by a minister named Martin Luther King, Jr.

Finally, the United States Sumpreme Court ruled that the law was wrong. This important decision meant that all people of all races and colors would have to be treated fairly in hotels, restaurants, and other public places. The courage of one woman led to this victory.

At this time provide a handout for each student about Rosa Parks. They will use it to formulate their questions. Questions they might generate are

(1) What does the word *protest* mean?
    ANSWER: *Protest* means to express disapproval of something that one has little power to prevent or to avoid.
(2) Where was Rosa Parks from?
    ANSWER: Montgomery, Alabama.
(3) When did she live?
    ANSWER: In the 1950s.
(4) Why was she arrested?
    ANSWER: She would not give her seat to a white man who asked for it.
(5) Why did Rosa feel she had the right to her seat on the bus?
    ANSWER: She had paid her fare, and the seat was empty.
(6) Why couldn't she sit at the front of the bus?
    ANSWER: The city's laws did not allow black people to sit in those seats.

Ask students where they could locate other information on Rosa Parks as part of the prewriting stage. Some of the students might say an encyclopedia, other reference books in the library, newspaper articles in the library, information from the NAACP, etc.

Next, the class needs to choose a title that will capture the meaning of the report. Some ideas might be "Rosa Parks," "Rosa: A Brave Woman," or "Rosa Parks and Segregation."

After all the information has been collected on cards (show them how to record on the card the source where they obtained the information), they can begin writing the draft copy. They might want to make each of the question/answer items into a separate paragraph. Have them write an opening paragraph explaining what city and state Rose Parks was from and where in the United States this is.

Collect a number of these paragraphs and read aloud. Have the class decide if any of them are acceptable the way they now are—or whether some revisions should be made to make it sound even better. Write the final version of the paragraph on the board, but include several intentional mistakes in spelling and punctuation. As a last step, have the class point out the errors and the corrections that should be made.

IV. *Conclusion*: **tells how to close or evaluate the day's lesson**

At this point have the students work on another question/answer item from Part III above. They should revise this draft copy of the paragraph to make it sound just right. They can exchange their paragraphs with a classmate to spot any errors in grammar, spelling, or punctuation.

At this time, inform the class that tomorrow they will begin the prewriting stage of their own report by visiting the school library to gather some information.

V. *Materials*: **tells what is needed for the day's lesson**

Handout on Rosa Parks.

Note: This lesson is adapted with permission from material by Bonnie Armbruster et al., found on pages 240 and 322 of the teacher's edition of *America's Regions and Regions of the World* (1986), a fourth grade text published by Ginn and Company.

ASSISTANCE POINTS

Questions for Action for the Administrator

1. An elementary school teacher made plans in the beginning of the school year for a unit of work dealing with UNICEF. The culminating activity, planned to coincide with Halloween, involved pupils in depicting representative "children around the world" dressed in native garb and expressing some universal themes of childhood—family life, games, and songs. A few days before the culminating activity, the teacher received calls from some of the parents objecting to any kind of educational activity that portrays UNICEF in a favorable light.

WHAT ACTION IS POSSIBLE REGARDING THIS CONTROVERSY?

ACTION: The parents were reacting to values regarding global education. They apparently were objecting to the image in their minds of this one-world organization. Despite mounting pressure, the teacher indicated her intention to proceed with her plans and sought backing, via two and one-half hours of phone calls, from her principal, school board members, and ultimately the superintendent of schools. Her pleas for backing were agreed to and the culminating activity was carried out as planned.

Note: This incident is taken from "Global Education: Charges and Counter-Charges," by Stanley Wronski in *Michigan Social Studies Journal*, p. 149, Spring 1988.

2. What implications for social studies does the following statement have?

> "Today's students come to school speaking over 100 different languages and dialects."

3. Look at the latest accreditation review that was done for your building/district. Do a discrepancy analysis for an item from this report. A suggested analysis format might be as follows:

A	B	C	D	E	F
Topic	What the school is doing	What the school should be doing	Discrepancy between B and C	Person who should be responsible for correcting the discrepancy	Date when the discrepancy should be corrected

Names and Addresses of Professional Organizations

Following are some addresses to which an educator can write to obtain information about topics beyond the six social sciences:

1. Population Institute
   110 Maryland Ave., NE
   Washington, DC 20002
   (PI distributes a newsletter called "Popline.")

2. The American Forum
   45 John St., Suite 1200
   New York, NY 10038

(American Forum publishes materials on global education and international studies, including *Next Steps in Global Education: A Handbook for Curriculum Development*, by Willard Kniep.)

3. Yale Center for International and Area Studies
   Yale University
   85 Trumbull St., Box 13A Yale Station
   New Haven, CT 06520
   (The Yale Center is a national resource center for the interdisciplinary study and teaching of international relations.)

4. Population Reference Bureau, Inc.
   2213 M St., NW
   Washington, DC 20037
   (The PRB is a nonprofit education organization established as a source of facts and implications of national and world population trends.)

5. National Women's History Project
   P.O. Box 3716
   Santa Rosa, CA 95402
   (The NWHP publishes materials on the heritage of women.)

6. General Learning Corporation
   P.O. Box 3060
   Northbrook, IL 60065-9931
   (GLC publishes a magazine called *Writing*, which teaches students to become more skillful writers.)

7. Center for Environmental Education
   624 Ninth St.
   Washington, DC 20001
   (The CEE publishes the *Directory of Environmental Education Resources*.)

8. United States Environmental Protection Agency
   Waterside Mall
   401 M St., SW
   Washington, DC 20460
   (The EPA publishes the *EPA Journal*.)

9. Heldref Publications
   4000 Albemarle St., NW
   Washington, DC 20016
   (Heidref publishes *Environment*.)

10. National Science Teachers Association
    1742 Connecticut Ave.
    Washington, DC 20009

(The NSTA distributes a number of publications, one of which is the *Energy and Education Newsletter*.)

11. Mershon Center
Ohio State University
Columbus, OH 43201
(The Mershon Center has a "Citizenship Development and Global Education Program.")

12. United Nations
Room DC2-853
New York, NY 10017
(The U.N. has a number of publications for distribution.)

13. Center for Teaching International Relations
University of Denver
Denver, CO 80208

14. Commission on Schooling for the 21st Century
Phi Delta Kappa
Eight & Union, P.O. Box 789
Bloomington, IN 47402
(PDK publishes *Handbook for Conducting Future Studies in Education*.)

15. World Future Society
4916 Elmo Ave.
Bethesda, MD 20814
(WFS publishes *The Study of the Future* and the monthly journal *Future Study*.)

16. Science, Technology & Society
The Pennsylvania State University
248 Calder Way, Room 303
University Park, PA 16801

Research: Implications for Educators

1. Chris Buethe (1986) surveyed teachers in a midwestern state and found out that

   (a) A majority of those who responded to his questionnaire did not know the meaning of terms such as *catalytic converter*, *biosphere*, *dioxin*, and *leaching*.

   (b) Approximately half the teachers could not recognize the principal expected 1990 fuel sources.

   (c) Most appeared not to know the meaning of the term *watershed*.

   (d) Most did not know if their state had nuclear power plants.

Some of Buethe's suggestions were to encourage teachers to read current news for environmental issues and content; use related cross-age tutoring from 4-H, FFA, and science clubs; and improve their own knowledge of environmental topics through university courses, local industries, government agencies, and guest speakers.

2. Mary Haas reviewed a number of research studies to find that "beginning as early as in the elementary grades, students at various ages hold identifiable views about war" (1985, 255). Students' attitudes toward war changed as they got older: young students reject a justification for war, but older students feel that there are acceptable reasons for war. The implication for educators is to make sure that teenagers are supplied with "examples of positive actions of people and institutions [to] lead students to believe that war is not inevitable" (Haas, 1985, 256).

REFERENCES

Abrams, Eileen. *A Curriculum Guide to Women's Studies for the Middle School Grades 5–9.* Old Westbury, NY:The Feminist Press (1981).

Anthony, Robert B. "Multinational Corporations and Global Awareness," *Social Studies*, pp. 59–61 (March/April 1985).

Buethe, Chris. "Are Social Studies Teachers Environmental Illiterates?" *Southern Social Studies Quarterly*, pp. 60–64 (Fall 1986).

Cannings, Terence R. "Is There a Future in Your Classroom?" *Social Studies Review*, pp. 74–84 (Winter 1983).

Cervino, Dennis R. "Future Studies: Why, What, Where, and How?" *Michigan Social Studies Journal*, pp. 91–93 (February 1987).

Chapman, John et al. "Position Statement on Global Education," of the National Council for the Social Studies. In *Social Education*, pp. 36–38 (January 1982).

Charles, Cheryl and Bob Samples, eds. *Science and Society: Knowing, Teaching, Learning.* Bulletin No. 57. Washington, DC:National Council for the Social Studies (1978).

Collins, H. Thomas and Sally Banks Zakariya. *Getting Started in Global Education: A Primer for Principals and Teachers.* Arlington, VA:National Association of Elementary School Principals (1982).

Cunningham, Patricia M. and James W. Cunningham. "Content Area Reading-Writing Lessons," *The Reading Teacher*, pp. 506–512 (February 1987).

Fitch, Robert M. and Cordell M. Svengalis. *Futures Unlimited: Teaching about Worlds to Come.* Bulletin No. 59. Washington, DC:National Council for the Social Studies (1979).

Fleisher, Paul. "Teaching Children about Nuclear War," *Phi Delta Kappan*, pp. 215–216 (November 1985).

Goodlad, John I. "The Learner at the World's Center," *Social Education*, pp. 424–436 (October 1986).

Grambs, Jean D., ed. *Teaching about Women in the Social Studies.* Bulletin No. 48. Washington, DC:National Council for the Social Studies (1976).

Haas, Mary E. "Considerations for Curriculum Development in Teaching War and Peace," *Social Studies*, pp. 254–256 (November/December 1985).

Haessly, Jacqueline. "Peace-Making Goes to School," *The History and Social Science Teacher*, pp. 49–52 (Spring 1985).

Hunkins, Francis P. et al. *Social Studies in the Elementary School*. Columbus, OH: Merrill (1982).

Jarolimek, John. *Social Studies in Elementary Education, 7th edition*. New York:Macmillan (1986).

Johnson, Jacquelyn and John Benegar. "Global Issues in the Intermediate School," *Social Education*, pp. 131–137 (February 1983).

Kaltsounis, Theodore. *Teaching Social Studies in the Elementary School*. Englewood Cliffs, NJ:Prentice-Hall, Inc. (1987).

Kasschau, Richard A. "Pressures and Principles: How Shall We Teach Psychology?" *Social Education*, pp. 13–16 (January 1985).

Kauffman, Draper L., Jr. *Teaching the Future*. Palm Springs, CA:ETC Publications (1976).

Kniep, Willard M. "Defining a Global Education by Its Content," *Social Education*, pp. 437–446 (October 1986).

LaConte, Ronald T. "Teaching the Future," *Educational Leadership*, pp. 40–44 (September 1983).

Lamy, Steven L. "Resources for Global Perspectives Education: A Practitioner's View," *Social Studies Review*, pp. 43–49 (Winter 1983).

Lane, Kathleen R. "Energy Education Evaluation Checklist," *Indiana Social Studies Quarterly*, pp. 61–63 (Winter 1982–83).

Lipman, Matthew et al. *Philosophy in the Classroom*. Upper Montclair, NJ:Institute for the Advancement of Philosophy for Children, Montclair State College (1977).

Long, Cathryn and Fred R. Czarra, eds. "Food We Need and How to Get It," *Social Studies*, pp. 144–159 (July/August 1983).

Mallea, Kathleen. "Educating for Peace," *Middle School Journal*, pp. 11–13 (November 1985).

Maxim, George W. *Social Studies and the Elementary School Child*. Columbus, OH: Merrill (1983).

McCumsey, Janet. *Exploring the Future*. Carthage, IL:Good Apple, Inc. (1984).

National Council for the Social Studies. "Guidelines for Energy Education in Social Studies," in *Social Education*, pp. 558–561 (November/December 1981).

National Council for the Social Studies. "Guidelines for Teaching Science-Related Social Issues," in *Social Education*, pp. 258–261 (April 1983).

National Council for the Social Studies, Ad Hoc Committee on Global Education. "Global Education: In Bounds or Out?" in *Social Education*, pp. 242–249 (April/May 1987).

Neubert, Gloria A. and Sally J. McNelis. "Improving Writing in the Disciplines," *Educational Leadership*, pp. 54–58 (April 1986).

Nickell, Pat and Mike Kennedy. "Global Perspectives through Children's Games," *How to Do It Series*, Washington, DC:National Council for the Social Studies, Series 5, No. 3 (1987).

Otto, Robert. "Teaching Science-Related Social Issues," *How to Do It Series*, Washington, DC:National Council for the Social Studies, Series 5, No. 4 (1987).

Passe, Jeff. "The Role of Internal Factors in the Teaching of Current Events," *Theory and Research in Social Education*, pp. 83–89 (Winter 1988).

Passe, Jeff. "Developing Current Events Awareness in Children," *Social Education*, pp. 531–533 (November/December 1988).

Schuncke, George M. "Global Awareness and Younger Children: Beginning the Process," *Social Studies*, pp. 248–251 (November/December 1984).

Shermis, S. Samuel. "Criteria for Selecting Controversial Curricula," *Indiana Social Studies Quarterly*, pp. 33–39 (Autumn 1983).

Smiley, Bill "Psychology and the Social Science Curriculum," *Social Studies Review*, pp. 19–28 (Fall 1983).

Sweeney, Jo Ann Cutler and Peter A. Zandan. "Comparing Ourselves to Others: International Knowledge and Attitudes," *Social Studies*, pp. 135–142 (May/June 1982).

Vocke, David E. "Those Varying Perspectives on Global Education," *Social Studies*, pp. 18–20 (January/February 1988).

Vriens, Lennart and Robert Aspeslagh. "Peace Education as Alternating between the Person and the Structure," *The History and Social Science Teacher*, pp. 11–19 (Spring 1985).

Wertheimer, Michael et al. "Psychology: Social Science, Natural Science, and Profession," in *Social Studies and Social Sciences: A Fifty-Year Perspective*. Bulletin No. 78, Washington, DC: National Council for the Social Studies, pp. 165–178 (1986).

Women's History: Curriculum Guide. Santa Rosa, CA: National Women's History Project (1986).

Wronski, Stanley P. "Global Education: Charges and Countercharges," *Michigan Social Studies Journal*, pp. 147–150 (Spring 1988).

Zarnowski, Myra. "Learning about Contemporary Women," *Social Studies*, pp. 61–63 (March/April 1988).

12 | EVALUATION: LINKAGES TO INSTRUCTION

Chapter Preview of Key Ideas

★ Formative and summative are two kinds of evaluation.

★ Formative is used to monitor an operation as it proceeds.

★ Summative is used to assess an operation at its conclusion.

★ Student performance can be based on the results of standardized tests or teacher-made tests.

★ Standardized tests allow students in a district to be compared with outside standards.

★ Teacher-made tests are used within a classroom.

★ Teachers use objective devices to evaluate students.

★ Multiple choice items, alternate choice items, and matching items are some examples.

★ Teachers use subjective devices to evaluate students.

★ Essay tests are the most common examples.

★ Program evaluation is performed on the social studies curriculum.

★ Curriculum mapping describes the curriculum as it is taught.

★ Results of mapping are used to align the curriculum with national and state objectives, textbook content, and tests that the district administers.

This final chapter, entitled "Evaluation," deals with assessing individual students in social studies classes as well as with assessing the worth of social studies programs in the school. To begin with, there are some associated terms that should be discussed.

FORMATIVE EVALUATION. This is an evaluation that is made during a program or during instruction. Its purpose is to enable an administrator to monitor how well the social studies program is operating or to give a teacher an idea of how well the students are learning. By checking frequently throughout a specified time period, and educator can better make adjustments and determine how well goals are being met.

SUMMATIVE EVALUATION. Summative evaluation is a "summing up" at the end of a program or a period of instruction, which is in contrast to formative evaluation. This type of evaluation is often based on surveys, reports, or test results.

STANDARDIZED TESTS. These can be of two types. The first is a norm-referenced test, that is, results for students are stated in relation to a norm (standard for a large sample of students of the same age and grade). The second is criterion-referenced test, which means that the performance of a student is measured in relation to how well she has attained the criterion (mastery level) of specific objectives. Comparisons are not necessarily made with the performance of students in other parts of the country, as is done with norm-referenced tests.

The chief benefit of standardized tests is that an administrator can determine how the achievements of a student, class, grade, building, or district compare to a standard that has been established. The main drawback to standardized tests lies in the fact that the standard has been established for a large group of students in a different part of the country. Therefore, there is a possibility that this large group has been exposed to a different curriculum or a different set of objectives from the local students. Another drawback is that performance on standardized tests relies heavily on reading ability. Therefore, scores on the test might be distorted for students who do not read well.

The names of some frequently used standardized tests for social studies appear in Chart 12.1.

STUDENT EVALUATION

Evaluation of students should be carried out in ways so that feedback is given to the educator for the purpose of designing instruction. Paper and pencil tests afford one source of feedback; however, there are many other methods for evaluating students. Following are evaluation examples for administrators to explore. These can be used to evaluate understandings, attitudes, and skills in the social studies curriculum.

Observation

This is a very commonly used technique, which can be improved if several guidelines are followed. First, a teacher should have specific be-

Name of Test	Address
Iowa Test of Basic Skills	Riverside Publishing Co. 1919 South Highland Ave. Lombard, IL 60148
California Achievement Tests	CTB/McGraw-Hill Del Monte Research Park Monterey, CA 93940
Metropolitan Achievement Tests	The Psychological Corp. 757 Third Avenue New York, NY 10017
Stanford Achievement Test	The Psychological Corp. 757 Third Avenue New York, NY 10017
SRA Achievement Series	Science Research Associates 155 N. Wacker Drive Chicago, IL 60606
Sequential Tests of Education Progress	Addison-Wesley Pub. Co. 2725 Sand Hill Rd. Menlo Park, CA 94025
Primary Social Studies	Houghton Mifflin One Beacon St. Boston, MA 02108
Stanford Early School Achievement Test	The Psychological Corp. 757 Third Avenue New York, NY 10017

Chart 12.1 Standardized tests for social studies.

haviors in mind as he observes; it should not be a disorganized, impression-getting activity. Second, make the observations manageable. This can be done by focusing on just a few students at a time, rather than taking on the unwieldy task of observing the entire class. Third, the teacher should systematically record the observations, e.g., with a checklist.

Checklist

This can be created so that either the teacher fills it out or the student fills it out. A sample of a checklist showing items to be observed is presented in Figure 12.1.

Student:_____ · _____   Date:_____

	Excellent	Good	Fair	Poor
Identifies the problem			✔	
Proposes possible solutions		✔		
Gathers data	✔			
Makes decisions based on alternatives and consequences		✔		

Figure 12.1 Check list for problem-solving skills.

Discussion

Even though a lesson has been presented, there is no guarantee that the students have assimilated it. The adage, "A lesson is taught, but not caught" is very meaningful in this situation. If students are not able to discuss the topic easily and knowledgeably, it might indicate to the teacher that the lesson should be retaught. This is a good formative technique to enable both the teacher and student to see what progress has been made toward the objective of that day.

Conference

Sometimes children are shy about participating in group discussion and respond better when talking individually with the teacher. A teacher/student conference can establish a climate whereby the student expresses the understandings he has acquired from the lessons while the teacher becomes a careful questioner and listener.

Log or Diary

Another avenue for evaluation of a child who is hesitant about orally participating in large group discussion is to have the student write. The teacher can instruct the class to write a paragraph every day (after the social studies class) describing (1) what they felt was the most important information they learned, (2) what new information they learned that day, (3) what changes they experienced about their feelings toward the topic, etc. These writings can be kept in a notebook to be gathered periodically by the teacher. It is best to call this a log or journal rather than a diary because the last term connotes a personal, secret account which youngsters can be reluctant to share with other people.

Experience Summary

Another approach allowing students to appraise their learning is to have them summarize in writing an experience they have had. For example, after the class has returned from a field trip, the teacher can ask the students to write some paragraphs about what they saw and what it meant to them. If students are too young to be able to write, the teacher can ask them questions (e.g., "How long did it take us to walk to the bakery?" "What were the names of some of the jobs that people had?" "How did they bake the rolls?") and then write key words, phrases, or complete sentences on large butcher paper. The paper can then be displayed for the students to later recall the field trip's value.

Anecdotal Record

Sometimes a teacher needs to keep written notes, or anecdotes, on the actions of students. This can be done by recording the name of the student, the action, and the date/time when it occurred. This provides a reminder when a teacher must later substantiate impressions about the student. An example of an anecdotal entry is shown in Figure 12.2 for a student named Daron.

Work Samples

Sometimes growth can be almost imperceptible; consequently, work samples allow a teacher to note the progress of a student over a period of time. Samples can be kept of homework assignments, written in-class

Oct. 12	Daron did not complete any of the map exercises.
Oct. 13	Same thing today—incomplete map exercises.
Oct. 14	Conferred with Daron for a few minutes; doesn't know how to find latitude & longitude—confuses the terms.
Oct. 19	Divided class into groups; Daron was placed in group of students who find latitude and longitude to be confusing.
Oct. 20	Daron has more difficulty than others in the group; can't remember which direction to go to find latitude or longitude numbers.
Oct. 21	Daron is glueing two flat sticks together in a cross figure, writing "latitude" on one and "longitude" on the other. Maybe this will help distinguish between the two terms when the sticks are placed on top of a map.

Figure 12.2 Anecdotal entries for a student.

papers, special projects, and quizzes. Audio and videotapes can also be made to show an increase in performance.

Questionnaire

This affords the teacher a look at the views of the students in the class. Questions can be assembled dealing with topics ranging from academic knowledge to opinions about issues. Sometimes a student can simply circle a response such as the following:

Circle the face that shows how you feel when

Learning about famous Americans

Reading your social studies book

Students can be asked to express a relative opinion:

Indicate how you feel about each of the statements by placing one of these on the line:

SA = strongly agree   D = disagree
A = agree   SD = strongly disagree
U = uncertain

_____ People in the world should cut down fewer trees.

_____ All cans should be recycled.

_____ I learn best when I work in a small group.

_____ The President of the United States should be paid more than any other person in our country.

Students can also rank their preferences:

Put a "1" beside the item you most like to do, a "2" beside the next favorite, a "3" beside the next, and "4" beside your least favorite.

_____ Working on a report on the school library.

_____ Reading a book in our room's "Book Corner."

_____ Trying out a challenge at the room's interest center.

_____ Answering the questions at the end of a social studies textbook chapter.

Sociogram

It is often difficult to evaluate the affective part of a student's education. Some of the previously mentioned techniques, e.g., observation, conference, log, and questionnaire, can be very helpful in assessing the attitudes or feelings of the students. Another technique is a sociometric device called a sociogram. Suppose that a teacher has established the following as one of her objectives for a unit:

> Students will develop a more tolerant attitude toward one another.

A sociogram can help determine if this has been accomplished. At the beginning of the unit the teacher can distribute index cards to the class and ask them to write their names on one of the sides. They should circle their names to indicate that they are preparing the card. On the backside of the index card, they should write the name of one person in class they would like to sit beside as a new seating arrangement is made for the room. Below this name they should write a second name of the person who would be their second choice. The teacher should collect the cards and later prepare a grid to display what students have been chosen by whom. It might appear as in Figure 12.3.

Students (such as Paul, who was chosen five times) with a high total of selections are called "social stars." There are some students (such as Dan and Myra) who are not chosen by anyone and are called "social isolates." If the teacher notices that a student is shunned by others, it is her responsibility to try to determine the cause and bring that student into the class's acceptance. The source of the problem might be that the student is unaccepted because of bullying behavior, insensitivity, etc. After the problem is worked on during the following weeks, the teacher can try another sociogram. Hopefully, the student in question has now modified his behavior so that he is tolerated more by his classmates.

OBJECTIVE TEACHER-MADE TESTS

Schools make extensive use of commercially prepared evaluation instruments. However, teachers prepare a great many quizzes and tests in order

	Paul	Mary	Dan	Kris	Jack	Sue	Bill	Myra	etc.
Paul									
Mary	1								
Dan							1		
Kris	.				1				
Jack	1								
Sue				1					
Bill	1								
Myra						1			
etc.									
Total	5	2	0	2	1	3	2	0	

Figure 12.3 A grid sociogram.

to assess the accomplishment of students in that particular classroom. This part of the chapter will describe some objective tests, which administrators should make sure their teachers are familiar with.

Matching

Matching items require a student to choose a series of correct responses from a series of question stems. They can be particularly good for younger students because reading proficiency does not have to be a consideration. Figure 12.4 shows how a question can be written for students who have difficulty reading. Notice that there is an extra item in the left-hand column. This eliminates the possibility of getting the last item correct simply by eliminating all the others. The items on the left are also listed in alphabetical order to make it easier for students to locate the word when re-reading the list.

Multiple Choice

Multiple choice items require a student to read a question stem and then choose a single correct answer from a series of plausible responses. Several suggestions for constructing a multiple choice test include

(1) Construct three to five plausible choices for each question stem.
(2) Arrange choices so that the correct response is not always in the same position.

Draw a line connecting the name of the tourist attraction with the name of the continent where it is found.

Africa   kangaroo

Asia   Big Ben, Leaning Tower of
                          Pisa, or Eiffel Tower
Australia
                          Taj Mahal
Europe
                          Statue of Liberty
North America

Draw a line to match the continents on the left with the pictures on the right.

Figure 12.4 Matching questions.

(3) Make sure the question stem does not give a grammatical clue to the correct answer.

Alternate Choice

Alternate choice items force a student to make a decision between two alternatives, e.g., true-false, yes-no, right-wrong, etc. These kinds of questions are very quick for a teacher to write, but they are susceptible to correct guessing by the students. Helpful suggestions which administrators can pass along to teachers who compose this type of question include

(1) Avoid statements that are partially true and partially false (these allow either answer to be correct).

(2) Include an equal number of yes-no questions.

(3) Avoid words that will signal the answer, e.g., all, never, none, always, etc.

Short-Answer

This type requires a student to generate a response, e.g., by filling in a blank line to complete a sentence or by writing a phrase to answer a question. Tips for creating these questions include

(1) Be prepared to accept more than one answer as being defensibly correct.

(2) Do not use statements with too many blanks.

(3) Avoid copying sentences directly from the book.

SUBJECTIVE TEACHER-MADE TESTS

Subjective tests (also called essay tests) do not require much time for the teacher to create, but they do take a lot of time to grade. This is because students must write an extended response to open-ended questions which require attention to analysis, synthesis, and critical judgment. Essay tests should only be given to older students, who are capable of writing to these ends. Guidelines for constructing and grading essay tests include

(1) Make the question clear to reduce the possibility that students will misinterpret what is asked. For example, the question "What can you say about immigration?" is too vague. It is much better to write an item such as "Discuss two reasons why people left European countries during the first part of this century to come to the United States."

(2) Write a sample answer before grading the papers; this will serve as a standard.

(3) Inform the class how much spelling and grammar will influence the scoring for the question. It is a good idea to assign a grade for the content and a separate grade for spelling/mechanics.

Chart 12.2 summarizes some important considerations for administrators as they monitor how their teachers evaluate students.

PROGRAM EVALUATION

The main purpose of social studies program evaluation is "to determine whether the curriculum goals and objectives are being carried out" (Olivia, 1988, 467). Some people feel that this can be done merely by having teachers follow the curriculum guides, which have been prepared at the district or state levels. But, as English points out, these guides often go unused because

(1) Most guides are not user friendly.
(2) Most guides are not quality documents.
(3) Most guides are based on the partially true premise that "teachers will use what they help make."
(4) Most guides are too costly and take too much time to create.
(5) Most guides are based on the myth that the will of the local community can be translated into local control (English, 1986/87, 50–51).

Rather than hope that social studies program quality can be achieved simply by asking teachers to follow written curriculum guides, it is a better alternative for an administrator to undertake curriculum mapping. As described by English (1980), it

. . . reveals to a staff, principal, or supervisor what is actually being taught, how long it is being taught, and the match between what is being taught and the district's testing program. Curriculum mapping invents or creates no "new" curriculum. Rather, it attempts to describe the curriculum that currently exists (p. 559).

Chart 12.3 sets out the steps that an administrator should follow to conduct curriculum mapping.

Figure 12.5 illustrates a typical format used for curriculum mapping at the elementary school level over a week's time. Social studies is listed on line 12. If Figure 12.5 were to be broken down to show only the social studies component, it might appear as shown in Figure 12.6.

If the teachers at all grade levels in the district were to complete such a map for social studies, then a supervisor could construct a picture of the curriculum for the district, which would include

	YES	NO

1. Do the teachers use diagnostic questions early in a unit to determine how much students already know both individually and collectively?

2. Do teachers know the functions and proper construction of questions in all formats—true-false, multiple choice, matching, completion, discussion, etc.?

3. Do teachers use evaluation approaches that take into account individual differences such as personal interviews with students?

4. Do teachers use informal means of testing such as checklists and direct teacher observation of student work?

5. Do teachers assess student attitudes using scales, semantic differentials, or unfinished sentences?

6. Do teachers use Socratic questioning techniques as a means of leading students to discover ideas?

7. Do teachers provide many-faceted "think tank" questions in which students in small groups collaborate on responses?

8. Do teachers encourage students to ask questions?

9. In making assignments, do teachers use the question patterns devised by developmental reading specialists?

10. Do teachers consciously build all levels of thinking into questions (Bloom's taxonomy or a similar system)?

11. Do teachers emphasize important ideas in their questions rather than details?

12. Do teachers test for skills as well as content?

13. Do teachers sometimes use formative tests only to see how well students are doing and not for grading?

14. Do teachers construct tests that are grammatically and stylistically correct and clearly reproduced?

15. Do teachers conduct tests in such a way that cheating is difficult and therefore not such a temptation?

16. Do teachers fairly evaluate responses to questions with subjective answers, judging not how much students agree with the teachers but how well the students develop their responses?

17. Do teachers construct questions clear in meaning? Do they deal fairly with students who read a reasonable meaning into the words other than the one anticipated?

18. Do teachers make comments on tests to show students an appreciation of their achievements as well as the nature of their errors?

19. Do teachers have a system for collecting and saving questions from a variety of sources so that they can refer to them later when building a new test?

Chart 12.2 Checklist for student evaluation. (This checklist is drawn from information on pages 131 and 132 of *A Guide to Curriculum Planning in Social Studies*, published by the Wisconsin Department of Public Instruction, Madison, WI, copyright 1986.)

	YES	NO
20. Do teachers use test results as the basis for reteaching?		
21. Do teachers keep anecdotal records in a notebook or log, which provide brief descriptions of how individual students are performing?		
22. Do teachers use individual student-teacher conferences as a way of diagnosing or evaluating student learning?		
23. Do teachers use individual interest inventories as a means of identifying student interest, knowledge, or skills that might relate to an upcoming social studies unit?		

Chart 12.2 (continued). Checklist for student evaluation. (This checklist is drawn from information on pages 131 and 132 of *A Guide to Curriculum Planning in Social Studies*, published by the Wisconsin Department of Public Instruction, Madison, WI, copyright 1986.)

(1) The number (and names) of the topics that were being taught

(2) The amount of time that each of the topics was being taught

(3) What teachers were covering certain topics and what teachers were neglecting certain topics

Administrators should decide how many grade levels they want to map. After the mapping is carried out, the results can be used to align the real curriculum (as actually taught by the teachers). This can be done by having teachers from each grade level prepare a curriculum alignment guide (English, 1986/87) for their grade. The approach should be as follows:

(1) List the social studies objectives that are mandated by the state.

(2) List the social studies objectives that are included in the standardized tests given by the district.

(3) List the objectives that are present in the social studies textbook.

(4) List the objectives that are recommended by the National Council for the Social Studies.

The merger of objectives from these four sources affords a comprehensive alignment guide that should serve as the basis for the social studies program in the school district. An alignment guide should be prepared for each grade level and should be placed in each classroom for the teacher's use. Each objective should have a coding system so that its source can be easily identified. Examples of several objectives appear in Figure 12.7.

The National Council for the Social Studies has prepared guidelines for analyzing a social studies program, and this checklist appears in Chart 12.4. When completed, the guidelines will let an administrator see any patterns in the social studies program. A large number of fours and fives

Step	What the School Administrator Does
1. Determine curricular areas to map.	Based on poor test scores, observation, survey data, or staff/student/parental complaints, designate specific curricular areas to map.
2. Determine level of specificity to employ.	Based on the desirability of matching test data to map data, determine the level of specificity required to develop maps and decisions to be made with the data.
3. Decide how often mapping is to occur.	Relate the types of decisions to be made with the mapping data to the necessary frequency of mapping (daily, weekly, monthly, semester, or yearly).
4. Determine how mapping data will be consolidated.	Decide who and how mapping data will be gathered and collated. Will automation be part of the collation process? Develop computer software if necessary.
5. Determine how the data will be interpreted and reported.	What does the data mean? Decisions will have to be interpreted in light of what the numbers really mean about the "taught" curriculum. What will be done with the data?
6. Determine the benefits of mapping to the school/ system.	Analyze the major anticipated benefits of engaging in mapping. Who specifically benefits? Do students and teachers benefit? How?
7. Determine the costs of mapping.	Determine the costs involved in conducting mapping. Include staff training, use of consultants, development of a computer program, teacher time, changes in curriculum guides, other changes that may be required. What are the sources of funds for mapping?
8. What follow-up activities are anticipated after mapping?	How will it be known if mapping was a success or a failure? Who will decide? What has to happen after mapping? Determine the criteria by which you will have to answer the above questions.
9. Determine policy changes that may be required.	Based on analysis of existing board policies or administrative regulations, what may have to be altered to engage in mapping? Consider policies pertaining to teacher evaluation, use of data, reporting of data, public review of the data, and so on. Develop new policies that will facilitate mapping.

Chart 12.3 Skills involved in curriculum mapping [taken from *Skills for Successful School Leaders*, by Hoyle, English, and Steffy, p. 87, published by AASA, Arlington, VA (1985)]. Reprinted with permission.

Instructions: Record each day the total minutes spent in each curricular area and noncurricular area. Compute totals in minutes by week for each line. Total vertically by day for curricular area (line 17) and noncurricular each day (line 28). Compute total time per week (line 29). Do not count any activity twice (in more than one category). Total instructional time per day cannot exceed 265 for kindergarten, 265 for grades 1–2, 275 for grade 3, or 310 for grades 4–6. For total maximum time, add noninstructional time for your school.

Time Distribution (in minutes)

Curriculum Area/Topic/Skill/Subject	May 24	25	26	27	28	Weekly Total
1. Reading (formal reading instruction, follow-up)						
2. Spelling						
3. Oral Language						
4. Written Language						
5. Handwriting (formal instruction, drill only)						
6. Mathematics (formal instruction, follow-up)						
7. Science (formal instruction)						
8. Health Education (formal instruction)						
9. Art (formal instruction and follow-up)						
10. Music (formal instruction, listening)						
11. Physical Education (instruction plus play)						
12. Social Studies (history, geography, gov.)						
13. Career Education (nonduplicative time)						
14. Multicultural Education (formal instruction)						
15.						
16.						
17. Total Minutes on All Curricular Areas (lines 1–16)						
18. Attendance						
19. Assemblies						
20. Classroom Discipline						
21. Testing						
22. Collections, Drives						
23. Announcements						
24. Recess						
25. Lunch						
26. Other (Specify)						
27. Total Time on Noncurricular (18–26)						
28. Total Time Minutes per Day (17+27)						
29. Total Time per Week (17+27)						

(lines 18–26 labeled vertically: Noncurricular Time)

Noncurricular Time

Figure 12.5 Sample: elementary school mapping format [taken from *Skills for Successful School Leaders*, by Hoyle, English, and Steffy, p. 84, published by AASA, Arlington, VA (1985)]. Reprinted with permission.

should be a cause of concern, whereas ones and twos are cause for gratification.

CONCLUDING COMMENTS

Evaluation can be like a hot potato. It can be tossed between a team of administrators and a team of teachers. Central office administrators (Sproull and Zubrow, 1981) believe that standardized test results are of most use to building-level personnel—especially classroom teachers. The feeling of teachers, however, is contrary to this for

. . . [teachers] rely most heavily on assessments provided as part of instructional materials and assessments they design and construct themselves—and very little on standardized tests or test scores (Stiggins, 1985, 69).

Teachers may spend as much as 20 percent to 30 percent of their time directly involved in assessment-related activities for the classroom (Stiggins, 1988). Administrators—as instructional leaders—can provide assistance to teachers in their district in the following areas:

(1) Clarifying the demands of various assessment purposes
(2) Selecting assessment methods to match purposes
(3) Designing or planning assessments that work

General Description: geography I taught the geography of the U.S. by working with four different kinds of maps: relief, landform, political, and historical. The students worked in committees and created an example of each kind of map.			Time A .50
Concepts	Skills	Attitudes	
Utilized time belts	Used string to measure distances on the globe	Developed an awareness of the need for international agreement on dates/times	Time B .50
Used longitude and latitude to locate cities and places as a concept	Made time estimates of how long it took to reach a place by various methods	Realized the need for uniformly understood map symbols	
Was able to utilize the International Date Line			
Time .20	Time .25	Time .05	Total .50

Time A is the total time for the topic which should be equal to Time B, the total time sub-divided into three categories. Time is expressed as the number of hours per week per school year. This teacher spends about one-half hour per week teaching social studies.

Figure 12.6 Sample classroom curriculum map: fifth grade social studies [taken from "Curriculum Mapping," by Fenwick English, published in *Educational Leadership*, p. 558 (April 1980). Reprinted with permission.

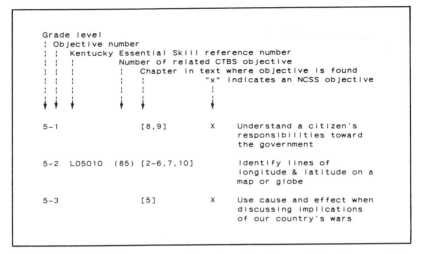

Figure 12.7 Sample objectives from a fifth grade social studies curriculum alignment guide.

(4) Ensuring the quality of those assessments

(5) Constructing assessments based on performance judgment

(6) Using modern technology in classroom assessment

(7) Promoting testwiseness among students

(8) Measuring higher order thinking skills (Stiggins, 1985, 73)

Just as an administrator must do the above eight because he is an *instructional leader*, he must also perform other duties when he "wears the hat" of an *accountability agent*. These duties include producing summaries of standardized test scores for public consumption as well as selecting and developing tests for district-wide use in policy making (Stiggins, 1988).

An administrator, then, who is concerned with both student assessment and program assessment should be prepared to answer the following questions (SSEC, 1983, 201–202):

(1) What are the strengths and weaknesses of the social studies program?

(2) Is the current social studies program achieving district-wide goals and objectives?

(3) What type of changes and/or experimentations should be conducted to improve the instructional program?

(4) What are the educational gains of our students as compared to those of students in other districts?

(5) What are the strengths and weaknesses of the social studies teachers?

(6) What in-service programs appear to be needed?

Circle the number that indicates how evident the following items are in your school district. A "1" reflects that it is carried out "very often," while a "5" indicates that it is carried out "very seldom."

I. Relationship of the Program to the Maturity and Concerns of Students

1.1 Students should be involved in the formulation of goals, the selection of activities and instructional strategies, and the assessment of curricular outcomes.	1	2	3	4	5
1.2 The school and its teachers should make steady efforts, through regularized channels and practices, to identify areas of concern to students.	1	2	3	4	5
1.3 Students should have some choices, some options within programs fitted to their needs, their concerns, and their social world.	1	2	3	4	5
1.4 Students should have a special studies experience at all grade levels, K–12.	1	2	3	4	5
1.5 The program should take into account the aptitudes, developmental capabilities, and psychological needs of the students.	1	2	3	4	5

II. Relationship of the Program to the Real Social World

2.1 The program should focus on the social world as it is, its flaws, its strengths, its dangers, and its promise.	1	2	3	4	5
2.2 The program should emphasize pervasive and enduring social issues.	1	2	3	4	5
2.3 The program should demonstrate the relationships between the local and global aspects of social issues.	1	2	3	4	5
2.4 The program should include analysis and attempts to formulate potential resolutions or present and controversial global problems such as racism, sexism, world resources, nuclear proliferation, and ecological imbalance.	1	2	3	4	5
2.5 The program should provide intensive and recurring cross-cultural study of groups to which students themselves belong and those to which they do not.	1	2	3	4	5
2.6 The program should offer opportunities for students to meet, discuss, study, and work with members of racial, ethnic, and national groups other than their own.	1	2	3	4	5
2.7 The program should build upon realities of the immediate school community.	1	2	3	4	5
2.8 Participation in the real social world both in school and out should be considered a part of the social studies program.	1	2	3	4	5

Chart 12.4 Social studies evaluation checklist. (This chart is adapted from "Needs Assessment Instrument Based on the Social Studies Curriculum Guidelines," on pp. 274–278 of the April 1979 issue of *Social Education*.)

II. Relationship of the Program to the Real Social World

2.9 The program should provide the opportunity for students to examine potential future conditions and problems.	1	2	3	4	5

III. Relationship of Program to Currently Valid Knowledge Representative of Human Beings' Experience, Culture, and Beliefs

3.1 The program should emphasize currently valid concepts, principles, and theories in the social sciences.	1	2	3	4	5
3.2 The program should develop proficiency in methods of inquiry in the social sciences and in techniques for processing social data.	1	2	3	4	5
3.3 The program should develop students' ability to distinguish among empirical, logical, definitional, and normative propositions and problems.	1	2	3	4	5
3.4 The program should draw upon all of the social sciences such as anthropology, economics, geography, political science, history, and the behavioral sciences.	1	2	3	4	5
3.5 The program should draw from other related fields such as law, the humanities, the natural and applied sciences, and religion.	1	2	3	4	5
3.6 The program should represent some balance between the immediate social environment of students and the larger social world; between small group and public issues; among local, national, and global affairs; among past, present, and future directions; among Western and non-Western cultures; and among economically developed and developing nations.	1	2	3	4	5
3.7 The program should include the study not only of human achievements, but also of human failures.	1	2	3	4	5

IV. Selection of Objectives; How Objectives Guide Program

4.1 Objectives should be carefully selected and formulated in the light of what is known about the students, their community, the real social world, and the fields of knowledge.	1	2	3	4	5
4.2 Knowledge, abilities, valuing, and social participation should all be represented in the stated objectives of social studies programs.	1	2	3	4	5
4.3 General statements of basic and long-range goals should be translated into more specific objectives conceived in terms of behavior and content.	1	2	3	4	5

Chart 12.4 (continued). Social studies evaluation checklist. (This chart is adapted from "Needs Assessment Instrument Based on the Social Studies Curriculum Guidelines," on pp. 274–278 of the April 1979 issue of *Social Education*.)

IV. Selection of Objectives; How Objectives Guide Program

	1	2	3	4	5
4.4 Classroom instruction should rely upon statements which identify clearly what students are to learn; learning activities and instructional material should be appropriate for achieving the stated objectives.	1	2	3	4	5
4.5 Classroom instruction should enable students to see their goals clearly in what is to be learned, whether in brief instructional sequences or lengthy units of study.	1	2	3	4	5
4.6 Instructional objectives should develop all aspects of the affective, cognitive, and psychomotor domains.	1	2	3	4	5
4.7 Objectives should be reconsidered and revised periodically.	1	2	3	4	5

V. Nature of Activities

	1	2	3	4	5
5.1 Students should have a wide and rich range of learning activities appropriate to the objectives of their social studies program.	1	2	3	4	5
5.2 Activities should include formulating hypotheses and testing them by gathering and analyzing data.	1	2	3	4	5
5.3 Activities should include using knowledge, examining values, communicating with others, and making decisions about social and civic affairs.	1	2	3	4	5
5.4 Students should be encouraged to become active participants in activities within their own communities.	1	2	3	4	5
5.5 Learning activities should be sufficiently varied and flexible to appeal to many kinds of students.	1	2	3	4	5
5.6 Activities should contribute to the students' perception of teachers as fellow inquirers.	1	2	3	4	5
5.7 Activities must be carried on in a climate which supports students' self-respect and opens opportunities to all.	1	2	3	4	5
5.8 Activities should stimulate students to investigate and to respond to the human condition in the contemporary world.	1	2	3	4	5
5.9 Activities which examine values, attitudes, and beliefs should be undertaken in an environment that respects each student's rights to privacy.	1	2	3	4	5

Chart 12.4 (continued). Social studies evaluation checklist. (This chart is adapted from "Need Assessment Instrument Based on the Social Studies Curriculum Guidelines," on pp. 274–278 the April 1979 issue of *Social Education*.)

VI. Relationship between Instruction and Range of Learning Resources

6.1 A social studies program requires a great wealth of appropriate instructional resources; no one textbook can be sufficient.	1	2	3	4	5
6.2 Printed materials must accommodate a wide range of reading abilities and interests, meet the requirements of learning activities, and include many kinds of material from primary as well as secondary sources, from social science and history as well as the humanities and related fields, from other nations and cultures as well as our own, from current as well as basic sources.	1	2	3	4	5
6.3 A variety of media should be available for learning through seeing, hearing, touching, and acting, and calling for thought and feeling.	1	2	3	4	5
6.4 Social studies classrooms should draw upon the potential contributions of many kinds of resource persons and organizations representing many points of view, a variety of abilities, and a mix of cultures and nationalities.	1	2	3	4	5
6.5 Classroom activities should use the school and community as a learning laboratory for gathering social data and for confronting knowledge and commitments in dealing with social problems.	1	2	3	4	5
6.6 The social studies program should have available many kinds of work space to facilitate variation in the size of groups, the use of several kinds of media, and a diversity of tasks.	1	2	3	4	5

VII. Relationship of Social Studies Program to Students' Experiences

7.1 Structure in the social studies program must help students organize their experiences to promote growth.	1	2	3	4	5
7.2 Learning experiences should be organized in such a manner that students will learn how to continue to learn.	1	2	3	4	5
7.3 The program must enable students to relate their experiences in social studies to other areas of experience.	1	2	3	4	5
7.4 The formal pattern of the program should offer choice and flexibility.	1	2	3	4	5

VIII. Nature of Local Program Evaluation

8.1 Evaluation should be based primarily on the school's own statements of objectives as the criteria for effectiveness.	1	2	3	4	5

Chart 12.4 (continued). Social studies evaluation checklist. (This chart is adapted from "Needs Assessment Instrument Based on the Social Studies Curriculum Guidelines," on pp. 274–278 of the April 1979 issue of *Social Education*.)

VIII. Nature of Local Program Evaluation

8.2 Included in the evaluation process should be assessment of progress not only in knowledge, but in skills and abilities including thinking, valuing, and social participation.	1	2	3	4	5
8.3 Evaluation data should come from many sources, not merely from paper-and-pencil tests, including observations of what students do outside as well as inside the classroom.	1	2	3	4	5
8.4 Regular, comprehensive, and continuous procedures should be developed for gathering evidence of significant growth in learning over time.	1	2	3	4	5
8.5 Evaluation data should be used for planning curricular improvements.	1	2	3	4	5
8.6 Evaluation data should offer students, teachers, and parents help in the course of learning and not merely at the conclusion of some marking period.	1	2	3	4	5
8.7 Both students and teachers should be involved in the process of evaluation.	1	2	3	4	5
8.8 Thoughtful and regular re-examination of the basic goals of the social studies curriculum should be an integral part of the evaluation program.	1	2	3	4	5

IX. Local Support for Social Studies Education as an Integral Part of the School Program

9.1 Appropriate instructional materials, time, and facilities must be provided for social studies education.	1	2	3	4	5
9.2 Teachers should not only be responsible but should be encouraged to try out and adapt for their own students promising innovations such as simulation, newer curricular plans, discovery, and actual social participation.	1	2	3	4	5
9.3 Decisions about the basic purposes of social studies education in any school should be as clearly related to the needs of its immediate community as to those of society at large.	1	2	3	4	5
9.4 Teachers should participate in active social studies curriculum committees with decision making as well as advisory responsibilities.	1	2	3	4	5
9.5 Teachers should participate regularly in activities which foster their professional competence in social studies education: in workshops or in-					

Chart 12.4 (continued). Social studies evaluation checklist. (This chart is adapted from "Needs Assessment Instrument Based on the Social Studies Curriculum Guidelines," on pp. 274–278 of the April 1979 issue of *Social Education*.)

IX. Local Support for Social Studies Education as an Integral Part of the School Program

service classes or community affairs or in reading, studying, and travel.	1	2	3	4	5
9.6 Teachers and others concerned with social studies education in the schools should have competent consultants available.	1	2	3	4	5
9.7 Teachers and schools should have and be able to rely upon a district-wide policy statement on academic freedom and professional responsibility.	1	2	3	4	5
9.8 Social studies education should expect to receive active support from administrators, teachers, board of education, and the community.	1	2	3	4	5
9.9 A specific minimal block of time should be allocated for social studies instruction each week.	1	2	3	4	5

Chart 12.4 (continued). Social studies evaluation checklist. (This chart is adapted from "Needs Assessment Instrument Based on the Social Studies Curriculum Guidelines," on pp. 274–278 of the April 1979 issue of *Social Education*.)

ASSISTANCE POINTS

Questions for Action for the Administrator

1. Explain how your schools' formal test results are communicated to teachers, parents, and the public.

2. From your position as an administrator, you are required to evaluate teachers and programs. As a related matter, what is your opinion about observation being one of the most useful student evaluation techniques a teacher can use?

3. Is pupil growth—shown by gains on paper and pencil tests—a valid way to appraise teacher effectiveness?

4. Using information from this chapter, how would evaluation of students differ for kindergarten, fourth grade, and eighth grade?

5. Assume you are an administrator who is going to use curriculum mapping. How will it help you determine whether your district's social studies goals and objectives are being carried out?

6. Look at a copy of your district's standardized test for social studies at a particular grade level. To what extent does the social studies curriculum for this grade match (or align) with the test?

Research about Evaluation: Implications for Educators

Torabi-Parizi and Campbell (1982) conducted a study with fifth grade students to determine effects of varying the number of options (three or four) available in multiple choice questions. One-half of a class took a test with four-response multiple choice items, while the other half of the class took a three-response multiple choice test. The following examples show how a question was rewritten:

Most factories are found in
a. cities
b. small towns
c. farming areas
d. mountain areas

Most factories are found in
a. cities
b. small towns
c. mountain areas

When the tests were scored, there was no significant difference in the results. The implication for educators is that three-response questions might be just as reliable as four-response questions. Advantages to using three-response questions are that (1) they are easier for teachers to write than four-response questions and (2) students should be able to read and complete them in a shorter period of time.

REFERENCES

Berg, Harry, ed. *Evaluation in Social Studies*. Thirty-Fifth Yearbook of the National Council for the Social Studies. Washington, DC:NCSS (1965).

Brown, Lena Boyd. "What Teachers Should Know about Standardized Tests," *Social Education*, pp. 509–516 (November/December 1976).

Buros, Oscar K., ed. *The Eighth Mental Measurements Yearbook*. Highland Park, NJ: Gryphon Press (1978).

English, Fenwick W. "Curriculum Mapping," *Educational Leadership*, pp. 558, 559 (April 1980).

English, Fenwick W. "It's Time to Abolish Conventional Curriculum Guides," *Educational Leadership*, pp. 50–52 (December 1986/January 1987).

English, Fenwick W. *Curriculum Auditing*. Lancaster, PA:Technomic Publishing Co. (1988).

Fleming, Margaret and Barbara Chambers. "Teacher-Made Tests: Windows on the

Classroom." In *Testing in the Schools: New Directions for Testing and Measurement*, No. 19. W. E. Hathaway, ed. San Francisco, CA:Jossey-Bass (1983).

Gronlund, Norman. *Measurement and Evaluation in Teaching, 5th edition*. New York: Macmillan (1985).

"Guide to Social Studies Program Evaluation: K–6," Albany, NY:New York State Education Dept., ERIC document number ED 290647 (1987).

Hartoonian, H. Michael (Task Force Chair). *A Guide to Curriculum Planning in Social Studies*. Madison, WI:Wisconsin Department of Public Instruction (1986).

Herlihy, John G. and Myra T. Herlihy. "Report from the Classroom," *Social Education*, pp. 576–581 (November/December 1976).

Hoyle, John R., Fenwick W. English, and Betty E. Steffy. *Skills for Successful School Leaders*. Arlington, VA:American Association of School Administrators (1985).

Hunkins, Francis P. "Rationales for Testing in the Social Studies," *Social Education*, pp. 504–508 (November/December 1976).

National Council for the Social Studies Position Statement. "How to Use the Guidelines for Social Studies Needs Assessment," *Social Education*, pp. 261–278 (April 1979).

Oliva, Peter F. *Developing the Curriculum, 2nd edition*. Glenview, IL: Scott, Foresman, & Co. (1988).

Paddock, Marie-Louise. "Full Accounting for Curriculum," *The School Administrator*, pp. 12, 13 (November 1988).

SSEC. "Planning a Social Studies Program: Activities, Guidelines, and Resources" (revised edition), Boulder, CO:Social Science Education Consortium, Inc. (1983).

SSEC. "Working Papers from Project SPAN," Boulder, CO:Social Science Education Consortium, Inc. (1982).

Sproull, Lee and David Zubrow. "Standardized Testing from the Administrative Perspective," *Phi Delta Kappan*, pp. 628–631 (May 1981).

Stiggins, Richard J. "Improving Assessment Where It Means the Most: In the Classroom," *Educational Leadership*, pp. 69–74 (October 1985).

Stiggins, Richard J. "The Ecology of Classroom Assessment," *Journal of Educational Measurement*, pp. 271–286 (Winter 1985).

Stiggins, Richard J. "Revitalizing Classroom Assessment," *Phi Delta Kappan*, pp. 363–368 (January 1988).

Superka, Douglas et al. *Social Studies Evaluation Sourcebook*. Boulder, CO:Social Science Education Consortium, Inc. (1978).

Torabi-Parizi, Rosa and Noma Jo Campbell. "Classroom Test Writing: Effects of Item Format on Test Quality," *The Elementary School Journal*, pp. 155–160 (November 1982).

Wiles, Jon and Joseph C. Bondi. *Curriculum Development, 2nd ed.* Columbus, OH: Merrill (1984).

Williams, Paul L. and Jerry R. Moore, eds. *Criterion-Referenced Testing for the Social Studies*, Bulletin 64. Washington, DC:National Council for the Social Studies (1980).

APPENDIX A

PROGRAM OF STUDIES (K–8) FOR THE STATE OF KENTUCKY

Kindergarten—Awareness of Self in a Special Setting: Myself and Others in My World

Home and school experiences provide the background for children as they learn about social patterns, families, and socioeconomic roles. Emphasis is placed on economic needs, social processes, and the interrelationship of individuals and groups. Comparisons to other countries and cultures may be made where appropriate to student and local needs. The program assists in building positive self-concepts in children, human relations skills in working with others, and adjustment to classrooms and school procedures and rules. Manipulative activities, role playing, resource persons, and relevant field trips help provide experiences for personal growth as a foundation for further social studies knowledge, skill, and attitude development.

Grade 1—The Individual in Primary Groups: Understanding School and Family Life in the World

The introduction to school in kindergarten is continued and extended in first grade. Students identify specialized roles and the division of labor.

Studying family life in early times and in other cultures provides opportunities for comparing ways of living. Children can study the specialized roles of school personnel as an example of the division of labor. Family life and structure, including variations of family structures, are to be included, as well as roles of family members. Essential activities of a family in meeting basic material and psychological needs should be stressed. Variations in the way families live are studied; e.g., urban, rural, self-employed, both parents employed, single-parent family arrangements, various housing options, and dependence of family members on each other and of the family on other families is to be stressed. The need for rules and law is taught as a natural extension of orderly group life.

333

Grade 2—Meeting Basic Needs in Nearby Social Groups: The Neighborhood in the World

The initial focus is on the student's neighborhood. This provides a basis for the introduction of a worldwide perspective through the study of life in another culture.

The study of social functions such as education, production, consumption, communication, and transportation in a neighborhood context is appropriate as children develop an understanding and appreciation of people living in groups. The need for rules and laws is stressed and illustrated by examples from the everyday lives of children. Geographic concepts relating to directionality and physical features need to be included. A historical perspective is developed by contrasting neighborhood life today with that of an earlier time.

Grade 3—Our Community and Other Communities in the World

An in-depth study of the local community is the major content focus. Primary studies are centered on community services, institutions, occupations, government, and the technology that enables the community to exist. In this study emphasis is given to building citizenship, respecting one's self, others, one's country, and group decisions. The study of people and groups extends from local communities to the world community, while developing an interdependence of people's respect for various cultures. The students will identify geo-political units (e.g., Kentucky and United States) and physical features (e.g., continents, oceans, peninsulas, islands) on maps and globes. Students will read and interpret information from maps, globes, charts, and graphs.

Grade 4—Kentucky: Its Relation to the United States and to the World

This course focuses on Kentucky's historical and geographical development in relationship to the rest of the United States. Students will conduct an in-depth examination of Kentucky's geographic regions and a comparative study of the regions of the United States. One state from each region will be selected by students for specialized investigation.

Kentucky's development from frontier times to the present will be examined through both events and individuals. Included will be minorities and women, as well as activities in economic, cultural, social, political, and educational areas. Students will also conduct a specialized study focusing on one aspect of local or state history.

Grade 5—The United States and the Western Hemisphere

The basic principles of the United State's government and of its economic system, as well as the diverse cultural, ethnic, and racial origins of the American people, shall be emphasized. Attention should be given to specific individuals who have contributed to the cultural, economic and political life of the nation.

A brief look at the history, geography, and culture of our neighboring countries in North America and of selected Latin American countries will enable students to compare the similarities and differences of American culture in the Western Hemisphere. Latin American countries will enable students to compare the similarities and differences of American culture in the Western Hemisphere.

This course is designed to establish a historical perspective of the Western Hemisphere.

Grade 6—A Changing World of Many Nations: World Geography

The focus of the sixth-grade program is on basic concepts, skills, and content from both human and physical geography, resource differentiation, and global interdependence.

All of the basic map and globe skills are taught. Upon completion of the sixth grade, students will have a cognitive map of Kentucky, the United States, and the world. Students will be able to associate nations with their world regions (e.g., Europe, Middle East, Africa, Asia, and the Pacific World).

The emphasis is on people and patterns of life, including government, economics, history, beliefs and attitudes, and global interdependence. There should be some variation in the regions selected for study in order to illustrate the adaptability of human beings to varied environments.

Grade 7—World Civilizations of the Past: Peoples and Cultures

The seventh grade program expands the students' geographic perspective and develops the historical perspective by identifying change over the centuries. The great civilizations of the past from each of the major geographical regions is introduced and is studied in depth. Students will identify the ways in which groups of people meet common needs and problems. Students will learn (1) where the different civilizations were located; (2) when the different civilizations existed, using a time line chart to depict the chronology; and (3) what the major contributions were to the world. Attention is focused on both the Western and the non-Western worlds prior to 1500.

Grade 8—Foundations of the United States History and Citizenship

Expanding on the content and skills developed in grades four and five, this course focuses on life in the United States from Colonization through the Reconstruction era. Students identify the historical roots of our democratic values by studying the ideas, values, critical episodes, and turning points associated with founding the nation and through the study of basic documents of the period. A study of the Declaration of Independence, Articles of the Confederation, and the

United States Constitution and its amendments shall give students a foundation on how governments are organized and function. Note: The study of American history through the Reconstruction era will be emphasized in grade 8. Twentieth century United States history including problems of democracy shall be taught in grades 9 through 12.

Note: Excerpt from "Program of Studies for Kentucky Schools, Grades K–12,; 704 KAR 3:304. Reprinted with permission of KDE.

APPENDIX B

PROFESSIONAL JOURNALS AND ORGANIZATIONS IN SOCIAL STUDIES

(1) Philip Hart, Journal Editor
Arizona Council for the Social Studies
Arizona Historical Society
949 E. Second St.
Tucson, Arizona 85719

(2) Dr. Pam Hronek, Journal Editor
Arkansas Council for the Social Studies
Jonesboro, Arkansas 72401

(3) Damon Nalty, Journal Editor
California Council for the Social Studies
849 Rockwood Drive
San Jose, California 94129

(4) Charles Wiggins, Journal Editor
Connecticut Council for the Social Studies
Brien McMahon High School
Highland Avenue
Norwalk, Connecticut 06584

(5) Dot Hudgens, Journal Editor
Florida Council for the Social Studies
2103 Veranda Circle
Orlando, Florida 32908

(6) Elmer Williams, Journal Editor
Georgia Council for the Social Studies
Dudley Hall
University of Georgia–Athens
Athens, Georgia 30602

(7) Roger LaRaus, Journal Editor
Illinois Council for the Social Studies
814 Reba Place
Evanston, Illinois 60202

(8) John E. Weakland, Journal Editor
Indiana Council for the Social Studies
Ball State University, History Dept.
Muncie, Indiana 47306

(9) John Wilson, Journal Editor
Kansas Council for the Social Studies
Wichita State University
Box 28
Wichita, Kansas 67208

(10) Charles Holt, Kent Feeland, Journal Editors
Morehead State University
Kentucky Council for the Social Studies
RA 114 UPO 738
Morehead, Kentucky 40351

(11) Dr. William Knipmeyer, Journal Editor
Louisiana Council for the Social Studies
Northwestern State University
Natchitoches, Louisiana 71457

(12) Dr. David Pierfy, Journal Editor
Middle States Council for the Social Studies
430 Belmont Avenue
Doylestown, Pennsylvania 18901

(13) Mike Young, Journal Editor
Nebraska Council for the Social Studies
Burke High School
12200 Burke
Omaha, Nebraska 68154

(14) Arthur Kennedy, Journal Editor
New England History Teachers' Association
18 Fiske St.
Waltham, Massachusetts 02154

(15) Edwin W. Reynolds, Journal Editor
New Jersey Council for the Social Studies
786 Estates Boulevard
Trenton, New Jersey 08619

(16) George Mehaffy, Journal Editor
New Mexico Council for the Social Studies
Eastern New Mexico University
School of Education
Portales, New Mexico 87106

(17) James Killoram, Journal Editor
Association of Teachers of Social Studies
United Federation of Teachers
20 Richard Avenue
Lake Ronkonkomo, New York 11779

(18) Tim Keely, Journal Editor
Capitol District Council for the Social Studies
Shenendehowa Schools
Clifton Park, New York 12065

(19) Douglas Wilms, Journal Editor
East Carolina University
Greenville, North Carolina 27834

(20) Editor, *Social Education*
National Council for the Social Studies
3501 Newark St., NW
Washington, DC 20016

(21) William Shorrock, Journal Editor
Ohio Council for the Social Studies
Cleveland State University
Department of History
Euclid Ave. at 24th
Cleveland, Ohio 44115

(22) Jerome Ruderman, Journal Editor
Philadelphia Social Studies Council
1901 John F. Kennedy Blvd.
#1903
Philadelphia, Pennsylvania 19103

(23) Patricia Mosley, Journal Editor
Texas Council for the Social Studies
1915 Mohican Ave.
Denton, Texas 76201

(24) Jacob Susskind, PACSS Journal Editor
Pennsylvania State University
Capitol Campus
Middletown, PA 17057

(25) Helen Snook, Journal Editor
Virginia Council for the Social Studies
1823 Edgewood Lane
Charlottesville, Virginia 22903

(26) George Farmakis (Editorial Board)
Michigan Council for the Social Studies
752 Trombley
Grosse Pointe Park, Michigan 48230

(27) Editor, *The Social Studies*
Heldref Publications
4000 Albemarle St., NW
Washington, DC 20016

I APPENDIX C

RESOURCE UNIT

The following resource unit represents a "bare bones" unit. A minimum number of items are used as examples, just to illustrate how the different parts fit together. For example, Part I would contain more than one short paragraph. Part II would have more than three concepts, more than one generalization to go with each concept, and more than three facts to accompany each generalization. This would then apply to the remaining Parts III–VIII. As mentioned in Chapter 2, there is no upper limit to the length of the parts of the resource unit.

I. OVERVIEW

This unit . . .

II. CONCEPTS, GENERALIZATIONS, AND FACTS

A. Currency

1. People use money to buy things.
   a. Mexico uses the peso for its unit of money.
   b. There are 2800 pesos to the U.S. dollar.
   c. Americans in border towns go to Mexico to shop for bargains.

B. Population

1. Rapid population growth presents problems.
   a. Mexico's population is growing at an annual rate of 3–4%.
   b. There are 90 million people living in Mexico.
   c. Unemployment in Mexico is high because of the large number of people looking for jobs.

C. Living Accommodations

1. Homes differ according to the geography of a country.
   a. Adobe houses are made of mud/clay which is found in the native soil of Mexico.
   b. Houses on large ranches are known as haciendas.
   c. In the tourist areas, such as Acapulco, there are expensive condominiums.

III. UNDERSTANDINGS, ATTITUDES, AND SKILLS

A. Understandings

1. Students will specify the rate of exchange between Mexican and U.S. money.
2. Students will know how fast Mexico's population is growing.
3. Students will understand that there are a variety of residences in Mexico.

B. Attitudes

1. Students will appreciate the stability of the U.S. dollar compared to Mexican currency.
2. Students will show sympathy for other people who live in crowded and cramped conditions.
3. Students will take pride in their own homes.

C. Skills

1. Students will be able to make change with Mexican money.
2. Students will be able to locate on a map the largest cities in Mexico.
3. Students will be able to make a model of a hacienda.

IV. MOTIVATIONAL ACTIVITIES

A. On the first day of the unit, the teacher will have a large outline map of Mexico attached to the bulletin board. Only a few of the largest cities will be shown on the map: Mexico City, Juarez, Acapulco, and Merida. The teacher will have some pictures cut out depicting an oil well, a mountain, a desert scene, an urban city, a cattle ranch, and a seaside resort. At the beginning of the day's lesson, the teacher will place each of these pictures at the top of the map, telling the class that each one shows an area of the country they are about to study. It will be up to the students—as the unit progresses—to be able to place the pictures in the proper location on the map. This activity will give the students a purpose for the unit and will motivate them to learn about the various aspects of the country of Mexico.

V. DEVELOPMENTAL ACTIVITIES

A. To teach about the population in Mexico, the teacher will have the students push their desks to the perimeter of the room and they will stand in a circle near their desks. The teacher will put strips of masking tape on the floor so that a large square—with sides that are roughly eight feet long—is created in the center of the room. The teacher will then ask a student to walk into the square. This solitary student represents a country with very sparse population, i.e., there is plenty of room for this person to move around. Ask another student to enter the square. Continue to do this until students can't be added without bumping into someone who is already in the circle. At this point the teacher should ask the students in the circle how they feel about having this number of people "in their country." This activity will demonstrate the increasing feeling of cramped conditions as people are gradually added to a limited area.

VI. EVALUATION TECHNIQUES

A. *Self-Evaluation Checklist.* As students work in small groups to build haciendas, they will be asked to evaluate their own efforts. When the project is completed, each member of the groups will complete the checklist shown below:

Self-Evaluation Checklist

| Date: _____ | Name: _____ | | |

In this unit I did the following	Always	Usually	Sometimes	Very Seldom
I contributed my share of effort to the group project				
I cooperated with the rest of the group				
I gave help or encouragement to others in my group				
I worked happily without getting angry				
I cleaned up the area at the end of each day				

B. At the end of the unit, each student will write a pen pal letter to a child in Mexico. The students will make a list of the things they learned about Mexico during the unit and then will include information about these items that correspond to their own area. For example, the students will need to mention the following information:

1. Population: Give the number of people who live in their hometown of Morehead and home state of Kentucky.
2. Homes: Tell about the kind of homes that they live in. They should tell what the house is made of, how many rooms it has, if it has a garage, if the child has a room of his own, etc.
3. Money: Write about the ways that they get spending money and the things they buy with it.

This concluding activity will allow the students to apply the concepts of the unit to their own surroundings. A tie will be made between the Mexican and U.S. examples for these concepts.

VII. BIBLIOGRAPHY

For the Students

Shannon, T. *A Trip to Mexico*
Pope, B. N. *Your World: Let's Visit Mexico*
Epstein, S. *The First Book of Mexico*
Koch, S. *Mexico*
Ross, P. *Mexico*
Johnson, W. W. and editors of *Life, Mexico*
Grossman, R. *Mexico: The Land, the Art, the People*
Tosi, F. *New Guide to Mexico*

For the Teacher

Riding, A. *Distant Neighbors: A Portrait of the Mexicans*
Montgomery, T. S. *Mexico Today*
Hofstadter, D. *Mexico 1946–73*
Hodges, D. and Ross Gandy. *Mexico 1910–1976: Reform or Revolution?*
Greenleaf, R. and Michael Meyer. *Research in Mexican History*
Dominguez, J. I. and Marc Lindenberg. *Central America: Current Crises and Future Prospects*
Cumberland, C. C. *Mexico: The Struggle for Modernity*
Quirk, R. E. *Mexico*
Brand, D. *Mexico, Land of Sunshine and Shadow*

VIII. OTHER SOURCES

Transparencies

"Mexico," CS Hammond

Records

"Spotlight on Latin America," Hy Zaret and Lou Singer

Kits

"Mexican Revolution of 1910," Multi Media Productions
"Conflicts of Culture," Multi Media Production
"Seeing Mexico Series," Coronet Films
"Mexican Arts and Crafts," Encore Visual Education, Inc.
"Mexico: Our Dynamic Neighbor," Teaching Resources Films

Filmstrips

"Mexico: Landforms, Climate, Vegetation," Budek Films and Slides, Inc.
"The Course of Mexico's Culture," Multi Media Productions
"Exploring Ancient Mexico," Imperial Film Co.
"Seeing Mexico," Coronet Instruction Films

Films

"Mexico: Four Views," Coronet Instructional Media.
"Crowded City: Mexico City," Lucerne Films.

| APPENDIX D

SOCIAL STUDIES SKILLS CHART

Skills	K	1	2	3	4	5	6	7	8	9	10	11	12
I. Locating information													
A. Work with books													
1. Use title of books as guide to contents	●■		■	■	■	■	■	◄	◄	◄	◄	◄	◄
2. Use table of contents	●■		■	■	■	■	■	■	■	■	◄	◄	◄
3. Alphabetize	●■		■	■	■	■	■	■	■	■	◄	◄	◄
4. Use index					●	■	■	■	■	■	◄	◄	◄
5. Use title page and copyright date					●	■	■	■	■	■	◄	◄	◄
6. Use glossary, appendix, map lists, illustration lists						●	■						◄
7. Distinguish between storybooks and factual books			●	■	■	■	■	■	■	■			◄
8. Choose a book appropriate for the purpose			●	■	■	■	■	■	■	■			◄
B. Find information in encyclopedias and other reference books													
1. Locate information in an encyclopedia by using key words, letters on volume, index, and cross references					●	■	■	■	■	■	◄	◄	◄

346

Skills	K	1	2	3	4	5	6	7	8	9	10	11	12
2. Use reference works, such as *World Almanac*, atlases, *Who's Who*, *Statesman's Yearbook*						●	■	■	■	■	▲	▲	▲
C. Make efficient use of the dictionary													
1. Alphabetize a list of words according to the first letter; according to the second and third letters			●	■	■	■	■	■	■	■	▲	▲	▲
2. Use guide words				●	■	■	■	■	■	■	▲	▲	▲
3. Learn correct pronunciation of a word				●	■	■	■	■	■	■	▲	▲	▲
4. Understand syllabication				●	■	■	■	■	■	■	▲	▲	▲
5. Choose the appropriate meaning of the word for the context in which it is used				●	■	■	■	■	■	■	▲	▲	▲
D. Read newspapers, magazines, and pamphlets with discrimination													
1. Recognize these materials as sources of information about many topics, especially current affairs				●	■	■	■	▲	▲	▲		▲	▲
2. Select important news items					●■	■	■	▲	▲	▲	▲	▲	▲

● Grade at which skill is introduced through planned readiness experiences.
■ Grade at which skill is developed systematically.
▲ Grade at which skill is retaught, maintained, and extended.

(continued)

347

Skills	K	1	2	3	4	5	6	7	8	9	10	11	12
3. Select from these sources material that is pertinent to class activities				●	■	■	■	■	■	■	◀	◀	◀
4. Learn the organization of a newspaper and how to use the index						●	■	■	■	■	◀	◀	◀
5. Learn about the sections of the newspaper					●	■	■	◀	◀	◀	◀	◀	◀
6. Recognize the differences in purpose and coverage of different magazines, papers, and pamphlets						●	■	■	■	■	◀	◀	◀
E. Know how to find material in a library, both school and public													
1. Locate appropriate books					●■	■	■	■	■	■	◀	◀	◀
2. Use a book card					●	■	■	■	■	■	■	■	■
3. Use the card catalogue to learn that—													
a. A book is listed in three ways—by subject, by author, and by title						●■	■	■	■	■	◀	◀	◀
b. All cards are arranged alphabetically						●■	■	■	■	■	◀	◀	◀
c. Cards have call numbers in upper left-hand corner which indicate the location on the shelf						●■	■	■	■	■	◀	◀	◀

Skills	K	1	2	3	4	5	6	7	8	9	10	11	12
d. Some author cards give more information than the title or subject card						●■	■	■	■	■	◀	◀	◀
e. Information such as publisher, date of publication, number of pages and of illustrations, and usually some annotation are provided						●■	■	■	■	■	◀	◀	◀
f. The Dewey Decimal System is a key to finding books						●■	■	■	■	■	◀	◀	◀
4. Use the *Reader's Guide to Periodical Literature* and other indexes								●■	■	■	◀	◀	◀
F. Gather facts from field trips and interviews													
1. Identify the purpose of the field trip or interview	●■	■	■	■	■	■	■	■	■	■	◀	◀	◀
2. Plan procedures, rules of behavior, questions to be asked, things to look for	●■	■	■	■	■	■	■	■	■	■	◀	◀	◀
3. Take increasingly greater initiative in the actual conduct of the field trip or interview			●■	■	■	■	■	■	■	■	◀	◀	◀

● Grade at which skill is introduced through planned readiness experiences.
■ Grade at which skill is developed systematically.
◀ Grade at which skill is retaught, maintained, and extended.

(continued)

349

Skills	K	1	2	3	4	5	6	7	8	9	10	11	12
4. Evaluate the planning and execution of the field trip or interview			●■	■	■	■	■	■	■	■	◀	◀	◀
5. Find acceptable ways to open and close an interview				●■	■	■	■	■	■	■	◀	◀	◀
6. Express appreciation for courtesies extended during the field trip or interview	●■	■	■	■	■	■	■	■	■	■	◀	◀	◀
7. Record, summarize, and evaluate information gained	●■	■	■	■	■	■	■	■	■	■	■	■	■
G. Be selective in using audiovisual materials**			●■	■	■	■	■	■	■	■	◀	◀	◀
II. Organizing information														
A. Make an outline of topics to be investigated and seek material about each major point, using more than one source					●■	■	■	■	■	■	◀	◀	◀
B. Select the main idea and supporting facts				●■	■	■	■	■	◀	■	◀	◀	◀
C. Compose a title for a story, picture, graph, map or chart	●■	■	■	■	■	■	■	◀	◀	◀	◀	◀	◀
D. Select answers to questions from material heard, viewed, or read	●■		■	■	■	■	■	■	■	■	◀	◀	◀

Skills	K	1	2	3	4	5	6	7	8	9	10	11	12
E. Take notes, making a record of the source by author, title, page					●■	■	■	■	■	■	▲	▲	▲
F. Classify pictures, facts, and events under main headings or in categories	●■	■	■	■	■	■	■	■	■	■	▲	▲	▲
G. Arrange events, facts, and ideas in sequence	●■	■	■	■	■	■	■	■	■	■	▲	▲	▲
H. Make simple outlines of material read, using correct outline form				●■	■	■	■	■	■	■	▲	▲	▲
I. Write a summary of main points encountered in material				●■	■	■	■	■	■	■	▲	▲	▲
J. Make a simple table of contents				●■	■	■	■	■	■	■	▲	▲	▲
K. Make a bibliography							●■	■	■	■	▲	▲	▲
III. Evaluating information													
A. Distinguish between facts and fiction	●■	■	■	■	■	■	■	■	■	■	▲	▲	▲
B. Distinguish between fact and opinion				●■	■	■	■	■	■	■	▲	▲	▲

● Grade at which skill is introduced through planned readiness experiences.
■ Grade at which skill is developed systematically.
▲ Grade at which skill is retaught, maintained, and extended.

(continued)

Skills	K	1	2	3	4	5	6	7	8	9	10	11	12
C. Compare information about a topic drawn from two or more sources to recognize agreement or contradiction				●■	■	■	■	■	■	■	▲	▲	▲
D. Consider which source of information is more acceptable and why				●■	■	■	■	■	■	■	▲	▲	▲
E. Examine reasons for contradictions, or seeming contradictions, in evidence						●■	■	■	■	■	▲	▲	▲
F. Examine material for consistency, reasonableness, and freedom from bias						●■	■	■	■	■	▲	▲	▲
G. Recognize propaganda and its purposes in a given context						●■	■	■	■	■	▲	▲	▲
H. Draw inferences and make generalizations from evidence	●■	■	■	■	■	■	■	■	■	■	▲	▲	▲
I. Reach tentative conclusions	●■	■	■	■	■	■	■	■	■	■	▲	▲	▲
IV. Acquiring information through reading													
A. Skim to find a particular word, get a general impression, or locate specific information						●■	■	■	■	■	▲	▲	▲
B. Read to find answers to questions		●■	■	■	■	■	■	■	■	■	▲	▲	▲

Skills	K	1	2	3	4	5	6	7	8	9	10	11	12
C. Make use of headings, topic sentences, and summary sentences to select main ideas and differentiate between main and subordinate ideas					●■	■	■	■	■	■	▲	▲	▲
D. Select the statements that are pertinent to the topic being studied				●■	■	■	■	■	■	■	▲	▲	▲
E. Make use of italics, marginal notes, and footnotes to discover emphasis by author							●■	■	■	■	▲	▲	▲
F. Understand an increasing number of Social Studies terms		●■	■	■	■	■	■	■	■	■	▲	▲	▲
G. Learn abbreviations commonly used in Social Studies materials				●■	■	■	■	■	■	■	▲	▲	▲
H. Consciously evaluate what is read, using the approaches suggested in Section III above							●■	■	■	■	▲	▲	▲
V. Acquiring information through listening and observing													
A. Learn to listen	●■	■	■	■	■	■	■	■	■	■	▲	▲	▲
B. Listen and observe with a purpose	●■	■	■	■	■	■	■	■	■	■	▲	▲	▲

● Grade at which skill is introduced through planned readiness experiences.
■ Grade at which skill is developed systematically.
▲ Grade at which skill is retaught, maintained, and extended.

(continued)

Skills	K	1	2	3	4	5	6	7	8	9	10	11	12
C. Listen attentively when others are speaking	●■	■	■	■	■	■	■	■	■	■	▲	▲	▲
D. Identify a sequence of ideas and select those that are most important			●■	■	■	■	■	■	■	■	▲	▲	▲
E. Relate, compare, and evaluate information gained through listening and observing with that gained from other sources of information				●	■	■	■	■	■	■	▲	▲	▲
F. Adjust to a speaker's voice and delivery and to the physical conditions of the situation				●■	■	■	■	■	■	■	▲	▲	▲
G. Reserve judgment until the speaker's entire presentation has been heard					●■	■	■	■	■	■	▲	▲	▲
H. Take notes while continuing to listen and observe					●■	■	■	■	■	■	▲	▲	▲
I. Analyze video and audio presentations, e.g., films, pictures, models, exhibits, and other graphic materials concerned with Social Studies topics						●■	■	■	■	■	▲	▲	▲
VI. Applying problem-solving and critical-thinking skills to social issues													
A. Recognize that a problem exists	●■	■	■	■	■	■	■	■	■	■	▲	▲	▲
B. Define the problem for study	●■	■	■	■	■	■	■	■	■	■	▲	▲	▲
C. Review known information about the problem	●■	■	■	■	■	■	■	■	■	■	▲	▲	▲

Skills	K	1	2	3	4	5	6	7	8	9	10	11	12
D. Plan how to study the problem	●■	■	■	■	■	■	■	■	■	■	▲	▲	▲
E. Locate, gather, and organize information (For detailed analysis, see Section I.)		●■	■	■	■	■	■	■	■	■	▲	▲	▲
F. Interpret and evaluate information (For detailed analysis, see Section III.)		●■	■	■	■	■	■	■	■	■	▲	▲	▲
G. Summarize and draw tentative conclusions	●■	■	■	■	■	■	■	■	■	■	▲	▲	▲
H. Recognize the need to change conclusions when new information warrants	●■	■	■	■	■	■	■	■	■	■	▲	▲	▲
I. Recognize areas for further study	●■	■	■	■	■	■	■	■	■	■	▲	▲	▲
J. Use problem-solving techniques in meeting personal and societal problems	●■	■	■	■	■	■	■	■	■	■	▲	▲	▲
VII. Communicating orally and in writing													
A. Speak with accuracy and poise													
1. Develop an adequate vocabulary	●■	■	■	■	■	■	■	■	■	■	▲	▲	▲
2. Choose the appropriate word				●■	■	■	■	■	■	■	▲	▲	▲

● Grade at which skill is introduced through planned readiness experiences.
■ Grade at which skill is developed systematically.
▲ Grade at which skill is retaught, maintained, and extended.

(continued)

Skills	K	1	2	3	4	5	6	7	8	9	10	11	12
3. Pronounce words correctly and enunciate clearly	●■	■	■	■	■	■	■	■	■	■	◀	◀	◀
4. Talk in sentences	●■	■	■	■	■	■	■	■	■	■	◀	◀	◀
5. Prepare and use notes in presenting an oral report, giving credit when material is quoted					●■	■	■	■	■	■	◀	◀	◀
6. Keep to the point in all situations involving oral expression	●■	■	■	■	■	■	■	■	■	■	◀	◀	◀
7. Develop self-confidence	●■	■	■	■	■	■	■	■	■	■	◀	◀	◀
8. Exchange ideas through discussion, either as leader or participant	●■	■	■	■	■	■	■	■	■	■	◀	◀	◀
9. Respect limitations of time and the right of others to be heard	●■	■	■	■	■	■	■		■	■	◀	◀	◀
B. Write with clarity and exactness													
1. Collect, evaluate, and organize information around a clearly defined topic (See Sections I–V above)					●■	■	■	■	■	■	◀	◀	◀
2. Write independently, avoiding copying from references					●■	■	■	■	■	■	◀	◀	◀
3. Give credit for quoted material					●■	■	■	■	■	■	◀	◀	◀

Skills	K	1	2	3	4	5	6	7	8	9	10	11	12
4. Use standard English					●■	■	■	■	■	■	▲	▲	▲
5. Include a bibliography to show source of information					●■	■	■	■	■	■	▲	▲	▲
6. Include footnotes when necessary					●■	■	■	■	■	■	▲	▲	▲
7. Apply the skills being developed in printing, writing, spelling, punctuating, capitalizing, and arranging written work			●■	■	■	■	■	■	■	■	▲	▲	▲
8. Proofread and revise		●■	■	■	■	■	■	■	■	■	▲	▲	▲
VIII. Interpreting pictures, charts, graphs, tables													
A. Interpret pictorial materials													
1. Recognize these materials as sources of information		●■	■	■	■	■	■	■	■	■	▲	▲	▲
2. Distinguish between types of pictorial material, recognize the advantages of each, and recognize the need for objectivity in interpretation					●■	■	■	■	■	■	▲	▲	▲

● Grade at which skill is introduced through planned readiness experiences.
■ Grade at which skill is developed systematically.
▲ Grade at which skill is retaught, maintained, and extended.

357

Skills	K	1	2	3	4	5	6	7	8	9	10	11	12
3. Note and describe the content of the material, both general and specific		●■	■	■	■	■	■	▲	▲	▲	▲	▲	▲
4. Interpret by applying related information, and use the material as one basis for drawing conclusions		●■	■	■	■	■	■	■	■	■	▲	▲	▲
B. Interpret cartoons													
1. Recognize these materials as expressing a point of view and interpret the view expressed							●■	■	■	■	▲	▲	▲
2. Note and interpret the common symbols used in cartoons							●■	■	■	■	▲	▲	▲
C. Study charts													
1. Understand the steps in development indicated					●■	■	■	■	■	■	▲	▲	▲
2. Trace the steps in the process shown						●	■	■	■	■	▲	▲	▲
3. Compare sizes and quantities						●	■	■	■	■	▲	▲	▲
4. Analyze the organization or structure							●■	■	■	■	▲	▲	▲
5. Identify the elements of change							●■	■	■	■	▲	▲	▲
D. Study graphs and tables													
1. Understand the significance of the title					●■	■	■	■	■	■	▲	▲	▲

Skills	K	1	2	3	4	5	6	7	8	9	10	11	12
2. Determine the basis on which the graph or table is built and the units of measure involved					●■	■	■	■	■	■	▲	▲	▲
3. Interpret the relationships shown					●■	■	■	■	■	■	▲	▲	▲
4. Draw inferences based on the data					●■	■	■	■	■	■	▲	▲	▲
E. Construct simple graphs, charts, tables, and other pictorial materials (including cartoons)					●■	■	■	■	■	■	▲	▲	▲
F. Relate information derived from pictures, charts, graphs, and tables with that gained from other sources							●■	■	■	■	▲	▲	▲
IX. Interpreting maps and globes													
A. Orient the map and note directions													
1. Use cardinal directions in classroom and neighborhood				●■		■	■	■	■	■	▲	▲	▲
2. Use intermediate directions as southeast, northwest					●■	■	■	■	■	■	▲	▲	▲
3. Use cardinal directions and intermediate directions in working with maps					●■	■	■	■	■	■	▲	▲	▲

● Grade at which skill is introduced through planned readiness experiences.
■ Grade at which skill is developed systematically.
▲ Grade at which skill is retaught, maintained, and extended.

(continued)

Skills	K	1	2	3	4	5	6	7	8	9	10	11	12
4. Use relative terms of location and direction, as near, far, above, below, up, down	●■	■	■	■	■	■	■	■	■	■	◄	◄	◄
5. Understand that north is toward the North Pole and south toward the South Pole on any map projection				●		■	■	■	■	■	◄	◄	◄
6. Understand the use of the compass for direction					●	■	■	■	■	■	◄	◄	◄
7. Use the north arrow on the map					●	■	■	■	■	■	◄	◄	◄
8. Orient desk outline, textbook, and atlas maps correctly to the north					●	■	■	■	■	■	◄	◄	◄
9. Use parallels and meridians in determining direction					●	■	■	■	■	■	◄	◄	◄
10. Use different map projections to learn how the pattern of meridians and that of parallels differ					●	■	■	■	■	■	◄	◄	◄
11. Construct simple maps which are properly oriented as to direction					●	■	■	■	■	■	◄	◄	◄
B. Locate places on maps and globes													
1. Recognize the home city and state on a map of the United States and on a globe				●		■	■	■	■	■	◄	◄	◄

Skills	K	1	2	3	4	5	6	7	8	9	10	11	12
2. Recognize land and water masses on a globe and on a variety of maps—physical-political, chalkboard, weather, space, etc.				●	■	■	■	■	■	■	▲	▲	▲
3. Identify on a globe and on a map of the world, the equator, tropics, circles, continents, oceans, large islands				●	■	■	■	■	■	■	▲	▲	▲
4. Use a highway map for locating places by number-and-key system; plan a trip using distance, direction, and locations					●■	■	■	■	■	■	▲	▲	▲
5. Relate low latitudes to the equator and high latitudes to the polar areas					●■	■	■	■	■	■	▲	▲	▲
6. Interpret abbreviations commonly found on maps					●■	■	■	■	■	■	▲	▲	▲
7. Use map vocabulary and key accurately					●■	■	■	■	■	■	▲	▲	▲
8. Use longitude and latitude in locating places on wall maps						●■	■	■	■	■	▲	▲	▲
9. Use an atlas to locate places						●■	■	■	■	■	▲	▲	▲

● Grade at which skill is introduced through planned readiness experiences.
■ Grade at which skill is developed systematically.
▲ Grade at which skill is retaught, maintained, and extended.

(continued)

361

Skills	K	1	2	3	4	5	6	7	8	9	10	11	12
10. Identify the time zones of the United States and relate them to longitude						●■	■	■	■	■	◄	◄	◄
11. Understand the reason for the International Date Line, and compute time problems of international travel								●	■	■	◄	◄	◄
12. Consult two or more maps to gather information about the same area						●■	■	■	■	■	◄	◄	◄
13. Recognize location of major cities of the world with respect to their physical setting					●■	■	■	■	■	■	◄	◄	◄
14. Trace routes of travel by different means of transportation					●■	■	■	■	■	■	◄	◄	◄
15. Develop a visual image of major continents, countries, land forms, and other map patterns studied					●■●■	■	■	■	■	■	◄	◄	◄
16. Read maps of various types which show elevation							■	■	■	■	◄	◄	◄
17. Understand the significance of relative location as it has affected national policies							●■				◄	◄	◄
18. Learn to make simple sketch maps to show location			●■	■	■	■	■	■	■	■	◄	◄	◄

Skills	K	1	2	3	4	5	6	7	8	9	10	11	12
C. Use scale and compute distances													
1. Use small objects to represent large ones, as a photograph compared to actual size	●■	●■	■	■	■	■	■	■	■	■	▲	▲	▲
2. Make simple large-scale maps of familiar areas, such as classroom, neighborhood		●■	■	■	■	■	■	■	■	■	▲	▲	▲
3. Compare actual length of a block or a mile with that shown on a large-scale map					●■	■	■	■	■	■	▲	▲	▲
4. Determine distance on a map by using a scale of miles					●■	■	■	■	■	■	▲	▲	▲
5. Compare maps of different size of the same area					●■	■	■	■	■	■	▲	▲	▲
6. Compare maps of different areas to note that a smaller scale must be used to map larger areas					●■	■	■	■	■	■	▲	▲	▲
7. Compute distance between two points on maps of different scale					●■	■	■	■	■	■	▲	▲	▲

● Grade at which skill is introduced through planned readiness experiences.
■ Grade at which skill is developed systematically.
▲ Grade at which skill is retaught, maintained, and extended.

(continued)

363

Skills	K	1	2	3	4	5	6	7	8	9	10	11	12
8. Estimate distances on a globe using latitude; estimate air distances by using a tape or a string to measure great circle routes						●■	■	■	■	■	▲	▲	▲
9. Understand and use map scale expressed as representative fraction, statement of scale, or bar scale						●■	■	■	■	■	▲	▲	▲
10. Develop the habit of checking the scale on all maps used					●■	■	■	■	■	■	▲	▲	▲
D. Interpret map symbols and visualize what they represent													
1. Understand that real objects can be represented by pictures or symbols on a map	●	■	■	■	■	■	■	■	■	■	▲	▲	▲
2. Learn to use legends on different kinds of maps					●■	■	■	■	■	■	▲	▲	▲
3. Identify the symbols used for water features to learn the source, mouth, direction of flow, depths, and ocean currents					●■	■	■	■	■	■	▲	▲	▲
4. Study color contour and visual relief maps and visualize the nature of the areas shown						●■	■	■	■	■	▲	▲	▲
5. Interpret the elevation of the land from the flow of rivers						●■	■	■	■	■	▲	▲	▲

Skills	K	1	2	3	4	5	6	7	8	9	10	11	12
6. Interpret dots, lines, colors, and other symbols used in addition to pictorial symbols					●■	■	■	■	■	■	▲	▲	▲
7. Use all parts of a world atlas								●■	■	■	▲	▲	▲
E. Compare maps and draw inferences													
1. Read into a map the relationships suggested by the data shown, as the factors which determine the location of cities					●■	■	■	■	■	■	▲	▲	▲
2. Compare two maps of the same area, combine the data shown on them, and draw conclusions based on the data					●■	■	■	■	■	■	▲	▲	▲
3. Recognize that there are many kinds of maps for many uses, and learn to choose the best map for the purpose at hand					●■	■	■	■	■	■	▲	▲	▲
4. Understand the differences in different map projections and recognize the distortions involved in any representation of the earth other than the globe						●■	■	■	■	■	▲	▲	▲

● Grade at which skill is introduced through planned readiness experiences.
■ Grade at which skill is developed systematically.
▲ Grade at which skill is retaught, maintained, and extended.

(continued)

Skills	K	1	2	3	4	5	6	7	8	9	10	11	12
5. Use maps and the globe to explain the geographic setting of historical and current events						●■	■	■	■	■	◀	◀	◀
6. Read a variety of special-purpose maps and draw inferences on the basis of data obtained from them and from other sources								●	■	■	◀	◀	◀
7. Infer man's activities or way of living from physical detail and from latitude						●	■	■	■	■	◀	◀	◀
X. Understanding time and chronology													
A. Develop an understanding of the time system and the calendar													
1. Learn to tell time by the clock	●	●	■	■	◀	◀	◀						
2. Use names of the days of the week in order		■	■	◀									
3. Use names of the months in sequence		●	■	◀									
4. Use calendar to find dates or special events and to determine length of time between important dates		●	■	■	■	■	■	◀	◀	◀			
5. Associate seasons with particular months in both northern and southern hemispheres			●		■	■	■	◀	◀	◀	◀	◀	◀

Skills	K	1	2	3	4	5	6	7	8	9	10	11	12
6. Understand the relation between rotation of the earth and day and night				●	■	■	■	■	■	■	◀	◀	◀
7. Understand the system of time zones as related to the rotation of the earth					●	■	■	■	■	■	◀	◀	◀
8. Understand the relation between the earth's revolution around the sun and a calendar year				●	■	■	■	■	■	■	◀	◀	◀
9. Accumulate some specific date-events as points of orientation in time						●	■	■	■	■	◀	◀	◀
10. Comprehend the Christian system of chronology—B.C. and A.D.						●	■	■	■	■	◀	◀	◀
a. Use such definite time concepts as second, minute, yesterday, decade, century					●	■	■	■	■	■	◀	◀	◀
b. Use such indefinite time concepts as past, future, long ago, before, after, meanwhile			●	■	■	■	■	■	■	■	◀	◀	◀
12. Acquire a sense of prehistoric and geological time							●				◀	◀	◀

● Grade at which skill is introduced through planned readiness experiences.
■ Grade at which skill is developed systematically.
◀ Grade at which skill is retaught, maintained, and extended.

(continued)

367

Skills	K	1	2	3	4	5	6	7	8	9	10	11	12
13. Learn to translate dates into centuries					●	■	■	■	■	■	◄	◄	◄
B. Develop an understanding of events as part of a chronological series of events and an understanding of the differences in duration of various periods of time													
1. Recognize sequence and chronology in personal experiences, as the school day, weekly schedule, etc.			●	■	■	■	■						
2. Learn to arrange personal experiences in order	●	■	■	■	■	■	■						
3. Comprehend sequence and order as expressed in first, second, third, etc.		●	■	■	■	■	■						
4. Learn to think of the separation of an event from the present in arithmetical terms					●	■	■	■	■	■	◄	◄	◄
5. Learn to figure the length of time between two given dates					●	■	■	■	■	■	◄	◄	◄
6. Understand differences in duration of various historical periods						●	■	■	■	■	◄	◄	◄
7. Understand and make simple time lines					●	■	■	■	■	■	◄	◄	◄
8. Use a few cluster date-events to establish time relationships among historic events						●	■	■	■	■	◄	◄	◄

Skills	K	1	2	3	4	5	6	7	8	9	10	11	12
9. Learn to relate the past to the present in the study of change and continuity in human affairs							■	■	■	■	◄	◄	◄
10. Learn to formulate generalizations and conclusions about time in studying the development of human affairs						●		●	■	■	◄	◄	◄
XI. Developing interpersonal relations and group participation													
A. Enhance personal growth	●	■	■	■	■	■	■	■	■	■	◄	◄	◄
1. Improve self-image	●	■	■	■	■	■	■	■	■	■	◄	◄	◄
2. Accept self-limitations	●	■	■	■	■	■	■	■	■	■	◄	◄	◄
3. Gain independence and skill in self-direction	●	■	■	■	■	■	■	■	■	■	◄	◄	◄
4. Make choices and decisions	●	■	■	■	■	■	■	■	■	■	◄	◄	◄
B. Work with others													
1. Know the simple rules of courtesy and act upon them	●	■	■	■	■	■	■	■	■	■	◄	◄	◄
2. Respect the rights and opinions of others	●	■	■	■	■	■	■	■	■	■	◄	◄	◄

● Grade at which skill is introduced through planned readiness experiences.

■ Grade at which skill is developed systematically.

◄ Grade at which skill is retaught, maintained, and extended.

(continued)

Skills	K	1	2	3	4	5	6	7	8	9	10	11	12
3. Know how to participate in a conversation	●	■	■	■	■	■	■	■	■	■	◀	◀	◀
4. Engage in fair play	●	■	■	■	■	■	■	■	■	■	◀	◀	◀
5. Show appreciation of others' efforts	●	■	■	■	■	■	■	■	■	■	◀	◀	◀
6. Learn to give and receive constructive criticism	●	■	■	■	■	■	■	■	■	■	◀	◀	◀
7. Find ways to include newcomers	●	■	■	■	■	■	■	■	■	■	◀	◀	◀
8. Learn to empathize with others	●	■	■	■	■	■	■	■	■	■	◀	◀	◀
C. Participate in a group													
1. Understand the need for laws and the necessity of observing them	●	■	■	■	■	■	■	■	■	■	◀	◀	◀
2. Accept responsibility and complete tasks	●	■	■	■	■	■	■	■	■	■	◀	◀	◀
3. Accept group decisions	●	■	■	■	■	■	■	■	■	■	◀	◀	◀
4. Anticipate the consequences of a group decision and become actively involved in the group process	●				■	■		■	■	■	◀		◀
5. Participate in planning and education	●	■	■	■	■	■		■	■	■	◀	◀	◀
6. Follow parliamentary procedure							●	■	■	■	◀	◀	◀

Skills	K	1	2	3	4	5	6	7	8	9	10	11	12
D. Develop leadership characteristics													
1. Accept the role and responsibilities of a leader	●	■	■	■	■	■	■	■	■	■	◄	◄	◄
2. Acquire group consensus for agreements				●	■	■	■	■	■	■	◄	◄	◄
3. Delegate responsibilities and check on progress of ensuing activities	●	■	■	■	■	■	■	■	■	■	◄	◄	◄
4. Keep group members informed	●	■	■	■	■	■	■	■	■	■	◄	◄	◄
5. Distinguish between work that can be done most effectively by individuals and that which calls for group effort			●	■	■	■	■	■	■	■	◄	◄	◄
6. Use rules of parliamentary procedure when needed							●	■	■	■	◄	◄	◄

● Grade at which skill is introduced through planned readiness experiences.

■ Grade at which skill is developed systematically.

◄ Grade at which skill is retaught, maintained, and extended.

*Adapted from *Skill Development in Social Studies*, the Thirty-Third Yearbook, 1963, of the National Council for the Social Studies.

**See Acquiring information through listening and observing; and Interpreting pictures, charts, graphs, tables; Sections V, VII.

INDEX